Scholarly Reprint Series

The Scholarly Reprint Series has been established to bring back into print valuable titles from the University of Toronto Press backlist for which a small but continuing demand is known to exist. Special techniques (including some developed by the University of Toronto Press Printing Department) have made it possible to reissue these works in uniform case bindings in runs as short as 50 copies. The cost is not low, but prices are far below what would have to be charged for such short-run reprints by normal methods.

The Scholarly Reprint Series has proved a valuable help to scholars and librarians, particularly those building new collections. We invite nominations of titles for reissue in this form, and look forward to the day when, with this series and other technological developments, the label 'out of print' will virtually disappear from our backlist.

BRITISH EMIGRATION TO BRITISH NORTH AMERICA

The First Hundred Years

By Helen I. Cowan

REVISED AND ENLARGED EDITION

UNIVERSITY OF TORONTO PRESS

*Coypright, Canada, 1961, by
University of Toronto Press*

SCHOLARLY REPRINT SERIES
ISBN 0-8020-7062-0
LC 61-19466
Printed in Canada

FOREWORD

IT GIVES ME singular pleasure to be asked to write the preface to this revised and enlarged edition of Miss Cowan's *British Emigration to British North America*; for I wrote the preface to the first edition of the book, when it was published a third of a century ago. I had, indeed, something to do with its publication. I was at that time Editor of the *Canadian Historical Review*; and when Miss Cowan returned to Canada in 1927, after two years of postgraduate work at the University of London's Institute of Historical Research, she submitted to me, for publication in the *Canadian Historical Review*, a chapter from her dissertation. It was the chapter dealing with Irish emigration to British North America. I was so struck by the freshness and originality of Miss Cowan's treatment of her subject that I asked to see the whole of the thesis. I ought to explain that I was at this time not only Editor of the *Canadian Historical Review*, but also, in my capacity as Librarian of the University of Toronto, Editor of the *University of Toronto Studies*. This was a series, in various fields, published by the University of Toronto Library, and used as exchanges for publications by other libraries. The *Studies* provided an outlet for a good deal of scholarly work which would not perhaps have found a commercial publisher; and they brought into the University of Toronto Library a great variety of similar publications published by other universities and by numerous learned societies.

When I read Miss Cowan's manuscript, I was so impressed by it that I recommended its publication to the Studies Committee of the University. It appeared in 1928, in an edition of only several hundred copies, most of which were sent out on exchange to libraries and learned societies. My only mistake was in ordering such a small number of copies to be printed. It was not long before the book was out of print; and in recent years copies have, on the rare occasions when they came into the second-hand market, been offered at ten times the published price.

I have therefore urged Miss Cowan to prepare a new, revised, and enlarged edition of her book; and I am glad that the University of Toronto Press should have undertaken to publish this edition. After all, if a book has weathered a third of a century, a new, revised, and enlarged edition ought to be welcomed. I congratulate Miss Cowan on the completion of what I can only describe as a *magnum opus*.

W. S. WALLACE
Librarian Emeritus
University of Toronto Library

INTRODUCTION

WHEN THE FIRST EDITION of *British Emigration to British North America* was written in London more than thirty years ago, it represented a venture in an almost untouched field. From the centres of work on British colonial history at the great universities in the British Isles, the United States, and Canada, there had come results of investigations in the political and constitutional aspects of the growth of the British North American colonies. Only at the London School of Economics, where Professor Lilian Knowles was expanding her work done under William Cunningham, had research in this field produced a book on British emigration: S. C. Johnson's *History of Emigration from the United Kingdom to North America, 1763–1912*, published in London the year before the outbreak of the First World War.

Some specialists in the history of the second empire believed that no extensive description of British emigration to the British American colonies, beyond Johnson's excellent survey, could be written because of the lack of first-hand sources. This belief was shattered by the discovery of the vastness of the manuscript materials which had been preserved in the Emigration Room of the old Colonial Office. The letters from British subjects, rich and powerful, poor and humble, which that material contained, the remarks upon the letters made by government officials, and the related administrative correspondence, completely destroyed the easy concept of a hit-and-miss emigration noticed by the government only between fits of concentration on vital problems of political administration. In the new light from this collection of sources, census statistics of this and that region in the British Isles, stories of beginnings preserved in Canada's first four provinces came alive, printed parliamentary papers took on new meaning, and even the mighty secretary of state responsible for colonial affairs and his aloof undersecretary appeared as human beings, fully aware of the often unfortunate plight of their fellow countrymen.

Within ten years of the end of the war, following Belcher and Williamson's survey of empire migration in 1924, the publications on British emigration began. In 1928 some of Frances Morehouse's work at the University of Manchester was given space in the *Canadian* and *American Historical Reviews*, and the first edition of this study was published. In 1929 came W. A. Carrothers' book, after his investigations from the University of Edinburgh; in 1930 Kathleen A. Walpole's prize-winning essay from the University of London; in 1931 Fred H. Hitchins' book published by the University of Pennsylvania Press; in 1932 William Forbes Adams' from the Yale University Press; and so on until before his death in 1938 Marcus Lee Hansen had broadened the base of exploration and, in his *The Atlantic Migration*, had made of emigration the epic story it is. Norman Macdonald's book appeared in 1939, the year before Hansen's masterpiece arrived from the Harvard University Press. The stream continued as late as the fifties. Brinley Thomas' work on migration then appeared in a study of Great Britain and the Atlantic economy, Wilbur S. Shepperson brought out two volumes, and some of Oliver MacDonagh's findings on Irish emigration and the regulation of the emigrant traffic were published in *Irish Historical Studies* and the *Transactions* of the Royal Historical Society. In 1956 the American Historical Association published I. C. C. Graham's *Colonists from Scotland*, in 1958 Arnold Schrier brought out his study of the effect of Irish emigration upon the Irish homeland, and in 1959 came Andrew Hill Clark's historical geography of the community on Prince Edward Island.

Of all these investigations, Hansen's alone had been a general study of the emigration of peoples in the same sense as the early works of Johnson and Carrothers. All the others had chosen some significant phase of the great movement. Kathleen Walpole had uncovered in living detail what before had been merely sketched in a chapter or less—the influence of the British humanitarian reforms on the transportation of emigrants on the Atlantic crossing. Professor Hitchins had described the operations of the agencies which the British government created between 1830 and 1873 to watch over the emigration of its subjects, a topic more critically developed twenty-five years later by Dr. Oliver MacDonagh. Dr. Adams had deepened and broadened, particularly by the use of rare Irish records and newspapers, the history of Irish removals begun by Frances Morehouse. Norman Macdonald alone had written specifically of the British North American colonies, and he with his eyes mainly on the procedures of new-world settlement not on old-world emigration. Meanwhile fine series of books on scholarly and statesmanlike subjects, the "Relations of Canada and the United States," "Canadian Frontiers of Settlement," were enlarging on the conclusions of earlier series and providing brilliantly for a variety of Canadian needs and interests. Authors of books in these series as well as others were writing important monographs on the Canadian forest and its industries, the fur trade, agriculture, and transportation, on commerce centring on the St. Lawrence, on vital regions and problems, as well as biographies by the dozen.

To these special and general studies, this author is greatly indebted. They have opened the pioneer historian's dark forest with a multitude of blazed trails in a fashion unimaginable when the first edition of this book was finished in 1928. All that existed to stir the searcher's interest in those days was the vision of Charles Buller and his contemporaries or the memory of a childhood peopled with strange-speaking Englishmen or Scots who measured all things in Canada by doings in a faraway place called HOME. Later those of us who studied in London, riding its buses and walking its historic streets, were impressed year after year by the swarms of women to be seen and the absence of men. No one then thought of the remarkable longevity of the female. When the subject was brought up in London University seminars, the gist of the answer was always the same: "That is the price of empire. The men must emigrate." Had the ability been present, the thoughts awakened by these experiences would undoubtedly have been set down in dramatic form or at least in historical fiction. Lacking that, the best that could be done was the tracing in cold fact of the movements of the men, and also the women, who left home and the thoughts and actions of those in authority and out of it who saw them go and aided or deplored their departure.

Interest in Canadian beginnings must be growing, for one hears more frequently now than formerly of a Canadian setting out to find his roots somewhere in the four older British American colonies or perhaps in the British Isles. Unless he has the good fortune to happen upon one of the excellent articles by careful local historians or a well-authenticated regional study, one may hear too of his fruitless search and his discouraged return. In the British Museum in his day, a professor of history of colonial expansion sometimes had to shock the tourist searching for her ancestors with the plain statement: "Madam, I've told you every place to look I can think of. If you've not found them, there's nowhere for you to go but to the prison lists." For some searchers the work of the genealogist would fill all needs; many, however, seek a broader view, a knowledge of the original old-world environment and of the forces that drove men and women from it on a trying voyage to an almost equally trying experience in the colonies. The search will continue, for it is characteristic not of the new but of the older, more firmly established society.

For that reason, words written in 1928 are as appropriate now as then. "We have been too prone to think that when emigrants arrived in the colonies, here a group and there a group, by some subtle process they became Canadians at the moment of arrival, and that here Canadian history must begin. As a matter of fact, all groups of emigrants formed part of a greater movement, all had characteristics in common, and all had been more uniformly influenced by the conditions that *drove* them from the home land than by those which *attracted* them to the colonies. Therefore, to study the essential, original characteristics of Canadian life one must follow the spreading colonial branches back to the root stock, or . . . shift the point of view from the circumference to the centre, and begin not at Halifax and St. John and Quebec, but in the Highland fisheries, the Irish farm, and the English factory."

The heroic quality of the human outpouring which peopled the British North American colonies still appeals to this student as it did when the graphic details of the story first began to unfold from the letters in C.O. 384 in the Public Record Office in Chancery Lane, London. That appeal and the fact that various scholars have been kind enough to say they found the early book useful are the main reasons for this new and enlarged edition. In extending the work to cover the years before Confederation the purpose has been, as it was before, to reveal the movement of the people—the conditions from which they came, the means they employed to reach the New World, their government's part in that removal and, to a less extent, their location in their new homes. Every effort has been made to continue the specific detail of persons and places and of programmes and policies for emigration which was said to be a helpful feature of the first study. But adding thirty years, the maximum years of mid-century emigration, created problems of space and choices had to be made. The writer hopes that the matter retained has been the most appropriate.

Of debts accumulated over the years, the first to be acknowledged should be that to the editors whose books for review have provided pleasant reading and required critical examination of theses and sources and to one of them, Dr. W. S. Wallace, who wrote the Editor's Preface to the book of 1928 and who has also read the manuscript of this revision and enlargement. During the same years, the specialized staffs of two great national institutions, the Public Archives and Library of Canada and the Library of Congress in Washington, D.C., have been unfailingly attentive and efficient. Only those students who have laboured year after year with the massive collections of British parliamentary papers in the British Museum and the Library of Congress or with the growing manuscript and microfilm materials in Ottawa can realize how continuous and exacting are the demands on the custodians of such sources, and only such students can appreciate the help so well given. In a lesser degree, because the British holdings though remarkable are smaller, the same is true of the Toronto Public Library in Canada, and the Johns Hopkins University and the Peabody Libraries in Baltimore.

H. I. C.

BRITISH EMIGRATION
TO BRITISH NORTH AMERICA

CONTENTS

FOREWORD	v
INTRODUCTION	vii
I. Settlement for Trade and Defence, 1765–1815	3
II. Unemployment, Overpopulation, Emigration	18
III. The Rising Tide: To the Military Settlements, 1815–1830	40
IV. The Rising Tide: To the Irish Settlements, 1823–1845	65
V. New Needs and New Theories	85
VI. Colonization Leaders and Colonization Companies	113
VII. The Emigrant Ship and the Emigrant Trade, 1815–1860	144
VIII. The Great Emigrations, 1830–1860	172
IX. Help for the Needy Emigrant	203
X. The Triumph of Laissez-Faire	228
NOTES	241
APPENDIXES	
A. For the Information of Emigrants	283
B. Statistical Tables	287
BIBLIOGRAPHICAL NOTE	305
INDEX	311

ILLUSTRATIONS

LINE-DRAWINGS

1. City of Quebec. Taken from the Harbour — 55
2. The Ejectment of Irish Tenantry — 76
3. Settlement, Canals, and Rail Lines, British North America, 1825–1860 — 130
4. Plan of the Betwixt Decks of the Ship, *Earl of Buckinghamshire* — 145
5. Emigration Vessel, Between Decks — 155
6. The Emigration Agent's Office — 181
7. The Embarkation, Waterloo Docks, Liverpool — 196
8. The Petition of the North-Quarter Glasgow Emigration Society, 1841 — 211

BLACK AND WHITE PLATES

Between pages 34 and 35

I. The Parting Cheer. Emigrants leaving Glasgow for the Colonies

II. The Emigrant's Welcome to Canada

III. Process of Clearing the Town Plot at Stanley, October, 1834

IV. View of Cholera Hospital and Telegraph, Grosse Isle Quarantine Station

I. SETTLEMENT FOR TRADE AND DEFENCE, 1765-1815

BY THE ACQUISITION of Canada in 1763, Great Britain completed the conquest of the French possessions in the North American continent, and relieved the Thirteen Colonies of a menace which had long threatened them. No one then could have foretold that Canada, inhabited by some sixty thousand people and fit only to be weighed against Guadeloupe in the negotiations which terminated the farspread Seven Years' War, would resist the revolutionary invitation of the English colonies to the south and, together with Nova Scotia, remain to form the goal of a new century of emigration from the British Isles. Yet even before the sound of war had passed, events were preparing for such a culmination.

In the years when Great Britain fought France for colonial and maritime supremacy, as well as in the succeeding period when she struggled to retain the rebelling American colonies and then faced them in battle along with Napoleon, every consideration demanded the strengthening of Britain's hold on her northern posts in America. Garrisons were sent in and an occasional trader, establishing himself where the French had hitherto held sway, began to see the possibility of opening up that intercourse with the West Indies which was to become an interest of the new British settlers on the Atlantic seaboard.

During the same years the foundations of future settlement were laid. The new and the old colonies in North America were to be welded into one people, British in trade and loyalty. Pioneers for the new lands were not actively sought in Great Britain because the population of the mother country was still looked upon as a resource to be cherished. Colonies could best be peopled by British subjects able to defend them, military men and experienced British civilians from the early North American settlements. Since the days of the Romans, armies had been recruited and military service rewarded by promises of free land. Cromwell had attempted to colonize Jamaica with soldiers and had used parts of the confiscated Irish estates to pay off the Commonwealth army.[1] The colonies of Massachusetts and Virginia had given lands to men on condition that they be prepared to defend them; Pennsylvania had enlisted soldiers to fight the French in 1755 by offering rewards of land. Even the name Nova Scotia, New Scotland, had been derived from the same practice when, in 1621, King James granted to Sir William Alexander the territory north of the two original colonizing companies in North America as an offset to French ambitions on the continent. Plans for colonizing with armed men were begun and expeditions sent out between 1622 and 1624, but the undertaking had to be abandoned in the reign of Charles II when France again obtained Nova Scotia.[2]

Though the Treaty of Utrecht had effected a nominal transference of allegiance to the British Crown and a garrison was placed at Annapolis Royal, it was not until the return of Louisbourg to the French in 1748 that the British government again undertook the peopling of Nova Scotia.[3] In spite of early recommendations by Governor Shirley of Massachusetts for the safeguarding of this northern peninsula by an ingrafted population of English-speaking settlers, preferably fishermen from the Massachusetts colony,[4] the Committee of the Privy Council for Trade and Plantations offered in the *Gazette* of March 7, 1749, transportation, arms and ammunition, and land to men recently "disbanded His Majesty's land and sea service." Parliament then voted £40,000 to begin the enterprise and the Honourable Edward Cornwallis set out for Nova Scotia in charge of some twenty-five hundred souls in thirteen vessels. Landing at a good harbour, Chebucto, where they were joined by the garrison from Louisbourg, they raised stockades, organized themselves into a militia, and named the new British post Halifax in honour of the First Lord of the Board of Trade who had sent them. Shortly afterwards a contract was made with a merchant of Rotterdam for procuring foreign Protestants as settlers. They came mainly from the Palatinate and the Duchy of Württemberg; after an uneasy sojourn at Halifax they were moved by Lieutenant-Governor Lawrence to a more promising area to the south, Lunenburg. Though the government's support was generous, the results of the settlement were disappointing.[5]

Upon the expulsion of the Acadians in 1755 and the subsequent opening of 200,000 acres of valuable lands on the Bay of Fundy, a plan possibly adapted from Governor Shirley's suggestion was undertaken. The British government still wished to send out disbanded soldiers. This Governor Lawrence opposed for, military man though he was, he believed that a soldier's habits prevented him from becoming a good settler. He hoped to see every vacated Acadian farmstead in the Annapolis Valley occupied by loyal, sturdy American settlers.[6] Accordingly, in late 1758 and again in 1759, Lawrence announced in New England the opening of the Bay of Fundy lands. The announcement attracted land prospectors in plenty. Lawrence died in 1760, but boom times had begun and individuals and groups were winning large grants of land. British colonists in New England, already on the move northward, now continued into Nova Scotia. Farmers took up the old lands of the Acadians in the Annapolis Valley, the Minas Basin, and the Isthmus of Chignecto; lumbermen went inland from the fishing stations operated by New England fishermen on the southwestern and the Bay of Fundy coasts. The Philadelphia Company was formed and received about 200,000 acres; it, as well as emigrant agents long accustomed to new-world colonization, brought in groups of American, Irish, and Scottish settlers.

Among the agents, one man has received the most attention—Alexander McNutt, an Ulsterman of Augusta County, Virginia, later of Boston, and as early as 1759 an active petitioner for Nova Scotia grants.[7] Fertile in schemes, persuasive in argument, and possessed of an amazing energy, he pleaded his case with Governor Lawrence and with men much less easy to move to action, the Lords of Trade in England. In the early 1760's, McNutt won permission to undertake the settlement of seven townships and the land granted to the Philadelphia Company. He won also a reservation upon a million acres in various parts of the colony. McNutt's British settlements began in 1760 with the conveyance of fifty families from Ireland to Truro and, after vigorous advertising in Londonderry and elsewhere in 1761 and 1762, he persuaded over six hundred needy Irish to lend themselves to the Nova Scotia venture. But in Londonderry, Truro, and Onslow where the agent had deposited his charges the life of the pioneer was too strenuous for the Irish to encounter unaided. In 1763 when the indefatigable McNutt was full of plans for his "New Jerusalem" to be founded at Cape Sable, £50,000 had already been spent to settle emigrants in the province and an order of the Lords of Trade and Plantations intimated that the colonization of Irish must come to an end. Apparently there was as yet no fear of overpopulation in Ireland, for in the spring of 1762 an Order in Council from Whitehall announced "the danger to Ireland of withdrawing so many of the population." In consequence, no lands were to be "granted in Nova Scotia to people from Ireland except to those who have lived there or in another Colony for five years."[8]

The Lords of Trade had not abandoned their belief in soldier settlement. Again following the peace of 1763, the government made special offers to disbanded troops, imperial and colonial, this time at the rate of 5,000 acres to captains, 2,000 to subalterns, 200 to non-commissioned officers, and 50 to privates.[9] While the Acadian lands were being opened to immigrants from New England, more than a dozen regiments of colonial and Highland troops were brought to the fertile areas around St. John and Fredericton.[10] By the end of 1766 the Londonderry, Truro, and Onslow areas had almost one thousand settlers, only three of the present counties, Pictou, Antigonish, and Digby were unbroken by the pioneer, and the population of the whole peninsula had risen to thirteen thousand.[11]

The policy by which Nova Scotia had been maintained as a naval base and strengthened by planned settlement had required that Cape Breton be left uninhabited for the better use of those resorting to the fisheries. This plan included neither the lands of modern New Brunswick nor those in the Island of St. John, later Prince Edward Island. In the mid-1760's most of the land on the St. John River on the mainland was secured to proprietors or companies. Soon small communities of New Englanders came to the grants on the River, and to Sackville, Portland, and Campobello; and Scottish merchants interested in the salmon fisheries brought groups of their own countrymen to Miramichi in 1764 and to Campbelltown in 1775.[12] Meanwhile in complete disregard of early settlers who eventually moved to Miramichi and Restigouche, the whole of the Island of St. John was granted in 1767 to a few absentee proprietors, and a desultory emigration then set in to the Island and the main coast. What settlement developed on the Island was the work of Scottish emigrants, some disbanded soldiers, others civilians. In 1769 a few of the Fraser Highlanders began home-building there. Shortly before the American War of Independence a Scottish chieftain, Captain John Macdonald of the Eighty-fourth Regiment, bought two townships and led in Roman Catholic Highlanders from Moydart and Uist. Other Scots made similar attempts to assist their countrymen and to develop the Island but none with the devotion displayed by Macdonald. In spite of these efforts, by 1779 fifty-one out of the sixty-seven townships lacked settlers and, under the government's terms of settlement, every lot was liable to forfeiture.[13]

In government offices in London it was perhaps natural to assume that Nova Scotia and indeed Quebec could be peopled easily and assimilated quickly with the older British colonies in North America. But neither the policy of the Board of Trade, by which the post at Halifax was founded, nor the system of land grants introduced for the province by Governor Lawrence was designed to bring about the satisfactory settlement of the maritime colonies. The first, in its plans for establishing a naval base and developing the fisheries, was intended primarily for defence; the second constituted a land system the terms of which, involving the stipulation for Protestant settlers and even the perpetual growth of hemp, were practically impossible of fulfilment.* Moreover the American Revolution cut off immigration from the colonies to the south while the first proprietors were making their efforts to bring in settlers. The result was obvious after 1783 when large grants, still undeveloped, gradually reverted to the Crown.

In the conquered French province, Canada, government policy had followed lines similar to those carried out in Nova Scotia. Here too the main purpose was defence and British trade, and the assimilation of the Quebec colony as a part of the unified British American dominions. For a time in 1763, it seemed that "the advantageous and effectual settlement" of the province would be undertaken as that of Halifax had been in 1749, with probably a similar end in view—the suppression of the French population.[14] By the Royal Proclamation of October 7, 1763, which marked the close of the Seven Years' War and Britain's victory over France in America, the British government made an appeal for settlers by offering to British officers and privates disbanded in North America free grants of land in the same proportions as those mentioned for Nova Scotia. Two months later the instructions issued to guide the Honourable James Murray, captain general and governor-in-chief of Quebec, outlined provisions for establishing soldiers on public lands "upon such terms, and under such moderate quit rents, services and acknowledgments as have been appointed in our other colonies." Since "great Inconveniences" had arisen in many of the older colonies from "granting excessive Quantities of Land" to persons who did not cultivate or live upon it, Murray was carefully instructed that grants must be made in proportion to the recipient's ability to cultivate. Heads of families were to receive 100 acres and 50 additional for members of the family to a maximum limit of 1,000 acres.[15] The Governor was to have townships laid out and the lands advertised in the other British American colonies. By this means the mother country proposed to use disbanded soldiers and pioneers from the older colonies to form the nucleus of a new loyal population in Quebec.

*These terms required that one-third of the grant be enclosed, planted, or improved within ten years and the remaining two-thirds within thirty years; that one rood of every thousand acres be planted and kept forever in hemp, and that one-quarter of the land be settled the first year, one Protestant settler to every two hundred acres, and the whole within four years; finally, unless the required conditions were fulfilled the land was to be forfeited.

General Murray had already made grants of land "en fief et seigneurie" in the name of two officers of the Fraser Highlanders, Captain John Nairne and Lieutenant Malcolm Fraser. The best known of the settlements of this famous regiment, the most picturesque of Wolfe's celebrated army, grew up at Murray Bay on the north shore of the St. Lawrence River; others were at Rivière du Loup, Lévis, Matapedia, and Restigouche.[16] Now, following the new instructions, Murray requested a lowering of quit rents and advertised the Quebec lands enthusiastically in a poster published in Massachusetts, New York, Pennsylvania, and Connecticut. As settlers from the old colonies failed to respond to this invitation to move north, Murray rose to the defence of those he had, the French.[17] He would not have them dissatisfied by the machinations of "four hundred and fifty contemptible sutlers and traders" who were pressing the claims of the small English population to special favour.

The "sutlers and traders" had arrived early and made themselves the most powerful influence in Quebec. Sensing the demand of the St. Lawrence population which had been isolated by the years of war, canny merchants from the old Thirteen Colonies and those purveyors who inevitably follow armies had arrived with their wares and remained to profit. In time they were to master the inland trade and hold its control until the breakdown of the British mercantile system and the rise of the interior agricultural economy. Now they were determined to assert their rights as Englishmen in a foreign but British community. But when the British traders at last obtained the removal of their governor, it was only to receive in his place a stronger advocate of the pro-French view in the person of Sir Guy Carleton, and by that time all possibility of settlement was destroyed by the controversy which preceded the American Revolution. Energies were accordingly concentrated on solidifying the loyalty of the French by assuring them in the Quebec Act of 1774 the preservation of their own language and customs, including the French land system. On the whole, however, the divergence from the course pursued in Nova Scotia was less than might be supposed. In each area the idea of encouraging settlement was accessory to the main object, defence. From 1774 until after 1783, Quebec was little more than a military outpost to be maintained against the Indians and the colonies now in revolt.

So it was that the coming of the United Empire Loyalists* brought the first great influx of population into the vast territories now comprised in the Maritime Provinces, Ontario, and Quebec. By sea to the Nova Scotia

---

*Though the name "United Empire Loyalists" is used here, it should be noted that the title was not officially granted to the refugees until 1789.

ports, by the St. Lawrence River and the Lake Champlain route to Canada, from Oswego and Sackett's Harbour across Lake Ontario, some forty thousand emigrants from the now independent states were assisted by the British government in their removal to the northern colonies.

Loyalists who reached Quebec before the fighting ended were enrolled, when possible, in local regiments. The backbone of the most distinguished of these, "the King's Royal Regiment of New York," commissioned by Sir Guy Carleton, consisted of tenants of Sir John Johnson's estates in western New York. Many of them, originally Highlanders, had been just the type needed for the uneasy New York frontier; now as Loyalists under Sir John Johnson they served for a guard to protect the colony of Quebec and give aid to other Loyalists desiring to reach it. Another group to become famous was the "Royal Highland" or Eighty-fourth Regiment. The first battalion under Lieutenant Colonel Allan MacLean came mainly from the Fraser Highlanders who had been disbanded following the Seven Years' War, the second from Highlanders in Nova Scotia. Various Loyalist volunteers found places in Butler's Rangers, Peter's Queen's Loyal Rangers, and other regiments.[18] The land allotments promised these men on enlistment varied slightly, but after the peace of 1783, a uniform rate of 100 acres for each disbanded soldier and Loyalist, with 50 acres additional for persons in his family, became the general rule. Officers, of course, were rewarded more generously.

In the colony of Quebec the able and far-seeing Governor, Frederick Haldimand, bore the responsibility for placing, feeding, and even clothing the hordes of newcomers. The duty could scarcely have fallen upon a man with a finer sense of responsibility and understanding. Choosing and preparing the lands for regulars and militia became a complicated task requiring excellent organization and diplomacy. Already Haldimand had permitted many of the early arrivals to remain in that strategically vital area, Sorel, at the junction of the Richelieu and St. Lawrence rivers which, through his own foresight, had become government property. After considering possible locations for the Loyalists in Cape Breton, the Eastern Townships, and the lands stretching all the way from Gaspé to Niagara and Detroit, and after lengthy correspondence with the British government in London and the Indians in the West, Haldimand finally decided to use first the vacant lands which lay westward from the upper boundary of the seigniory of Longueuil above Lake St. Francis, and promising areas about the old outpost of Cataraqui, the modern Kingston. As need arose other regions would be opened. The task of surveying the fourteen townships deemed necessary for the reception of the expected Loyalists fell upon the shoulders of the experienced Surveyor-General, Major Samuel Holland. Organizing and holding the Loyalist groups together, an even more exacting job, was the work of the veteran patriarch of war and settlement, Sir John Johnson.[19]

Haldimand's judicious policy of maintaining the Loyalists in their units proved wise for the colony since it prevented an uncontrolled scramble for land grants, and helpful for the Loyalists because it continued the old associations which are often lost in pioneer life. In accord with this policy, most of Butler's Rangers were allowed to remain at Niagara where they wished to be placed on lands already purchased from the Indians. Johnson had requested for his regiment the lands above the Longueuil seigniory; consequently his first battalion occupied the first five townships there: the Roman Catholic Highlanders, the Scottish Presbyterians, the German Calvinists, the Lutherans, and the Anglicans each separately located in their own townships. Most of Major Jessup's Corps arrived to fill up the next three townships. Of the townships around Cataraqui, Johnson's second battalion took up numbers 3 and 4; Captain Michael Grass's six militia companies of "nondescript refugees" from New York number 1; disbanded regulars, part of them German, number 5; and the remainder of Major Jessup's men along with some of Colonel MacLean's Eighty-fourth Regiment, of whom others had gone to Chatham township north of the Ottawa River, took up number 2. So efficiently was this rearranging of human lives carried out by Haldimand and his aides that by the autumn of 1785 the townships above Longueuil and around Cataraqui contained eighteen hundred families and those at Niagara about three hundred. In the remainder of the huge colony under Governor Haldimand there were a few hundred Loyalists under Governor Cox down on the Gaspé, on Cape Breton Island a few more, and opposite Detroit an even smaller group with Captain Alexander McKee, the Indian agent.

Nowhere in these areas had it been possible to obtain complete separation between military and civilian Loyalists nor indeed to confine settlement to the regions mentioned. And as the immigration of the late Loyalists continued after the peace of 1783, new regions were set aside for them, some immediately south of the St. Lawrence River, some few across in the Eastern Townships. In 1787 the Governor, Sir Guy Carleton, now Lord Dorchester, rewarded the head of each Loyalist family who had improved his original land grant with the gift of an additional 200 acres.[20] From London Lord North urged the importance of planning for military protection, both by leaving accessible border areas wild and unbroken and by holding others with a population of unquestionable loyalty. In short, the formation of settlements was still to be subordinate to the need for defence.[21]

Even before the western part of old Quebec became the colony of Upper Canada, the movement of Loyalists into the west of the province had required the opening of townships along the St. Lawrence River and the Bay of Quinte, west along the lake front to York, and on around the head of the lake from Burlington Bay to the early post at Niagara. Surveys and some few settlers were also proceeding up the north bank of the Ottawa River and west and south to the River Thames and Lake St. Clair. Everywhere, except in the townships adjoining the present province of Quebec and in the Niagara peninsula, settlers were so sparsely spread that in the whole upper region in 1791 the total population was only about fourteen thousand.

The main purpose however had been served. The vital areas had been claimed by people whose British loyalty had been tested. More than that, nuclei of settlement had been formed which, if necessary, would be useful as centres for future settlers. The value of such nuclei was seen in 1786 when a shipload of five hundred Highlanders from Glengarry arrived with their priest, Alexander Macdonell, to join their clansmen in the new-world Glengarry. Similarly to Pictou in Nova Scotia where the ship *Hector* had brought a little cargo of Scots before the American Revolution, there now were drawn Scots from Ross, Perthshire, and Inverness; and to Prince Edward Island more Highlanders came to make homes near Captain Macdonald's early contingents.[22]

In Upper Canada after the arrival of the first lieutenant-governor, the ambitious and martial-minded John Graves Simcoe, the planning for military defence was continued and enlarged. Simcoe thought of Upper Canada as "the Bulwark of the British Empire in America."[23] He proposed to protect it by means of military roads and well-placed settlements of loyal British subjects built up with the assistance of his special military force, the Queen's Rangers. The old highway from Montreal was run on to York and Niagara, and from York west; to the north, Lake Ontario was joined to Lake Huron by a trail cut from York to Lake Simcoe and beyond to Penetanguishene. Though the Rangers did aid in the building of Simcoe's new capital at York and in work on the roads nearby, the plan for semi-military, semi-civilian settlements soon broke down.[24] But nothing could dampen the drawing power of the Proclamation of February 7, 1792, which promised generous land grants to new settlers. Hundreds of land-hungry men and women from the old New England colonies made their way across New York State, Lake Ontario, and the Niagara River to join the first Loyalists on Upper

Canada's rich lands. Though the original Loyalist refugees in the colony had numbered six thousand or less, by the outbreak of war in 1812, that colony alone had perhaps eighty thousand inhabitants.[25]

To Nova Scotia which had long been an outpost of New England more than twenty thousand Loyalists, largely civilian but some military, made their way just before and after the peace. The second battalion of the Royal Highland, the Eighty-fourth Regiment, demanded large grants of land and in the end received almost 100,000 acres, mainly around Pictou, but also on Prince Edward Island and near Halifax. Of the nearly 300,000 acres set aside as rewards for military service, Hamilton's Eighty-second Regiment took up acreage south of Pictou, and local militia and the Duke of Cumberland's regiment with representatives of a few voluntary groups absorbed the remainder.[26] On the whole these disbanded soldiers, mainly Scots, proved to be loyal citizens but indifferent settlers. In Nova Scotia as in western Quebec, later Upper Canada, their ultimate service was to be of another sort, to form a link between Canada and Scotland and to be the means of drawing to British North America others of their clansmen.

In the hope that the peninsula would be "practically fringed with vigorous townships," shiploads of Loyalists were sent to the Bay of Fundy shores west and east of Annapolis, and to the Atlantic coast east of Cape Sable. Some of these newcomers to the Annapolis Basin were well-to-do and able to purchase farms, and their lands were quickly improved. Some were men of training and experience in the professions. However, at Shelburne on the Atlantic coast ten thousand hopeful patriots did not succeed well. The failure of the cod fishery, a special project for the training of seamen dear to London policy-makers, race riots on the arrival of Negroes, and the prospect of pioneer hardships soon caused the group to scatter to more promising locations, leaving behind a town of only a few hundred. On Prince Edward Island, too, hopes for the growth of the Loyalist population were unfulfilled because lack of funds to alienate lands held by the proprietors limited the Loyalist immigration. For Cape Breton the new population of Loyalist refugees numbered about three thousand.[27]

When in 1784 the lands north of the Bay of Fundy were created a separate colony, New Brunswick, on the British plan of *divide et impera*, new regions were in need of a trustworthy population. In St. John at the mouth of the river and on rich meadow lands farther up thousands of Loyalists, some from the old colonies, others from disbanded Scottish regiments, now made homes. All in all between eleven and fourteen thousand settled in this new colony, in accord with the mother country's policy of forming a reliable backbone of people and useful soldier settlements for the colony's exposed areas on the coast and along the St. Croix River.[28]

In brief, after the peace of 1783 preparations for the protection of Canada and the maritime colonies went on as before. During the years of the American Revolutionary War, the doctrines of Adam Smith, Dean Tucker, Major Cartwright,[29] and other critics of the Old Colonial System had had every opportunity to gain wide acceptance. The possession of colonies was said to be of no advantage to the mother country; their maintenance required an expenditure the only return for which would be found in the profits of trade with them; and these profits would be as great were the colonies themselves under a foreign flag. But there is no evidence that such theories had penetrated far into the system by which the colonial empire was bound to Whitehall.

The creation of strategic settlements in New Brunswick, Cape Breton, Nova Scotia, and western Quebec, the plan to run an inland road and mail route from New Brunswick to Quebec which would be safe from attack by the United States,[30] the opening of military highways to the west of Cataraqui, all indicate the official determination to maintain permanent occupation, by force if necessary. Although Governor Haldimand had believed that the evacuation of the posts in the upper country would ruin commerce and greatly lessen the value of Canada to the empire, committees of the Council under Lord Dorchester had reported on population, agriculture, commerce, and settlement.[31] Dorchester himself had written in 1786, "A passive demeanour in these Provinces would prove ruinous to Great Britain in case of a war on the continent; their hearty concurrence, and the most active measures . . . are necessary or we cannot expect to maintain the dominion; good policy therefore requires we should leave as little for them to gain by a separation as possible."[32] Such preparations for the continuance of dominion and the furtherance of trade could not have been made by men converted to the theories which had appeared since Halifax was founded on the principles of the Old Colonial System.

Nor was there any great change with respect to the emigration of British subjects. It is true that Chief Justice Smith wrote from Canada to Evan Nepean in London that "one can scarcely conceive many words necessary to show that *Men* and not *Trees* constitute the strength of a Country. . . . It is in your power to make Canada the residence of *Scores* of millions, all dependent upon your Island for *Cloathing*, and able to pay for it in raw materials to the comfort of your Manufactures and the Expansion of your Commerce."[33] Another too advised that "relief or aid" be given to emigrants removing to the British colonies in order to offset the loss of citizens which was annually taking place through removal to the United States.[34] But the day for emigration had not yet come. For a few years more the prevailing spirit was to be that of guarding population on the old principle set down again in 1790, "as the People of every Nation constitute its strength and wealth, the Parent State suffers a loss when an industrious Individual leaves it."[35]

The attitude of Henry Dundas, the secretary of state for war and the colonies, towards settlement abroad is indicative of the times. To Lord Dorchester in 1791 he expressed his conviction that it was undoubtedly the duty of the government at home to adopt every plan which could promote the wealth and population of its colonies;[36] nevertheless in 1792 when Lieutenant-Governor Simcoe desired an aggressive immigration policy for Upper Canada, Dundas condemned the proposal vigorously. "An ingrafted population," he wrote, would necessarily be attended "with a want of that regularity and stability which all, but particularly Colonial Governments require." Settlers sufficient for the needs of the new provinces would come of their own accord and, as for emigration from the British Isles, proper steps would be taken to put a stop to it.[37] Admonitions such as this would not deter a man of Simcoe's energetic devotion to the interests of his colony. Catching the spirit of the far-visioned merchants and speculators who were already assessing possibilities near and distant, he warned the legislators of Upper Canada to provide "clear and evident Security to the Possessor of Capitals in the British Empire" who might invest in colonial lands.[38]

Egoistic or not, Simcoe saw the future more clearly than the secretaries in the British offices above him. These were the years in which the face of England was transformed by the new activities of the Industrial Revolution, and her trade and finance put on the basis which enabled her to come successfully through the commercial crisis of the Napoleonic Wars. In view of such circumstances, it is not surprising that the government should believe that loss of citizens meant loss of power and that there should be no movement of Englishmen abroad. It was not until the results of war and the fruits of industrial and other great changes, seen in an increase of population, brought an undeniable demand for a new economic and political organization that a different attitude appeared towards the emigration of British subjects.

In the northern colonies in America however, new interests were at work. The coming of the United Empire Loyalists, the first and their successors, was changing the character of the economy developing on the upper St. Lawrence River and the north shore of Lake Ontario. These newcomers along with some of the military settlers were making homes, clearing away the forest, and preparing agricultural products. Soon there would be a surplus for export. From 1787 on, merchants and traders on the St. Lawrence urged their claims to British favour by petitions which described the future of commerce and settlement in glowing terms. In 1790 a committee of the Council of Lower Canada advocated the encouragement of immigration from Europe; in 1791 the Quebec Agricultural Society vigorously pushed the cultivation of hemp and advised the direction of Scottish settlers to Canada.[39] The strongest advocates of settlement were not those interested in the defence of the colonies or in the general advancement of their prosperity. They were, as big promoters generally are, men personally interested—merchants, shipowners, and land speculators. After a visit to Kingston in 1794, Lieutenant-Governor John Graves Simcoe reported that he had found the "language" of the merchants very much enlarged: "The Fur Trade . . . seemed no longer the principal object of their attention." They looked forward to the produce of the country as the true source of their wealth. The land was rising in price and nothing was wanted but the introduction of British capital.[40]

In the Maritime Provinces business interests were especially active. Memorials from Cape Breton in 1803 dwelt upon the colony as the Gibraltar of the fisheries and upon the possibility of it becoming a depot for the produce of the countries of the American continent and the means by which the West Indian trade might be wrested from the Americans. Nova Scotia had advocates equally enthusiastic. In 1806 Richard Uniacke sent to the Colonial Office a memorial of nineteen manuscript pages in which he argued the necessity of directing British capital and enterprise from the United States to Nova Scotia and so securing to the empire the wealth and population which were annually passing from Great Britain to a foreign, perhaps an inimical, flag.[41] Land speculators too, men like Isaac Ogden and William Willcocks, were begging grants of land in proportion to the number of British emigrants they would bring into the colonies.

This was a period none the less when Canning could insist that "to fence and support, not to extend . . . was the obvious dictate of policy," and Pitt could mildly write, "Is it the wish of Lord Hobart to *discourage* the grant of lands in Canada, or to encourage *useful* men to go thither? If he wishes to discourage *wholly* such applications, I am silent." Even while they wrote, events of war were drawing the attention of the British government departments to a consideration of colonial resources. As the possibility of a break with the Baltic powers became imminent, an effort was made to find naval supplies within the empire. In 1800 a circular was sent out to the colonies in America giving instructions to attempt the growth of hemp. In Nova Scotia and Upper Canada the governors met their councils and finally granted a bounty on all hemp grown;[42] in Lower Canada also assistance was given. But in every case the results were disappointing. Though Joseph Banks was convinced that Russian hemp, the product of personal labour, would always surpass in quality the best the American colonies could produce, the hopes of the colonists did not die. Extravagant grants of land were made to men promising to grow hemp; directions were translated into French for the Canadians to follow in its culture, and year after year the legislatures were induced to make grants for its encouragement.[43]

Next came a call for Canadian timber. The Navy refused the white oak sent but pine masts were shipped from various points on the St. Lawrence River and from the Bay of Quinte.[44] In 1806 Napoleon announced the continental blockade; within two years the Scandinavian sources of timber supply had joined the continental system. The British government and its merchants turned perforce to the colonies. Soon the Nova Scotia and New Brunswick trade was on the increase. By 1808 British North America was furnishing 50,000 loads of timber a year,[45] and when in 1809 Great Britain laid a duty on Baltic timber the market was again enlarged. In 1810 the port of Quebec alone shipped almost 34,000 tons of oak and 70,000 tons of pine timber. The President of the Board of Trade had already shown the House of Commons that the North American colonies could practically supply the West Indies. Now Canning wrote that "this country has in itself, *in its own consumption* and *its own colonies*, ample means of self-existence."[46]

Whatever fortune the end of war might bring, whatever disgust with the maintenance of dominion at the price of souls, there would be left the traces of wealth revealed during the stress of war. In books of travel estimates of the resources of the empire had been appearing. Hugh Gray, John Lambert, and others had described North America; Bristed and Chalmers had discussed the empire. But it remained for a Scot, resident in London, Patrick Colquhoun, in a book more widely known and reviewed than any of its predecessors, to bring together the then absorbing questions which none before had noticed were coincident—the problem of apparent overpopulation, economic stagnation, and the development of the resources of the empire. Just before the peace, he wrote in words which might seem prophetic: "It is, therefore, through the medium of an increased demand for manufactures in the colonies and foreign countries that the most certain resource is to be found for the beneficial employment of the people, and when this and agriculture fail, the next best resource will be found in emigration." Emigration, he believed, would augment the resources of the parent state by "the consumption of British Manufactures, and by the exportation of the various productions of the soil in Timber, Corn, Hemp, Flax, Flaxseed, Potashes and other valuable articles of Commerce." Emigration would render the labour of emigrants as beneficial to the parent state as if they remained in their native country.[47]

Such an argument placed the case for emigration on the old mercantile doctrine of a self-sufficing empire. It was in the years after Colquhoun's statement, the years immediately following the peace, that this doctrine was replaced by the newer one of free trade. The emigration which began under the auspices of the first system continued and increased under the second. Advocates of the new, as well as of the old, attempted to justify the outward movement. Emigration undoubtedly proceeded from causes working deeply in the life of the nation.

II. UNEMPLOYMENT, OVERPOPULATION, EMIGRATION

FAR FROM BRINGING the end of British dominion in North America, the peace of 1783 made inevitable the retention and peopling of the northern part of the continent by Great Britain. The War of American Independence interrupted but did not stop an outward movement of population which sprang from need in the mother country and opportunity in the New World. Such a movement once begun provides momentum for its own continuance. Scottish Highland regiments disbanded and given lands in Nova Scotia and Quebec after the wars, in accord with the government's plans for military defence, soon welcomed kinsmen newly arrived from Scotland. And in Scotland the poverty which drove population outward before 1776 remained as compelling as ever after 1783 when peace again permitted the opening of the way to North America.

In the pre-Revolutionary year that the ship *Hector* brought its destitute little cargo of Scots to Pictou, Nova Scotia, Samuel Johnson journeyed slowly across from Inverness to the Hebrides. Noting the crumbling hovel, the furrow grown in grass, and the vessel taking on its sad passengers in the Isle of Skye, he wrote with a caustic pen:

To hinder insurrection by driving away the people, and to govern peaceably by having no subjects is an expedient that argues no great profundity of politicks; . . . it affords a legislator little self applause to consider that where there was formerly an insurrection, there is now a wilderness.[1]

Before the failure of the Stuart cause, the Highland tribal chieftain had been the leader in war, the judge in peace. He counted his wealth not in lands, flocks, or rents, but in the number of men he could call out against an enemy raider.[2] The need for men encouraged him in the subdivision of his property and his farmers continued the process until the Highland estates were supporting as large a population as could draw a bare subsistence from the soil. With the Disarming Act, the Abolition of Heritable Jurisdictions, and the Forfeiture of Estates Act[3] the landlords ceased to be petty monarchs requiring the services of followers for defence. At the same time was removed the most potent check upon population, the petty Highland warfare, and this, together with the growing use of the potato, combined to increase population at the very moment when the proprietors, forcibly divested of their prerogatives, turned their attention towards bettering their own positions. Whether they determined to make the old system of farming pay by raising their terms to the tacksmen who now formed an unnecessary link between proprietor and tenant, whether they adopted new farming methods—"engrossing"—or whether they took up sheep-farming, the resultant changes were bound to cause a readjustment of population.

Some Highland landowners, it is true, desired to increase population on their coastal estates in order to have plentiful labour available for the short kelp season. Though this practice enriched the proprietors generously, it could do nothing but impoverish the labourers, now left without any full-time occupation or sufficient land to support themselves. The rise in rents largely explains the emigration of the sixties and seventies, for the emigrants were tacksmen, often relatives of the former chieftain, who took along with them the lower and lesser tenantry. In 1769, for example, all the tenants of Lord Macdonald's estate in Skye emigrated.[4] The outbreak of war in 1776 checked emigration for a time, but when the peace of 1783 freed the Scot from army service his native land, still faced with the problem of a numerous population and a scanty production, was enduring the results of the disastrous famine of 1782.[5] Newspapers of the day tell the story in its barest, yet most essential, details. In the advertising column one reads: "For rent or sale 1,000 acres of arable farm land capable of maintaining 9,000 sheep," and in the next column, a notice of equal size: "The *Caledonian Mercury* hears that about 500 young men . . . who have waited two years for employment in the fisheries or elsewhere are about to emigrate from the West Coast."[6]

The rumour of this departure roused opposition in England and Scotland. At a meeting of the Highland Society of London in May, 1786, the Earl of Breadalbane secured the agreement of those members present to co-operate with the government in frustrating emigration from the estates of Macdonald of Glengarry and to recommend that the principal noblemen in the Highlands endeavour to prevent further emigration.[7] The *Caledonian Mercury* subsequently contradicted the report of the emigration. But two months later the Quebec *Gazette* announced the arrival in the ship *Macdonald*, from Greenock, of 520 Highland Scottish emigrants with their priest, the Rev. Alexander Macdonell, and Hugh Finlay wrote to Evan Nepean, under-secretary in the Home Office, that the men were "young, stout, hale and hearty; a brave and loyal people. . . . Their Highland friends who evacuated Sir John Johnson's lands on the Mohawk River gave them encouragement to come over to Canada." Before another month passed, the government at Quebec had agreed to provide lands, rations, and the transportation necessary for the Glengarry emigrants to join their friends.[8] Not until 1790 is there equally authentic record of another emigration to Quebec. There can be little doubt, however, that during the intervening period small groups made their way to Canada and Nova Scotia.

As sheep-farming progressed northward from the Lowlands, emigration increased. Ninety-six Highlanders, who had been evicted from their small farms at Arisaig and on the Island of Eigg when the proprietors turned their holdings into grazing grounds, landed at Quebec on the *British Queen* in 1790. The little fund of £200 which they had possessed on departure was exhausted by January, 1791, and, though offered situations by Panet on his seigniory of Argenteuil, the Highlanders preferred to accept government aid to join their friends who had settled at Johnstown in 1785 and 1786.[9]

A much larger emigration was going on at the same time to the Atlantic provinces. Situated as they were just off the old well-travelled route to the New England states and employing a considerable shipping in their own fishing and timber trade, Nova Scotia, New Brunswick, and Cape Breton had the advantage of cheaper passage rates than the St. Lawrence port of Quebec. When the little subscriptions had been collected in the Highlands, and the representative of the prospective emigrants went down to make his bargain with the ship agent, the cost of transportation was an important factor in determining the party's destination.[10] Those who had least to spend went perforce to the Scottish Lowlands, next in price came Newfoundland, and higher still the other maritime colonies. Highland families reached Pictou, Nova Scotia, in 1786 and Knoydart in 1787, and Lowlanders came from Dumfries in 1788. In 1791 through tempting promises of free land and provisions made by an agent in Glasgow, four shiploads of almost one thousand persons were directed to Nova Scotia and Prince Edward Island. The *Caledonian Mercury* believed that the ship agents cleared twelve shillings on each steerage passage, "a very decent sum to their pockets on the trade of emigration in 1791." But the emigrants landed at Pictou in September practically penniless and though that small community, itself containing only seven hundred individuals, made an effort to support the newcomers, eventually it was necessary to appeal for aid to the colonial government. The petition addressed to Lieutenant-Governor Parr showed clearly that unless the British emigrant's way were made agreeable in the British colonies, they would follow the line of least resistance and make their new homes under a foreign flag in the United States, "where every possible Encouragement [was] given them."

"My heart bleeds for the poor Wretches," Parr wrote to Evan Nepean, "and I am distressed to know what to do with them. If they are not assisted, they must inevitably perish upon the Beach where they are now hutted; humanity says that cannot be the case in a Christian Country."[11] In the end the Lieutenant-Governor himself provided Indian meal and herrings to ward off starvation and in the spring, at the advice of Father McEachern of St. John, those who did not embrace the Protestant gospel of the Rev. Dr. MacGregor, minister at Pictou, scattered to Antigonish and various parts of the province.[12]

Again in 1801 Pictou received a group of Roman Catholic Highlanders, many of whom had been evicted by the chief of the Chisholms. Their emigration was managed by an agent, Hugh Dunoon, who appears to have misled them with wild tales of a Nova Scotian tree that would yield them sugar, soap, and fuel,[13] and with the idea of a voyage so short that before they were out of sight of the Western Islands, they inquired if "this be Ameriky." Dunoon's two chartered vessels, the *Sarah* and the *Pigeon*, sailed from Fort William with over six hundred passengers, badly overcrowded and short of rations. Pictou was no more able to support these than the emigrants of 1791 and they ultimately went, as had their predecessors of the same faith, to the settlement at Antigonish, and farther to the east.

So great was the discontent now spreading in the Highlands that when the estate of Appin, Argyll, passed from its former landlord to the Marquess of Tweedale, six thousand of the old tenants sent Duncan Moir Campbell of Ardsheat to New Brunswick, Canada, and the western United States in search of lands.[14] When the extension of sheep-farming into Ross and Sutherland the following year brought on the riots in which the dispossessed tenants tried to drive the sheep down into the sea, further colour was given to the rumour that great emigrations were about to take place.[15] Emigration agents and land speculators had already approached the Lower Canadian government with proposals to conduct Highlanders to the province, if the land committee would reward them with grants of land in proportion to the number of settlers brought in. The outbreak of war put an end to these plans, for when the drum beat to arms in the Highlands the emigrant agent's trade languished. Though the most frequent notices in the northern publications are those of the recruiting sergeant* and the emigrant agent, they never appear in papers of the same date.[16]

The whole subject of emigration had come up for review when the Highland Society, founded for the purpose of studying and improving Highland conditions, set out in the nineties to put an end to depopulation. Certain Scottish newspapers supported the Society's aims. In the opinion of the *Caledonian Mercury* none were enriched by the emigrations but the agents and they at the expense of the public. In the *Edinburgh Evening Courant*, presently, an "Emigrant" contended that in return for his increase in rents the proprietor gave back nothing, that the Highlander could not improve his farming "for nothing and with nothing," and that the new sheep-farming must reduce population. To this the "Man of Ross" replied that the Highlander was backward and unprogressive.[17] By 1802 Alexander Irvine had statistics to show that in one area on the western coast population was greater in 1801 than in 1791 though five hundred residents had departed in the interval.[18] Three years later Thomas Douglas, Earl of Selkirk, an intelligent but perhaps not disinterested native, argued, and the *Edinburgh Review* agreed, that in the midst of the prevailing political and economic adjustments the Highlander could remove either to find work in the new manufactories of the Lowlands or to find land in the New World. To men of the Highlanders' habits, of course, land was preferable.[19] Modern historians, who have analysed the facts and the theories of these and other contemporary authorities—Sir John Sinclair and Thomas Telford, for example—have concluded that nothing could have stopped the movement, that the "Highland population was overrunning its resources," and that in spite of the efforts of Highland proprietors, the Highland Society, and the British government, neither the capital nor the brains were to be found to solve a problem "which is still perplexing the statesmen of the twentieth century."[20]

The Highland Society, however, assisted as it was by a government grant from the restitution of the Highland estates,[21] and closely in touch with the ministry through Henry Dundas, wielded an authoritative publicity against emigration. In 1789 it recommended that proprietors who adopted sheep-farming should build villages for the displaced tenants and occupy them in fishing or the manufacture of kelp.[22] It encouraged better farming methods, black cattle, home manufactures, and even

---

*The Highlands were called the nursery of soldiers. Between 1745 and 1815 fifty battalions of soldiers besides fencibles were raised; see MacKeggie, *Social Progress in the Old Highlands*, 38.

the playing of the bagpipes by annually awarded premiums. It advocated the opening of the Highland country by roads and canals. It appointed a committee which investigated the "momentous and delicate" subject of emigration and made two recommendations. The first was a request for a law to regulate the conveyance of passengers on ships sailing to the colonies, since by no other means would it be possible to control "the arts of deceit" by which interested men encouraged emigration. A striking comparison was drawn between ships in which emigrants were conveyed and those in which the law obliged traders to transport their cargoes of slaves, and it was the opinion of the Society that "preferable accommodation ... was afforded to the latter."[23] In 1773 on board a vessel of 300 tons carrying 450 passengers to North Carolina, 25 emigrants were without berths until 23 sleeping places were vacated by the death of as many emigrants. In 1791 a 270-ton emigrant ship sailed from the Isle of Skye with 400 passengers. The berths placed in three tiers were eighteen inches wide and two feet high; there were only two cooking vessels, pots of twenty-four pints each. After twelve days at sea the ship was dismasted and forced to put back into Greenock.[24] In 1801 two ships left the western Highlands which, if subjected to the act regulating the slave trade, would have carried between them 489 slaves; instead they carried 700 Scottish emigrants; on one vessel the death rate was 14 per cent.[25]

As a second recommendation, preventive measures to control the emigration movement were suggested: "various employments and encouragements to industry ... might be offered by an improvement of the fishery, ... the establishment of simple manufactures, ... the opening of proper communications through these remote districts by roads and ... canals."[26] After copies of the Society's report were sent to the Home Office and the Exchequer in London, the Treasury dispatched the engineer, Thomas Telford, to the coasts and central Highlands. His examinations there convinced him of the inevitability of the progression from more and more sheep walks to dispossession and emigration. It was a real hardship, "if not a great injustice," that the inhabitants should be driven from their native country, "but it was to the interest of the empire that this district should produce as much human food as possible." When Telford's findings were referred to a committee of the House of Commons, it was possible to use his more scientific investigations as a justification for adopting the recommendations of the Highland Society. Information was received from the Society and witnesses were called.[27] Comprehensive reports on the Highlands were presented to Parliament in May 1803. Along with them came a bill prepared by the Lord Advocate of Scotland, Charles Hope, for the purpose of "regulating the Vessels carrying Passengers from the United Kingdom to His Majesty's Plantations and Settlements abroad or to Foreign parts, with respect to the number of Passengers which they shall be allowed to take on board, in proportion to the tonnage of such Vessels, as well as with respect to the provision of proper necessaries for the voyage."[28] The result was soon apparent in the Passenger Vessel Act of 1803,[29] in the vote of £20,000 for defraying the expense of making an inland navigation from the eastern to the western sea by Inverness and Fort William, and in the building of roads and highways undertaken after the passing of the Scottish Highlands Roads Bill.

Extensive and prophetic though the title and terms of the Passenger Vessel Act were, the bill had encountered no opposition from vested interests and passed without being recorded in the debates, while Parliament gave its attention to discussions concerning France.[30] And whatever the original motives that prompted the agitation for the law, the Act was ostensibly designed to protect the Highlander from the rapacity of men who engaged in the emigrant trade "with the same views of mercantile advantage which they would have turned to any other transportable commodity."[31] By its terms, it became an offence punishable with a penalty of £50 for a vessel to carry to any parts beyond the seas more than one person, child or adult, for every two tons' burden; to sail without submitting to the Customs a muster of all on board, or without provisions sufficient to give a specified quantity of food to each passenger. A surgeon was to be carried, and whenever possible bedding was to be aired and the ship fumigated. Both surgeon and captain were to keep a journal of the voyage to be handed over to the Customs on return, and no ship should be cleared until bonds were given that the vessel was seaworthy and that passengers could be landed at the ports for which they had contracted. Such terms necessarily increased the cost of equipping a ship for sea. Shipowners soon made it evident that the Highland emigrant would have to pay for this, even pointing out—what certain interests had possibly hoped to hear—that the higher passage rates would probably act as a complete prohibition on emigration.

Before war again employed the Highlander, or the Passenger Vessel Act made the Atlantic crossing too costly for many, a renewed outburst of emigration set in. The course most easily pursued was that to Nova Scotia and New Brunswick for changes in trade routes following the American Revolutionary War had shifted some timber vessels to that run. Timber vessels going west in ballast carried the Scots to Pictou in 1801. In 1802 ten vessels sailed to British North America from Fort William, Knoydart, Ullapool, Stornaway, Moidart, Barra, and Uist; in 1803 there were ten more. Before 1803, too, small groups of Scots followed kinsmen into lands bordering the Ottawa River in Canada, some at St. Andrews and Lachute, others in the township of Grenville. To the latter in 1802 and to Suffolk and Templeton townships, Archibald MacMillan of Lochaber, Scotland, brought five hundred Scots and obtained for them lots of 200 acres each. Though their first years proved to be very difficult because of MacMillan's engagement in lumbering, Scottish emigration to the region eventually continued.[32] One reads of the steady stream of Highlanders leaving for British America; and Dorothy Wordsworth, wandering through the Scottish lake country, notes the deserted estate of Glengyle, and is told that emigration is "a glorious thing for them who have the money."[33]

In the year when these shiploads were preparing without the assistance of the government, Alexander Macdonell, chaplain of the Glengarry Fencibles disbanded in Ayr, July 8, 1801,[34] applied directly to London for aid in settling his men with their kin in Canada. Dispossessed of their small properties in 1791, some of the Glengarry Highlanders had determined to remove to North America when Macdonell, a priest of their clan, persuaded them to seek a living in Glasgow and nearby manufacturing towns. The priest himself remained with them, though no clergyman of the Roman Catholic faith had passed a night in Glasgow since the riots of 1780. On the outbreak of war in 1793, when Scotland was so roused by the theories of the new political freedom that many of the Fencible Corps refused to march to England, Father Macdonell offered his men for service. They were formed into the Glengarry Fencible Regiment, saw service in Ireland, and now in 1801 were again unemployed. As the government was at the time strongly pressed to act against Highland emigration, Macdonell was first urged to keep his men at home, then advised to settle them in Trinidad. At last Lord Hobart, secretary for war and the colonies, convinced that the Fencibles would go nowhere but to Canada, instructed Lieutenant-Governor Hunter of Upper Canada to grant 1,200 acres to Macdonell and 200 to each family he might introduce into the colony. The renewal of war and the terms of the new Passenger Vessel Act prevented the company from sailing as one group, but some of the Glengarries arrived in Lower Canada in 1804, "literally smuggled away, unknown to Hobart or Hunter."[35]

While the ministry was thus with one hand helping the Highland Society to put an end to emigration and with the other providing lands for the emigration of the Glengarries, it received from Thomas Douglas,

Earl of Selkirk, a memorial requesting assistance for emigration from Ireland. Selkirk urged that Ireland, in forced quiet after the rebellion and union of 1801, would profit from the removal of those who might become leaders of disaffection. In Canada, new surroundings, property of their own, and religious freedom might make good citizens out of bad.[36] To this unusual proposal, Hobart replied that the government was opposed to colonization *en masse*, and that there would be "great difficulties and objections to Government undertaking to transport and settle people from Ireland or elsewhere in either of the Canadas."[37] Though Selkirk retorted to this edict by threatening to take his emigrants to the United States, in the end he agreed to Hobart's suggestion to spend his efforts in redirecting to British North America those Scots who were already decided upon emigration. Before the last of November, he had succeeded in inducing one hundred families, principally from the Isle of Skye, a district which had long sent settlers to Canada, to promise to change their destination to Prince Edward Island where, in accord with the government policy of developing the maritime colonies, he had applied for lands.[38] Of the ten ships known to have carried emigrants to the British colonies in 1803, three sailed to Prince Edward Island with Selkirk's settlers, in all about eight hundred persons.[39] When, after a visit to the United States,[40] Selkirk transferred his colonizing and emigration energies to Upper Canada[41] and then to the Red River in the Hudson's Bay territory of the West,[42] his assistance to Scottish Highlanders continued.[43] No colonizer of the day, perhaps, knew so well as Selkirk the needs of the Scottish worker and the opportunities to be found in the British colonies in North America.[44]

In Scotland conditions were rendering it more and more necessary for the Highlander to seek an asylum overseas. The demand for increased production after the hard years of 1799, 1800, and 1801, when the poor were largely dependent upon charity,[45] encouraged proprietors in further adoption of the new methods of farming which otherwise might have been delayed until after the peace. In 1806 Sir George Mackenzie of Coul, Ross-shire, petitioned the government for lands in Prince Edward Island on which he wished to place certain of his too numerous tenants whose leases expired in the spring and whose support he could no longer undertake. Nothing came of the proposal, but it was evident that Lord Selkirk had set an example that was to be followed, as later events proved, far into the nineteenth century. Moreover, emigration had become popular, almost a craze. James Headrick might write in a prize essay for the Highland Society that "whether he chooses to work on sea or land, above ground or below it," the Highlander was not likely to want for employment,⁴⁶ but a people's movement once started is not easily stopped. Departure from one's native land was no longer exile. Glengarry followed Glengarry to New York and afterwards to Canada; the men from Argyll went out to their kin in Carolina; and Inverness kept up a steady intercourse with Nova Scotia. None understood better than Samuel Johnson how this influence would spread. "He that goes thus accompanied carries with him all that makes life pleasant: ... language, ... opinions, ... popular songs and hereditary monuments; they change nothing but the place of their abode; and of that change they perceive the benefit."⁴⁷

As the Napoleonic Wars drew to their close, even the extractions made by the army and the press gang did not keep pace with evictions and this growing desire for emigration. In 1810 four shiploads of "deluded Highlanders" (according to the *Caledonian Mercury*) were led by emigration agents to exchange the overpopulation of the Highlands for the fresh lands of Prince Edward Island.⁴⁸ In the winter of 1812–13 evictions from the Sutherland estate began on a large scale. A deputation of tenants returning from London was met by Lord Selkirk who offered conveyance to the Red River to one hundred of the seven hundred who had just demanded redress. Each succeeding year until 1815, the Earl sent another small group to carry on the fight for settlement on the western plains. And though the exodus may have been greater than that recorded, in 1812, 1813, and 1814, the Customs records showed annually the departure of a few hundred.⁴⁹

From England in this early period no emigration occurred comparable to that from Scotland. Though continuous wars and the Industrial Revolution together provided occupation for the population, nevertheless conditions were preparing which would bring about unprecedented unemployment. From 1750 the decline in mortality had been perceptible. Birth rate and death rate had generally cancelled each other at about 30 in 1,000, but after 1750 the loss by deaths gradually fell behind the gain by births. Better water, better drainage, less disease, better diet including fresh meat in winter, all helped to increase the numbers surviving each year to work and to be fed. The population of England and Wales which had been less than 7,000,000 when England took over Canada in 1763 had risen to about 8,750,000 by the time Upper Canada was established in 1791. It reached approximately 10,000,000 by 1811 and almost 13,750,000 in 1831.⁵⁰

Migration if not emigration went on during these years, of course, for the whole face of England was being transformed by an agricultural as well as an industrial revolution. Wartime demand and the reforms of Arthur Young and others stimulated agricultural production. When corn stood at 126s. 6d. the quarter as it did in 1796, enclosure of common and waste lands proceeded apace until even the moorland and the sands turned in their golden harvest. Between 1761 and 1801 there were two thousand acts of enclosure, between 1810 and 1844 at least eighteen hundred more.[51] Together with industrial improvements and Pitt's financial genius they brought Britain through the wars. They did not harm the small farmer greatly until after 1815 because he could still supplement agriculture with other work and the price of foodstuffs remained so high that all but the least efficient could produce at a profit. But the villager was losing his grazing fields and his bit of wood-cutting and this at the same time that the Industrial Revolution was taking his by-industries from him.[52] Some men indeed saw the danger in the future. The Board of Agriculture, formed in 1793 by the influence of Sir John Sinclair, had attempted to provide for a possible increase in population by reserving waste lands and stipulating that some land should never be alienated from the cottage, but Parliament struck all these clauses out of the enclosure bills. An abundant supply of labour was then considered a source of wealth and strength. Not until 1845 did the government provide by law that small plots of land be granted to workers removed by the enclosure of estates.[53]

Gradually opportunities for non-agricultural employment began to shift from south to north. The iron industry in Sussex closed down from lack of wood and moved to South Yorkshire and Shropshire. Silk-weaving went northward to Coventry and Cheshire, hosiery to Nottingham, calico-printing to Lancashire, and the fire-arms industry to the blast furnaces of Birmingham in time for Nelson to hammer the French with improved guns. Workers for the newly established industries were drawn from nearby and the gaps so created were filled by similar short-distance migrants. As time went on the cottage industries, spinning, weaving, and glove-making, by which the small holder or tenant had helped support himself were swept into the new factories. This succession of migrations left the workers of the removing industries like the villagers to find a living in agriculture or fall upon the Poor Law.[54]

Since 1796 an innovation in the system of poor relief had authorized weekly payments in proportion to the size of a worker's family and the cost of bread, if the worker's earnings did not reach a prescribed level. This pernicious practice had developed throughout the country from the misguided but humanitarian decision of the Berkshire magistrates who met at Speenhamland near Newbury in 1795 to consider the wartime rise in prices and the low wages prevailing. By ancient custom the magistrates should have fixed a wage in accordance with the cost of living; instead they left the inadequate wage unaltered and drew up a scale of doles. Henceforth every farm labourer became a pauper, "perpetually in receipt of parish relief," relief which was contributed by all ratepayers alike. The farmer who employed no paid labour thus was penalized to support his richer competitors. The "small owner went down whilst the big one went up." The Speenhamland system was meant to be a temporary device, but the wars lasted twenty years and the system persisted for twenty more after the wars. Small farmers who had survived during wartime shortages collapsed when prices fell with the peace. In 1815 the landed interests were supreme in Parliament. They obtained the passage of the Corn Law which forbade the importation of foreign corn until the domestic product reached 80s. a quarter. But this enactment merely raised the price of bread for those who were already nearing starvation level. Low wages and unemployment for the labourer, high rates and agricultural depression for the farmer, were soon to make emigration necessary.[55]

By the end of the year 1815, the true position of the villager and the small farmer could be concealed no longer. The village contained a "mass of labourers, all of them underpaid, whom the parish had to keep alive in the way most convenient to the farmers." In Kent, Wilts, Oxford, Hereford, and Lancashire, the disappearance of the small landholder was evident from 1802 onward. In 1817 in the parish of Swanage the rate was a guinea on the pound and "every occupier but one had given notice to abandon."[56] County landlords raised their voices against the rates. In the years 1820, 1821, and 1822 almost five hundred agricultural petitions were sent to the House of Commons. Matthenson and other shipping agents in Liverpool reported to the Colonial Office that small farmers were daily requesting conveyance to British America.[57] During the same years, three select committees of the House of Commons reported upon the distressed state of agriculture. To the third of these was presented a plan for the relief of the farmer by means of emigration.[58] Agricultural interests were the last to succumb to the full meaning of the new theories of economic freedom, and the opposition here was sufficient to prevent the inclusion of the emigration plan in the report of 1822 and to forbid any recommendation for the free movement of labour such as had already been put forth by the Poor Law Committee of 1819.[59]

The part of the population engaged in the various sorts of manufactures had gradually fallen into the same difficulties as that employed in agriculture. The introduction of power machines and labour-saving devices in the last half of the eighteenth century had brought changes in conditions for which there came no corresponding change in the laws regulating the manufacturing industries. Historical comparisons are often misleading, especially those involving an age when contemporary values were affected by the rise of a new point of view such as that of the early nineteenth-century humanitarians. In spite of this danger, one modern scholar has written that not since the days when whole races were taken into slavery has such a scourge visited the earth as the process by which the Midlands of England were covered with the scarring works of the Industrial Revolution. Within the space of a man's life all that stood for the old freedom was taken from the manufacturing labourer. Before the advent of machines he had worked in his own house; his garden was about him and his wife and children. Machines took his property from him and crowded him into a segregated community. This change and the new employment eventually brought more advantages than the oft-regretted old freedom.

The increased use of steam brought the miners too into the same system. As the war went on problems created by the new industry became more acute. "At times it [the war] was conducted directly by economic weapons.... Nobody can read the evidence given before the Committee on the Orders-in-Council in 1812 without appreciating the difficulties of an employer who suddenly found himself denuded of orders for his five or six hundred workers."[60] A contemporary has described the effect of the new cotton mill:

By the building of the cotton mill, and the rising up of the new town of Cayenneville, we had intromitted so much with the concerns of trade that we were become a part of the great web of commercial reciprocities, and felt in our corner and extremity every touch or stir that was made in any part of the texture. In 1808 when the local mill owner . . . was forced to close his doors, the bread in a moment was snatched from more than a thousand mouths. . . . What could our parish fund do in the way of helping a whole town thus thrown out of bread.[61]

Strong protests and then pleas for aid to emigrate soon came from the weavers. For years their condition had been deteriorating. From 1797 to 1804 a wage of 26s. 8d. a week spent on flour, oatmeal, potatoes, and meat purchased 281 pounds of provisions, but by 1820 a weaver's average receipts had so fallen that the comparable purchase was only 101 pounds.[62] As early as 1801 when the clamour for peace was great and food riots were occurring all over the country, the weavers were in particular distress, and a movement was set on foot for a wage regulation act. When an Arbitration Act was given in 1804 the weavers began to work for the minimum wage. Parliament from that time forth was flooded with petitions from manufacturing workers. Certain men, Romilly, Bennet, Whitbread, Curwen, and others, were ready to protest in favour of the poor, but the general temper of the age was that which prompted Lord Sheffield to write, "Nothing, surely, is more disgusting than the new system of being instructed and governed by petitions from those, who, from their stations in life, are the least informed, and perfectly incapable of judging of their real, permanent interest."[63]

After the minimum wage bill failed in 1808 the Lowlands of Scotland, the Midlands, and particularly Lancashire were in a most serious state. Riots broke out, and then a strike ending in the monster agitation of 1811 with its Manchester petition signed by 40,000 and the Scottish petition signed by 30,000.[64] In Manchester alone 24,000 had received parish relief in 1811. When presenting the petitions from Paisley and Lanark, Lord Archibald Hamilton announced that 12,000 out of 30,000 families in that district were in receipt of relief. But again the agitation was a failure. Lord Sidmouth quelled resistance by increasing the powers of the magistrates and the numbers of the military force. Lord Stanley reported that the committee which had considered the petitions deeply regretted the distress but that Parliament could not interfere with the freedom of trade or the perfect liberty of every individual to dispose of his time as he wished.[65]

At the very moment when the theory of free competition in all branches of trade was thus being formulated for literal adoption, the market was swamped with labour. Though convinced of the abominations of the slave trade and converted to the theories of Adam Smith, men could still think poverty a disease, the natural and inevitable consequence of war, perhaps an evidence that society must endure the poverty and pain which were the final remedy for overpopulation explained by Thomas Robert Malthus. With the results of the census of 1801 and 1811 before them, it is not surprising that those who read and thought should have been dismayed by the condition of England. The great mass of the people, who cared little for statistics and denied the truth of the Malthusian principle when they chanced to hear it,[66] were equally alarmed by the plain fact that the country did not provide a living for all. The very activities which up to 1815 had been the most powerful factors in employing and increasing the population were now suffering an eclipse which rendered redundant the workers they had helped to produce. If proof were necessary for the truth of the principle that population presses against subsistence so that it is only restrained by the want of produce, the English had merely to look about them. To reply that the increase of wealth had kept pace with the increase of population was not to the point, while wealth remained in the hands of a few and neither agriculture nor the manufactures could employ the many. It was this *The Times* wished the government to study when it wrote:

... a population is redundant, not abstractedly or absolutely, but relatively—that is, so far as it exceeds the means of support afforded by the earth under the existing system of agriculture. But if we look upon our country at the present time—there is still sufficient space of uncultivated or imperfectly cultivated land left for practise; and yet those by whose hands this earth ought to be tilled for their own nourishment, quit it in unusual numbers, encounter the dangers of a long voyage and fix their abode in far distant regions....
Whatever we have said of peasants, or labourers of the earth, applies also to artificers. There are the same means of forcing trade as of forcing natural production: only remove the burdens, facilitate the operations, and even study the tempers of those who are engaged in the two pursuits. But to make men love a thing, even though that thing is their native land, it is not sufficient to tell them they ought to love it; no, it must be rendered lovely.[67]

Later events were to show that *The Times* had seen aright, for after a reinvigoration of trade England was to support numbers unthought of at the beginning of the century. Indeed, before it was half gone, Lord Grey pointedly assured Parliament that he had never believed there was "any real or permanent excess of population." But the fact remains that a population which had been carefully cherished and kept from emigrating since the seventeenth century was not in 1815 regarded as an unmixed blessing.

Until 1824 when Joseph Hume, William Huskisson, Francis Place, and others won the fight against the laws prohibiting either the combination or emigration of artisans, it was illegal for an artisan to leave the country.[68] Long before that time, however, many had found their way to North America. Some of the Glengarry Fencibles whom Father Macdonell took to Canada had been weavers for a few years. In the Colonial Office papers of 1807, there is a petition with twelve signatures from Oldham, Manchester, which begs for land in Upper Canada, since the petitioners were "much short of imploy." Nothing was done for the applicants, but by the winter of 1811–12 the emigration of artisans and manufacturers had become so common that *The Times* published a warning that those who had already removed to America from Lancashire and the West Riding of Yorkshire in the hope of bettering their fortune had made a sorry exchange of country.[69] However, in staying the movement that was now under way, such warnings were useless.

UNEMPLOYMENT, OVERPOPULATION, EMIGRATION

The first official recommendation for the freedom of movement for labour and thus for emigration came from attempts to administer and reform the Poor Law. Those who considered the state of agriculture and the manufactures dwelt upon the good of the industries concerned; economic theory then justified them in disregarding the labourer as a human being. But for those considering poor relief, the problem of increasing expenditure and unemployment had to be faced in its relation to the state of the nation. By 1803 the human and money cost of the new system of poor relief was alarming. When Samuel Whitbread brought in his bill for reform in 1807, he could state as proof of the need for change that in 1803, out of a population of 8,870,000 in England and Wales, 1,234,000 were partakers of relief, and that in the same year £4,267,000 had been raised for that purpose, a sum almost double the average for the years 1783 to 1785. By 1815, this expenditure had risen to about £7,000,000.[70] In 1817 John Christian Curwen, a northern member of Parliament who had spoken frequently on distress was able to obtain the appointment of a select committee on the Poor Law which presented its report on July 4, 1817. In addition to pointing out that the increasing assessments to aid the poor would ultimately absorb all profits and ruin the lands that paid for them, the report recommended that "all obstacles to seeking employment wherever it can be found even out of the realm, should be removed; and every facility that is reasonable afforded to those who may wish to resort to some of our colonies." In 1818 and 1819 committees carried on the investigation begun in 1817; poor relief expenditure had risen to £7,870,000 and distress was still increasing.[71] The personnel and methods of the 1818 committee resembled those of 1817, but the recommendations of 1819 struck a broader note favouring an end to aid for able-bodied poor and the removal of all restrictions on the free circulation of labour. As even this would not give sufficient relief because of the overstocking of the labour market, the following was added to the earlier recommendation of 1817:

It seems not unnatural that this country should, at such a time, recur to an expedient which has been adopted successfully in other times, and in other countries, especially as it has facilities for this purpose which no other state has perhaps enjoyed to the same extent, by the possession of colonies affording an extent of unoccupied territory in which the labour of man assisted by a gentle and healthy climate would produce an early and abundant return.

The committee of 1819 examined witnesses for the purpose of ascertaining if "any considerable number of persons could be taken off in a few years" by emigration. Three witnesses who were in a position to report upon the possibilities of the Cape of Good Hope were questioned, and Henry Nourse's evidence appears to have been promising enough to justify the rejection of Canada and the recommendation for the vote to "assist unemployed workmen removing" to the Cape.[72] If the words of the committee are to be understood at their full value some people at least had realized that the resources of the colonies might be used to supplement those of the mother country with advantage to both. Parliament had not recognized the fact, it is true, and years were to elapse before a group of men were to interest themselves in emigration to the colonies as a subject in itself worthy of consideration. But here in 1819 is the first sign of that change in attitude towards labour and the colonies which foreshadowed the legislation for the removal of restriction on emigration in 1824 and the full investigation of the problem in the emigration committees of 1826 and 1827.

From Ireland before 1783 emigration was slight. The annual average exodus may not have been above five or six thousand and these were mainly Scottish-Irish. During the long wars between 1793 and 1815, emigration in large numbers occurred only in the interval of the temporary peace of 1801-2. But with the peace of 1815 the movement quickly rose to more than six thousand, though for that year passage could be obtained no farther than Newfoundland.

Beneath the squalor and savagery, disease and disorder which all observers noted in Ireland lay conditions of life and causes for emigration which few contemporaries cared to or knew how to interpret. Many of those who attempted the task found a neat explanation in absentee landlordism or the character of the Irish and stopped to look no deeper. Only gradually the simple facts of population growth became known. Excessive population had been induced by the very nature of the Irish climate, by the character of the agricultural system developed since the middle of the eighteenth century, and by the facility with which a bare subsistence could be obtained from the growth of the potato, the staple food which permitted the lowest ratio of land to the population unit then known in the temperate zone.[73] The removal of restrictions on Irish trade, the removal of the disqualifying statutes affecting Roman Catholics, and the encouragement given to agriculture by the bounties offered in the last quarter of the eighteenth century were also causing an increase in the land under tillage and consequently an increase in population.[74]

So long as a meagre living could be gained from a small patch of ground, the Irish peasant apparently continued to rent a few acres, build his wretched hovel, and add mouths to the superabundant population.

PLATE I. The Parting Cheer. Emigrants leaving Glasgow for the Colonies. By Henry O'Neil, A.R.A., 1861. (Courtesy of M. Newman, Limited, London, England.)

PLATE II. The Emigrant's Welcome to Canada. (Courtesy of Coverdale Collection, Manoir Richelieu, Quebec.)

PLATE III. Process of Clearing the Town Plot at Stanley, Oct. 1834. (New Brunswick and Nova Scotia Land Company, *Sketches in New Brunswick*, London, 1836. Courtesy of New Brunswick Museum, St. John, N.B.)

PLATE IV. View of Cholera Hospital and Telegraph, Grosse Isle Quarantine Station. Sketch by Captain R. Carr Alderson, 1832. (Courtesy of Public Archives of Canada.)

Bishop Doyle had no words to describe the misery he found in the crowded cottages. English observers, Wakefield in particular, believed that the positive check on population was at work as early as 1812.[75] He had been assured by the Bishop of Londonderry that subdivision of land, intermarriage, and increase had gone on in his diocese until population had exceeded produce and the enterprising had removed themselves to America. The census of 1821,* such as it was, gave proof of these assertions. Since the Union, population had risen from perhaps 4,500,000 to 7,000,000. Even by 1815, the total had probably reached more than 6,000,000, and these had to extract a living from only 13,500,000 acres of usable land.[76] In 1821, through one cause or another but largely through the increase in small farms, Ireland had more mouths to feed per square mile than any country in Europe. Twenty years later, the province of Leinster with its grazing lands had 281 persons per square mile, Munster 396, Connaught 411, and Ulster where some manufactures flourished had 434. For most areas Lecky described a "dense, improvident, impoverished and anarchical population," Halévy a "vast proletariat, ignorant, miserably poor, superstitious and disorderly."

At least 90 per cent of the people depended for a living directly or indirectly upon agriculture, in the main agriculture of a primitive sort untouched in the case of the small occupiers by the reformed methods spreading in England. Land ownership was in the hands of a more powerful group who, whether they spent their surplus in London or elsewhere, certainly did not reinvest it in Ireland.[77] Landlords had not been eager for change; political influence and large rentals sprang from a numerous tenantry. The tenant farmer who agreed to pay his thirty or forty shillings yearly as well as to work at five pence per day gave his vote as a matter of course to his landlord. The landlord held the principal political power; he served as resident magistrate in his local district; and he and his kind made up the grand juries. Their will against disturbers of the peace was frustrated now and again by the courage of the petty juries of small farmers acting to protect their friends, but on the whole "the lower orders" bowed subserviently to the gentry. And the landlord, as a matter of course, rented his land to the highest bidder, thus entrusting the collection of his due to a race of middlemen who made their living from the excess they could extract in the process of collection. Asked by his agent what method to use with the tenants, the Duke of Leinster is said to have replied, "Get all you can."[78]

---

*Before 1841 the censuses of Ireland appear to have been of dubious value.

Conditions varied on different estates, there is no doubt, but other extractions, the demands of the tithe collector or the proctor, were also reducing the renters of small cabins, the cottiers, to a state of utmost poverty. As disorder became widespread and returns fell off, the landlords began to see the dangers in the system and, with a determination to return to the larger farms of earlier days, the eviction of the tenantry commenced. Risings of tenants against unpopular landlords or more usually against middlemen or tenants who dared to rent from unpopular middlemen now multiplied. When to the tension engendered by these actual dangers were added despondency from lack of employment and weakness from lack of food, the poorer of the people were, in the words of the committee of the House of Commons, "highly predisposed to disease." During 1817, 1818, and 1819 the suffering from famine and fever was acute and relief in the form of money and food was furnished from England.[79]

After 1815 when wheat prices fell and large farms became more profitable than small and pasturage more profitable than either, new legislation in 1816 and 1819 brought down the legal cost of an eviction to one-quarter that in England. Those most disastrously affected by the bad condition of agriculture were the labourers or cottiers and the smallest farmers. The former, numbering perhaps somewhat less than three million, rented on an uncertain tenure small windowless hovels with little or no land. With a daily wage of six or eight pence and seldom more than two weeks of work a month, a diet of potatoes, perhaps herring or pork from the family pig, whisky or poteen and very occasionally milk, and without the few advantages of the Poor Law or the Industrial Revolution of England, these cottiers constituted a class lower than the English and scarcely higher than the Russian peasant. Lacking education and full of superstition and hatred, they fell easy members to the secret societies, Whiteboys, Ribbonmen, and the like which, whatever their leadership and higher purpose, were used for violence— to threaten evictions, attack the evictor, and spread terror. Clearly these millions could not provide the cash or the energy for emigration until after 1830 or later.[80] It was to consider their condition that the Committee on the State of the Poor was appointed in 1830 and it recommended emigration financed by the landlords. The great Poor Law commission of 1833 again advised relief by emigration, this time to be financed by the government, the landlords, and the poor rates, a favour which was sparingly granted in legislation of 1838.[81]

So it was that until about 1830 the great body of Irish emigrants consisted of small farmers and the tradesmen whose lot was linked to theirs, and some few artisans. Though the small farmer holding less than thirty acres appeared to be better off than the cottier because of his longer lease and general position, subdivision of his little acreage among his descendants often led to desperate overcrowding. For example, on a farm in County Clare which had been let in 1793 to one tenant for three lives, that is 61 years, subdivision had gone on from generation to generation until in 1841 the one farm pretended to support 96 tenants, "all of them legal heirs by Irish common law to fractions of the original holding," and 48 under-tenants, altogether between 700 and 800 souls, a few of them squatters evicted from neighbouring estates. One region differed from another. In thickly settled counties like Armagh and Monaghan where the average farm was less than ten acres and the majority were under five, the poverty-stricken farmers in their hovels made up the principal population. In addition to overcrowding, lack of scientific agriculture and high rents reduced the farmer to serious want. During the Napoleonic Wars, high prices hid this precarious condition but with 1815 the disclosure of reality began. In Limerick after 1815, E. G. Stanley found some 600 persons on 400 acres, "cleared" almost half of them, and by 1826 was forced to provide food to prevent starvation.[82]

The manual industries everywhere and especially in Ulster where they had been widely dispersed survived under protection until 1830. But the fight against the machine industry across the water and the absence of risk capital in Ireland doomed the Irish artisan unless he moved his skill to Great Britain or across the Atlantic to America. As early as 1793 the Secretary for War and the Colonies, Henry Dundas, was warned that the Americans had agents in Ireland for the purpose of "enticing . . . artists abroad." Thousands, it was reported, artisans and others, had sailed for North America in 1792 and 1793. Will Willcocks, one-time mayor of Cork, urged upon the British government a plan for redirecting these Irish workers to British North America and Lord Selkirk did the same after the Union.[83] Nothing was done for the petitioners nor was any similar plan developed until the Horton experiments of 1823 and 1825.

In Ulster, the seat of the most important Irish industry, linen, the independent weavers and the farmer-weavers were already losing out to the large farmer-weaver who could employ more and more journeymen and to the bleacher-merchant who hired his own weavers to make his cloth. Some emigration from the Belfast area was of long standing. Arthur Young wrote of it in 1779 as being dependent upon two circumstances, linen and the Presbyterian religion. It had not come with high rents and it did not attract Roman Catholics who seemed tied to the parish in which their ancestors had lived. When the linen trade was low, emigration increased, for the weaver being part farmer with property in cattle to sell was inclined to better his position by emigration rather than to submit to enlistment.[84] In 1812 Edward Wakefield felt no alarm, for he found Belfast which had lost more than any other district the most flourishing town in the island. Robert Peel in the Irish Office, however, thought this diminution of the Protestant population very unfortunate and "still more unfortunate—that the United States should reap the advantage of their departure."[85] For the woollen and cotton industry in other parts of Ireland, the future was equally uncertain. Between 1800 and 1820, for instance, more than nine thousand weavers of broadcloth in and around Cork gave up work.

So while the most dejected and the least experienced of the Irish drifted to the village or the town slums or wandered the country over, the farmer with a few pounds or the skilled artisan with experience and courage read the ship advertisements, made his way to the ports, and set off for the new world of better opportunities. Hard hit by the ruinous harvests of 1816 and 1817, the agrarian disturbances which followed, and by changes in the textile industry, farmers and farmer-weavers began to emigrate in numbers in 1817 and 1818. On the Irish coasts the prohibition on the emigration of artisans was not enforced and many got away with ease. Perhaps two-thirds of all Irish emigrants in the five years after 1815 were Ulstermen. Some observers have maintained that these first emigrants were superior economically to the average in Ireland and were leaving in time to save what little they had. Others have noted that the Ulster area with its Scottish settlers, like the Dublin with its English and Welsh, may have produced men of outstanding initiative.

From Monaghan and Cavan and the other southwestern counties of Ulster, these early emigrants travelled to the timber and general cargo vessels waiting to sail from Belfast, Dublin, Sligo, or Londonderry. From Londonderry, too, went the Presbyterian small farmer and the tradesman of Tyrone and above all of Derry which alone furnished perhaps one-fifth of all the Irish emigrants of that time. Belfast shippers drawing from a wide area of Ulster could offer the better vessels. They practically monopolized the St. Andrews trade, provided nearly half of the emigration to Quebec, and carried out in these first years almost half of all the Irish emigrants to the New World. Another quarter of the emigrants of the period went down from Wexford, Queens, and Kings counties, and Dublin and the Ulster plateau to sail from Dublin's port.[86]

In 1818 this first post-war emigration reached its height, perhaps

20,000. Of these between 13,000 and 15,000 sailed to British North America, for British shipping regulations had been manipulated to lower the emigrant's fare in British ships bound to British ports. In 1818 about 5,000 Irish took ship to Quebec alone. In the maritime colonies, St. John received almost as many as Quebec while other Nova Scotian and New Brunswick ports lost out.[87] The great majority of those Irish who landed at Quebec and Montreal went on to Upper Canada or the United States, what proportion to each one can only guess.

By 1819 panic in the United States had decreased temporarily the attractions in that country but bad potato crops in Ireland were driving the poorer to seek means of emigration even by remittances from America or the aid of landlords like Richard Talbot or W. K. Newenham in Ireland. So, before the government acted to assist Irish emigration, a pace had been set that might fluctuate but would not greatly slacken during the first half of the nineteenth century.

III. THE RISING TIDE:
TO THE MILITARY SETTLEMENTS,
1815-1830

THE YEARS immediately following the peace of 1815 have been described as the most miserable in modern English history. No longer sustained by the news of successive victories, the public slowly began to realize the cost at which those victories had been won. The weight of the debt fell upon the farmer at the same time as the price of corn dropped from 120 to 68s. a quarter and it fell, though with less force, upon the manufacturer at the moment when the war contracts were removed and the foreign markets collapsed. Upon the lower middle and labouring classes the effect was serious. They were not in a mood to submit to poverty without protest, for they had hoped for change even when distress was greatest. The fulfilment of their hopes was denied by the government in power. "Ere we asked them their complaints or their wishes," someone has written, "we took away their liberties." By the suspension of Habeas Corpus, by Peterloo, and the Six Acts, the government replied to the agricultural petitions, the meetings of the manufacturing labourers, and the protests that had been growing in volume for over twenty years.

Measures of relief were discussed, but change came slowly. Before political and economic conditions improved, thousands of British subjects sought opportunities in a new world, a form of relief that had long been practised. No one conversant with the history of emigration would assume that the search for relief was the only incentive taking men outward after 1815. There was the call to follow the path to America which had been closed off and on since 1776; there was the natural restlessness which follows war; and there was that spirit, chance, economic determinism, whatever it may be, which has made the inhabitants of the British Isles more than any other people of modern times the colonists of the world.

Something of this spirit may have penetrated, as the years went on, to the government office from which Britain's colonial possessions were administered. Since 1792 the government had been urged to direct the outward flow of population to British possessions and so prevent loss of citizens to the empire. The War of 1812 had shown the colonies' need for an increase in population. While the war was still under way Lord Bathurst, secretary for war and the colonies, consulted British American officials about his plan for turning to the advantage of the empire the spirit of emigration which then prevailed in the Scottish Highlands, particularly in Sutherland and Caithness. Would the emigrants' value as a military defence and a future means of prosperity be sufficient to counterbalance the expenditure required for their establishment?[1] According to some few theorists, the vast undeveloped wastelands of the colonies could so be used for the good of the whole empire, of the landlords with overcrowded estates, of the manufacturers seeking new markets, of a government striving to quiet agitators, and of the colonies themselves which needed population.

A Trial of Liberal Encouragement for Settlers

When both Governor Sir George Prevost and Lieutenant General Gordon Drummond had replied in favour of bringing British settlers into a "country already too much inhabited by Aliens from the United States,"[2] Lord Bathurst gave instructions for enlarging the preparations being made for placing demobilized soldiers on lands in British North America. In anticipation of the shipping which would be available at the peace, terms for "Settlers Proceeding to Canada" were drawn up in November 1813.[3] The Hundred Days prevented the fulfilment of the plan in 1814; Lord Liverpool, the prime minister, did not sanction it until January 16, 1815, the Treasury not until February 10; and Parliament does not appear to have been consulted until a Mr. Horner in June called upon Henry Goulburn, under-secretary for the Colonial Office, to refute the charge of "encouraging emigration." This phrase had been used again and again in Bathurst's correspondence with the colonies and in the advertisements which had been published in Scottish newspapers. It is therefore some indication of the feeling which the Colonial Office had to meet that both the Chancellor of the Exchequer and Goulburn assured the House carefully that no encouragement to emigration had been given but that, "as the danger in which Canada was during the last war had arisen from its scanty population, the object of the government was merely to direct those determined to emigrate and change their destination from the United States to His Majesty's possessions."[4]

Whether because of this questioning or from some other cause, the emigration carried out in 1815 was much smaller than the four thousand persons contemplated in the first plans. From the Irish Office, Robert Peel had advised that loyalists from the north of Ireland be rewarded by aid in emigration and the Prime Minister had authorized a larger removal. However, the shortage of ships and the uncertainty in that uneasy land forbade the adoption of this part of the plan.[5] Though no publicity was given the scheme in England, thirty settlers went out from Deptford under regulations similar to those published in Scotland[6] but, as these at once lost their identity as a group, it was with the Scots that this government experiment in assisted emigration was tried out.

Under the heading, "Liberal Encouragement to Settlers," the first official notice on emigration since 1749 appeared in the Edinburgh newspapers on February 25, 1815. Throughout March and April sheriffs and ministers were requested to "take an early opportunity of giving Publicity to the advertisements," as many of the persons "most interested in this notice have no access to Newspapers."[7] Of the thousands who made first application to John Campbell, W.S., government commissioner for the emigration in Scotland, less than one thousand persisted when they learned the full terms of the government offer. These were mainly farmers and labourers from Edinburgh, Glasgow, Paisley, Knoydart, Glenelg, and Callander,[8] districts which then had fair means of communication with Glasgow, where all were to gather in April.

The inducements offered the emigrants in 1815 were liberal: transportation to the colony; free grants of 100 acres of land to each head of a family, and to the sons on coming of age; rations for eight months or until establishment; axes, plows, and other implements at prime cost; and a minister and school-teacher on government salary. In return the emigrant was to produce a satisfactory recommendation of character to the government agent, John Campbell, at his office in Glasgow or Edinburgh, and deposit with the government on his departure £16 for himself and £2 for his wife, the whole sum so deposited to be returned two years later in Canada when he was satisfactorily settled on his land.[9]

During late April and early May, 758 applicants made their way on foot and in small boats to Glasgow, paid their deposit money, and placed their names on the agent's list. But it was not until late June that the Transport Board could spare four vessels and during the interval of waiting Campbell lost fifty-nine of the applicants, though he had fed all with rations from the government stores.[10] Relaxation of the terms of the Passenger Act of 1803 were necessary to permit the carriage of arms, settlers' tools, and other equipment, but surgeons were provided for each vessel and the required inspections were made before sailing.[11] In passing it might be noted that after this experience of the government with the Passenger Act of 1803 (an Act passed after prolonged agitation by the Highland Society with the intention of restricting emigration), legislation was enacted imposing less stringent terms.[12]

From Quebec the Scottish emigrants were conveyed at public expense to Cornwall where they were housed in government huts under the superintendence of Major General Sir Sidney Beckwith, quarter-master general of the forces. There during the winter he had to see to their supply of rations from the Army Victualling Office and adjust their complaints regarding stoves, windows, and even school-teachers.[13] While the emigrants thus spent their first months in idleness, a time which might have been better employed in clearing land, as it was later under Sir John Colborne, the Upper Canadian Council arranged for the survey of lands for the settlement. The result was a clash between civil and military authorities in which the welfare of the Scots and that of the colony of Upper Canada were almost wholly submerged. Imperial military officers had recommended the development of the Rideau waterway and lands as a highway between the upper and lower colonies which would be safe in time of war. But eventually the emigrants were placed in the new townships of Bathurst, Drummond, and Beckwith, which had been purchased from the Indians west of the Rideau and to which they had to cut their way through twenty miles of unbroken bush, not because the situation had peculiar military significance but because the lands closer in had already been granted to absentee proprietors.[14]

By October 1816 upwards of fourteen hundred emigrants and demobilized soldiers were established in the new townships, the first settlements in the county of Lanark.[15] But a year had elapsed since the Scots' arrival, a planting season had been wasted, and a land speculator, David Parish, was urging the newcomers to cross the St. Lawrence River and take up lands near Ogdensburg in the United States. Under these circumstances the British government agreed to continue its assistance. Two years later, when repayments of their deposits fell due, most of the emigrants were occupying their own log houses with clearings averaging ten acres each, and were in possession of some few cows and oxen.[16] Nevertheless, on the whole the experiment had proved expensive. The government agent, Campbell, had received £500 over and above all his expenses; the commissariat department had been enlarged and four vessels taken from regular transport duty; army rations had been provided for two years to almost seven hundred civilians as well as farming and building implements, seed grains, ministers, and school-teachers; later the settlers' deposits had to be repaid. This expenditure, along with that for the settlements of disbanded soldiers in Nova Scotia and New Brunswick, came out of the Military Chest at a time when Nicholas Vansittart in the Treasury was vainly trying to adjust the nation's post-war debt.[17] In February, while the Scots were still in government huts, Bathurst had warned Governor Sir John Sherbrooke that though the first expense had been "politic," all further expenditure "unless provided for out of the Colonial Revenue" must be deferred till a "Season of less financial Difficulty." Indeed "economical considerations had induced them to abandon the 1815 plan, and persons wishing to settle in British North America must proceed thither at their own expense."[18]

When Bathurst soon instructed colonial officials to assist arriving emigrants, they replied that emigrants most needed relief from the cost of land surveys and titles.[19] The Colonial Office and the Treasury accordingly devised a plan for granting land only to those who could provide some capital and engage persons to emigrate with them.[20] Though the plan was not adopted in British North America to the extent of superseding the land granting system, it is of importance as an early attempt to secure the balance between land, capital, and labour which was to receive much attention in later years. On February 23, 1818, the Colonial Office sent out to an applicant the first of its printed circular letters promising free transportation and land on the following terms:

> Such grants will only be made to those who can engage to take out and locate upon the Land granted, Ten Settlers at the least and the quantity of Land granted in each case will be in proportion of 100 Acres for every Settler proposed to be taken out.
>
> In order to prevent any evasion of this condition, the persons applying for a grant of Land will be required to pay down a sum at the rate of £10 for every Settler, which sum will be repaid to him so soon after his arrival in the Colony, as the Settlers shall have been located upon the Land assigned.[21]

Three groups, one English, one Scottish, one Irish, accepted the offer. In each case, the Colonial Office negotiated with the leader of the party, receiving £10 for each family consisting of man and wife and not more than two children; the Navy engaged the tonnage for the passage; and the embarkation was carried out under the direction of the acting agents for transport at Whitehaven, Greenock, and Cork.[22] In the English group there were about nineteen families from Alston, Cumberland; they sailed from Whitehaven towards the first of June,[23] and from Montreal proceeded at their own expense, by Rice Lake and the Otonabee, to lands newly surveyed in Smith township, Upper Canada. In this far-removed district the early experiences of the English party differed only slightly from those of unassisted emigrants, but eight years later Captain Basil Hall found them comfortably settled and able to aid newly arrived Irish emigrants.[24]

The Scottish emigrants came mainly from Breadalbane, where in a thirty-mile circuit around Loch Tay the inhabitants numbered some three thousand and many of the farmers had been "reduced to such a state of extreme poverty as to be able to procure but one scanty meal per day."[25] Funds required for the emigration of about one hundred families were obtained by one Robertson of Breadalbane, either from the emigrants themselves or from a general subscription, such as was then common in Scotland.[26] When the little band from Dull, Comrie, Balaquidder, Kincardine, and Callander was mustered at Greenock, 106 for the *Sofia* and 205 for the *Curlew*, they could not supply the provisions required by the new Passenger Act of 1817. While the whole party waited for permission to sail, many suffered real hardship.[27] Once in Canada some of the Scots were placed on land, undoubtedly bad, in Beckwith township, but with Lord Bathurst's promise of support.[28] Others arrived in Montreal so dismally discouraged that they determined to turn about and go to Cape Breton and "on their being out of Provisions and quite in distress, they called at Prince Edward Island where [they] . . . and their families . . . yet remained," according to their plea for help in 1820, "in a most deplorable state of poverty." Though they applied at once for the repayment of their deposits, it was not until 1827 that all their accounts were closed.[29]

The Irish emigration of 1818 was carried out with somewhat better luck under the leadership of Richard Talbot of Cloghjordan. Having deposited the necessary £440 with the Colonial Office, he arrived in Cork on May 6 along with his charges. When he had waited one month in lodgings at a loss of £20 to 30 a day, the Navy at last despatched to Cork a fine vessel, the *Brunswick*, of 541 tons.[30] It was "elegantly fitted up," with a large dining-room, two staterooms with berths for four persons each and two bedchambers with berths for nearly twenty persons. As was customary, the fifty steerage berths were much larger, "capable of accommodating six men or a proportionate number of women and children," in all 240 steerage passengers. Talbot brought only 172 and for them provisions for three months. In spite of these careful precautions, before the *Brunswick* docked at Quebec on July 27, more than twenty persons had been "consigned to a watery grave" or buried on St. Lawrence islands.[31]

After taking possession of the blankets and provisions on the *Brunswick* Talbot and his party moved up to Montreal by a steamboat,* the *Telegraph*.[32] At Lachine thirty-one of the emigrants, dreading the expense of the trip to Upper Canada,† accepted Lieutenant Colonel

*Seven steamboats, five of which were as large as forty-gun frigates, then plied the river between Quebec and Montreal. The trip usually took thirty-six hours up and twenty-two down. The price of cabin passage was £3, of steerage 10s.

†Though there were fifty government boats idle at Lachine, the Duke of Richmond had received no orders and could not permit the use of them.

Cockburn's offer of settlement at Perth.[33] The remainder of the party spent two weeks in open Durham boats travelling from Lachine to Prescott, six days on the schooner *Caledonia* running from Prescott to York, and thence they went *via* Niagara across to Lake Erie, by water to Port Talbot, and at last on to London. There they obtained land in a district being developed by Colonel Thomas Talbot.[34]

By 1825 the Richard Talbot emigrants were comfortably established. This success was due partly to the government insistence upon the possession of at least £10 capital, partly to the saving enjoyed by receiving free transportation, and partly to their organization under a leader of experience and initiative. These were all features of the scheme of 1818 and, though they played no part in the larger settlement of Canada, perhaps because leaders and conducted parties smacked too much of the old order and America stood only for the new individualistic independence, there can be no doubt that the scheme had advantages. During 1819 the operation of the ten-pound plan was transferred to the Cape of Good Hope and emigration to British North America was left to conduct itself, as most of it had all along, on the old principle of personal effort. Unless a particular need was strongly urged, the Liverpool government opposed interference with local conditions in the British Isles, especially to give aid to an emigration movement that was prospering passably well without it.[35]

The only official attempt to maintain control over voluntary emigration was made through the imposition of land terms, notices of which were sent out to private inquirers and were occasionally published in the newspapers. The first plan, based no doubt on the liberal encouragement given to discharged soldiers who received transportation, rations, and 100 acres of land, offered other settlers a similar land grant and certain agricultural implements, and required each emigrant to carry to the colonial governor a recommendation from the Colonial Office in London. In 1818 a radical change was made. For civilian settlers supervision and assistance from London ceased; on arrival in the colony the emigrant received a "mere grant of land in proportion to the means of cultivation" which he appeared to possess.[36] By 1825 dissatisfaction with the methods of granting land pursued by the Colonial Office was severe and farspread, and some plans for the adoption of a land sale system had been discussed.[37] Until such a plan had been fully developed, however, the Colonial Office was compelled to insist upon the terms of its most recent arrangements for requiring the emigrant to possess capital. When the departing British subject troubled to consult his government, the Colonial Office sent out the form reply and sometimes added a word of advice concerning the dangers of poverty in the colonies. Practically, the land terms offered by the London office seem to have had little effect in controlling the character of the voluntary emigration. Under the systems in use from time to time, a pauper with £3 to pay his fare and faith in himself or in colonial charity could emigrate as easily as the professional patriot or ambitious capitalist who secured a 2,000-acre grant with the promise of growing hemp for the empire or with the aid of a powerful friend in the offices in London.*

Scottish and English Emigration Under Way

The free emigration movement after 1815 picked up more quickly from Scotland than from England. One of the greatest inducements to

---

*L. J. Jennings, ed., *The Croker Papers* (3 vols., London, 1884), I, 147–8, gives the following example of the unofficial procedure by which would-be emigrants obtained favours in the colonies:

September 8th, 1819

Dear Goulburn,

"Accept a miracle of wit." I send you a very dull and almost illegible piece of Walter Scott's composition, but dull and difficult as it is, I hope his name and my request will induce you to wade through the enclosed packet.

The argument of this new "Tale of my Landlord" is as follows:

One Pringle, a Scotch Tory, born lame, dedicates himself to literature—sets up a magazine—quarrels with his publisher—is turned off, abused and ridiculed. Sets up a new magazine in opposition to the former, engages with the new publisher for a salary of five years, on the strength of which he marries—The new publisher as bad as the old—another dismissal . . . the little all of the increasing family £100, . . . present difficulties—dreadful projects—emigration to Canada or the Cape—prefers Canada—changes his mind—prefers the Cape—how to get there? Applies to Walter Scott, for whom he has done some little literary jobs—and on whose family he had some kind of dependence—sets forth his wishes and his means—the former a grant of land—the latter £500, and a dozen experienced farmers and their wives, his own relations or servants. Walter Scott receives the proposal, and conveys it to the first Lord of the Admiralty. His Lordship advises Scott to interest Mr. Croker, who can interest Mr. Goulburn, who can interest Lord Bathurst, who can interest Lord Charles Somerset to do something for the interest of the intended colony of the Pringles.

Croker, who himself is bored with reading three long letters and one short one on the subject, writes a longer letter than any of them to Goulburn, and bores him with the whole galiamatias. Goulburn in a rage writes a hasty refusal without reading the letters; next day dreadfully wet, can't go abroad; thinks he may as well endeavour to decipher Walter Scott's letter, and wade through Pringle's. Does so in two hours, ten minutes, fifteen seconds. Writes a favourable answer to say the proposals promise reasonably well, and that he will do all he can. Croker acquaints Scott—Scott tells Pringle. Pringle in ecstasies of joy runs to tell his wife, big with child—rapture accelerates her labour. She is brought to bed of a fine boy, who is christened Henry-Scott-Bathurst-Goulburn-Pringle.

Finis of the first volume,
Yours ever,
J.W.C.

emigration is preceding emigration, and the Scots had at first the benefit of this. They had neither the advantages nor the disadvantages of the English poor relief system, and so were thrown often upon their own resources.[38] Nor did they feel as sensitively as the English the temporary prosperity which came with the early 1820's, only to disappear in 1825. Undoubtedly, too, the emigrant agent and the shipper found the less frequented coasts and harbours of Scotland profitable shelters for taking on a cargo which the customs officers of the regular ports would not have permitted.

In spite of the important precedence in early emigration possessed by the Scots, the London *Times* and local newspapers were giving publicity to the agricultural distress which most frequently led to the emigration of the small farmer. At a meeting held in Cambridge the month that Bathurst announced his first change in policy, the owners and occupiers of land in the county protested against the low prices of produce, the high rents and taxes, the whole accumulation of misfortune under which they struggled.[39] They sent a petition to Parliament and in March Mr. Western told the House of Commons that within the last few years farmers in the Isle of Ely in Cambridgeshire who had failed had left debts amounting to £72,500. Nineteen farms in Ely and the parishes adjoining were without tenants; the wage for strong, healthy single men was 8*d*. a day. In one hundred in 1812-13 arrests numbered 50; in the same hundred in 1814-15 they were 203. The last ratepayer in the parish, being unable to bear the burdens laid upon him, had come to ask what to do. The occupiers of land, "worn out by the wretchedness of the times," would not touch the land. "Whole parishes had been deserted, and the crowd of paupers increasing in numbers as they went from parish to parish, spread wider and wider this awful desolation."[40]

Parliament did nothing; perhaps it was too late to do anything in a short time. Lord Bathurst contented himself with explaining that the state of the nation was not worse than should be expected since "it was notorious, that no war had ever terminated without occasioning distress." Meanwhile rioting, "a mere blind outbreak of starvation," Conybeare has called it, broke out in Norfolk, Suffolk, Huntingdon, and with special severity in the Isle of Ely.[41] Houses were attacked and money was extracted, a clergyman magistrate was driven out, and after two days of anarchy the rioters came to blows with the law in a battle in Littleport. Two rioters were killed, 72 taken prisoner. On June 26 *The Times* reported the trial. The prisoners went before a commission: 24 were capitally convicted, of these five were hanged, five were transported for life, one for 14 years, and 10 were imprisoned for 12 months in Ely gaol. "The spirit in which . . . Mr. Christian, the Chief Justice . . . conducted the proceedings may be gathered from the closing speech in which he said that the rioters were receiving 'great wages' and that 'any change in the price of provisions could only lessen that superfluity which, I fear, they too frequently wasted in drunkenness.' "[42]

For the government the matter ended here. As for the people, some sought their relief in their own fashion.[43] They emigrated. In May 1817, *The Times* wrote again: "The rage for emigration from the Isle of Ely to America has not yet subsided. Farmers, tradesmen and merchants are continually quitting their native Isle to seek a livelihood in a distant land. A vessel lately came around to Wisbeach for passengers, and in a few days upwards of ninety applications were made."

Persons brought up to agriculture, many of them small farmers, make up a considerable number of the English mentioned in the emigration notices which appear in publications of the period. The year of the emigration from Wisbeach, the Colonial Office was informed by shipping merchants that farmers from all parts of the kingdom were applying for conveyance to British America. Nevertheless in 1821 William Cobbett believed that English farmers were still hanging on "like sailors to the masts of a wreck—to finish them would not take long," but their time had not quite come.[44]

Up to this time, the majority of the ruling order in Great Britain had accepted those parts of the theories of Adam Smith, David Ricardo, and T. R. Malthus and the ideas implied in free competition which suited their own ends but had shut their eyes to the fact that freedom worked two ways, for the labourer as well as for the employer. In 1817 however, the Duke of Beaufort was brought to apply to the Home Office for assistance in the emigration of 242 families of miners from Kingswood Bitton, some of whom had had but one day's work in a year and others who had walked 300 miles "without earning a shilling." The same year Lord Lascelles presented to the House of Commons an emigration petition from the cloth workers of Yorkshire. To the Home Office he insisted that the law to prohibit the emigration of artisans was no longer necessary, since other nations were manufacturing now without the aid of British workmen.[45] But the government, through the opinion of Lords Sidmouth and Liverpool, decided that no special favour in emigration or otherwise could be given to the Yorkshire workers who were unemployed because of the increased use of machines.[46]

The refusal of aid did not stop emigration. Before the middle of the year 740 persons had sailed from the Yorkshire port of Hull to British North America; by December 31 the total from all the ports of the

British Isles had climbed to almost 10,000, and that was a mere start. In 1818 more than 15,000 British subjects left their homes for the British American colonies, in 1819 more than 25,000.[47] Ultimately the government could not hold out against the demands for assistance. In 1819 it won the first vote for emigration and, in spite of the unwillingness of the workmen to accept what seemed to be only another form of Poor Law relief, some three hundred families were enabled to remove to the Cape of Good Hope.[48] The vote, however, was carried as a government measure without discussion of the policy of giving relief by means of emigration at state expense. The action must be taken, therefore, as one of those measures of relief which the Liverpool administration found itself compelled to adopt in spite of its avowed determination not to interfere with the operation of free competition. When in the spring of 1819, John C. Curwen, M.P., brought in the first petition ever to be presented to Parliament "to supplicate the House to devise means for expatriating large bodies of people," the petition was promptly tabled.[49]

In the files of both the Home Office and the Colonial Office ministers must have seen plentiful evidence of the temper of the people. During 1818 and 1819 while Home Office spies watched the districts where unemployment and discontent were serious, the Colonial Office was flooded with all manner of protests and petitions, some asking directly for the terms upon which emigration assistance would be given. For the year 1817 one volume of these containing about five hundred communications has been preserved; for 1818 and 1819 there are two volumes each, a number unequalled until 1831 and 1832, years of maximum exodus.[50] Demobilized soldiers ask for transportation to the colonies and land upon arrival; tradesmen cannot support their families, and many raise a plea similar to the following: "Feeling at this crisis the great difficulty of supporting our families owing to the scarcity of employment and the lowness of wages, and apprehensive we may in a short time be obliged to apply to our respective parishes for pecuniary relief, thereby adding to the already overgrown rates—it pains us to think instead of being useful to ourselves we should in the prime of our lives be a burden to our Country."[51]

More remarkable in this early period than private petitions are those received from parishes requesting government help in the removal of families desirous of emigrating. A Somerset vestry writes of twenty persons with families who have applied for recommendations for emigration to Canada and continues that the idea is acceptable to the parishioners if the government will assist them in the removal. Charles Taylor reports from another parish that "the owners and occupiers of land would willingly raise a sum of money, to rid the parish of this burden [of rates and population] every way injurious, if Government will afford facility in exporting them."[52] To the latter Goulburn replied from the Colonial Office that nothing could be done by his department unless some private individual undertook the pecuniary responsibility of the emigration. These parish proposals assume special significance when it is realized that in the House of Commons a plan for parish-aided emigration had been mentioned as merely having "been considered,"[53] but that no such plan was widely known until discussion of Wilmot Horton's ideas in 1823 and later.

Travellers' accounts of new-world experiences illustrate the character of another part of this emigration movement. In August 1817, Henry Bradshaw Fearon landed in the United States as the emissary of thirty-nine educated, intelligent English families who desired information on North American opportunities before leaving home. Fearon travelled through the eastern parts of the United States and west to Illinois and Indiana, but before he completed his survey, most of the thirty-nine families had been induced by the publications of another traveller, Morris Birkbeck, to invest in Illinois. There at Albion where Birkbeck had been building up a "New England," some four hundred fairly well-to-do English emigrants had already founded a British community which, in spite of schisms, continued to grow.[54] Fearon, Birkbeck, and another travelling author, Lieutenant Francis Hall, observed United States democracy without dismay and saw economic advantage in emigration to the United States.[55] Their point of view was opposed by William Cobbett and Charles F. Grece of Longue Pointe on the Island of Montreal. Cobbett could describe the United States from residence there, and through his *Political Register* and his volume, *A Year's Residence in America* (1819), he had means to expose the hardships of emigrants in the American West and the materialistic motives of promoters which Birkbeck's publication had failed to recount.[56] Grece had lived in Canada since 1807, knew its trackless forests as well as its progressive agricultural societies, its inland transportation, its free lands, and its value for British emigrants. All these he set forth vigorously in print in 1819 in the hope that he could "divert the tide of emigration from . . . the United States to the more hospitable, contiguous and accessible districts of the Upper and Lower Canadas."[57]

How great the loss of British subjects to the United States was in this early era, no one can say accurately. Records of departure from the British Isles indicate that between 1818 and 1826 sailings to the British

American colonies were greater than those to the United States in the proportion of sometimes two to one. But the records are incomplete, especially for vessels trying to avoid the Customs officers, and the drain from the British American colonies to the United States has been estimated as very great. Although a considerable immigration into Upper Canada from the United States must be counted as gain against the loss of population, probably Grece was justified in his concern.

Because of their early ties with Canada and Nova Scotia, fewer Scottish emigrants appear to have gone to the United States in this period than English and Irish. In Scotland public opinion had swung around from the opposition to emigration prevalent in 1803 to the new feeling of the "northern philosophers" and the Highland proprietors who, Selkirk writes, were now "as eager for the people emigrating as they were formerly to throw obstacles in their way."[58] This is the more remarkable since in the first six years after the peace, according to government report some nineteen thousand passengers had sailed from the Customs ports of Scotland to British North America.[59] It should be noted here that many Irish sailed with the Scots from the northern coasts and that a good proportion of these passed on from the British colonies to the United States. The Scottish movement in 1816 and 1817, had been from the Caithness and Sutherland port, Thurso, to Pictou in Nova Scotia,[60] where Lord Dalhousie was in favour of developing the province by opening roads and giving easier land terms to new arrivals. In 1819 consequent upon the removal of the Marquess of Stafford's tenants from their farms inland to small holdings on the coast, an even greater emigration took place to the same colony. Notices of eviction were served in 1817; local papers gave touching accounts of the cruelty of removals, though it now appears that all tenants removed were given an opportunity to take up coast lands at low rentals.[61]

Some Scots were enabled to emigrate by the activities of Donald Logan, a kinsman from Pictou; some by the efforts of Donald Cameron who managed the emigration of 690 Highlanders from Fort William and carried on a thriving passenger trade among those who could pay for their passage;[62] others had the assistance of the Sutherland and Trans-Atlantic Association which had been formed at Meikle-ferry-inn.[63] By 1820 small tradesmen, mechanics, men of every occupation were joining the throngs of emigrating small farmers, and every port in the north and west was sending hundreds annually to Nova Scotia and Quebec. One day in 1819, the *Hope* and the *Harmony* carried 525 natives of Argyll out of Crinan on their way to the St. Lawrence port; in one week 581 departed from Dumfries to British North America.[64] In the same year, St. John, New Brunswick, received 7,000 Scottish and Irish emigrants, 3,000 of them as late as October.

The emigration movement had grown so strong by the early 1820's, overpopulation or hard times so pressing, and the government's previous assistance so well known that in the west of Scotland proprietors themselves petitioned the Colonial Office for aid in removing their tenants. In 1825 Archibald McNab, though already insolvent himself, requested government help in transporting his clansmen to the establishment he planned to found in Canada. At the same time McLean of Coll in the Hebrides solicited a similar favour for his overcrowded tenantry who, without fishing or manufactures, were dependent upon the produce of their meagre land and the kindness of their landlord.[65] After consulting the Home Office and the Lord Advocate of Scotland, the colonial officials decided that the "same political expediency" as might exist for facilitating emigration from Ireland did not prevail in the Hebrides. Accordingly McLean and other Highland petitioners were left to join the ranks of the voluntary emigrants by whatever means they could.[66]

Bearing in mind the stories of Highland evictions and labourers' distress which bulk so large in contemporary sources, one might be led to believe that all Scots emigrants of the period were poor. Such was not the case. An authority of the day pointed out that one-quarter of the Scottish settlers on their way to British North America brought money and other resources. Other estimates place the proportion higher. The greater part of the emigrants, small farmers and all, had been accustomed to have property and were determined to have it again. Farmers who emigrated from Kintail and Lochalsh, as sheep-farming became widespread, were men of £150 property and removed from choice.[67] The tenants from Sutherland and Ross and Argyll had a few sheep and cows of which they could dispose. Many who went from Argyll to Upper Canada were in fair circumstances. The *Harmony* mentioned above carried in specie about £12,000, one man alone having exchanged £1,500 in gold and silver.[68] A Greenock correspondent, describing the emigrants he saw daily, gives a forecast of that fear which was soon to spread through agricultural interests:

By far the greater proportion of the whole are respectable agriculturalists, and possessed of considerable property. The *Ben Lomond* carries out a sum in specie little short of £30,000 belonging to persons on board. We have already expressed an opinion that this is not the sort of emigration which we should desire to see extended—they are in fact the very sinew of the country's strength.[69]

In settlement policy that was ever to be the point of difference between colony and mother country: what capital and experience the new lands needed the mother country wished to retain; what the mother country wished to rid itself of, the colonies looked upon as a useless addition, probably a burden. The destitute and enfeebled condition of emigrants arriving at Halifax and Quebec was early remarked, and the fear expressed that with the permission of the authorities in England the weak and the useless of the mother country would be thrown upon the colonies. Many of these protests and complaints might better have been directed against the abuses of the passenger trade or silenced in an attempt to appreciate the stupendous experiences which emigration brought into the lives of men and women who had never been beyond their own parish until they found their bewildered way to the emigrant ship. Much of their helplessness and apparent shiftlessness was due to the discouragement induced by their miserable condition—the result of a trying passage and the wrenching days of deprivation and farewell which preceded it. Of the voyage, one passenger wrote:

We were completely shut up in the hold. At the commencement of the storm the weather became very cold. This circumstance, providentially, was greatly in our favour, from our being so much crowded together, which in several respects was very disagreeable to our feelings. This cold state of the weather continued till we approached the mouth of the St. Lawrence, when it became so warm, that I was nearly suffocated from the smell and heat below deck. I was consequently compelled to sleep on deck, together with many others.[70]

The power to endure the breaking of old ties and to survive these first trials soon came to be acknowledged as a necessary asset for the emigrant, and the lack of it a sufficient explanation for the unhappiness and illness of many pioneers, especially women.[71] Add to these the worry from the impossibility of obtaining reliable information concerning the best course to be followed in the colony, and it is not surprising that early nineteenth-century observers dwell upon the initial uncertainty as the greatest test of the poor emigrant. Howison believed that many who arrived with funds to convey them inland found their way into the hovels of Quebec and Montreal, "the slaves of vague reports and false and exaggerated descriptions." Halifax, a town of less than ten thousand population, received in each of the four years 1816 to 1819 some two thousand Irish and Scottish emigrants who landed in this condition and were soon in actual need.[72]

Whatever the various causes of the unfortunate state of certain emigrants on arrival in the British American colonies, the problem became a matter of concern for the colonial officials. In 1817 and 1818 Lord Dalhousie from Nova Scotia and the Duke of Richmond from Quebec

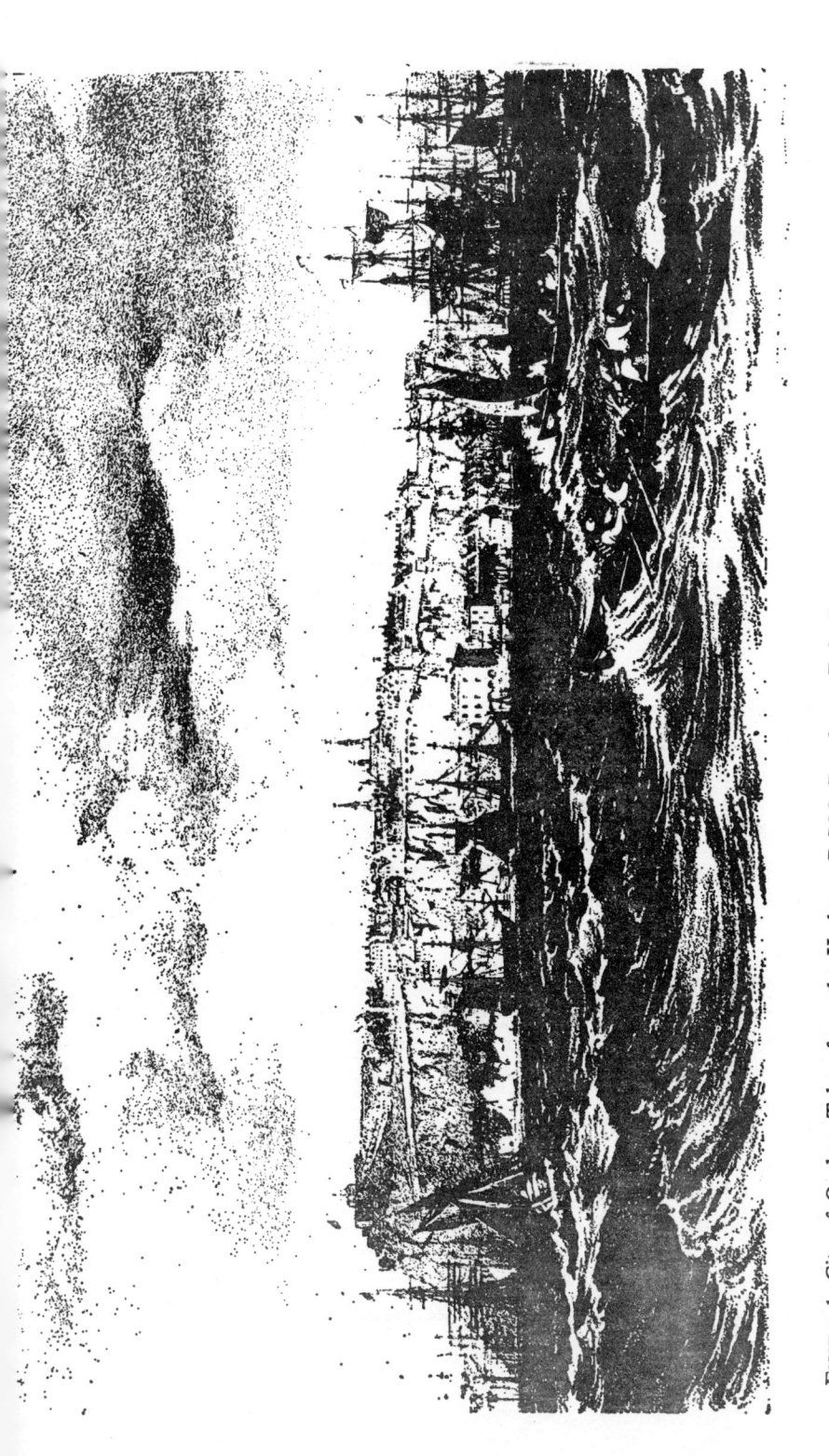

FIGURE 1. City of Quebec. Taken from the Harbour. R.S.M. Bouchette, Del., Day & Haghe, Lithographer to the King. (J. Bouchette, *The British Dominions in North America*, London, 1832.)

brought cases of distress to the attention of the Colonial Office. In the port of Quebec, the Duke was authorized to grant relief "as economically as possible."[73] At the same time, humanity and common sense prompted Canadians to form emigrant societies. At Kingston in 1818 a committee was appointed and a subscription taken to assist British emigrants in finding employment and so prevent their discomfort or departure. In 1819 New Brunswick founded the Fredericton Emigrant Society. Nova Scotia had organized a poor relief system, and in 1820 Walter Bromley founded in Halifax a Poor Man's Friend Society. Despite opposition from the current Malthusian enthusiasts, this voluntary society before its demise in 1827 visited and provided help for hundreds, in some years for thousands, of emigrants.[74] Montreal was forced to form a relief organization too.

A strong organization, the Quebec Emigrant Society, was set up in Quebec to meet the heavy problems of that busy port. Notwithstanding the accusations of misdirected humanitarianism and interested cupidity which were later levelled at that society, particularly by the Emigration Agent, A. C. Buchanan, and the French press, there can be little doubt that its founders were actuated by worthy motives. The scenes on the wharves in 1819 might well have caused alarm. In one day, Sunday, August 2, eight vessels brought in 1,337 emigrants; the total arrivals in the port of Quebec in the same year were 12,000, a number equal to two-thirds of the whole population of the city. Many of these, from their own scanty preparation, the crowded condition of the ships, the change of climate, shipwreck or loss by death, were in a state of poverty or disease serious enough to cause the Society to fear that "as the winter closed in the Inhabitants of . . . the City" would have on their hands "an accumulation of misery and distress" for which they could provide no adequate remedy.[75]

At first the funds of the society had come only from private subscription; later, in 1823, they were increased by legislative grant and an emigrant hospital was organized.[76] In short by 1823, this necessary demonstration of charity had become an annual contribution of a nature to alarm Canadians. While it was compelled to enlarge its grant to £950 in 1826 and £1,000 in 1827, the legislature was inclined to limit its assistance to the sick and finally withdrew even the salary previously allowed for the health officer of the port of Quebec. Under such circumstances, the British Treasury authorized the expenditure of £1,000 which later became the yearly grant for relief in Quebec,[77] and for the disbursal of which the Quebec Emigrant Society originally gave a regular account. The first report shows the principle on which assistance was

THE MILITARY SETTLEMENTS, 1815–1830

dispensed. All expenses were classified under three heads: "The Relief of Helpless Indigence," "The Providing of Work," and the "Aiding and Settlement of Emigrants." Actual money was seldom given and the object in every instance seems to have been "to promote the permanent advantage of the Emigrant, by inciting him to good habits or preserving them if already acquired, and by aiding him in the actual Settlement of his family."[78]

It was essential for the success of settlement that immigrants should leave for the interior in good condition. Beyond the St. Lawrence ports, population was so meagre and scattered that few facilities for assisting new arrivals were available. The trip up the river by steamboat, by bateau, or on foot was, as every contemporary emphasized, most trying to unacclimatized Europeans.[79] It was also expensive. One could not travel from Quebec by river, stage, and lake to the western limits of the upper province, a distance of 800 miles, for less than £14 or 15, exclusive of provisions and luggage. The comforts of cabin and stage from Quebec to Prescott came to about £6. Steerage, usually on the deck of the new, 140-foot steamboats which after 1817 plied regularly between Quebec and Montreal, and then on foot from Montreal to Lachine, and in slow boats up to Prescott, cost one-third less.[80] From Prescott many routes were possible: by land to the Rideau military settlements; up the river to Kingston and beyond to Rice Lake, Cavan, Monaghan, and the settlements in the Newcastle district; to York, or the promising districts in the rich western parts of the colony. But to reach any of these transportation, together with the expenses en route and on arrival, was sufficiently costly to appal all but those who came possessed of at least £300 capital.[81]

The locating of land* was an equally difficult undertaking. In New Brunswick after Surveyor-General Lockwood placed in Cardigan the Welsh emigrants† whom he found stranded at Fredericton,[82] the colonial legislature appropriated sums for the encouragement of settlement by the building of roads and the assistance of emigrants. In 1803 the Assembly had appointed eleven immigration commissioners; eventually it voted £1,000 for paying the ocean fares of British emigrants. Under Sir Howard Douglas, when many emigrants were passing on to the United

---

*"Locating land" is used in the following sense given by Murray: "to mark the position or boundaries, to enter or take possession of (a land-claim, a gold-mine, etc.) U.S."

†On his arrival in 1819, Lockwood found the Welsh who had emigrated with Lord Bathurst's consent stranded in Fredericton; he placed them on land, procured food, and got the legislature to assume the expense. In 1827 the Cardigan settlement had 37 log buildings and 717 acres of land cleared.

States, emigrant societies were formed to receive the new arrivals and aid them judiciously until they were established. In Nova Scotia, the legislature raised £500 to assist the destitute Scots who arrived at Pictou in 1815, and soon Cape Breton similarly aided the emigrants whom Simon Fraser, with Bathurst's permission, had encouraged to remove from Barra to Sydney. Later Lieutenant-Governor Sir James Kempt set aside lands for settlers to which in 1824–5 some three hundred emigrants from northern Scotland made their way at their own expense.[83] In Upper Canada, the emigrant could obtain from the local land boards maps and information respecting lands opened by the government. But frequently these lands were separated by large tracts of closed lands. The long distances to be travelled, often on foot because of poverty and lack of roads, entailed a strain so exhausting that Europeans in the colonies began to advise none who could remain at home to emigrate.

The increase in land fees gave strength to this argument. Since the report was prevalent that land was given free, Talbot and others asserted that hundreds emigrated without means to meet this additional expense.[84] Fees which at the beginning of 1819 were slightly over £8 on a 200-acre grant were raised to £16 in 1820 and by 1823 to £30. By that time discontent with the fees, which brought little revenue to the Treasury and merely increased the income of civil servants, and with the colonies' systems of opening lands, caused the home government to institute (partially in 1828 and fully in 1831), a policy of sale on four-year annual credit. A commissioner of Crown lands was now to select and announce lands for sale at auction. But this system too penalized the emigrant of small means who could seldom afford to wait for the auction and, when he could, was often outbid by speculators. After taking into consideration the nature of the payments and settlement duties required,* settlers often found it cheaper to buy land from private owners than to deal with the government.[85] Contemporary writers were almost unanimous in recommending private purchase. Assuming however that it was possible to raise funds to obtain land by purchase or grant or that, as later regulations permitted, the emigrant obtained a 50-acre grant free, the work and expense of establishment to be undertaken made British North America a desirable land for two classes of people, the man of small capital who could remove, secure his land, and

---

*In Upper Canada one-third of the land fees was payable at the time of receiving the location ticket, one-third when settlement duties were finished (two years being allowed to build a house eighteen feet square, and clear the road in front of each concession and three and one-half acres out of every hundred), and the final third on the receipt of the patent for the land: Q 396, 425–37; C. P. Lucas, ed., *Lord Durham's Report* (3 vols., London, 1912), III, 54–5.

set up his farm for from £200 to 900, according to the quantity of land acquired, or the labourer who was willing to emigrate steerage and work for wages on the farms of men of capital.

It was good policy, in one sense, for the colonies to permit or even create conditions which would keep out a great influx of unemployed paupers from the mother country, and it was quite in keeping with the spirit of the age that a labourer should remain a labourer. But what happened in the colonies was not what was to be expected from the spirit of the times, for a new spirit and indeed a new age were already in sight. The result was that, by a process of adaptation developed from the very needs of the situation in the British Isles and the opportunities in America, the British American colonies received many of their labourers and landowners from the same source. After 1830 this plan of producing land purchasers from the labourers who saved their wages was hailed as a new discovery. As a matter of fact, it was an expedient resorted to by penniless emigrants ten years before and during the same length of time commented upon by understanding writers and reported to the Colonial Office. It was to a large extent the method by which a good part of those colonial lands was settled.

Assistance for Weavers—The Growth of Lanark Settlement

For years before this outcome was obvious, before the home government fully accepted the policy of laissez-faire as far as emigration to British America was concerned, the Colonial Office faced a recurrent dilemma: should it refuse to give aid to needy applicants or should it send out to the colonies, or even permit the emigration of, the indigent to whom the colonists loudly objected. For example, while small farmers were financing their own removal overseas by the sale of their few possessions, unemployed weavers, living on relief or reduced to short time and starvation wages, could provide not even the food or clothing required for emigration. During 1819 the state of the northern weavers became so serious and the pressure brought by members of Parliament so strong that the colonial officials were again compelled to provide emigration assistance. In July 1816 the *Scots Magazine* had written: "The situation of the country becomes more and more deplorable."[86] The period has been described as one of "Soup and Reform Agitation." For the benefit of the government, Henry G. Bennet spoke at length of the march of "radical doctrine" through Scotland and northern England where wages had dropped since 1803 from 25 to 5s. a week and even pawnbrokers were being driven to bankruptcy.[87] The ministry in

London had decided to suspend Habeas Corpus, but repressive measures directed by Lord Sidmouth from the Home Office did not prevent the weavers' strike of 1818 or the mass meeting of protest at St. Peter's Fields in Manchester in 1819. When government troops were sent into the gathered crowds, this deed of prowess was derisively christened "Peterloo." The extreme Tories in power replied by the Six Acts: gatherings for drill and unauthorized meetings were forbidden, and open expression of radical opinions muzzled.[88]

From this year the weavers divided into two parties. The first "sought salvation through Reform, the other . . . made efforts to secure a minimum wage at home, or, failing that, asked assistance for emigration."[89] Resolutions favouring emigration were read at a meeting of thirty thousand weavers in Glasgow in June 1819. One speaker, an advocate of Reform, told the advocates of emigration that "the low wages . . . did not arrive from a superabundant supply of hands, . . . but from excessive taxation and misrepresentation in Parliament . . . even were their petitions [for emigration] answered, it would not, by diminishing the number of hands have any effect in raising wages of those who remained. He instanced the Irish, who were not, he said, in the least benefitted by the emigrations to Scotland. He moved an amendment to the resolution, that there should be annual parliaments, universal suffrage, and a diminution of taxation."[90]

Above that indeterminate mass which forms the centre of every community there now stood forth two groups differing vitally in principle, men who would fight and men who would compromise. The first group believed that improvement, whether social or economic, could be won only by gaining political freedom and they were willing to give their lives to the winning of it; the second group was willing to negotiate with the government and in this case to accept land in the colonies in compensation for what was denied at home. It is scarcely necessary to remark upon the contempt with which the Reformers regarded the emigrants or to explain that the government acted first with the advocates of compromise and, twelve years before it granted Reform, assisted in the removal of more than two thousand weavers to British North America.

Assistance for emigration to British America in 1815 and 1818 and to the Cape of Good Hope in 1819 had been given without bringing Parliament to a decision on the theory of relief. For aiding the weavers in 1820 it seemed that private negotiations would be best because many members still opposed the minimum wage, public employment for the poor, and parliamentary grants for relieving distress. Such devices, they argued, would counteract the natural checks on increasing population which were the only means of effectual, lasting relief. During the winter the weavers of Glasgow, Paisley, Hamilton, Lanark, Carlisle, Whitehaven and thereabouts had formed emigration societies and addressed petitions for aid to the Colonial Office and northern members of Parliament.[91] On May 24, 1819, John Christian Curwen had risen in the House of Commons, as noted above, to beg for twelve hundred petitioning weavers "as a boon, that which bespeaks the extinction of one of the most powerful feelings of the human heart. In despair of obtaining bread at home, they ask you," he said, "to expatriate them—to convey them to your colonies."[92] Now a year later Lord Archibald Hamilton and the Lord Advocate of Scotland came to an agreement with the Prime Minister and the Chancellor of the Exchequer, Nicholas Vansittart, by the terms of which Kirkman Finlay, M.P., was to arrange details with the Colonial Office and the emigration societies for the removal to Canada of one thousand of the needy workers. Land grants of 100 acres were promised subject to the usual duties but free of the expense of survey; seed corn and implements were to be offered at prime cost; and capital was to be provided, not by leaders as before but by the government in successive instalments of three, three, and two pounds, for the repayment of which at the expiration of ten years the societies bound themselves jointly.[93]

The weavers had expected free transportation to the colony and when the emigration societies came to make selections from their members, funds to engage the necessary shipping had to be raised by private subscription and an advance from the government.[94] In the Glasgow neighbourhood in the winter of 1819–20, Reform agitation and even proclamations for a provisional government caused the ministry to increase the military in garrison and in St. George's and St. Enoch's squares.[95] Leaving this "peaceable but gloomy" atmosphere, twelve hundred emigrants embarked on the Glasgow steamboat in June and July and went down to the emigrant vessels. All were in high spirits, "the weavers' wives in particular rejoiced in the prospect of 'getting quat o' the prin' wheel.' "[96]

By this embarkation about 12,000 ells were removed from the Lancashire market. But the improvement was as purely theoretic as the Reform party weavers and men of Robert Peel's way of thinking had prophesied. Before Christmas 1821, the Colonial Office had received another lot of petitions from the weavers' emigrant societies.[97] At a meeting in the Black Ball Inn in October a list of 6,281 applicants was presented and during the winter Kirkman Finlay and a committee of local men accepted 2,000 weavers desiring emigration, mainly from the counties of Renfrew and Lanark and a few from the western Highlands.[98] Vessels were hired and their equipment and loading supervised by Robert Lamond, secretary of the emigrant societies, so that within thirty days 1,833 persons from Lanark, Dumbarton, Stirling, Clackmannan, and Linlithgow were enabled, as the *Scots Magazine* put it, to remove "in search of subsistence on the other side of the Atlantic."[99] Though the *Quebec Mercury* reported the emigrants' "appearance of health, neatness, and comfort" on their arrival, John M'Donald has described the overcrowding, bad air, seasickness, and lack of food during storms at sea, the whole trying routine on the long crossing of his vessel, the *David of London*.[100]

At Quebec M'Donald's group, about four hundred, transferred in a heavy downpour of rain to the deck of a river steamboat. Twenty-four hours later in Montreal they moved women, children, and baggage to wagons, and the cavalcade proceeded, the men walking, to Lachine. There they transferred again, this time to open Durham boats, and conveyance was undertaken now by the colonial government. The Scots suffered severely from the heat, from drinking the local water, and from wading in wet garments to haul the boats. At night the party "remained on the river side . . . by far the most part of them lodged out in the fields for six nights," the time required to reach Prescott. At this spot, they waited for three weeks with six hundred Scots from other vessels for the wagons which were to move them to Perth, the heart of the military settlements.[101]

From this thriving place, with its two churches, two bakers, three smiths, stores, post office, and quarter-master general's department, the Scottish emigrants of 1821 had to travel fourteen miles through unbroken woods to New Lanark on the Clyde. At that little clearing in 1820 the settling department had placed about fifteen hundred settlers, some demobilized soldiers, some emigrants of independent means, and the rest the weavers of 1820.[102] From there again, all soon scattered to lands in the townships of Lanark and Dalhousie. By 1821 the desirable lands near New Lanark had been taken and the new arrivals often waited in temporary shelters until snow and frost had come before the family acreage was found and the clearing of trees and home building begun in the townships of Ramsay and Sherbrooke.[103]

While the weavers were beginning their new life, the government in London and Lieutenant Colonel Cockburn, as superintendent of the military settlements, were both counting the cost. In May, 1821, Cockburn reckoned total expenditure on the weavers, including the opening of roads, surveys, buildings, transportation, and money advances at

£11,832 11s. 7d., or about £16 per family on each 100-acre farm.[104] By 1829 another report, this by the superintendent, Captain William Marshall, had placed the expenditure on the New Lanark settlers above £22,000, in addition to the actual cost of settlement in Canada.[105] On the theory of Lord Dalhousie and Sir Peregrine Maitland that aid should be withdrawn as soon as the settlers could provide their own subsistence, the Perth military establishment was discontinued at Christmas, 1822, though for the Lanark settlers a superintendent, clerk, doctor, and schoolmaster were maintained until 1829.[106] None of the cash advanced to the settlers had been repaid by that year and in 1831, after various settlers had abandoned their unproductive land and the colonial government still protected its investment in the others by withholding title deeds, the settlers of Ramsay, Lanark, Dalhousie, and North Sherbrooke made a claim for remission of payments. Captain Marshall, in charge of the settlement, suggested payments and rent in proportion to the value of the land, much of which was none too good. But the Treasury in London declined to countenance the Colonial Office's recommendation for clemency; not until 1836 did it agree to Sir John Colborne's advice to cancel the weavers' debts of some £22,000 to the government.[107]

As actual money investments, therefore, it must be acknowledged that these schemes for assisting emigrants failed. Not one penny of the capital advances made by the government was ever returned. In the announced purpose of forming a military barrier on the water communication between Upper Canada and the lower province the settlements were also unsuccessful. Five years after they were opened, the waterway was still uncompleted and Lord Dalhousie was appealing to the home government for a means of protecting the settlers who had been put in to form a defence. As late as December, 1825, the Duke of Wellington made a new report in favour of the old recommendation, a safe highway between Upper and Lower Canada, now only "less important in a Civil and Commercial than in a Military point of view."[108] Not even in another predominant purpose, that of giving relief to the overcrowded ranks of the trade at home, did the aid to emigrant weavers bring satisfaction, for the result of this small removal was negligible. Later investigation seemed to show that improvement came from change of conditions within the trade itself, such as the return of prosperity which rendered unnecessary a similar grant in 1827, rather than from any lessening of competition caused by emigration.

If, however, these experiments be looked upon as a means of bringing relief and comfort to the worker so taken from distress in the older country, or as the founding of a nucleus of settlement about which later emigrants would gather, the whole aspect of success and value is changed. Lanark township in 1824 had a population of 1,560 living in comparative plenty.[109] There were already 275 oxen and 1,338 cows in the township, and taxes were trifling. Some of the emigrants had their looms set up; all were better dressed than tradesmen in Scotland. "J. S." describes heavily laden dinner tables, houses packed with "indian corn, pease, wheat and oats . . . several hams resting in nooks." When asked if she would be willing to return, one Scottish emigrant woman replied, "Aften when I am feeding the dogs an' cats wi' meat that I hae seen the day we wad hae been blythe to hae had for oursells, the tears are like to rin owre my cheeks for the poor starvin' folk at home."[110]

Though the Lanark area was not to become one of the famed agricultural regions of Upper Canada, the progress of the whole Rideau settlement was in general sound and steady. At first in their ignorance some of the assisted emigrants located on rocky or swampy lands; some sold out, and others crossed the St. Lawrence River in search of high wages in the United States. But the arrival of the new settlers stimulated the progress of the older Perth settlement by providing a market for surplus produce and at the same time it supplied the poorer settlers with the employment and other essentials which Colonel Cockburn, superintendent of the military settlements from 1818 to 1822, realized they could not find for themselves. Though the annual totals of new arrivals in the British American colonies declined after 1819, falling from approximately 18,000 in 1820 to about 9,000 in 1825, the new emigrants were sufficient to fill in all unoccupied, surveyed lands around the older settlements. And after 1823 the rising tide of newcomers often overstripped the preparations made by the colonies. By 1831, this scattering of isolated groups in a wilderness had become, through natural increase and new arrivals, a community of 18,000 more or less prosperous British subjects.[111] John Richards found Brockville a thriving town of 1,500, "supported by the rich back country of Perth and other settlements." In 1836 after further increase from voluntary emigration the flourishing Bathurst district, according to Thomas Rolph, "abounded in villages and new settlements."[112]

IV. THE RISING TIDE:
TO THE IRISH SETTLEMENTS,
1823-1845

DURING THE YEARS when the Colonial Office was experimenting with plans to aid demobilized soldiers, unemployed weavers, and others desiring to emigrate, the government faced a more urgent need in Ireland. In the last quarter century, apparent overpopulation, unemployment, poverty and famine, risings of the people against landlords and agents, and all manner of activities of secret groups had reduced parts of the country to a more or less continuous state of insurrection. In London parliamentary committees studied the Irish economy and the poor; food and money were sent as relief.[1] In spite of these efforts, until after 1823 the main reliance for improvement had been placed on the Insurrection Act; of the twenty-seven years between 1796 and 1823, the Act had been in force for sixteen. Yet by 1822, conditions were worse than ever. The government of Ireland, according to Parnell, was nothing but "a continual scuffle between the magistrates and the multitude."[2] In 1822 Henry Goulburn, the chief secretary for Ireland, wrote to the Home Office requesting a convict ship for three hundred Whiteboy offenders in the county of Cork. After a disquieting conspiracy in Doneraile and a bad riot in Dublin, Lord Wellesley recommended the suspension of Habeas Corpus and the renewal of the Insurrection Act.[3]

Robert Peel, in the Home Office after six years as secretary for Ireland, was sceptical of improving anything within that unhappy island. In the Irish Office he had worked to keep down the forces of anarchy with a strong hand, a policy thoroughly agreeable to his superiors in office, Lord Sidmouth and the Duke of Wellington. He had brought efficiency and honesty to the administration of government but no improvement in agriculture, no appeasement of religious strife.[4] Now he could write comfortably from London that he had heard of more "shots through the hat in Ireland without the head being affected than in any other Country"; in his opinion another vote of money for employment of the poor would be "an invitation to be Poor and Distressed." But of emigration Peel did approve, especially if it were directed to British colonies; to Goulburn he wrote of it as "one of the Remedies for Irish Misery."[5]

THE BEGINNING OF IRISH EMIGRATIONS

The peace of 1815 had already opened this form of relief to Irish emigrants. In one day the Irish Council which met weekly in 1816 considered seven hundred applications for permission to emigrate. Though few vessels were available in 1815, fish and oil boats on the Newfoundland run had taken out more than three thousand Irish, mainly from Waterford. Except for some of the timber hulks, the Newfoundland boats were the poorest on the Atlantic and their fares the lowest, 30 to 40s., sometimes less. The most poverty-stricken of the emigrants used them, some transferring in St. John's to anything that would carry them to New York, Quebec, or the British maritime colonies. In spite of Londonderry's flax trade with Philadelphia, its sailings in 1815 were to New York and along with those from Belfast and Dublin they took to the United States between one and two thousand Irish. By 1816 the post-war opening of trade and the easing of passenger vessel regulations furnished shipping accommodation for some two thousand emigrants each from Belfast and Londonderry to New York and sizable numbers from other ports to the United States.[6]

Few Irish emigrants went direct to Quebec or any British North American port until new passenger vessel legislation raised travel rates to the United States and the tariff preference on British North American timber increased the sailings to New Brunswick and Quebec.[7] As a result, in 1817 Belfast, Londonderry, and Dublin sent twenty shiploads of emigrants to the maritime colonies and more than 1,300 emigrants to Quebec. Soon the majority of the emigrants landing at St. John were Irish. Passage from Ireland to New Brunswick could now be had for £5 in contrast with £10 to New York, and in 1818 from Belfast alone more than 4,000 sailed to British North America while but 1,600 went to the United States.[8] Except for those to Newfoundland, these first emigrants were largely farmers, tradesmen, farmer-weavers, and artisans who had not yet, like the cottiers, lost all. After the potato famine of 1817 and the resultant typhus, a fierce uneasiness arose among even the more apathetic of the poor and some of them found means for removal by binding themselves for payment of their fares to the shipmasters, as had the indentured servants of earlier days.[9]

British North America retained few of these emigrants; some contemporaries estimated that as many as six-tenths passed on from the colonial ports to the United States.[10] In 1817 however the British consul in New York, James Buchanan, a member of a shipping family from the north of Ireland, set on foot a reverse migration. When his patriotism was aroused in 1816 by the great number of British subjects landing in New York, he won permission to expend ten dollars on each one he could send on to Upper Canada.[11] Though Lieutenant-Governor Gore strongly opposed immigration from the United States and would accept Buchanan's emigrants only when the consul vouched for their loyalty, Buchanan was enabled by an arrangement with the Foreign Office[12] to forward to Upper Canada 3,663 British emigrants in the years 1817 to 1819. The greater part were Irish from the Ulster counties of Cavan and Monaghan. By the time they reached York, most of them were penniless and they went to work in the brick-yard there. Presently when the townships later to be known as Cavan and Monaghan were surveyed in the Rice Lake region, these emigrants obtained lots of their own in a growing community where additional work could be had at road and canal building.[13]

As the movement for emigration spread from Ulster outward and emigration ports of less importance began to send a quota, as emigrant agents spread their advertisements far and wide, and reports of success began to return from the New World, the discontented, the ambitious, in fact almost all types of Irish looked more and more to North America as the solution of their growing difficulties at home.[14] Presently the movement from the south began to catch up with that from the north. Passage was cheap to Amboy, New Jersey, near New York; American representatives were busy and as *The Times* reported the Irish went because they would not stay in Ireland. Many communicated with the Colonial Office protesting their loyalty and desire for land in Canada. Before 1820, perhaps, one-half of the petitions filed in London were from western and southern Ireland.[15] In memorials varying in size from a few inches with ten or twenty words to monstrous sheets containing eight square feet and over three thousand signatures, the story of the misfortunes of Ireland is set forth—"the Slavery of Rents, Tythes and Leases," the "murders and house burnings," the "stalking Starvation in this our native Land."[16]

Private merchants giving particulars of their own passenger trade showed records of thousands—one of 7,000—of emigrants conveyed to America in the first five years after the peace. A large shipowner of Dublin, John Astle, is authority that though the exodus varied from year to year with certain districts sending greater numbers at certain times, Dublin shipped annually 4,000 persons and the whole of Ireland

20,000.[17] It was his opinion also that only the better class of tenantry with some little capital dared to risk the difficulties and uncertainties of emigration to British North America. But the colonial under-secretary took a different view: scarcely one-twentieth, he believed, of the Irish emigrating to the colonies had more capital than a small provision of clothes and bedding.[18]

The government which fought Catholic Emancipation appears to have felt little concern over these departures. Robert Peel, on whose shoulders fell a great part of the responsibility of enforcing order until 1818, felt that Ireland would not suffer were the emigration from the south ten times the extent of that which was taking place.[19] Suggestions came in plenty for directing "the current of emigration from the United States to our own colonies,"[20] but with the exception of the redirection by James Buchanan in New York and the assisted emigrations of 1823 and 1825 described below no action was taken for the purpose. For this reason as well as a complication of other causes the southern Irish emigrant, a great colonizer elsewhere, did not play a part commensurate with his numbers in the colonization of British North America.

Peel was no believer in panaceas, but because of his work with Ireland he was in constant touch with the new secretary for that island, Henry Goulburn, and Goulburn had come to the Irish Office from an experience in directing the government-aided emigrations to British America from 1815 to 1821. Both men therefore were well fitted to co-operate with the new emigration enthusiast, the Under-Secretary in the Colonial Office, Robert John Wilmot Horton. Through their influence probably, the committee appointed in 1823 to inquire into the condition of the labouring classes had heard witnesses on emigration and recommended it as a means of relief. If it tended to the tranquillity of the country, it might lead to the introduction of British capital by means of which principally the economists believed the condition of labour could be improved. Except in evidence, no mention was made of the fear that England would suffer from an inundation of Irish workers, but it was hoped that "some slight additional demand for labour" would result in areas from which the emigrants were taken.[21] A plan for such an emigration to the New World was included in the report.

AID FOR EMIGRATION FROM SOUTHERN IRELAND

Before the report was in print, Goulburn and Horton had a scheme in progress for assisting Irish emigration. Wilmot Horton who had developed his emigration theories for the relief of English parishes spoke of the undertaking as an experiment financed by the government for the purpose of planning a great system of emigration for England.[22] In the light of contemporary evidence it is difficult to consider the Irish emigration which followed in 1823 and 1825 as the mere experiments here represented. Reference has already been made to the attitude and experience of Peel and Goulburn on Irish emigration. Early in 1822 the Secretary for War and the Colonies, Lord Bathurst, had been approached by Irish landlords who desired the encouragement of emigration from overpopulated districts.[23] Before parliamentary committees the same gentlemen gave evidence in favour of emigration. Presently at Goulburn's they were read a plan, adapted or drawn up by Horton, for government-aided emigration. Finally, if the motive stated by Horton were the only one, it is inexplicable why an emigration scheme planned for English parishes should have been hastily arranged for Ireland and tried out with emigrants from the "most disturbed district," when upon the success of the venture depended the future policy of Parliament towards the whole problem of relief by emigration. It would seem therefore that whatever the ideals of Horton, the motives of the government officials above him were not entirely those of experimentation but that, as in the case of the northern weavers, it was found expedient to offer a means of partial relief to a district where severe political danger was imminent.

The plan given to the Irish gentlemen at Goulburn's stated as a premise that "Government desirous of alleviating the inconveniences of excessive population in Ireland, and at the same time of giving the Provinces of Canada an accession of Emigrants capable of improving the advantages afforded by those Colonies to active and industrious men, has taken into consideration the expediency of providing for the transport and location of a certain number of Settlers on a system which will best insure their immediate comfort, and their future prosperity." To those disposed to emigrate from the south, who were under forty-five years of age and acceptable to the superintendent of emigration, the government promised to the number of 500 passage to Canada and conveyance to their lands free of expense, provisions and medical attendance on their journey and for one year after their arrival on their land; also, seventy acres of land subject to the usual conditions of fee and residence, with a 30-acre pre-emption reserved adjoining, and utensils necessary for a new settler, all furnished at the public expense. The advantages to be gained by one proceeding under these terms rather than as a casual emigrant were emphasized. Finally, as it was the desire of the government that this system should prove satisfactory to the emigrant and beneficial to the public, the terms concluded with the warning that the continuance of assistance must depend upon the "good conduct in the colony" of those who availed themselves of the offer as well as upon that of future claimants for similar assistance whom it was out of the power of the government to remove the first year.[24]

Towards the end of May Peter Robinson, brother of Attorney-General John B. Robinson of Upper Canada, who was selected by the Colonial Office to superintend the emigration and settlement in Canada, proceeded to Fermoy, Cork. There he was introduced by Lord Kingston, Lord Doneraile, and other proprietors. The greatest objection these gentlemen made to the emigration plan was that "the most industrious and best disposed" would be most likely to take up the offer. They believed however that the magistrates and landowners could guard against this "by recommending only those who, if not actually connected with the disturbances," were almost sure to be so from their situation and lack of employment.[25] Robinson was advised therefore to take as many persons as possible from the worst district, the barony of Fermoy. Accordingly Fermoy, Ballyhooly, Mallow, Newmarket, Charleville, Killdorrery, Doneraile, Killworth, and nearby villages were visited, the terms of the emigration made public, and a list opened from which Robinson and the magistrates would later select the emigrants to receive aid.[26]

The scheme was not at first well received by the Irish. Though they willingly approached Robinson, they would not place their names on the magistrates' lists. This was due, Robinson wrote, to the necessity for "the Magistrates to be almost daily sitting as judges to enforce the law."[27] Stories respecting the government's intention were soon widespread: "It was a *gental* way of transporting them. . . . Government found they could not get rid of them fast enough by the Insurrection Act." As Robinson stated, the good to be effected by exporting five hundred would depend entirely upon their description; he felt it would be wrong "openly to hold out a bounty to persons of bad character," but since he had to procure candidates he was forced to expedients. He told applicants that as for character no questions would be asked; and with the consent of Thomas Arbuthnot, commanding officer of the district, he accepted a few persons of means in order to show the others that it was not a trick to get them out of the country.[28]

Within two weeks, in which Robinson had the assistance of the landlords and the priests, the people evinced "a perfect mania for going to Canada." "All so many questions to ask." Was Mr. Robinson an American? Was he quite sure there was no catch in it? Were there potatoes, priests, etc.? In Fermoy in one day there were two hundred applicants, some of whom had come fifty miles. The whole number desired might have been enlisted without going over half the territory Robinson visited in order to spread the opportunity throughout a wide district. Even in Buttevant and Doneraile—decidedly the most disturbed regions—the full quota was obtained. Most encouraging of all, it appeared that the few taken in 1823 would do "a great deal of good in relieving the small towns." For ten days there had been neither fire nor murders in the barony of Fermoy.[29]

So the *Hebe* and the *Stakesby* were enabled to sail on July 8 with all accommodations filled. Some who had promised failed to arrive at the port, it is true, but Robinson had prepared for this contingency by accepting more than he could carry. Though many came on board in dread and terror, other applicants crowded around the vessels in boats offering to go to Canada until the anchors were up and the ships put to sea. After an average crossing on which eight children and one woman were lost by death, the two vessels reached Quebec on the last day of September.[30] Conveyances ordered by the Quebec officials on instructions from Lord Bathurst were ready and the emigrants transferred directly from the *Hebe* and the *Stakesby* to the river steamboats and travelled at once to Montreal. From that port they went forward without stop, now on foot and in wagons to Lachine; here only two days were spent in rest and loading. Again the party set out, this time in large river boats the crews of which consisted of the Irish emigrants and two Canadians to guide and steer. Nothwithstanding the rapidity of the river and the unskilfulness of the men, few of whom had ever been in a boat, Prescott was reached on October 15, two weeks after the emigrants had entered Quebec harbour.[31]

At Prescott one month's provisions were taken over from the representatives of the quarter-master general's department who were waiting there. On October 18 the journey across country to Ramsay and Packenham townships in the Rideau settlements was begun. Four days later Robinson reported his arrival. A few settlers from Glasgow with a party of discharged soldiers had cleared the first land in Ramsay in 1820 and Sir Peregrine Maitland had given orders that Robinson use the remainder of their old stores.[32] There were neither barracks nor government buildings in the neighbourhood and the party was without shelter of any sort until log huts were put up, first in the central encampment and gradually on the various lots. As the Irish were unskilled in the use of the axe, it was necessary to pay old settlers to perform this work. The experience of choosing land upon which the home was to be reared, of receiving tools for work, and of being free men appears to have been fully appreciated.

John Mara wrote of his land grant: "to my judgment [it] was as good land as any in the Country." As for Robinson, the superintendent, "he has served us out with Beds and Blankets, all kinds of Carpenter's Tools, Farming Utensils and a Cow to the head of every Family next Spring." Writing home the same year, Carrol O'Sullivan extended the customary invitation for others to emigrate and added that even the cold Canadian winter was easier "to put up with" than "the rebuke of a landlord and the frown of a proctor at home."[33]

From the success of this pioneering in the Canadian woods, it had been said, would be decided the government's policy towards expenditure on emigration. Horton wrote of the Irish settlers:

If the accounts of them continue favourable, if instead of verifying the predictions which proceed from very high Canadian authority now in England that these men all run away from their Grants as soon as they cease to be provisioned by Government, the Settlers betake themselves to regular industry and proceed with the cultivation of their Grants, North American Emigrants will become a part of our National Policy. If the contrary event take place we shall be brought to disgrace, and as far as any individual will suffer, I am sorry to say that I shall be the most prominent one.[34]

The adoption of a large emigration scheme, however, depended upon Parliament and Parliament was interested, as it turned out, not in any colonial experiment but in conditions and opinions at home. Nevertheless it rested with the Colonial Office to justify its experiment.

From the first, contradictory reports regarding its success were spread. Lord Dalhousie, the high Canadian authority referred to above, had believed that such an addition of poor settlers at a time when the Canadas were already "overwhelmed by a Voluntary Emigration" would enlarge seriously the difficulties consequent upon all sudden, great increases of population. He objected particularly to the expense and when in the spring of 1824 quarrels arose between the neighbouring Scottish settlers and the Irish newcomers, he felt his fears had been fully realized. He and Captain Marshall, the former local superintendent of the Lanark settlers, were convinced that the Irish were little less than banditti. They advised that the scheme under Peter Robinson "be stopped at once as a Waste of Public Monies, and a most serious mischief done to the Canadas."[35]

The reports of Sir Peregrine Maitland, lieutenant-governor of Upper Canada, were as glowing as those of Lord Dalhousie had been gloomy. Although the rationing had been done by the commissariat, the management of the Irish settlement had been very much more in the hands of Upper Canadian officials than that of the military settlements. Maitland commended Robinson's efforts and the industry of the Irish. When in the spring the magistrates of Bathurst sent in protests against the habits of the newcomers in quarrelling with the early Scottish settlers, Maitland pointed out that there had been great jealousy of the Irish because they were assisted more liberally by the government than were the first settlers.[36]

Bare statistics of this venture in government colonization are inconclusive. Of the 567 souls brought out from Ireland only 477, of whom 63 were newly born, were on land in the Bathurst district in 1825; in other words, of the 182 heads of families located in 1823 only 120 were living on their farms in 1825. Eight of the 62 deserted farms had been vacated by death, 9 by departure to the United States, 12 by departure without leave, and 32 by departure of men to work for other settlers, a practice almost universal among penniless settlers.[37] Had the 567 emigrants remained effective settlers, the cost of the emigration would have fallen within the sum estimated, £13,974, or an average of £22 1s. 6d. Allowing for the expenditure on the emigration to the Cape and for the failure of the Navy Board to call for a full account for conveyance, Robinson's outlay was only £750 beyond the sum available from the vote, since his total expense for transporting, locating, equipping, and rationing the emigrants for one year had been £12,539 3s.[38] But if only 477 of the 567 became settlers on the land the whole calculation was altered and the average expense of settling one emigrant rose to something over £26.

Meanwhile the Irish at home were finding their own means for emigrating. After the first burst of departures, the outward movement slackened. In 1821 as wages rose in Great Britain and steamboat fares from Ireland to England fell, Irish removals to North America hit a record low for the nineteenth century: to Quebec only four thousand and to the United States only fifteen hundred. Near famine in Munster the next year and very cheap rates to British America, however, reversed the current and the arrivals at Quebec in each of the years 1822 and 1823 numbered about eight thousand.[39] Then while the government was shipping the assisted Irish in vessels it provided, the Passenger Vessel Act of 1823 put into effect severe regulations which raised the lowest fares to British America to £3 10s. This was beyond the means of the poor cottiers and labourers who had been sailing west on the timber vessels to the St. Lawrence. It almost equalized costs between British American and United States ports, and foretold in a way the tremendous exodus to the United States which was to come. Liverpool shippers now often gave free steamboat passage from Irish ports to their Liverpool docks and so were winning the Irish emigrant to their New York run. The shipbroker too who chartered part of a timber vessel and sold passage locally in Ireland was becoming characteristic of the Liverpool trade.[40]

In spite of changing British duties on Canadian and Baltic timber, vessels in that business continued to ply the St. Lawrence route and, no matter what cargo they were able to carry east especially after the New Brunswick trade collapsed, they could be sure of an emigrant cargo on the westward voyage. General as well as timber merchants advertised their St. Lawrence sailings widely in Irish newspapers, and the government experiments directed by Peter Robinson broadened Irish knowledge of the British American colonies. According to government evidence, about three-quarters of the casual emigrants arriving at the port of Quebec in the mid-1820's were Irish born and of these less than three thousand were assisted by the British government.[41]

Preparations for a second government-sponsored emigration had been made before the accounts of the first were fully balanced. Robinson returned to England in the spring. Just before him came a letter from Lieutenant-Governor Maitland looking forward to a continuance of the emigration; by means of it he hoped the important line of communication between Richmond Landing on the Ottawa and Lake Simcoe could be settled.[42] To promote this object and in order not to disappoint certain Irish who had been promised assistance, Lord Bathurst favoured an emigration in 1824. But Horton and Robinson wanted delay, the former because of "the comparatively tranquil state of Ireland making it unnecessary as a means of relief," and the latter because it would give the Canadian officers time to prepare food and shelter and the magistrates of Ireland a chance to make a careful selection of the most deserving for the emigration favour.[43] The Irish authorities were consequently instructed to announce the government's intention to aid in the emigration of fifteen hundred Irish in 1825 and to impress upon those chosen that they would be "immediately struck off the List of Settlers if at any time previous to the period of embarkation their conduct should in any respect afford the ground of complaint."[44]

In the House of Commons on April 15, 1825, Horton spoke of emigration as a matter of wide possibilities, of national concern which in the present instance might bring relief to Ireland.[45] Neither the Lords nor the Commons took the empire view. A committee of the House of Lords showed its interest in the project by inquiring if the promotion of emigration in a district where disturbances prevailed might be expected to contrbute to produce quiet.[46] In the House of Commons, one member spoke of the bad government of Ireland, another of the need of working for unity and prosperity at home, and another favoured emigration "on the simple ground that he should thereby be rescuing that number of persons from hopeless misery."[47] So Horton's vote for £30,000 for a second Irish emigration was agreed to, as many a vote on colonial subjects, in a very thin House.[48]

During the autumn of 1824 before Parliament or the Treasury had sanctioned the grant of money for the second venture, Peter Robinson had been in correspondence with landlords of the district from which the emigrants of 1823 had been taken. W. W. Beecher, Lord Mount Cashell of Killworth, Lord Doneraile, Lord Ennismore, Lord Kingston, and other proprietors had sent in lists of individuals who were willing to emigrate and who, being reduced to the state of paupers and in most cases being farmers and Roman Catholics, were "just the sort of persons" they believed Robinson wished to have in America.[49] In spite of Horton's warning not to encourage hopes before the decision of Parliament was taken, by the opening of the year Robinson had pledged himself for the emigration of 1,600: From Lords Kingston, Doneraile, Ennismore, and Mount Cashell 400, 200, 200, and 100 individuals respectively, from Mallow, Charleville, and Ballygibbin 200 each, and from Newmarket 100. Private petitioners too urged their claims to Robinson's favour. From Newmarket-on-Fergus John Burke wrote to remind Robinson that, with his wife and "four Sons and as many Daughters, rising gradually from 11 to 21 years of age . . . all well educated and industrious," he was awaiting the permission to emigrate which he had lost in 1823. William Croak of Milthrea parish of Buttevant, also with four boys and four girls, reported that he had "disposed of his potaties and Furniture and reduced himself to a State of Beggary" and had no refuge "under Heaven but relying on your Honrs. Goodness and Humane Character."[50]

At the same time Horton was harassed by allusions made in the House of Commons to favouritism in dispensing the privilege of emigration. Though he warned Robinson at once to "take special and particular care to have the sanction of the Collective Magistracy as a Warrant of the Persons taken coming within the rules prescribed,"[51] Lord Kingston shortly brought to town "very long details" of sixteen families who, having received emigration tickets and sold all their little property, were now refused by Robinson.[52] The regulations governing acceptance of emigrants were essentially the same as those of 1823 but with renewed emphasis on the necessity for accepting none who could pay for their passage and the desirability of taking Roman Catholics rather than

FIGURE 2. The Evictions of Irish Tenantry. (Illustrated London News, Dec. 16, 1848.)

Protestants. Try as he would Robinson could not down the rumour that the selection of emigrants was in the hands of a few gentlemen who had no right to exclusive patronage. At Killworth some 3,000 tenants were eager to go, at Doneraile 974, and Robinson could take only 397 without doing injustice to candidates elsewhere. "Those rejected were very clamorous," the work of selection a most unpleasant duty.[53] So in the end the superintendent accepted 2,034 emigrants though the vote of the House had provided for only 1,500.

Management of the expedition was as efficient as one could expect. Magistrates furnished certificates to show that candidates had been chosen in conformity with regulations and a final muster to check all was made on shipboard. In addition a deputation from Cork reported to the Colonial Office that none of the 306 heads of families embarked, the majority of whom were small farmers recently dispossessed, could have supported themselves at home.[54] The nine vessels used had been chartered by Navy tender and it was arranged that blankets and excess food were to go to the settlers.[55] In spite of all precautions and the presence of a surgeon on each transport, many emigrants who had been on a starvation diet for months before sailing collapsed with typhus and smallpox on the voyage, the death rate was heavy, and the Irish reached Prescott "generally in a very Weak State."[56]

At Kingston where the shiploads of emigrants were soon encamped, 300 cases of fever and 33 deaths occurred before Robinson arrived to move the new arrivals on to Cobourg.[57] Travelling *via* New York, Niagara, and York, Robinson had tried to arrange for supplies for the settlers. Once in Cobourg after a 70-mile journey from York, he had gone out to explore the Rice Lake and Otonabee River waterways and parts of the townships of Smith, Douro, Emily, Ennismore, Asphodel, Otonabee, and the rest of the tract in the old Newcastle district upon which it had been decided to place the settlers. In Kingston on August 11, he embarked the first load of about 500 emigrants upon a steamboat for the trip of 100 miles to Cobourg. Then, while the emigrants were transferred one boatload per week to encampments near Cobourg, Robinson obtained the help of the magistrates and the settlers already in the district in repairing the road for the wagons from Lake Ontario to Rice Lake and in building a flat-boat for moving freight to the head of the River.[58]

From the time of his arrival at Cobourg on August 15, 1825 until March of 1827 Superintendent Peter Robinson resided constantly with the emigrants, "a greater part of that time under Canvass." By early October, 1825, he had his charges encamped in huts of poles and branches plastered over with mud on the plains at the spot which he designated as the head of the "Otonabee River," and which one of the first settlers in Douro township, Thomas Alexander Stewart, later a member of the Legislative Council of Upper Canada, called Scott's Mills. Robinson thought that the plain, the "prettiest place" he had ever seen, should be named Wilmot Horton after the father of the Irish emigration plan.[59] But before his work in the rising settlement was finished, Scott's Mills had become known as Peterborough.

Locating the families on farm lots turned out to be Robinson's heaviest task. Though the colonial government, through Lieutenant-Governor Maitland's willing co-operation, furnished the essential surveyors, and the local magistrates were helpful, the building of a log cabin for each family and transporting supplies to it could not have been accomplished without the help of early settlers from Douro, Cavan, and other nearby townships. The Irish knew nothing of the pioneer woodsman's axe, and besides many were incapacitated by the sickness which began on shipboard, the 100-degree heat encountered in the encampments, and the flies that swarmed in the forest. Nor did they know that three years would see one-third of their adults in their graves, dead from those dangers met by all colonists. Nevertheless, before the winter snows fell, the families had been placed in separate log shelters on the land they were to cultivate. A year later in 1826 Robinson could report 142 locations in the township of Emily, 67 in Ennismore, 60 in Douro, 51 in Otonabee, 36 in Asphodel, 34 in Smith, and a few others farther distant from Peterborough.

Robinson understood the risk he bore with two thousand emigrants from "the most disturbed" part of Ireland on his hands in a remote, sparsely settled community. At Ile Perreau on the way up, a riot had broken out over the right to boil a kettle and doors and windows of a house and men's heads were smashed. Quiet was restored when Dr. Reade, the devoted surgeon who remained with the emigrants in the Peterborough neighbourhood, dismissed Cotter and Casey, the originators of the strife.[60] At the encampment on the plains, Robinson soon found "many idle rascals from Ireland frequently exciting our people to mischief and leading them astray." As superintendent he was determined to be obeyed and apparently with the help of a few strong settlers and Captain Charles Rubidge who had settled in Otonabee township in 1820 and who now became an assistant superintendent, he succeeded fairly well.[61]

At least two circumstances led to bad publicity for the Irish settlement of 1825. In the first place, the assisted settlements of 1815 and thereafter had been carried out largely under the supervision of the commissariat and the military. In the Irish emigration of 1825, the home government had co-operated mainly with the civilian authorities of Upper Canada. Lord Dalhousie, the governor-general, still believed the early system the better. Lieutenant-Governor Maitland of Upper Canada and his friends enthusiastically supported the later system. In the second place, Irish Roman Catholic emigrants of 1825 had been settled close to Protestant Irish who had been in Cavan and Monaghan since 1817 and 1818 and the belief was widely accepted that the two could not live peaceably side by side. Again, loss of population to the United States which continued almost as a matter of course was a delicate subject in the colony and a few of the emigrants of 1825 left the settlement for that destination. Naturally many rumours were afloat. Down at Sir Peregrine Maitland's cottage, Colonel Talbot told Peter Robinson's brother that the Irish were dying thirty a day. The *Colonial Advocate*, W. L. Mackenzie's paper, came out with a violent attack on the whole undertaking,[62] and Lord Dalhousie advised Horton far away in England that the Irish of 1825 would do as the Irish of 1823 had done, take their rations and decamp to the United States. The whole scheme, according to Dalhousie, gained "no other end than relieving the South of Ireland of a burden which [was] thrown upon the industrious classes of this young country."[63]

Such statements uncontradicted by Peter Robinson placed Horton in a difficult position as the defender of emigration before the committee on that subject then sitting. Lieutenant-Governor Maitland however soon came to his rescue with more favourable reports. He had visited the Irish emigrants of 1825 in the spring of 1826: they were at work, satisfactorily settled on their lands, and on friendly terms with their neighbours. Addresses presented to him by residents in the district and in Kingston expressed approval of a system of emigration which in relieving the United Kingdom of a redundant population might at the same time transform the Canadian wastes into "fruitful fields."[64] The *Colonial Advocate* too had been answered by Thomas Alexander Stewart who lived "in the very midst" of the Irish settlers. "From 20 to 30 pass my door almost every day," he wrote. "Some of them have told me with tears in their eyes that they never knew what happiness was until now. In general they are making great exertions in clearing land. . . . Not one complaint has there been against them by any of the old settlers. . . . When we heard of their coming among us we did not like the idea, and immediately began to think it necessary to put bolts and bars on our doors and windows; all these fears have vanished."[65] Finally as for the rumours regarding the death rate, when records of the first year were compiled it appeared that this had not been greater than one in twenty-one, a lower average than that of Carlisle, the healthiest locality in England.[66]

For Horton's experiment and the investigations of the Emigration Committee in London, statements of expenditure were of as much importance as those concerning the progress of the settlement. But, as it was impossible to close the accounts until after the committee had made its report and Horton himself had departed to a new appointment in Ceylon, no complete balancing of the accounts or averaging of per capita costs were ever made. Counting the additional vote of £10,480 which was required for the number of emigrants above 1,500 taken, the total vote for the emigration of 1825 was £40,480. More than £1,500 of this had gone to the Navy, some £8,000 to the commissariat in Canada, and a handsome lump sum of £29,000 to Peter Robinson who did not make his last payments to the Military Chest until 1833.[67] By calculating that the produce of the Irish settlement was valued at £11,272 8s. 3d. one year after the location, Robinson sought to prove that his settlers could have repaid the outlay on them, something that the weavers under the system defended by Lord Dalhousie could not do. But contemporary evidence belied Robinson's statistics and indicated that any advantage the Irish of 1825 had lay in the superiority of their land. Financially Robinson's estimate that a family of five could be established in British North America for £60[68] was practically the same as that of Lieutenant Colonel Cockburn whose experience had been gained in the military settlements.

Spreading Benefits for All

While controversy over the two systems of assisting emigrants divided rival advocates in Canada and discussion of the advisability of adopting any system engaged British officials in London, the emigrants themselves benefited from the relief given by emigration. The Irish selected in 1823 and 1825 were mainly small farmers who had been ruined by the fall in the price of produce or recently dispossessed by their landlords, labourers out of employment, or tradesmen in poor circumstances from the general badness of the times. Many of them had known what it was to be in actual need of food; it was necessary to provide most of them with clothes and bedding before sailing. They were taken from a district where life and property had not been safe for many years, where it had been impossible to preserve order even by the continual presence of soldiery and the frequent exportation of offenders to the convict colonies.[69] They were placed in a new land where a certain living could be obtained by industry, and where disorder and murder were little known. According to their own testimony they were removed "from misery and want and put into independence and happiness."

Around Rice Lake, the whole district and the earlier settlers shared the benefits enjoyed by the Irish. Before their arrival in 1825, voluntary emigrants had striven, some for eight years, without visible reward. Roads were mere trails, the essential mills—Scott's on the site of modern Peterborough, "an apology for a mill" in Smith township—so few and primitive that some pioneers ground their grain in a coffee hand mill or used boiled Indian corn.[70] In the townships of Cavan and Monaghan, emigrants redirected from New York by James Buchanan in 1817 and a scattering of Scottish and English settlers had made all too little progress; in Smith township the small group of English emigrants, mainly miners from Cumberland whom the British government had aided in 1818 and a few voluntary emigrant settlers, were able to support themselves from their own produce but scarcely more.[71] In Douro township where Thomas Stewart and his brother-in-law, Robert Reid, brought their families to settle north of Scott's Mills in 1822, Stewart's wife Frances spent more than a year without seeing "a female of any description" except her sister. In Otonabee township the first settler, Captain Charles Rubidge, R.N., told almost the same story of lonely pioneering and felt the same relief when the Irish emigration brought government improvements to the community.[72]

Three years had passed without any settler taking up land near him and Stewart had decided to remove his family from "this hopeless retirement," when in 1825 Peter Robinson came to his house and disclosed the government plan. At once "all our difficulties seemed over," Stewart wrote in 1828. Scott's Mills soon had two thousand inhabitants: "All became bustle and activity; houses and stores erected; a clergyman, priest, doctor, besides various kinds of tradesmen, were soon established." Frances Stewart, author of *Our Forest Home* (1889), wrote of the emigrants' humane, friendly Doctor Reade and his gentle wife. Captain Rubidge felt equal satisfaction at the sight of the town growing up near him: "roads are improving, bridges are built; one of the best mills in the province is just finished at Peterborough, another within three miles of me," he wrote two years after the arrival of the Irish. "Boards, and all description of lumber, are cheap—about five dollars 1,000 feet, four saw-mills being in operation." Besides these improvements, he listed also stores, a tannery, and of course, a distillery. As

Wilmot Horton said in far-away England, "Speculators flocked to the neighbouring townships ... and life, bustle and civilization went on with spirit."[73]

From 1826 onward the land around Rice Lake and the Otonabee River and indeed throughout much of the Newcastle district developed rapidly. Lumbering and milling provided an early income while farm lands were being cleared. The promotion of transportation services, work on the Trent Canal, improvement of the waterway north towards Lake Simcoe, and work on badly needed roads gave remunerative employment for many. The Canada Company began to advertise its lands in the area and made use of the versatile Major Samuel Strickland in spite of his preoccupation with the training of English gentlemen farmers on his property in Douro township.[74]

In the main British emigration to the area after the Irish of 1825 was voluntary and unassisted, and included a good number of men of means and retired British military officers, as well as the Stewarts and Stricklands, Susanna Strickland and her husband, J. W. Dunbar Moodie, Catherine Parr Traill, and John Langton, later a member of the provincial legislature, vice-chancellor of the University of Toronto, and auditor-general of the province, and others whose influence spread far beyond their local community.[75] A small emigration of the very poor, many of whom had received aid from parishes or proprietors in England, continued. Lieutenant-Governor Sir John Colborne developed a plan for providing near-indigent emigrants with small allotments in the township of Ops.[76] He placed some three thousand assisted emigrants from Wiltshire and Yorkshire in Douro, Oro, and Dummer townships,[77] and Captain Rubidge who had his first experience of the sort with Robinson's Irish helped with the settlement of these English poor as he did later in 1839 with some dispossessed Irish tenants from the estates of Colonel Wyndham in Clare and Limerick counties.

Through the arrival of such emigrants as these from the British Isles, the population of the Newcastle district had risen to 27,404, in 1837.[78] Total emigration to the British North American colonies, which had stood at 12,000 to 13,000 annually after 1825, soared to 30,000, 58,000, and 66,000 respectively in the years 1830, 1831, and 1832. Except for the Rebellion years, it was to rise intermittently until the famine flight of 1847. All the older settlements obtained a share of these new arrivals, but the convenient location, the timber and good lands, the investment in the improvement of transportation, and in aid for the Irish of 1825 gave the Newcastle district special attractions. By 1837 the townships which had been practically unbroken when Peter Robinson brought in his settlers were supporting 11,000 souls. Emily township where the greatest proportion of Robinson's group were placed had then a population of 2,341 with almost 36,000 acres "settled", 13,800 of them by the Irish. In Otonabee, Smith, and the other four townships the Irish, though far outnumbered by the newcomers, had increased their cultivated acreage at about the same rate as in Emily.[79]

In the space of one lifetime pioneers in the Rice Lake region had passed from the most primitive forest economy to the railroad age. Catharine Parr Traill recalled in 1853 the canoe by which the early settlers crossed the lake, the flat-bottomed scow the Irish and the other pioneers had propelled up the river; the coming of the steamboat and its successive improvements; and finally as she wrote the appearance of the railroad and the building of the great bridge across the same lake.

Whether this progress would have been hastened or improved by a continuance of assistance from the British government is a theoretical question to which the answer would depend almost purely on a personal point of view. While the British Parliament was declining to provide more aid for emigrants to British North America, in spite of early support of plans for assistance by Viscount Howick and the systematic colonizers, Lieutenant-Governor Sir John Colborne and various agencies and private settlers were producing their own system of assistance. At the same time, scores of travellers with interests mainly mercantile and sometimes of a broad national character passed through the colonies forming estimates of their possibilities for settlement and for trade. No matter how reluctant they were to send their own families to a pioneer world so long as they had means to remain comfortably in the British Isles, no matter how inclined they were to believe with the economists in England that the colonies would not long remain under the British flag, a perusal of their publications leaves the conviction that they were greatly impressed with the promising resources of the colonies. Some believed that in them would be found ample accommodation for any number of emigrants with which Great Britain might care to part.

This realization of future possibilties led to the formation of many private colonization plans and, as the fever of speculation spread, to plans for the chartering of the land companies. Of the early settlement schemes, some were contrived with the hope of procuring great gains for the capitalists interested,[80] others, such as that of John Bannister, with a view to receiving the whole pauper population of Great Britain, but all had characteristics of the Horton experiment with the Irish. All hoped to make the emigrant a producing settler from the moment of his arrival and depended on capital from external sources to accomplish that object. This was not the method pointed out by the action of colonial governments or that of many independent emigrants. For example, Thomas and Frances Stewart, mentioned above, took up a 1,200-acre land grant in Douro and were able to hire Highlanders of less means to work for them.[81] In Upper Canada and New Brunswick projects gradually undertaken by the colonies, like those in the Trent Valley, road and canal building, clearing of land for the reception of expected emigrants, were designed to develop the colonies and assist new colonists.

As the great emigrations began and the British government, ceasing after the Horton experiments to conduct settlement plans for British North America, left those colonies as a free field for voluntary, unassisted emigrants, the colonies themselves bore the responsibility for care of the incoming population. The first years after 1815 with their experiments in government emigration were a preparatory period, and the experiences then gained were the foundation upon which the later structure of colonial life was to be raised.

V. NEW NEEDS AND NEW THEORIES

THE FIGHT FOR PAUPER EMIGRATION

AFTER 1825 MANY EVENTS conspired to strengthen the arguments of those who supported emigration as a means of relief for the unemployment prevailing in the British Isles. Ten years of post-war disturbances had witnessed in turn the government committees investigating agriculture, the Poor Laws, and the Irish troubles, and then the beginning of trade reform, only to see the rising structure of Peel and Huskisson crumble into apparent failure in the distress of 1825. During the same years more than two hundred thousand persons had made their way to a new world of greater opportunities; six times the government had assisted in the removal of emigrants. By 1825 too, the theories of the economists as well as the principles of Thomas R. Malthus that population tends to increase beyond the means of subsistence had won, if not a large body of converts, at least a large circulation among certain classes of thinking men. In the reviews, the *Scots Magazine*, the reports of the Poor Law committees, and the words of John Ramsay McCulloch, David Ricardo, and others appeared in varied form the doctrine which the *Edinburgh Review* laid down when advocating Irish emigration to the British colonies, the United States, Colombia, and any other country: "What is wanted is, the adoption of a system that will effectually relieve the immediate pressure of pauperism, without throwing it upon Great Britain and which will, at the same time, enable such further measures to be adopted as will ensure the future and lasting prosperity of the country."[1] Finally, however faultily he interpreted the principles of the economists or the views of the government, for the time being the emigration movement had found its "oracle" in the parliamentary Under-Secretary of the Colonial Office, Robert John Wilmot Horton.[2]

Horton had entered Parliament in 1818 as member for Newcastle-under-Lyme in Staffordshire where Robert Peel's influence was strong. Taking office practically as the nominee of Henry Goulburn, on Goulburn's removal to the Irish Office which followed Peel's departure in 1818, Robert John Wilmot* had interested himself in the abortive Cana-

---

*Robert John Wilmot took the surname of his wife, Anne Horton, in 1823, in compliance with the directions of the will of his father-in-law, Eusebius Horton of Catton.

dian union bill of 1822. He was soon impressed with "the utter insufficiency of the colonies, as to self-support and self-defence, unless it were possible to give them an addition of population more rapid than their natural rate of increase." Like other young men who had leanings towards the theories of the economists, Horton had for some years taken an interest in the condition of the working classes. Now he saw the two problems in relation to each other: lack of population in the colonies, surplus of population in the mother country. As a practical man, he followed the policy of his predecessors, the ideas of relief and direction of emigration from the United States to British possessions. He endeavoured by emigration to make "the redundant labour and curse of the mother country, the active labour and blessing of the colonies."[3]

Two circumstances coloured Horton's thought and action for the next ten years and indeed until 1840. In the first place, he was an imperialist. With a large body of information before them that was unavailable to ordinary men, it is not surprising that Horton should turn a deaf ear to one tenet of the economists, "Emancipate your Colonies," or that William Huskisson in his brief tenure of the colonial secretaryship should have delivered the most eloquent appeal of the period in favour of maintaining the colonial connection.[4] In opposition to Malthus, McCulloch, and others who believed that it mattered little to what country the surplus population of Great Britain was conveyed, Horton stated his conviction that he would always consider the colonies "an integral part of the mother country," and that by their common participation in common benefits he could look forward to the "perpetual union" of colonies and mother country.[5]

In the second place, Wilmot Horton fell more and more under the influence of the economic theories of the time. He believed that Parliament would never approve any measure of colonization "unless the principles upon which that measure was founded had received the sanction of scientific men."[6] It was inevitable therefore that in his appeal to win the approval of the economists something of the original character of Horton's views should be lost and that, in place of receiving credit for his early humane interest in the welfare of the colonies and those in need of relief in the mother country, he should lay himself open to the accusation which might more properly have been levelled at the most zealous economists—the accusation of "shovelling out paupers."

The parliamentary committees on the Poor Law which had shown a tendency to advocate freedom of movement for labour were the stepping stones on which public opinion, or a certain section of it, crossed to the hitherto revolutionary idea of a committee on emigration, and the last stones were the Irish committees of 1823 and 1825. Before the former Wilmot Horton made the first public avowal of his faith in emigration. The committee of 1823, appointed to report on the state of Ireland, soon recommended the extension of the linen trade, the fisheries, and roads and harbours. In 1825 further investigations brought out the possibility of relieving Irish unemployment by the introduction of capital or the removal of population.[7] Certainly measures other than the Insurrection Act and the "composite politics of Lord Wellesley and Mr. Goulburn" would be necessary for Ireland and, indeed, for Great Britain. Pauperism could not be heaped up in Ireland; like water, it would find its own level. Already Glasgow alone had a population of twenty-five thousand Irish.[8]

Two methods of immediate relief had been heard in 1823: that of Robert Owen and the emigration plan of Wilmot Horton. It was the third appearance of the plan. Refused by the Agriculture Committee in 1822, it had received in 1823 at the home of the Irish secretary, Henry Goulburn, the approval which merited the experiment in emigration undertaken in County Cork in the same year.[9] Now a frequent correspondence passed between Goulburn in the Irish and Peel in the Home Office. Though Goulburn may have directed the government-aided emigrations of 1815, 1818, and 1820-1 without any settled beliefs regarding the problems of political economy involved, Peel was closely in touch with those who were changing England's commercial policy. Just before the Irish Committee began its sittings in 1823, he wrote to Goulburn, "Could nothing be done for . . . Ireland, by relieving her of some of her Population? I wish you would talk to Wilmot. . . . He has turned his attention to it. The Government must take . . . the measure into their own hands."[10]

The details of Horton's plan—the carrying out, rationing, and settling of paupers at the expense of the parish or local bodies, individual or collective, to which they were an encumbrance, and the proposal for raising the money by an annuity charged upon the rates—were all stated in the outline handed in to the committee in 1823.[11] The committee were far from agreement. Lord Palmerston suggested that the vacuum created by emigration might immediately fill up. John R. McCulloch believed that unless emigration were accompanied by measures for preventing the splitting of farms and a plan for disfranchising the forty-shilling freeholders and taking away all temptations to multiply the people in any way, the vacuum must fill up and "the expenditure on emigration by itself would be entailing a useless expense upon the country."

A second objection, characteristic of the day, was the fear that an addition of population to the British American colonies would hasten the time when those colonies must leave the British empire to join the United States. Here Horton was definite and, as events have shown, a better prophet than his critics. Nothing, he believed, would so much tend to have a contrary effect as an increase of colonial population. "We have colonies requiring population, which feel every hour that it is the want of population that prevents their resources from coming into play . . . ; and I should imagine that, so far from the expense of that four millions [for the cost of emigration] being lost to the country, if traced accurately for a series of years, this capital would be found to have reproduced itself in the colonies in the most beneficial manner."[12] Once set in motion, this sort of emigration and settlement might go on indefinitely, transforming the poor into landowners and wealth-producers and consumers, "until all the colonies of the British empire are saturated and millions added to those who speak the English language, and carry with them the liberty and the laws and the sympathies of their native country." This perhaps more than any other aspect of his theories was Horton's best case for emigration. It made no appeal to the scientific men of his day and consciously or unconsciously he came to dwell less and less upon it, and to bring forward those arguments which had already been accepted by such theorists as the editors of the *Edinburgh Review*.[13]

The years during which this change occurred were difficult years for Horton. While a host of commercial reforms were leading to that freedom of trade which it seemed the government had in emigration applied to labour, and the struggle to legalize the workers' freedom was being fought out in Hume's committee on the Combination Laws, Horton was busied with the direction of his experiments in Canada and the popularization of his theories in England. From Peter Robinson's settlers the reports during 1823 and 1824 were contradictory; from the settlers of 1825 no reports whatever arrived.[14] After sizable opposition, Parliament had agreed to vote £30,000 for the emigration from the south of Ireland, but only "on the understanding that a Committee should be appointed early in the next Session to inquire into and report upon the subject of Emigration generally."[15] For the expenditure of the vote Horton was to give account; upon its success he had staked his theories.

Horton directed the investigations of the Emigration Committee to the establishment of the truth of his doctrine. He believed that the British Isles were suffering the evils of a redundant population, though not overpopulation in the Malthusian sense. Labour, Horton declared, was a marketable commodity subject to the same laws as any other commodity. The result of an excessive supply of labour must be pauperism; as national capital increased this excess would be partly absorbed. But the degradation through which a people must pass in such an ordeal could not be "contemplated by any wise Government with indifference."[16] The remedy proposed by those who believed that an artificial remedy was possible was the introduction of capital, as the Irish Committee had suggested, or "the abstraction of the excess of labour" on the principle which the government had followed in the emigration of the Scottish weavers in 1820-1 and the Irish in 1823 and 1825. While accepting both principles, Horton was led to become the exponent of the latter remedy—"free trade in labour." To this he added his belief that the emigrants should be established as agricultural colonists on land prepared for them.[17]

The Emigration Committee began its sittings on March 20, 1826, it reported May 26, and Horton moved for its renewal on February 15, 1827. It investigated conditions in the north and closed a special report in April; then after further study, a third and final report appeared on June 29, 1827. Many of the members of the committee had previously served on the Irish committees and some as well on the earlier Poor Law Committee.[18] Some witnesses called were men who had been engaged formerly in the examination of relief in the British Isles; the final report, as a matter of fact, was an emigration report only in name. Horton wrote in 1830 that "the functions of the Emigration Committee of 1827 were also mainly directed to a specific inquiry into the condition of the Poor. That inquiry occupies four-fifths of the evidence, as well as a considerable portion of the reports; and, after the causes of the evil had been duly investigated, Emigration, the expediency of encouraging which the Committee had been appointed to consider, was recommended in connection with other measures."[19]

Opinions of witnesses differed only in the nature of the relief to be applied. Landlords on the whole favoured emigration, though they were not unanimous on undertaking the cost themselves. Alexander Nimmo, an engineer, advised relief by means of labour provided at home, such as Thomas Telford had instituted in the Scottish Highlands. This plan the final committee thought insufficient to supersede emigration. For England Horton, supported by the evidence of Malthus and convinced that emigration would be cheaper than settling the surplus on poor lands at home, reported in favour of emigration as the best means of relief.[20]

In Scotland, despite evidence on the crofters' scanty living on small islands, it was true that the fisheries were being encouraged. As for the manufacturing districts, when the Manufacturers' Committee offered to contribute £25,000 if Parliament would vote £50,000, the Emigration Committee closed its first hearings and recommended a vote for emigration. Before the report was tabled however a return of prosperity had removed, as Canning stated in the House of Commons, "the urgency of the distress, which alone would justify the interference called for." Horton, confirming the decision of the government to withhold the grant, recommended the elimination of the causes of distress at home as more suitable for Scotland than a system of state-aided emigration.[21]

To show that the British North American colonies could support the great influx of settlers which must be sent, Richard Uniacke for the maritime provinces and William B. Felton for Lower Canada boldly placed the powers of absorption of their colonies at from fifteen to twenty thousand a year.* H. J. Boulton and Colonel Cockburn, it is true, saw limitations: it might be necessary to import food from the United States.[22] Sir Howard Douglas, lieutenant-governor of New Brunswick, pointed out that the surplus population which the committee wished to remove was not the type the colonies needed; it might bring misery to colonies and emigrants and merely transfer British population to the United States.[23] But this protest was made in private; the enthusiasts on the committee had no cause to feel that their project was unwelcome to the colonies.

A second important consideration was that of expenditure. Neither proprietors nor others personally interested in emigration favoured contributing to this burden of expense. Failure here meant the failure of the whole scheme as far as Ireland was concerned. In England the parish machinery could be utilized. Horton insisted on colonizing, settling emigrants aided by some capital on soil prepared to receive them. He admitted finally that the emigrant's passage might be paid only to the colony, where expense would end if employment were available. But he did not believe the colonial labour demand would occupy the emigrants which should be sent and he clung to his original and more humane plea of establishing emigrants as landed proprietors.[24]

The evidence of 1827 showed that the cost of locating settlers could be lowered from the £20 per person spent in the Irish settlements to £60 per family of five. Tables which were drawn up for settling 19,000 families in three years, at an expense of £1,140,000, illustrated a method for raising the sum by a mortgage on the poor rate which the parish first, and the settler finally, could repay in thirty years with 4 per cent interest accruing on the capital. A first vote of £240,000

---

*The Australian and South African colonies were considered but only as fields for the reception of labourers, not for independent settlers. Felton saw no reason why 100,000 acres could not be settled as easily as 10,000.

would be required in 1828-9.[25] Peel believed that even this provision for 19,000 families would entail upon the country a permanent charge of £57,000 a year. Many denied the wisdom of the expenditure, especially because at home the parish could demand the paupers' labour. Though Horton was sure that the emigrant could begin to repay the outlay at the rate of 10s. per annum and increase this to £5, he never explained the fact that nothing of the advances to the settlers in the Rideau district was ever repaid.

The only possible means for lowering expenses was revealed in the statements of shipowners, W. Fitzhugh of Liverpool and John Astle of Dublin. English emigrants had been sent out, passage and food included, for £10 10s. each, Scots from the estates of Maclean of Coll for £5 14s., and in 1824-5 other Scots who had spent only 50s. on their crossing reached Nova Scotia in good health. The Irish emigrated even more cheaply, especially since exempted from the terms of the Act of 1825; according to one witness, they required no space on shipboard except their own length on deck to lie down upon. Colonel Cockburn, who was consistently conservative, believed that £6 would cover all expenses to Quebec and A. C. Buchanan showed that he could victual emigrants at £2 per head. Moreover shipowners stated that a vessel capable of carrying 200 passengers could be equipped and hired for £510,[26] if the requirements of the existing Passengers' Act could be removed.

Of the two motives that may be said to have actuated the government in enacting passenger vessel regulations, namely, the desire to control the outward movement of population and a humanitarian interest in the welfare of the passengers, the first was now removed* by the repeal of the Act forbidding the emigration of artisans,[27] and the second was about to be eclipsed by other considerations. When a verbal recommendation for the elimination of all control on the emigrant trade resulted in the repeal of the passenger vessel law, freedom of labour had been fully granted.† For a short time, the fear of overpopulation seemed to have overcome the humanitarian spirit of the age. But the experiment in unrestricted emigration which the repeal permitted proved too danger-

---

*While Peel, Huskisson, and Canning were working for the removal of obstacles to trade and Hume in the House of Commons and Place outside of it were anxious to free labour from all restrictions, it was not difficult to obtain the appointment of a committee to consider the laws relating to the emigration of artisans, the exportation of machinery, and the combination among workmen: *Parliamentary Report*, 1824, V (51).

†The Quebec Emigrant Society sent in a paper, and other protests against the inhumanities of the passenger trade lay in the Colonial Office, but this aspect of emigration was not placed before the committees and the repeal became law in 7 and 8 Geo. IV, c. 19.

ous at sea, and in March, 1828, Horton brought in a bill with mild terms which was agreed to in spite of the opposition of the shipping interests.[28]

In brief, the first report of the Emigration Committee points out that the illimitable land supply of the colonies could be developed advantageously by population from the British Isles which was useless at home and that state-aided emigration should be voluntary, confined to permanent pauperism, and its expense should be repaid by the emigrant. The final report concludes with definite recommendations: first, the adoption of the plan for parish emigration financed by a loan from the government, and second, the appointment of a board of emigration with agents in the British Isles and colonies to carry out the uniform system adopted.[29]

After winning, as he believed, the confidence of practical men in the committees, Horton undertook a long campaign to show that his theories had also met the approval of scientific men. He mailed the reports and his sets of lithographed letters to acquaintances at home, assuring such sceptics as Peel that he would yet effect their "ultimate conversion."[30] Some conversions did follow. The Duke of Wellington read the reports and informed the Chancellor of the Exchequer, Frederick Robinson, later Viscount Goderich, that he believed in the recommendations. The ministers too felt that Ireland could not remain as it was; according to Lord William Russell they "would gladly listen to any man who would point out the way to relieve her."[31] The reports went also to governors in the colonies with a request for their criticism and advice. In 1827, with the co-operation of Bathurst and Peel, Horton was able to despatch Colonel Cockburn to North America to prepare districts for the reception of ten thousand emigrants, "in the event of such a measure being finally decided upon by His Majesty's Government."[32]

In early 1828 the discussion of emigration became widespread. Publications like the *Edinburgh Review* might deprecate Horton's failure to touch the causes of the evil he planned to remove and the impossibility of conducting emigration on a scale large enough to be of real value, but unanimously they favoured emigration for paupers, even at government expense. "The money will be spent on them," the *Edinburgh Review* wrote, "the only question is, shall it be wasted here to their misery and our total loss, or thus advanced for their certain happiness and with every probability of great national advantages." At Oxford, lecturing in the spring of 1828, Nassau Senior seemed to defend Horton's plans and principles.[33]

To some opponents of Horton's plan, the Emigration Committee's recommendations meant state control of population, a radical innovation.

Horton repeated again and again that emigration should be voluntary only. Michael Sadler, a Christian socialist, and the author of various works in refutation of the Malthusian theories of population, railed at Horton in a book apparently specially prepared for the purpose: the committees had been inhumane in discussing surplus population and the clearing of estates; they would transport the best customers of British manufacturers. Though Horton took the trouble to reply to these accusations,[34] he could not remove the fact that Sadler's views represented the natural feelings of many of the common folk of Great Britain. In his own office lay protests to prove it.

Of that revulsion of the people against theories which made poverty a crime and transportation its punishment, William Cobbett was the chief exponent. In the *Weekly Political Register* he assured the workers that it was "something rather damnable . . . to talk of *transporting* Englishmen on account of the *excess* of their numbers." Here Cobbett represented the opinions of such men as the weavers of Glasgow, who refused to work for emigration in 1819 and set out deliberately to win the political and economic reforms that they believed would solve the workingman's troubles in the British Isles. To them the emigration committees were the work of pseudo-gentlemen who said not a word against the debt, the pensioners, or the taxes. "To be considered Redundant and be taunted in Misery and Ruin" with such an insult was, as they put it, too much. Casting their eyes over England they saw redundancy of another sort. "Have we not a Redundancy of Legislators, . . . of Clergy, . . . of Nobility, . . . of Landed Aristocracy, . . . of Sinecure Place-men and Pensioners," they wrote, "of Loan Jobbers, and Gamblers of every description, all living luxurious and fattening on the spoil of Industry and the very vitals of the People?" To the day of his last appearance as the advocate of this emigration scheme, Horton was unable to free himself from the suspicions with which a gentleman of his station, "bred up and fostered by the ruling aristocracy of the nation," was regarded when he condescended "to reason with his inferiors upon the propriety of removing a million or two of human beings from the country."[35]

Other opponents favoured emigration but refused to support it at public expense. As Horton failed to convince the government that a return of the funds invested would be made, it was apparent that the expenditure must fall upon the mother country. When he offered the plan for mortgaging the poor rates, Peel saw various reasons for refusing new facilities for mortgage. Hume warned the House that "If this measure was adopted, it would place the landed proprietors in the same condition as the country was placed and from the same cause."[36]

By April, 1828, when Horton brought in his first bill "to enable

Parishes in England, under given regulations, and for a limited period, to mortgage their Poor-rates, for the purpose of assisting Voluntary Emigration," the fall of the Liverpool ministry, successive changes in government offices, and the return to power of Wellington and Peel, had left Horton without office or organized support. He himself had moved from the Colonial Office to the vice-presidency of the Board of Trade and, for a time, had enjoyed the approval of Huskisson. Wellington thought it "very desirable to obtain" his assistance, and would have named him secretary for war and the colonies in May, 1828. But nothing came of that, and late in May he refused the Irish Office.[37] Now gone from the Board of Trade, he could rely only on Peel's polite, but lukewarm, advice and his own work as chairman of the Emigration Committee.

During two months discussion was intermittent and lively, but inconclusive. When Horton rose again in June, it was merely to bring in a motion pledging the House, early in the next session, to take measures of emigration or otherwise to prevent pauperism in Ireland and the spread of its evils to England. Peel did not underrate the importance of the subject, but he saw faults in Horton's scheme and finally obtained its withdrawal.[38] In spite of the gathering cloud which hung over Parliament until after 1832, and in spite of the insecurity of his own position, Horton persisted. Distress was still prevalent; Irish affairs were in a precarious state; and reform of the Poor Law had not been won. Horton accordingly addressed himself to the correction of these evils and, omitting any reference to emigration, in 1829 he had entered upon the *Journals of the House of Commons* resolutions embodying his remedy for decreasing unemployment, "either by the increase of the funds for the employment of labour, or by the diminution of the supply of labour, or by the compound operation of these two causes."

Though two petitions from parishes requesting aid for emigration of their paupers were soon presented in the Commons, Horton was forced to withdraw his motion for a committee of the whole House on the state of the poor in the United Kingdom. He failed to carry his promised emigration bill as far as the stage of discussion.[39] Until December he continued to advocate his principles in print and before the London Mechanics' Institution. But when his successor as under-secretary, Henry George Grey (Viscount Howick), son of the Whig Prime Minister, in February, 1831, introduced an emigration bill on the same lines, the Wakefieldian paper, the *Spectator*, could rejoice that one obstacle in the way of the adoption of "rational views" was eliminated, for Horton had been appointed to the governorship of Ceylon.[40]

In the last months of the fight for his bill, Horton had met powerful opposition organized by the followers of a new colonial theorist, Edward Gibbon Wakefield who, under the name of a fellow believer, Robert Gouger, began the advocacy of systematic colonization in 1829 and 1830. By means of a colonization society and through their own publications and the columns of the *Spectator*,[41] the Wakefield group carried on their attack until they gradually won to their side many men whose allegiance had long been sought by Horton. To this group colonization meant the creation of everything but land where nothing but land had existed. Their proposal to remove population by a plan which would pay for itself could be accomplished, they argued, by means of a fund from the sale of colonial lands at a price so fixed as to keep available land, capital, and labour in proper proportion.[42] They objected to setting up paupers as landed proprietors; the question was how to "remove the greatest number from a state of abject misery, dependence, and temptation." Again, Horton did not provide for the selection of emigrants. In comparison with their own method of building up the resources of the empire and solving the problem of surplus population without expense to the mother country, the systematic colonizers looked upon Horton's scheme as an imperfect theory good only for shovelling out paupers. Moreover, Horton's plan, since it did not include a theory for the disposal of colonial lands, was not, in their opinion, a plan for colonization at all.[43]

The accusations were unjust. Horton's plan failed with Parliament precisely because, not content with shovelling out paupers, Horton with his emphasis on thousands of emigrants and million-pound costs, had demanded assistance which was too expensive for the leaders of the day. The Agent-General for Emigration, Thomas Frederick Elliot, acknowledged the fact as late as 1838: "If reason were sought why inquiries so ably and perseveringly conducted were not productive of more immediate fruit, it might perhaps be found in the assumption which pervaded these reports, that in order to [ensure] the welfare of the people assisted to emigrate, it was necessary to establish them upon land and (almost a necessary corollary from an opinion so fraught with expense) that repayment should be required of the funds laid out for their benefit."[44] But it was not the custom of reformers, Wakefieldians or not, to admit debts to a predecessor in reform, especially when that predecessor might return in the guise of a rival, as Horton did in 1838.

The system of colonization advocated by the group sprang essentially from the brilliant mind of Edward Gibbon Wakefield. Before his plan, as he said, British colonizing in America and Australia and the government's preoccupation with emigration had brought nothing but "long experience without a system, immense results without a plan, vast doings but no principles."[45] Here at last was a system, new, it is true, only in the combination of its principles: Adam Smith's basic land, capital, and labour, to be kept in right relations necessarily; Robert Gourlay's belief in the sale of colonial lands, with its sale and tax funds to be used in bringing selected emigrants to the colonies, all developed while Gourlay himself was vainly petitioning Parliament on Poor Law reform and emigration.[46] Refinements added to the principles included compact settlements, self-government, a sufficient labour force always available. So persuasively were these ideas blended by Wakefield's powerful logic and eloquence that, though he was himself barred from political life by the stigma of a prison term, his writings and the Colonization Society his followers founded in London in 1830 won support from such men as John Stuart Mill, Jeremy Bentham, Charles Tennant, Sir Francis Burdett, Robert Stephen Rintoul, editor of the *Spectator*, Lord Durham, George Grote, Colonel Robert Torrens, a prolific writer on colonization. And in Parliament Wakefield could rely on Charles Buller, Sir William Molesworth, and others to support his theories.

Regulations requiring the sale of British American Crown lands had already been considered in the Colonial Office, partly as a result of reports from the colonies, and sale was authorized partially in 1827 and fully in 1831.[47] But that the full Wakefield plan was ill-adapted to conditions in those American colonies was probably suspected by Wakefield himself. Horton had seized upon this possibility too. At first he appears to have wished to negotiate with his opponents, attending their meetings, and proposing that the sphere of colonial activities should be divided, South Africa and Australia going to the systematic colonizers, and British North America remaining his own field. The emigration committees, he explained, did not recommend sale of land at a fixed price as the Wakefieldians proposed, because under such a system no land could be sold in a colony near the United States. He hoped to bring up a bill for supplying Australia and South Africa with labour. But compromise failed and Horton, himself taking the chair at a public meeting of the Colonization Society, zealously condemned the objects of those with whom he had professed to unite and finally brought about the dissolution of the Society.[48] Thereupon the quarrel became more virulent; while Horton was making the final, ineffective attempt to save his scheme from utter failure, he was loudly berated by the Wakefield group as an "insufferable political bore," whose experiments and theories the public had voted intolerable.

Though the Wakefieldians, who owed more to Horton than they would ever acknowledge, were already in touch with the Colonial Office and Howick has been described as an early convert to their views, Howick's bill bore no mark of their principles. It would facilitate voluntary emigration and "empower the Crown to appoint commissioners for the purpose of supervising the business of emigration, and regulating its details." All the features of the earlier bill were present. Even Horton's interest in Ireland seemed evident in Howick's admonition that a similar plan should be undertaken for that country. Finally Howick insisted that the government "only claimed the merit of having adopted the ideas of the right hon. gentleman [Mr. Wilmot Horton], who had so long and so perseveringly urged on the country the consideration of the subject."[49] Though the exodus by emigration was rising (from 26,000 in 1828 to 57,000 in 1830 and 83,000 in 1831) and the vigour of the new Whig ministry was pervasive,[50] the old opponents, Sadler, Hunt, Bennett, and Henry Warburton, again came forward; problems of another sort were pressing in 1831, and again the bill failed to reach a second reading.

The next year, 1832, the great Poor Law Committee began its work; in 1834 the new Poor Law bill was enacted and here in clauses LXII and LXIII provision was made for certain types of emigration under the direction and at the indirect expense of parish authorities. In a sense this was the culmination of Horton's work, the goal towards which his activities had been pointing; but in view of its limitations it was a poor monument to the young under-secretary who had begun with imperial interests and a dream of building up the empire by supplying the needs of one part with the produce of another. Ever in pursuit of an end truly great, Horton ever contrived to adopt means which defeated perfect fulfilment of his purpose.

The Collapse of Later Schemes

Though the Howick bill came to nothing the Secretary for the Colonies, Viscount Goderich, carried out one of its principles in June 1831, by appointing a commission of five members, F. T. Baring, Henry Ellis, R. W. Hay, Lord Howick, and the Duke of Richmond.[51] They were to collect information regarding opportunities in the colonies for British subjects desirous of emigrating and inform the Secretary regarding emigration. Eventually they reported their conviction that to be useful to Great Britain government-aided emigration would have to be undertaken on a scale so enormous that its cost would be prohibitive. For the time, that opinion ended government consideration of expenditure on emigration. After a little more than a year, the Commissioners were relieved of their task, and their work was returned along with their secretary, Thomas Frederick Elliot, to the Colonial Office. In dismissing them Goderich gave an opinion, probably from Under-Secretary Howick whose influence was already decisive,[52] which may be cited as prophetic for Whig and Peelite policy on emigration to British North America: "In the case of the North American colonies there are many reasons why the intervention of a Government Board, in providing the conveyance of emigrants, would be neither desirable nor, unless with the aid of a large and expensive establishment, practicable."[53]

The Commissioners had scarcely left office before Lord Grey's government appointed a commission of another, more urgent sort. Once the Whigs were in office, as some one has said, the Benthamites and the humanitarians laid lustily about them, attacking old abuses. One problem was to persist: Ireland. Agrarian agitation in the island was spreading, aid for emigration was being demanded, and Poor Law debates were continuing, when in 1833 Lord John Russell obtained the creation of a parliamentary committee to consider the condition of Ireland. The commission of twelve—the two archbishops of Dublin, a few Irish country gentlemen, and a few authorities on Irish affairs and the English Poor Law—recommended: first, the creation of a board to promote "national improvements" for Ireland; and second, reforms in land tenure, tithes, and poor relief, though without the introduction of the English system.[54] As for emigration, the chairman of the commission, Richard Whately, Archbishop of Dublin, formerly professor of political economy at Oxford University, had advocated assisted emigration in the *Quarterly Review* as early as 1820, and Irish landlords in general favoured the ideas originally introduced to them by Wilmot Horton. The commission therefore advised, as a temporary "essential auxiliary to a commencing course of amelioration" for Ireland's condition, that "those who desire to emigrate should be furnished with the means of doing so in safety." Only thus could the labour market "be relieved from the weight that is now upon it, or the labourer be raised from his present prostrate state." Half of the expense of emigration was to be borne by the imperial treasury, half by the Irish poor rates and the landlords of emigrants; plans were included for depots to house all able-bodied unemployed Irish and for the appointment of commissioners to look after settlement of the emigrants.[55]

Such an extensive development of part of the idea underlying Horton's plans, though it was supported by George Poulett Scrope (Stroud), W. Smith O'Brien (Limerick), and various other members, was denounced by Melbourne as impractical and by Peel as absurd.[56] In short, the energetic government intervention in Irish life which the Whately recommendations outlined was foreign to the economic convictions of the government in office. Discussion on the issue was delayed by Lord John Russell while George Nicholls, an English Poor Law commissioner, took a bird's-eye glance at Ireland in a six-week tour, and returned to advise a limited workhouse system rather than the reforms and emigration recommended by the commission.

When on February 13, 1837, Russell introduced a Poor Law bill which did not provide for emigration, he explained that the colonies were deeply opposed to immigration of paupers. Howick, too, though a moderate believer in emigration, wished to separate the idea of Irish emigration from that of the Poor Law.[57] This official opposition to the Irish belief in emigration brought an outburst from Daniel O'Connell on the possibility of emigration conducted on Wakefieldian lines: "Why not take the waste lands of Canada?" he asked, "Why not dispose of them in such a way as to promote an effective emigration? . . . It would enrich the Canadian people by sending out to them great numbers of able-bodied labourers." After the Wakefield group, and especially Colonel Robert Torrens, had campaigned openly for an Irish emigration system and after Nicholls had made a second visit to Ireland, Russell late in 1837 added a new clause to his bill. Too mild for the Irish, it provided merely that the majority of the rate-payers in a district might spend one shilling on the pound of their assessment to aid emigration to British colonies.[58] So Ireland received a poor relief and workhouse system which, as Nicholls himself intimated, would prove inadequate to deal with famine. At the same time, the theories of the advocates of emigration were watered down and the colonies saved from an inundation of government-propelled needy Irish emigrants.

Meanwhile a select committee of Parliament began investigations in 1836 of that subject vital to Wakefield's theories, the use of colonial lands. For Wakefield the hearings were "of great personal advantage," for they gave members of Parliament an opportunity to know him in the flesh and the public a sight of the real man behind the publications. Henry George Ward, a confirmed believer in the master's ideas, sat as chairman of the committee; he saw to it that the recommendations contained the main essentials of the systematic colonizers' beliefs: the sale of Crown lands and the use of the sale funds to finance emigration. Members of the committee, W. E. Gladstone, Daniel O'Connell, Sir George Grey, F. Baring, and others, thought highly of the United States land sale methods and stressed the bad results of land disposal in British

America. For the administration of the system recommended, the committee advised the creation in London of a land board and in the colonies of local boards to take charge of the sale of land and direct emigrants to the colonies in accord with the demand for labour there.[59]

Neither the Colonial Office nor the Whig government was inclined to take the responsibility of such a scheme for selling and peopling the British American colonial lands. The Secretary for the Colonies was Charles Grant, Lord Glenelg, whom the clear-minded Howick regarded as incompetent and vacillating. The permanent Under-Secretary, meticulous and thorough James Stephen, could not bring himself to trust Wakefield or his fertile theorizing; the value of the colonies as an asylum for Great Britain's surplus numbers could not be denied, but the promotion of colonization was not the business of government.[60] In partial response to the recommendations of the committee therefore, an agent-general for emigration was appointed in 1837 to run a small office financed separately from the colonial department. The Agent-General, the same Thomas Frederick Elliot who had served the previous office, soon introduced practices in the supervision of emigration and shipping which were to become permanent and valuable.[61]

When the Canadian differences and demands for fuller self-government flamed into rebellion in 1837, the Whig ministry chose as its investigator and advisory commissioner John George Lambton, Earl of Durham, a brother-in-law of Viscount Howick. Durham took to Canada on his mission Charles Buller, Wakefield's ablest lieutenant in Parliament and also, unofficially, Wakefield himself. The report on Canadian affairs which followed in 1839 was a testament to Durham's faith, a faith that was to be justified not by his own friends, the laissez-faire statesmen, but by the plain British emigrants who were building up their colonial communities on the British model. Durham recommended the grant of responsible government to the united provinces of Upper and Lower Canada and he foresaw as a result of that grant the growth of a Canadian nation under the British Crown. The evils of the land granting system with its vast blocks of idle lands were described at length, as was the conduct of emigration without foresight, preparation, or method of any kind. But the solutions offered, signed by Charles Buller, probably dictated by Wakefield, suggested the sale of Crown lands on Wakefieldian principles and the support of emigration by the proceeds from the land sales.[62] In Canada however, this policy could not be implemented because Crown lands had been recklessly granted to various types of claimants and, with the exception of the Clergy Reserves, sold in large acreages to land companies. And, by the terms of the Union Act adopted in 1841, territorial and certain other revenues were to be handed over to the Assembly in return for the promise of a civil list of £75,000.[63] The funds necessary for the promotion of emigration to Canada on the plan developed for South Australia were therefore unavailable unless the Canadian Assembly chose to make them so; and under Durham's logic, the British government must not force the policy upon the colony. Fortunately for the statesmen defending their policy for the colonies in need of population, the size of the spontaneous emigration to British North America rendered artificial stimulation unnecessary.

The vision of Lord John Russell, now secretary for the colonies, may not have reached as far as Durham's. But so long as Sydenham's strength and assurance were moving mountains in Canada and land companies in London were pressing colonial officials for action on emigration, Russell produced one plan after another for the development of the colonies. When Sir George Arthur suggested the "cementing of the British connection" by British emigration, Russell wrote firmly on the despatch, "The Govt. [sic] should do all in its power to promote the object." When the land companies' suggestions for assisted emigration proved unacceptable to British opinion, Russell offered a plan by which the government would give a veiled assistance by voting annually five shillings per head to cover the colonies' head tax, up to 32,000 indigent emigrants. He approved Sydenham's departure from land sale principles in order to give 50-acre land grants on colonization roads to poor emigrants. He assured Sydenham that the imperial government would help provide a fund for assisting newly arrived emigrants to reach places where their labour was needed, a policy which Sydenham did not approve.[64] Though he withstood Howick's revolutionary suggestion that Upper Canada use the sacrosanct Clergy Reserves in lieu of a loan for public works,[65] he did put through the less radical plan for the guarantee of an imperial loan of £1,500,000 for the same purpose, and with cabinet approval which Peel's government did not ignore.[66] A few months after Russell became secretary for the colonies, too, the government created the Colonial Land and Emigration Commission on a plan which had been recommended by Horton and the Emigration Committee, and since by the colonial land committee, the Durham Report, and in Parliament by Henry George Ward, Sir William Molesworth, and others. The commission was to combine with the office of the Commissioners for South Australia who had been engaged since 1834 in an experiment in systematic colonization.[67] For the British American colonies, the Commissioners' work was limited by the lack of an emigration fund, as that of the Agent-General's had been, but theirs was a busy and useful office of which the labours were not terminated until 1877. In 1853, for example, when the House of Commons questioned their activities, the Commissioners reported their correspondence for 1852 as 91,092 letters on emigration received and 97,453 despatched, with the daily total in the season rising as high as 1,707.[68]

In general, Russell instructed the Commissioners that government had "no right to interpose actively to promote emigration," nevertheless "ignorant and helpless" British subjects should not be left unadvised. Specifically he set the group, Edward E. Villiers, Colonel Robert Torrens, and again Thomas Frederick Elliot, to study the wisdom of undertaking a government-sponsored plan for systematic colonization. In spite of the public demand for assisted emigration and the colonial need for population, the Commissioners believed that lack of funds and the danger that emigrants would use the colonies as a route to the United States rendered state-supported emigration to North America exceedingly unwise. They suggested instead a grant of £50,000 to be used under their guidance for transporting poor emigrants. This suggestion they later modified in order to obtain the cost of emigration, one-half from the home government and interested individuals and one-half from the colonies; and they advised also co-operation with the land companies. Russell and Stephen disapproved of the first idea but supported the second. Presently Russell advised the New Brunswick government of the profit to be gained by using the proceeds of the proposed land sales to the North American Colonial Association for the aid of emigration. He agreed with Sydenham and the Emigration Commissioners that once the emigrants were landed the colonies should bear all responsibilities.[69] The Canada Company, however, shrewdly refused to assist in the Commissioners' plan unless its instalments due the government could be used for assisting emigration, and the Canadian government, probably just as shrewdly, preferred the money to the experiment. The British American Land Company, badly involved financially, could give no help except on stiffer terms than the Canada Company, and the condition of the New Brunswick and Nova Scotia Land Company was even worse. The North American Colonial Association of Ireland in which the Wakefield followers had a powerful hand could not but agree to the plan, though its activities appear to have been negligible.[70]

In 1838 as Irish members of Parliament were urging action to allay the distress in their counties, Wilmot Horton reappeared, returned from his governorship of Ceylon.[71] Though he had been suggested for the position in Canada which went to Charles Poulett Thomson, Lord Melbourne had dismissed the idea as inappropriate, and Horton had busied himself again with the advocacy of emigration. Thomas Spring Rice, Lord Monteagle, entertained him and helped renew his friendships with Irish landlords.[72] With a man of Horton's energies and persistence, the result was the publication of a new pamphlet, *Ireland and Canada: Supported by Local Evidence* (London, 1839), and the development of another elaborate plan for government-aided emigration. But when on July 11, 1839, following Ward's resolution of June on colonial lands and emigration, Horton called for a select committee to consider emigration, he did not win attention.[73] By his new plan, Horton proposed to remove a million persons from Ireland at a cost of £12 million, the sum to be raised by an annuity of £537,400 for forty years, at first payable by the landlords and eventually by the emigrants. The plan might work for small farmers, W. S. O'Brien argued as he reviewed it in Parliament, but not with the labourers with whom government was concerned. For himself, O'Brien favoured the plan of the Wakefieldians. As usual Henry G. Ward and William Hutt rose to support the principles of systematic colonization and Lord John Russell finally refused the support of the government.[74] And Horton, having found the expense of membership burdensome, did not stand again for Parliament. By June, 1841, he was dead at 57 years of age.

Before another year had passed, a new select committee was at work investigating unemployment and poverty, this time in the Highlands of Scotland where Dr. Rolph had encouraged Henry J. Baillie (Invernessshire) to call for the committee. Baillie contended that he was no enthusiast for large-scale emigration: he favoured emigration only when some "very urgent, special, and peculiar case" could be made out for it. This the decline of the kelp industry and the ruin of many proprietors now did for Scotland. Canada should be the destination, for the Scots had many friends there. Warburton feared such a committee would excite false hopes. Hume objected to assisted emigration for Highland distress because such relief would "be in opposition to all the principles upon which they had acted since Sir William [Wilmot] Horton's emigration scheme." Peel agreed to the committee only because he believed that findings would prove the impossibility of undertaking an extensive aided emigration programme.[75]

Members of the committee, Baillie, Colquhoun, Stewart, Ward, O'Brien, knew well the extent of the Scottish famine of 1837 and the heavy charitable collections then necessary to stave off starvation. To prevent the recurrence of such a disaster, they believed that a "well-organized system of Emigration" would be of "primary importance." They had printed too a report of the Agent-General for Emigration of

July 29, 1837, on the *Applicability of Emigration to Relieve Distress in the Highlands*. In that report the Agent-General had quoted evidence from the Horton experiments to show that "very comprehensive arrangements" would have to be made and parliamentary funds voted, if great damage were not to be done to the colony by a large Highland emigration.[76] Consequently the Baillie committee suggested not only government aid for emigration but also the development of public works for Canada which would enable that colony to take in fifty thousand persons annually. Though the government had in its files an unprecedented mass of emigration petitions from Scotland, the weak Whig ministry was in its last days and nothing was done to implement the recommendations of the committee. Unemployment and stark poverty continued in the Highlands. In 1851 under Earl Grey, the former Viscount Howick, as secretary for the colonies, landlords who had been assisting their tenants to emigrate won legislation, referred to as the Emigration Advances Act, by which a landowner could obtain government funds for the removal to the colonies of needy, would-be emigrants in his parish.[77]

The ministry of Robert Peel brought no new inspiration on the problems harassing the supporters of emigration as a means of relief for the British Isles or of development for the British American colonies. Experienced, commercial-minded, and intent upon fiscal reform, Peel had little time for the theories of colonial government as Durham had understood them. In the speeches of Lord Stanley, his secretary in the Colonial Office, modern readers have heard the "swan-song of the old imperialism."[78] Though Stanley could dally with the idea of systematic colonization, he would take no responsibility for stimulating the emigration movement. In 1842 when almost 1,000,000 were receiving outdoor relief in England and Wales and 159,000 indoor relief, and parish emigration under the Poor Law or by the charity of landlords offered the only assistance available, Stanley more than once summarized the government's position. "It might be, and it was," he said, "wise to attempt to assume the direction of the manner in which this emigration should be conducted; but to attempt to force it . . . was at once impolitic and injurious to the very persons whom they desired to serve." The government had no funds for assisting emigration to British America (such as were used for Australia) because the proceeds of the land sales were paid over to the local legislature and it controlled their use.[79]

Here, of course, Stanley voiced the opinion of the government experts who had investigated the problem off and on since Horton's expensive Irish experiments in 1823 and 1825. At the same time, protests from the colonial governments and British emigration agents in British America were proving with every mail that poverty-stricken British subjects were better off in the mother country where they had a claim than in colonies which were not organized to help them. Even the propaganda for a government-supported emigration stirred up by Dr. Thomas Rolph, one-time agent for emigration of the Canadian government, with his prominent backers and imposing British American Association, could not move Lord Stanley from his position. He quickly squelched the rumour of government aid.[80] In 1842 as hard times caused a renewed flood of Scottish emigration petitions and elaborate plans for assisted emigration by John Silk Buckingham and a friend of Dr. Rolph, John Crawford of Paisley, Stanley still stood firm.[81]

When, in an effort begun in the House of Commons in April, 1843, and continued in August after an illness, Charles Buller elucidated the possibility of relieving distress in the British Isles by means of systematic colonization, the government appeared willing to consider a motion for the purpose. After the speech was printed and read by some hundred thousand interested British subjects, the influence of the systematic colonizers had probably reached its height.[82] Buller wished, first, for an experiment on the Australian lines to be undertaken in the British American colonies, necessarily with the consent of the colonial legislatures. In its final form, his plan would have had the Canadian government take over all wild lands in the colony, compensate the owners by debentures producing dividends from the sale of the land, and use the surplus from the sales for public works to employ British emigrant labour and develop the colony. The speech and the plan were magnificent portrayals of the best the colonial reformers could offer for the difficult problem of emigration; but no practical result followed.

In Canada Wakefield, now member for Beauharnois and pushing his land company in the Eastern Townships, referred Buller's proposal in the British Parliament to a committee of the Canadian Assembly. There it died. Henceforth according to Francis Hincks, Wakefield fought the Canadian ministry bitterly.[83] In the British Isles business trends reversed themselves and a short return of prosperity together with the strength of the anti–Corn Law members of Parliament ended the chance for action on emigration. Howick had supported the idea and was later to make part of it his own. Peel wanted delay: let it be known, he advised, that the ministry was thinking of emigration even if there were "valid reasons for our caution." Stanley spoke for the Colonial Office; to him Buller's plan was objectionable and impractical.[84]

In Ireland the Whig Poor Law Act of 1838 had brought vigorous action in the construction of 122 workhouses, but little effect upon emigration. Efforts of the Cork board of guardians to undertake pauper emigration were hamstrung by squabbles with the Poor Law Commissioners over the interpretation of section 51 which permitted an increase in the poor rates for use in emigration, and by an official rebuke from the Emigration Commissioners who pointed out that "habitual paupers were not likely to prove enterprising emigrants." When in the winter of 1842 the Belfast guardians attempted to raise rates for the same purpose, the local rate-payers replied with the poetic warning that such a favour offered the paupers only "a cold grave and a snowy winding sheet."[85]

Meanwhile Daniel O'Connell had responded to the declining power of the Whigs and the rise of the Tories by founding the National Repeal Association. Peel's long experience with Ireland enabled him to see that more than force would be necessary to right economic and social evils in the island.[86] Accordingly in 1843 the Tories began to prepare for reforms in education, religion, and tenant rights. A Landlord and Tenant Commission under Lord Devon was appointed and reported in 1845. It made another minute survey of conditions, then recommended extensive changes in agriculture and relations of landlord and tenant and, after listening to John Robert Godley, "a well organized system of emigration." This time the system was to provide not only transportation for the emigrants, but also employment in the colonies, and eventually land at a low price.[87] In Parliament Lord Stanley introduced a bill designed to give Irish tenant farmers some of the security recommended, but for the proposal on emigration he had the old reply. "As a means of proportioning the population of Ireland to its means of giving employment," he announced June 9, 1845, "emigration is not to be thought of for a moment."[88]

By late June, 1846, Peel had won the repeal of the Corn Laws, the Whigs were back in office, and the last great test of early nineteenth-century emigration theory was upon them. The crisis came, as crises had before, in Ireland. When severe unemployment and near famine spread throughout that country and parts of Scotland, hundreds of memorials requesting assistance for emigration accumulated in government offices. Colonization groups proposing emigration schemes begged hearings in the Colonial Office. In Parliament demands for the same panacea rose. Lord Monteagle, close to the Whigs, urged the Colonial Secretary, Earl Grey, to speed up emigration through the use of the Poor Law clauses and other measures.[89] Grey was already preparing, together with Buller, a comprehensive colonization plan, remarkable for its inclusion of the hard lessons learned in long experience with parliamentary and colonial rejection of such planning.

Since Grey deplored the wasteful fashion in which the first occupiers of the wilderness were "scattered over the surface of the country removed from civilizing influences," compelled to walk miles to a mill or a smithy, since he realized "the pain which must ever attend the breaking of the ties" that "bind men to their native country," he proposed group settlement of sixty or so families in village communities.[90] After obtaining from Lord Monteagle the assurance that Irish landlords would provide transportation for their tenant farmers, Grey authorized Lord Elgin, governor of Canada, to send out agents to offer land proprietors £50,000 in all for preparing the village settlements and providing the first employment. The houses built and the lands prepared were to be sold later to the emigrants.[91]

In spite of the effort to avoid earlier pitfalls, by January 28, 1847, this proposal had foundered on the old obstacles: the unwillingness of the mother country to increase expenditure, the scepticism of the land companies in Canada regarding employment and suitably situated land. To Buller, Grey confessed privately, "It is mortifying to the last degree, but I am beginning to come to the conclusion that I can do nothing to promote systematic colonization. There is not a farthing to be had from the Treasury." In that crucial spot, it should be added, Grey's brother-in-law, Charles Wood, held office and practised traditional Whig economics.[92] However in the official explanation sent to another relative, Elgin in Canada, Grey expounded the theories of the Emigration Commissioners and the permanent officials in the office of which he was the head. Insisting that these theories had developed from experience and not "from any doubt of the great importance . . . of giving every possible encouragement to emigration," Grey stated his faith in the voluntary emigration by which British America had mainly been peopled. To give assistance even in transportation might induce the unfit to remove; it might stop the remittances by which emigrants in America sent for their friends; and worst of all it would develop dependence upon government and discourage self-reliance. It was the strong and enterprising that emigrated. In short, "under the existing system of spontaneous emigration, emigrants are aware that on their arrival in Canada, they have only themselves to trust to. . . . Hence they are led to make every possible exertion to maintain themselves, and the result is that a very large number . . . annually find the means of doing so."[93]

Pressed as he was by Irish landlords, Monteagle received the failure of the emigration plan badly, and in March, 1847, there appeared on Russell's desk John Robert Godley's scheme for community settlements.* In these the emigrant communities were to be financed by a

---

*J. R. Godley was the idealistic son of a Sligo county landlord; he believed that the Irish "great circle of evil" could not be broken unless by heavy mortality or emigration: O. MacDonagh in *Irish Historical Studies*, V (1946–7), 291.

loan of £9 million secured on Irish property and an Irish income tax. The familiar methods, transportation provided by government and land companies, employment on public works to be developed by guarantees of British capital, all were present in Godley's plan, so worked out that 1,500,000 persons could be moved to the colonies in three or four years. Though the Colonial Office, the Treasury, and the Canadians arrayed themselves against Godley, as they had against similar planners before,[94] the pressure for action continued. Godley was soon to embark on his New Zealand colonization with Wakefield, but he found time to use Rintoul's *Spectator* for his Canadian plans. William Hutt and Lord Lincoln, who now bought the *Morning Chronicle* and published more articles by Godley, supported his plan in the Commons. In the Lords, Lord Monteagle finally carried his motion for a select committee[95] to consider colonization as a means for promoting the welfare of Ireland and the colonies. Grey's consent to the motion, given because he believed the result would disabuse men's minds of extravagant hopes, was justified by the findings of the committee. Refusing to support any scheme, it sounded a clear warning against undertaking large measures rashly.

While Monteagle took his revenge, reviewing step by step government action on emigration since 1826 right up to its ignominious end in 1847, noting Grey's early support and his recent supine withdrawal,[96] Grey concentrated on new plans. Monteagle could satisfy himself with aid for Ireland. Grey's duty led him to more complex problems: the related welfare of mother country and colony. For Vancouver Island in the Pacific, he tried to assure British settlement by the new grant to the Hudson's Bay Company and this in the face of opposition by Godley's cousin, J. E. Fitzgerald, and Molesworth, and Gladstone. On Canada, he analysed reports in his office and Buchanan's and Draper's proposals sent him by Elgin. He appealed to Elgin to obtain suggestions from his Council. He drew up a scheme by which the colonial parishes were to report names of British subjects for whom they would provide first support if the Poor Law commissioners sent them out. He summarized his thoughts in thirty-page despatches to Canada, finally reaching the conclusion, supported by Elgin, that expenditure on public works would be the best investment in emigration the colonies and mother country could undertake. In the end, he adopted an earlier proposal for building a railroad from Quebec to Halifax. In 1846, the three colonies concerned had approved the idea, and an imperial guarantee of funds had been discussed. Grey now convinced himself that the imperial government might advance £5 million for the road, the interest on the advance to be paid from the sale of land bordering the railroad and from an increase in the duty on colonial timber.[97]

As Grey could not be sure of the cabinet and "ultra economists [did] not conceal their wish to get rid of the Colonies rather than continue to incur any expense for them," Grey wrote Elgin privately. Elgin must propose the idea for financial support to his Council in "strictest confidence" and, if they approved, report back as if the proposal came from Canada. Elgin performed the miracle. In December a Council minute recommended all that Grey wished. But it was too late.[98]

Before this last of Grey's emigration projects was complete Russell, seldom forgetful of Ireland, capitulated to the Irish emigration enthusiasts. It was a critical moment. Colonial problems that had troubled the government for years were now urgent, public criticism was sharpened by a revival of the Wakefieldians, and all at a time when the Irish danger reached a new intensity, not only economic and social but also political. William Smith O'Brien, member for the county of Limerick and for years a vigorous supporter of the emigration theorists inside and outside the House of Commons, had split with the O'Connell men, joined Gavan Duffy in founding the Irish confederation movement, and visited the French revolutionaries in Paris. In April in his last speech in the House, he warned the government that it must take the chance of a republic in Ireland.[99] In August the Irish insurrection fizzled out; O'Brien gave himself up. Everywhere uneasiness lingered. As soon as the session ended, Russell hurried to Ireland. There while he observed and conferred, O'Brien had him subpoenaed to appear as a witness at his trial. In October O'Brien was found guilty and ordered to be transported. Later, on May 18, 1849, Russell brought a motion in Parliament for a writ of election in Limerick county, "in the room of William Smith O'Brien, adjudged guilty of High Treason."[100]

Russell in truth was having a lesson in realities in Ireland. In December, 1846, he had believed that emigration should be carried on only under the poor rates and the Emigration Commissioners, "established by me in 1838"; those who were so eager for large-scale emigration "should recollect that the colonies cannot be prepared at once to receive large masses of helpless beings, and there is no use in sending them from starving at Skibbereen to starve at Montreal."[101] Now in 1848, he proposed a broad plan for local aid and heavy emigration. A fund of not more than £5 million was to be raised by an Irish land and house tax and administration of emigration placed in the hands of the Poor Law unions. With the cabinet split between them, the rival projects facing criticism, and the Treasury determined to spend no money at all,[102] Grey and Russell had to abandon their plans, both in deep disappointment. According to Wood of the Treasury, the thing to do was to do nothing: create no new market for labour and let natural laws correct Ireland's overpopulation. The railroad proposal of course was to reappear in other form and with success. But the day for state-supported pauper emigration to British America, if it ever existed, had passed.

In spite of the government's contention that emigration, presumably with state aid, could never draw off sufficient population to ease the pressure in the mother country, the immense exodus of voluntary emigrants, combined with the loss from famine, was doing exactly that for Ireland. By 1851 the Emigration Commissioners feared that the country would be deserted by its original population. In a century remarkable for massive migrations, Irish emigration was the only population movement to cause a "definitive population decline."[103]

For the systematic colonizers, the future was not bright. Charles Buller, spokesman for systematic colonization though he was, had agreed with the ministry's decision to withhold government aid for Irish emigration because of the extent of the voluntary movement from the country. He had pointed out also the impossibility of developing a large colonization scheme in Canada where little free land could be found.[104] James Stephen, that intellectual balance wheel in the Colonial Office since 1836, had resigned in 1847, worn down by trying duties and finally by the death of his son. Though Buller had pilloried him mercilessly as an incompetent, officious "Mr. Mother Country," Stephen visualized the relationships and advantages of the imperial connection as clearly as Buller himself.[105] And Molesworth, who might have been of use to the Wakefieldians, was in delicate health. By the time Buller died in 1848, it was all but inevitable that laissez-faire economics and the policies of the Manchester School should be accepted as a matter of course.

The work of the Wakefieldians nevertheless had met a need of the times. They had raised the cloud of apprehension spread by Poor Law-aided emigration. It has been suggested that they saved the empire for they were imperialists in a day when influential leaders thought of emigrants only as potential consumers and cared not at all under what flag they came to rest. In the face of this claim it must be remembered that even in moments of disillusionment when Grey could write that in the highest quarters the distaste for empire was growing, even then no government, Whig or Tory, showed the slightest inclination to cease planning for the colonies' future. It must be remembered too that colonial secretaries and Grey in particular had to deal with changing practical problems in which Wakefield's fine theories were inapplicable.

They had to deal also with Wakefield himself, his superb gifts as a propagandist and his uncertain temperament. Within the year while Ireland, New Zealand, Australia, and British America were still heavy responsibilities for the government, Wakefield vented his feelings upon Grey and the Colonial Office in the attack published in 1849 in his *View of the Art of Colonization*. Little wonder that Stephen wrote from his retirement, "I have spent my life in a chaos of colonial controversies. I would not return to them for the wealth of the Rothschilds."[106]

While Molesworth and the remaining systematic colonizers suggested a Royal Commission on colonization and founded their Society for the Reform of Colonial Government in 1850, while the *London Times* felt the ground shifting under it, Grey certainly lost popularity. From Parliament and the press, he faced the consequences of his long experience in adjusting theory to practice. Why had he grown more conservative with the years, Lord Monteagle asked. Why was he discouraging emigration by permitting a high colonial immigrant head tax which could do nothing but drive British subjects to the United States? In reply Grey gave Parliament a lesson in the reforms that were at work in the new empire. The emigrant head tax was heavier in colonial than in United States ports because the British colonies needed the income. The colonies provided free hospital care and often food and transportation for British emigrants, as might be seen by any member who read the printed parliamentary papers on the colonies, or Dr. Douglas' report from Quebec which had just been presented. In short, Grey announced his belief that colonial affairs, including immigration, could not be administered from Downing Street.[107] He was telling members politely and publicly what Under-Secretary Stephen had told Secretary Stanley privately: "For my own part I have reached a firm conviction that our superior wisdom, if such it be, is utterly wasted in the attempt to make the people of North America as wise as we are." "I would leave them," Stephen had written, "to grow wise by experience."[108]

This was the voice of the new age. With Peel in opposition but practically in the cabinet and consulted on Irish and trade affairs,[109] a combination of the new imperialism and responsible government with the theses of Cobden and Bright in a sort of Manchester School liberalism came naturally. If Russell and Grey may be said to have practised no emigration policy for the British American colonies but that of a veiled laissez-faire, their proposals like Horton's showed their willingness to use imperial credit for colonization. Appalling necessity had compelled them to break through the rules of prevailing economic theory so far as to provide food for the starving in Ireland, but for the more radical plans suggested the Whig ministry lacked the requisite boldness, perhaps fortunately. Grey assured Monteagle in the Lords in 1848 that "the proper function of a government . . . is not to supersede the efforts of individuals, but rather to guide and assist individual exertion."[110] After thirty years of theorizing and experimenting, the government had returned almost word for word to the policy of Liverpool and Goulburn. Able, ardent patriot though he was, Grey could do little more than Horton, a lesser man, had done—bow to the spirit of the times.

As he observed the increasing prosperity of the British Isles and the development of the British American colonies in the last years of his office, Grey may have come with satisfaction to the conclusions he published in 1852. The result of leaving emigration to proceed spontaneously had been, he then wrote, "to effect a transfer of population from one side of the Atlantic to the other to an extent far beyond what could have been thought of, had it been left to be accomplished by the direct agency of the State,"[111] and that without expense and to the advantage of British trade with all parts of North America.* Whether or not the modern observer regards the vastness of that spontaneous emigration as resulting partially from the "callous" policy of the Whig ministry, he will acknowledge that up to the middle of the twentieth century vast colonization schemes have not proved practicable in the western world.

When the Russell government fell in 1852 and was followed within the decade by ten ministerial changes in the Colonial Office and by war and economic revolution outside it, no policy unless a limited laissez-faire was possible. The advocates of full systematic colonization had failed with the Peel and Russell governments as Horton had failed with the earlier. But the experiments of both had taught government officials the need for a policy of "judicious regulation and vigilant superintendence" of the emigration movement. It left local parishes and landlords in the British Isles and governments in the colonies virtually free to promote what policy they wished so long as they financed it themselves and conformed to the humanitarian standards established since 1805. By 1854 the British American colonies were themselves appropriating money for the encouragement of immigration.

The random emigration of the first half of the nineteenth century very probably permitted waste of human and material resources. Nevertheless it accorded well with the development of responsible government in the colonies, the practice of free enterprise then prevalent, and the breakdown of imperial trade control which ended the Old Colonial System in 1849.

*British steerage passengers and the friends who helped them were supporting the emigration and the British shipping business at the rate of £650,000 annually.

VI. COLONIZATION LEADERS AND COLONIZATION COMPANIES

FROM THE BEGINNING of its control in British North America, the imperial government approved settlement of the American lands by associated companies or individual leaders possessing the capital and other assets necessary to establish numbers of emigrants. A few times after 1815 the government itself, as has been seen, provided the capital required to place British subjects on colonial lands. As the years went on and the theories of laissez-faire came to dominate the British economy, imperial officials relied more and more on private enterprise for developing American resources. The government-assisted settlements had proved expensive, the land grant system unjust; neither method brought in the income needed to relieve the mother country of the cost of colonial administration. With these results in mind and one eye always on the rival land sale system of the United States, the government began to appeal to man's purely selfish instincts by making his reward depend solely upon his own efforts. Land was now to be sold outright and the individual or corporate purchaser left to earn what return he could by cultivating or selling land himself. In 1828, William Huskisson as secretary at the Colonial Office was glad to defend the policy: if by it unproductive lands could be brought under cultivation, "the result would be not only beneficial to the colony, but to the general interests of this country."[1]

A vision of the future, of population and homes, gardens and herds, springing up where only lonely plains or forests have been inspires the real colonizers. In modern times, depending upon the personal characteristics of the individual, such men have become selfish schemers like Archibald McNab, able administrators like Thomas Talbot, or perhaps unselfish planners wholly devoted to their cause. Ranging up the scale, one might find intermediate types. All had two things in common: all hoped to make their fortune, few ever did.

Individual Leaders: Successful and Unsuccessful

The Proclamation of February 7, 1792, by which Lieutenant-Governors John Graves Simcoe of Upper Canada and Alured Clarke of Lower

Canada invited colonizers to bring in settlers and receive grants of land was the first of its kind to receive wide distribution.[2] Nevertheless the policy which it announced, colonization by groups of associates under able leaders, was as old as British settlement in North America. Since the founding of the Virginia Companies in 1606 British subjects had formed groups and, depending on the policy of the government in power, had made their own arrangements for emigration. Unfortunately for the newly created colonies of Upper and Lower Canada, the land grants offered to leaders under the Proclamation of 1792 were so generous, the habits of land speculation so strong, and the lack of government machinery to supervise settlement so tempting that in return for handing over a great part of its patrimony in lands the government received astonishingly small increments of population.

The fate of an early petitioner for land, William Willcocks of Cork, Ireland, illustrates the ill-luck for both petitioner and government that dogged this venture in planned colonization. Willcocks's petition for land was approved at the last meeting of the Executive Council of Upper Canada in 1792. Back in Cork, Willcocks advertised for emigrants, but the war with France and his own election as mayor of that city prevented departures in 1793 and 1794. However, in 1795 some one hundred would-be settlers managed to sail. The first group landed in New York instead of Quebec and were enticed away from Upper Canada by United States land agents; the second shipload of 1795 was captured by the French at sea, and after release they reached Upper Canada only to find that their leader's grant of land had been cancelled under the government's new policy of rescinding lands granted but not settled. For his good intentions Willcocks received grants of 1,200 acres each for himself, his wife, his son, and his three daughters on the sole condition that he and his family reside in Upper Canada.[3] So the colony parted with 7,200 acres of land without provision for its development.

Another settlement conducted under the terms of the Proclamation brought in emigrants whose pioneering work ultimately became effective but who did not for some years meet official approbation. These were the well-known founders of Markham, Upper Canada, and their leader, William Berczy, né Wilhelm Albert von Moll, who had been a sub-agent of Sir William Johnstone Pulteney, M.P., on his 1,000,000-acre property in western New York. Berczy had placed about 160 German settlers on farm lots near the Genesee River when reports of the generous land regulations of 1792 began to spread from Upper Canada.[4] After he fell in with a Connecticut man, well-connected with Canadian officials, and a few German merchants and Americans resident in New York City, Berczy organized an association for land settlement in Upper Canada.

With cash from this German Company, he travelled to Niagara. There his ambitious proposal for a grant of 1,000,000 acres was cut down by the Council to 64,000 acres conditional on settlement,[5] and Berczy agreed with Lieutenant-Governor Simcoe to place his German settlers on the line running north from York now known as Yonge Street.

Following an idyllic encampment in British army quarters at Niagara, Berczy and the Germans reached their lands only in the winter of 1794-5. Their first two years were extraordinarily difficult and Berczy proved an exasperating superintendent, especially to the officers of Upper Canada. When the Executive Council decided to rescind undeveloped land grants in 1797 Berczy's German Company lost its acreage, and that after the expenditure of some £14,000. But while Willcocks received generous personal grants, Berczy got nothing.* The German settlers did well enough, gradually earning their lands by performing the prescribed duties and at the same time forming a nucleus around which later settlers could gather.[6]

While Berczy was coming to grief in his settlement schemes, the government in London began to foster rather similar projects for French Royalist refugees who had fled to England. A plan for bringing out refugee priests, much desired by Monsignor Hubert, the bishop of Quebec,[7] was being tried out when in 1797 Joseph Geneviève, Comte de Puisaye, made a proposal which combined many of the features later adopted in British American settlement. Expenses of a first group of three to four hundred French were to be borne by the British government as they were later borne for the Military and Irish settlements and repayment of this expenditure on them was expected. The terms for obtaining land resembled those under which Colonel Thomas Talbot was to carry on his settlement, de Puisaye himself assigning the land to the settlers. Some forty of the refugees began their Canadian journey in October 1798, and by mid-January 1799, with the warm assistance of Peter Russell in York, de Puisaye had men busy clearing the forest away for his colony of Windham near Whitby. By mid-October only twenty men remained in the place; lands not occupied by the remaining settlers were thrown open to the public in 1803. Between 1807 and 1827 a few of the original group received their land titles, and de Puisaye died in England a British subject.[8]

In no part of the Canadas during these years did the Proclamation of 1792 bring noteworthy results in British emigration or settlement. The first outstanding colonizers, Colonel Thomas Talbot and Thomas Douglas, Earl of Selkirk, were individual leaders who had influence in London,

---

*Berczy obtained rights to lands as a settler and an associate, but he forfeited these lands to satisfy creditors.

superior knowledge of economic conditions in mother country or colony, and the good fortune to work in a time of growing emigration.

Thomas Talbot, the first of these two to take possession of colonial lands, gained his knowledge of the New World during trips to Detroit and the Miami River as aide to Lieutenant-Governor Simcoe in 1793 and 1794. Though bred to army service, after the Peace of Amiens Talbot sold his commission as lieutenant colonel, and in 1803 obtained a grant of 5,000 acres of land due his rank under the regulations dating from the Seven Years' War. Since he wished to grow hemp for the Navy and to redirect British emigrants from the United States to Upper Canada, he was appointed a government agent, through the influence of his patrons, the Dukes of Kent and Cumberland, and promised 200 acres of land for every settler he placed on 50 acres.[9] He took his 5,000 acres in the township of Dunwich situated half way between the two ends of Lake Erie, an area which was for climate and fertility probably the best in Upper Canada. In addition to this grant, half of Aldborough and Dunwich townships were set aside for his settlers, and in 1818 all the ungranted lands remaining in the same townships were added to the first reservation for settlers he might introduce.

For his work in opening and peopling this western part of Upper Canada, Talbot has received credit as the greatest colonizer of his era. Under his system the settler, in return for his lot, had to build a house, clear and sow ten acres within three years, and open a road suitable for traffic fronting on half of his lot.[10] If these duties were not fulfilled, Talbot would not certify the settler and he could not obtain his patent from the government. So great was Talbot's influence that, after difficulties with various proposals, he convinced Lieutenant-Governor Francis Gore and later officials that he could finish the long road from Niagara to Detroit, provided that Crown land reserves were removed from the road-side in the regions of his interest. The government not only agreed to the policy but bit by bit placed the supervision of townships bordering on the road in Talbot's hands. Eventually through the approving co-operation of the government in London, Talbot became supervisor in twenty-four and by 1836 in twenty-eight townships in the London and Western districts.[11]

Though his task of filling up the two original townships, Aldborough and Dunwich, was finished by 1820 when 240 families were established on 50-acre lots, Talbot continued to supervise the great area stretching along the Talbot Road from Long Point until 1840. By 1830 that observer of British American conditions, John Richards, could describe a fine country in which the population was to be set at 40,000 in 1831 by Talbot himself.[12] In 1838, Mrs. Jameson reported her enjoyment at the sight of homes, barns, schools, and churches spreading out, at ten-year-old London with its 200 houses and 1,300 people, its architecture, "somewhat Gothic," and its five places of worship, and St. Thomas with its Mansion Hall Hotel and its view over a fertile, well-settled country.[13]

To build up this community of British institutions, Talbot had spent thirty years of his life as a log-cabin dictator and fought numberless battles with the local government officials. Through the favour of the home government, he had ruled in lieu of government itself, assigning 50-acre lots to applicants whom he trusted, expelling and "rubbing out" from his map those who neglected to perform the roadwork and settlement duties he believed essential.[14] The Executive Council resented this interference with governmental prerogatives; but after he had taken the quarrel to the fount of power in London, Talbot went back more or less vindicated to his wilderness realm.[15]

However successful he might be in transforming this vast area, almost one-quarter of the colony's best lands, into thriving farmsteads, as the years passed Talbot's "imperium in imperio," as John Strachan described it, was less and less in accord with the spirit of the day. In 1831, only 785 of 6,000 settlers placed by Talbot had taken out patents and almost £40,000 of their fees were unpaid. Investigations by the Assembly followed complaints about Talbot's arbitrary rule, a power the radicals said "infinitely more to be dreaded than that of the King in Great Britain." Lieutenant-Governors Maitland, Colborne, and Bond Head, one after another reported to London, until finally Lord Glenelg in the Colonial Office agreed to discontinue Talbot's superintendence. Because of the disturbances in the colony, these instructions could not be carried out until after 1840.[16]

As his accusers maintained, Talbot had very probably held his own immense acreage, in the end about 300,000 acres, until it gained value from neighbouring improvements; probably he manipulated allotments along the Talbot Road to enhance the value of the lands due him.[17] But the fact remained that no other large landholder had fostered settlement with the same devotion and success as he.*

Remarkable similarities and differences mark the work of Talbot and Thomas Douglas, Earl of Selkirk. Both developed their interest in British North America in the early 1790's, both received their first land

---

*As early as 1826, the British government had recognized Talbot's work and rewarded him with a pension of £400, for which see F. C. Hamil, *Lake Erie Baron* (Toronto, 1955), 17, quoting Bathurst's despatch, June 8, 1826.

grants early in 1803, and both devoted the remainder of their lives to colonization. Like Talbot, Selkirk wished to develop British colonial lands to offset the drawing power of land in the United States. But Selkirk, working with a broader perspective than Talbot and after years of study of the Scottish Highland population problem, viewed the empire as a whole and hoped to use the unpeopled lands as a refuge for the unfortunate in the Old World. Both men had visions of the future which were ultimately realized but, while Talbot built up a Canadian estate for himself and died an old man in possession of it, Selkirk's motives were partly philanthropic, his pecuniary losses great, and he died young, broken by his labours for his ideals.

Selkirk's sympathies for the under-privileged Scottish Highlanders had already been aroused when in 1796 he bought a piece of land near Fort Oswego in central New York.[18] After the temporary peace of Amiens reopened Atlantic shipping, Selkirk's interest turned to Ireland where conditions were making far-reaching reform or emigration necessary. He consequently sounded out the government on the possibility of settling Irish emigrants in the far west near Lake Winnipeg; he believed hemp could be produced there and imperial revenue gained by breaking the monopoly of the Hudson's Bay Company. Instead of this proposal, the government approved a plan for redirecting Scottish emigrants from the United States to Upper Canada.[19] Selkirk at once published emigration terms so attractive that Highland proprietors protested and he was warned that he must take only emigrants who were already determined to go to the United States and place them in a maritime colony, preferably Prince Edward Island. Generous and patriotic, Selkirk then purchased land from the original proprietors of the Island.[20]

In August, 1803, some eight hundred emigrants from Skye, Ross, Argyll, and Inverness disembarked at a spot where until 1758 a French village had stood. Few if any accounts mention the deeper significance of that romantic landing. A quarter century was to elapse before the theories of the systematic colonizers were fully developed, yet here in 1803 at his own expense Selkirk introduced almost every essential of colonization they advanced: the assisted transportation of emigrants, land at reasonable purchase terms, work as labourers for those who needed it, and preparation for settlement by providing surveying, provisions, and shelter. Selkirk offered, besides the essentials, a sincere interest in the human beings whose lives he was endeavouring to direct. He arrived in one of the first of the three ships. He visited the settlement again in 1804, after deciding to sell his New York lands. He so convinced the settlers of his good faith that, when other shiploads of Scots arrived in 1807 and 1808 and the inevitable disasters overtook them, the little group continued, built its roads and mills, and lived in comparative contentment.[21]

For the organizer of the settlement the undertaking was costly. To recoup his unexpectedly heavy expenditure and the failure of the settlers to pay up quickly, Selkirk purchased 143,000 acres which had been taken over by the Crown. For lands valued at £12,000, his expenditures were £35,000. Years after his death in 1820, his heirs still held 97,000 acres of his unfortunate purchase.[22]

After negotiations in 1803 and 1804, Selkirk obtained from Lord Hobart, secretary for war and the colonies, a personal grant of 1,200 acres of land in Upper Canada and the reservation for emigrants he would bring in of certain of the ungranted lands in the townships of Dover and Chatham between the Thames River and Lake St. Clair and also in Harwich township. For a period of five years, Selkirk was to receive 200 acres on condition that 50 of every 200 he received would be turned over to a *bona fide* settler.[23] But his plan to build a road from York to Amherstburg in return for compensation in lands, the Council declined to approve. Other hopeful projects did not mature, and to Selkirk's mental anguish the Highland families whom he assisted in removal to Baldoon in Dover township found themselves located on swampy land. In spite of lavish expense in aiding the settlers and his pleas to the Upper Canadian Council for easier terms, mismanagement, bad weather, and bad luck rendered Selkirk's colonization of Baldoon a total loss. Fewer than ten of the original Scottish settlers remained on the lands in 1817 and by the time of his death Selkirk had had to part with nearly all of his Upper Canadian property to satisfy creditors.[24]

Selkirk's first intention had been to colonize in the northwest territories where until then fur-trading interests had been dominant. He had picked on a strategic site near the falls of St. Mary between Lakes Superior and Huron which, like the Oswego land and the Baldoon lands near Lake St. Clair, seemed valuable for building up British commerce near the rival United States. The government received plans for the West with the pronouncement that existing policy for the fur trade was satisfactory, since "salutary neglect in such cases beats all the care in the world." Nevertheless by 1811 Selkirk held through marriage and purchase sufficient of the shares of the Hudson's Bay Company to dominate its policy. This victory brought his plans for colonization in "disastrous conflict with the purely mercantile interests of a trading company."[25] The result was a compromise by which Selkirk was to undertake the whole charge of forming the western settlement, in return for indemnification in land from the Company. In the spring of 1812 Selkirk's agent, Miles Macdonell, newly appointed superintendent of his colony, arrived with a few Scots at the forks of the Red River in what is now the province of Manitoba, to take over Selkirk's lands, a tract almost as large as the United Kingdom. A second group made up of Irish and Scots from the Hebrides under Selkirk's supervision managed to join the first party on the Red River as planned.[26] From 1813 onward, however, the early history of the Red River settlement becomes a part of the great story of rivalry between the two fur-trading companies of the West.

The lure of possible profits and the irregularity and favouritism by which the colonial land regulations were administered tempted some men possessing neither the perseverance of Talbot nor the humane vision of Selkirk to foist themselves upon the government as disinterested colonizers. Among speculators of this type, Archibald McNab of Kinnel House, Killin, Perthshire, received the most notice—notice that was often controversial but which none the less helped to publicize and people British North America. Like Selkirk, McNab assured the British government that his interest in colonization sprang from his desire to assist his unfortunate countrymen. When he arrived in Upper Canada in 1822, a fugitive from creditors in Scotland, he proposed to bring out Scots at his own expense, if the government would reimburse him in lands and allow him to issue deeds on his own certification. In the little capital of York, McNab's promoter's arts or his plausibility as "the McNab" proved effective with officials.[27] He won himself an arrangement, clearly set down in an Order in Council of November 5, 1823, by which he was to receive 1,200 acres at once and 3,800 acres additional later. Settlement in a township on the Ottawa River next to Fitzroy township was to be superintended for eighteen months solely by McNab. Patents to the land—100 acres to each adult male—were to be issued as on Talbot's lands, when the superintendent, McNab, reported that the settler had conformed to the colony's requirements.[28]

In the summer of 1824, a relative of McNab, Dr. Francis Buchanan Hamilton, laird of Leney near Callander, began gathering up emigrants in Scotland. Each emigrant signed a bond by which he agreed to the cash debt he would owe for transportation and other assistance: £35, £25, and £15 respectively for each adult male, each person over, and each under 14 years of age.[29] Before the first group sailed from Greenock in April, 1825, Hamilton put to McNab's credit the sum of £3,000. Such contributions to aid emigrants were customary and, accidentally or intentionally, the whole procedure so far did not differ greatly from the methods followed in legitimate government-aided emigration.

In Canada the contingent of 101 McNabs, McFarlanes, McIntyres, and other Scots travelled from Lachine to Point Fortune by bateau, thence to Hawkesbury on foot, by steamboat to Hull, and then by foot again to McNab Township.[30] At Kinnel lodge high above Lake Chats on the Ottawa, they gave their laird a mortgage on their assigned lands and agreed to pay him a quit rent of a bushel of their produce per cleared acre in perpetuity.[31] Soon McNab refused to supply provisions on credit, and when he insisted that timber on his settlers' lots was his not theirs and that no settler could leave his lot even to work to obtain food for his family, the Scottish emigrants learned that such treatment was not the custom in Canada. Presently Dr. Hamilton in Scotland realized it too, and the stream of assisted emigrants ceased to flow. But down in Montreal in 1827 and in later years the McNab, exerting his glamour as a Highland chieftain, induced newly arrived Scots to sign agreements like the first, though they had paid their own way from Scotland and were under no obligation to him.

In spite of these old-time practices, the government supported the McNab. He was made a justice of the peace. The government extended the eighteen months originally granted him for bringing in settlers. The authorities continued to legalize his arbitrary arrests of tenants who displeased him, even after their acquittal by local juries and pleas for rescue from feudal tyranny which were sent to Lieutenant-Governor Sir John Colborne. Over at Perth meanwhile, another community of Scots was prospering, and a government agent who viewed McNab's township soon found it less well developed than its neighbours.[32] Yet when McNab applied for a deed of trust for 10,000 acres, presumably land for his settlers, the Council authorized his ejectment actions against various of the settlers on the same land. Lord Durham was now in the colony and in answer to a memorial from the tenants, a special commission recommended that those settlers who emigrated at McNab's expense should pay what was due on their lots, that those who came at their own cost should be freed from arrangements with McNab, and finally that he should be deprived of all power.[33]

Though his claim to the 5,000 acres due him for settling the township had already been surrendered in return for timber rights, in 1839 McNab applied for his deed. To this application the government replied that McNab should give up all his claims and accept a cash compensation, finally reduced to £4,000, which was to come from the sale of the land to the settlers on it.[34] Even after McNab had agreed to these terms in a Minute in Council of September 27, 1839, the settlers demanded another investigation.[35] In 1840 Governor Charles Poulett Thomson appointed a new investigator, Charles Allan, Crown land agent at Perth. When Allan's report became public and Francis Hincks published a summary of the settlers' grievances in the *Examiner*, McNab brought a suit for libel, and the resulting publicity marked his final downfall. In 1841 an Order in Council gave his original settlers nine years to pay up and the colony an opportunity to meditate upon the anomalies of its land system.

The tight control the British government held over colonial lands and the variety of schemes permitted under the competing United States land sale system limited the number of independent colonizers in British North America. Of these none is more puzzling than Donald Cameron of Lancaster, Upper Canada. If certain colonists are to be believed, Cameron had their best welfare at heart; if the Executive Council was justified in its decisions, Cameron deserved the gaol sentence he got. For the modern observer, one fact is important: the two verdicts came from the two opposing forces—the humble colonist and the mighty Council—in the years of bitterest warfare between the two.

Cameron began his adventures in colonization in the most lucrative phase of that hazardous business, the emigrant-carrying trade. In June, 1823, after transporting about 600 Highlanders from Fort William, Cameron appealed to the Colonial Office for land in Upper Canada upon which to settle the Scots he had helped to emigrate.[36] Following a brush-off by Lord Bathurst, Cameron got from R. J. Wilmot Horton almost the same terms as the Irish emigrants under Peter Robinson were to receive.[37] Cameron then obtained from the Executive Council of the colony the promise of 1,200 acres for himself and 200 and 100 acres respectively for large and small families he might place, within one year, on the unassigned lots in the townships of Thorah in the Home and Eldon in the Newcastle districts.[38] When Cameron could not meet the time limit set he pled the usual misfortunes, poverty, illness, lack of supplies, and the temporary scattering of his emigrants to find immediate, paying work. Extensions were granted until the Council in 1829 closed the lots to all emigrants who had not put in an appearance and permitted those who had begun settlement duties only twelve months to finish.

By this time, the Council suspected that Cameron had misrepresented the number of his settlers. When investigation of the progress in Eldon and Thorah was made by a neighbour, Smalley, Cameron was deemed guilty of perjury and committed to gaol.[39] According to further accusations, Cameron had also reported names of settlers without compelling them to appear in York,[40] exactly the procedure followed by Colonel Talbot with the Council's apparent support. From the gaol in York, Cameron appealed again and again to the Lieutenant-Governor and the

British Parliament for delivery from the corrupt gang who controlled the colony. As the case dragged on year after year, Cameron's settlers added their pleas to his in at least six petitions, one of November, 1834, signed by 260 names.[41]

While the welfare of the Scottish settlers was all but forgotten, the Colonial Office reprimanded the Governor for not having Cameron's pleas answered; an Assembly committee insisted in 1836-7 that Cameron's case should be examined once more.[42] After repeated referrals to Mr. Mother Country and from Mr. Mother Country back to the colony, the Council refused in 1849 to reconsider the decision of its predecessor.[43] Certainly if Cameron's success as a colonizer were measured by the attention directed to the lots he lost, he would have no peer.

Emigrants were often urged to buy land privately rather than submit to changing government practices. Had such methods been possible, McNab could never have played his game as gentleman laird; Talbot's colonizing dictatorship would not have developed. At least one colonizer who bought land outright appears to have served his community as well as the better known men who received government support. William Dickson, as early a pioneer as Talbot, had practised law at Niagara and been a legislative councillor before he bought in 1816 the township of Dumfries northwest of Hamilton. A Scot himself, Dumfries bred, he advertised widely and sent an agent to Scotland to recruit emigrants. His letters on emigration went to prominent Scotsmen and appeared in the influential *Chamber's Journal*.[44] When emigrants arrived they were provided with essential supplies on easy credit. Dickson spent much time in his settlements. Saw and flour mills, roads and schools were built. According to Wilmot Horton of the Colonial Office, by 1825 Dickson had sold lands worth about £40,000. By 1834 the population of the township had risen to 2,000, by 1842 to 6,000 and cleared acreage to 60,000. In the latter year, cultivation had so improved land values that some farms were selling at over 20s. an acre and none lower than 15s.[45]

If any one of the lesser characters engaged in British colonization combined the qualities of an energetic emigration agent, an avid land salesman, and a tireless manipulator of settlement schemes, it was Thomas Rolph, M.D. A newcomer to Upper Canada in 1833, he familiarized himself with that colony by serving in the army there and by compiling a statistical account of it which was published in Dundas in 1836. His study of Canadian life convinced him that only by a vast increase in its British population would the divisions that split Upper Canada be healed and its lagging economy enlivened.[46] For the five years following his departure from army duty, Dr. Rolph expended his enthusiasm on a whirlwind campaign to redirect British emigrants to British America and incidentally, it is supposed, to enrich himself and his associates.

Back in England on his chosen mission in 1839, Rolph published a defence of British North America as a field for British emigration, stressing particularly its advantages over its current competitor, Australia.[47] In Scotland in the same year, he ventured to explain to the members of the Highland and Agricultural Society how greatly the Highlanders would benefit by emigration to Canada, a problem which had held and divided their attention for some thirty years. After a swift swing through Glasgow, Greenock, and parts of Ireland, gathering well-placed acquaintances and scattering newly formed emigration societies on the way, Rolph returned to England. There in the south, he was made an honorary member of the Central Agricultural Society of Great Britain and Ireland, and he received what he most desired, invitations galore to speak in public on agricultural distress, emigration, and the British colonies. In Upper Canada meanwhile, the *Patriot* described Rolph's "unremitting exertions . . . to bring before the British public the resources and capabilities of this Province."[48]

For emigration, the time was propitious. The Corn Law repeal agitation was in the air, agricultural reforms were spreading, societies and publications largely dedicated to promotion of the colonies were forming, and the Poor Law legislation had suggested a new type of aid for the emigration of the needy. When in January the Duke of Argyll, Rolph, and various advocates of emigration addressed prominent landlords and members of Parliament at the Hopetoun Rooms, Edinburgh, the gathering quickly resolved to petition Parliament for help in the removal of their labourers.[49] After members of the Highland and Agricultural Society joined with representatives of the Canada Company, the British American Land Company, and the North American Colonial Association of Ireland to organize the North American Colonial Committee, Lord John Russell, the colonial secretary, received their imposing group of emigration enthusiasts, the Duke of Argyll, company officers, Henry J. Baillie, M.P., Sir A. d'Este, and W. S. O'Brien, M.P.[50]

So far as government aid for emigration went, nothing came of the interview, except for Russell's interest in the North American Colonial Association of Ireland which will be noted later. But other master strokes of publicity enabled Rolph to reappear in Canada in mid-1840 as a famous man. Following a banquet offered by 170 citizens of Upper Canada in his honour in Toronto and others in Hamilton, Woodstock, and Brantford, immigration supporters in October, 1840, set up a

Canada Emigration Association for the purpose of preparing for the poor British workers who would be assisted to emigrate.[51] Rolph's success as a propagandist impressed the Governor Charles Poulett Thomson, later Lord Sydenham. He was convinced that some one should travel through the British Isles and explain viva voce "the advantages which . . . Canada holds out to the industrious and well conducted." Late in 1840 he appointed Rolph the official emigration agent for Canada. Rolph was instructed that the Governor wished to promote voluntary emigration with the aid of landlords, but that Canada would provide neither transportation nor any help beyond small grants of land.[52]

When Rolph returned to England early in 1841, he continued his addresses to Scottish emigration societies, wrote articles, and published along with a collaborator, Norman MacLeod, a Gaelic magazine which stressed the value of emigration, and also appeared as a witness before a select committee on conditions in the Highlands.[53] Early in the year, he co-operated with Sir Richard Broun (honorary secretary of the Central Agricultural Society and of the Scottish Baronets) in the organization of a commercial association, the British American Association for Emigration and Colonization, of which the Duke of Argyll became president. The principles of the Association were Wakefieldian, its stated object noble: "the Settlement and Colonization of the waste lands of our North American provinces by the suffering and redundant population of the United Kingdom."[54]

Lord Sydenham had already sent both Lord John Russell and Dr. Rolph his forthright condemnation of the Association's proposal to promote emigration of the poor with the help of government and to use the colonial land and timber revenue to assist settlement in Canada.[55] It would take more than that, however, to break the impetus gained by the Association. Perhaps from the impression that the Association was connected with the well-known Highland societies as well as with the Baronets of Scotland, who since 1836 had been reviving their early colonization plans for Nova Scotia, so many leading men in Great Britain permitted the use of their names that the Association membership included thirty-nine baronets, four earls, four marquesses, the lords provosts of Glasgow and Edinburgh, one duke, and various other personages and institutions. Capitalization was to be £500,000, shares £25. Four seigniories of some 200,000 acres were to be purchased in old Quebec and a large acreage taken up in Prince Edward Island. Sir Allan McNab, as an advocate of population increase for Upper Canada, was to be chief commissioner in Canada where he would sell ten thousand shares. No Canadian problem had ever received more distinguished attention. Rolph was presented to the Queen. A farewell dinner for McNab brought out members of Parliament and London aldermen, three former governors of Canada, a cabinet minister, and the Duke of Richmond.[56]

In mid-summer of 1842, the Board of the Association which was meeting daily in Sir Richard Broun's office sent the *Lady Wood* with emigrants to begin settlement on the lands the Association was planning to develop in Prince Edward Island. In September it chartered the *Barbadoes* to carry out emigrants, indentured to one Halden, who were to prepare for the reception of destitute tenants of the Duke of Argyll from the Isles of Mull and Tyree. Broun who had been out of town returned in time to visit the *Barbadoes* at Gravesend; but the vessel was delayed, a few of the emigrants complained at the Mansion House about the arrangements with Halden, and the Lord Mayor wrote to the Duke of Argyll. As the New Zealand Company held a mortgage on the vessel and foreclosed, Rolph charged foul play involving even the Lord Mayor, a supporter of emigration to New Zealand.[57] The Emigration Commissioners investigated both ship and emigrants and permitted their departure. However, before December 23 when storms drove the *Barbadoes* into the harbour of Cork, the Commissioners had learned that the Association, as charterer of the vessel and protector of the emigrants, was absolutely insolvent and thus "committing a fraud upon the emigrants." Though the Treasury was instructed to act, there were "no solvent persons against whom proceedings could be taken." Five hundred pounds would have saved all, but only Rolph and Broun had paid their £25 for Association stock, the Duke of Argyll withdrew from his position, and in the spring the Association was broken up. Printing of the papers on the *Barbadoes* was ordered by the government. Lord Stanley, secretary of war and the colonies, facing criticism from the Lord Mayor, eloquently announced that in its imposition on the emigrants and "unsuspecting people" the case was one of the "grossest hardship and oppression that had ever come under his notice." He could only hope that the "high and honourable personages" who had sanctioned the Association by permitting the use of their names would feel a moral if not a legal obligation.[58]

Some of the high personages did feel the obligation, particularly Sir Richard Broun who vigorously defended the sailing of the *Barbadoes* and the integrity of the Association's management. But it was too late to save the project or Thomas Rolph. In the summer of 1842 opposition to the Association's emigration plans had appeared in print as well as in the Colonial Office. Though Governor Sir Charles Bagot had reappointed

Rolph as emigration agent for Canada only at the beginning of 1842, in July the Colonial Office advised that Rolph's official duties might well be discontinued, and the suggestion was carried out in December. Within ten years, it should be remarked, the Canadian government made an appropriation for promoting immigration and within twelve it again sent an emigration agent to Great Britain. Soon after his dismissal Rolph obtained an appointment to help in the removal of Negroes from Canada to the Island of Trinidad. But he removed no Negroes and soon returned to his earlier interest. What he could not accomplish in real life, he now described in writing for the magazines of the day.[59]

Companies: Pleas and Profits

Of the many colonization schemes presented to colonial officials by corporate groups, only three reached full maturity: the Canada Company, the British American Land Company, and the New Brunswick and Nova Scotia Land Company. But for the three that lived, many like Rolph's were stillborn. One group hoped to make a settlement on the banks of the Rideau Canal; H. William Hobhouse urged in support of the plan that the increase in population would greatly enlarge the business of the canal.[60] Another which offered to colonize the upper Ottawa Valley was soon branded as a venture in lumbering. Practically all applicants declared their determination to relieve the "distressed classes" of the mother country. Lord Egremont, for example, who had already assisted tenants to emigrate, now employed an agent, James Marr Brydone. Brydone proposed to buy 60,000 acres, if the government would invest one quarter of the cost in improvements and reserve 100,000 acres additional until he succeeded with the first allotment. Other applicants were prepared to convey workers free and support them while they built houses for the company which would be formed. Still others proposed to take paupers from English parishes, place them upon land, and loan them money while they cleared the land of trees and built their own shelters.[61]

One colonization company, the North American Colonial Association of Ireland, sprang from the efforts of Irish landlords who approached Lords Stanley and Spring Rice in 1833 and 1834. After official rebuffs and disaffection among their own members, they had their bill for incorporation introduced in Parliament by Messrs. O'Connell and Barron and it won approval in September, 1835. When sufficient capital could not be raised by the original founders, a Wakefieldian group took over a controlling interest.[62] A new directorate included Lord Durham,

Sommes, the deputy governor of the New Zealand Company, and the main founders of the South Australia Company, Wakefield, Hutt, and Colonel Kingscote who was made the governor of the Association. New capital had been subscribed before the end of 1838 and Colonel Kingscote, having bought the seigniory of Beauharnois near Montreal from Lord Durham's friend, Edward Ellice, turned it over to the Association in August 1839. Meanwhile through Wakefield's intervention, it became known that the famous Durham Report recommended not only political reforms for Canada but also an influx of British capital and its active use. Presently Wakefield's new organ, the *Colonial Gazette* now published from Rintoul's *Spectator* office, reviewed a pamphlet of the North American Colonial Association of Ireland which revealed the plan for the Beauharnois property: the supplying of British capital and population and the employment of the capital to develop public works, make loans, and carry on banking. The Association was ready to loan money for building a canal, provided its route would cross the Beauharnois seigniory.[63]

While Wakefield was preparing to sail for Canada in 1841, an agent of his, John Abel Smith, met with directors of the Canada Company, the British American Land Company, and the North American Colonial Association. Co-operating with the Canadian government emigration agent, Dr. Rolph, and the Committee of the London Colonial Association, they petitioned the Canadian government *via* Lord John Russell to implement a programme of capital investment in public works. Russell was impressed. He sent Lord Sydenham in Canada advance word of the arrival of an Association "agent."[64] To Sydenham, however, the humanitarian and the profit-taking motives of such groups as these were contradictory. The operations of the North American Colonial Association had been "very much kept out of view" in Canada; in January Sydenham had assured Russell that he would be sorry to see the government in any way "countenancing them." But by July after Wakefield's descent upon Canada, the sceptical specialists in the Colonial Office could note down on Sydenham's latest despatch, "Mr. Wakefield has won." The Governor-General had been happy to avail himself of Mr. Wakefield's presence to learn the present view of the Association with which Mr. Wakefield "was connected." On July 26, he wrote Russell with his customary assurance that the Association's plans for advancing capital to improve its own and public property were likely "to be attended with great advantage to the Province." He would now be grateful to see Russell and the home government support the bill before Parliament to revise the Association's powers and omit the controversial clause on banking.[65]

So Charles Buller's bill for enabling the Association to loan money for public improvements became law in 1842. A bill permitting the same passed the Canadian legislature on August 30. Of all the plans submitted to the imperial government, the Emigration Commissioners believed that none appeared "more advantageous to the public, and more sound in principle" than this of the Association. In addition to the original proposal for conveying emigrants, the Wakefieldians now planned to run a railroad from Beauharnois to Lake St. Francis and to aid emigrants by providing labour on public works and in building homes for future emigrants. Similar plans probably lay behind the Association's purchase of land on a proposed railway route for which the New Brunswick Assembly passed enabling legislation.[66]

In implementing that part of his programme which required public works, Wakefield's activities in Canada brought speedy results. He drew up a comprehensive plan for the development of inland navigation and influenced Sydenham to remove one canal project from those to be financed by the £1,500,000 guaranteed loan. This project was the Beauharnois canal. The Canadian legislature had already considered a new canal to join the old Lachine Canal–Lake St. Louis waterway with Lake St. Francis, but local interests were seriously split over the choice of a route. Robert Unwin Harwood, seigneur at Vaudreuil since his marriage in 1823 with the de Lotbinière heir, insisted on the north shore. Engineers' reports for some years had shown that route to be more expensive than the southern. Now land for excavating a canal on the south shore could be obtained gratuitously through the influence of the Association, which of course owned part of the lands needed. Governor Sir Charles Bagot, in a tight spot, decided for the southern route.[67]

Wakefield returned to Montreal from a trip to England on January 20; on February 15 the Chairman of the Board of Public Works announced that a survey for the canal would begin at once. Less than four months later, almost before the ice was out of the Quebec waterways, a committee of the Executive Council authorized the Board to proceed with a canal through the Beauharnois property. On June 14, one day after final authorization, the City Bank of which the member for Beauharnois, John W. Dunscomb, was a director, advanced £50,000 for the work.[68]

Though the select committee investigating these extraordinarily well-timed actions at once pilloried Bagot and his government, and Peter McGill and George Moffat of the British American Land Company opposed the Association, the committee failed to implicate Wakefield. Nevertheless in the advance of the money, Dunscomb's bank appears to have served as agent for Wakefield's Association. In the same summer,

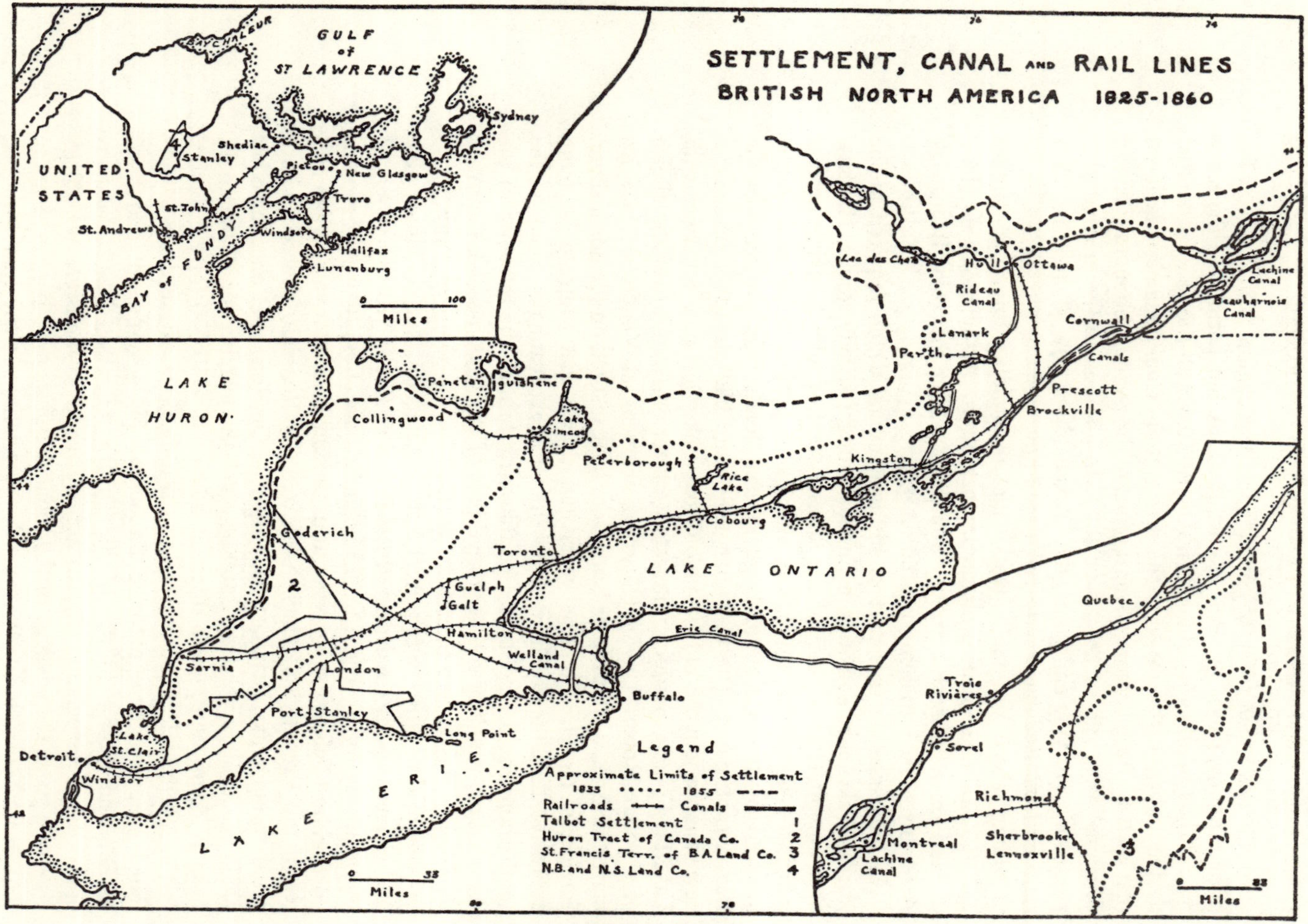
SETTLEMENT, CANAL AND RAIL LINES
BRITISH NORTH AMERICA 1825-1860
GULF of ST LAWRENCE
UNITED STATES
Shediac
Stanley
Pictou
New Glasgow
Sydney
Truro
St. John
St. Andrews
Windsor
Halifax
Lunenburg
BAY of FUNDY
Miles
LAKE HURON
Penetanguishene
Collingwood
Lake Simcoe
Lac des Chats
Hull
Ottawa
Rideau Canal
Lanark
Perth
Lachine Canal
Beauharnois Canal
Cornwall
Canals
Prescott
Brockville
Kingston
Peterborough
Rice Lake
Cobourg
Goderich
Toronto
LAKE ONTARIO
Guelph
Galt
Hamilton
Eric Canal
Welland Canal
Sarnia
London
Buffalo
Port Stanley
Long Point
Lake St. Clair
Detroit
Windsor
LAKE ERIE
Quebec
Trois Rivières
Sorel
Richmond
Sherbrooke
Lennoxville
Montreal
Lachine Canal
Legend
Approximate Limits of Settlement
1835 1855
Railroads Canals
Talbot Settlement 1
Huron Tract of Canada Co. 2
St. Francis Terr. of B.A. Land Co. 3
N.B. and N.S. Land Co. 4

FIGURE 3.*

Dunscomb resigned the Beauharnois seat in the Legislature and by November of 1842, Wakefield himself was the member for Beauharnois. For a time he was close to the colonial executive, so close that he was described by Bagot's critics as the Mephistopheles of the cabinet; but he withdrew his allegiance, it was said, when the government refused to support his emigration plans.[69] For that reason or some other, in the ten years after the inauguration of operations in Canada, not one British emigrant was brought to the colony through the efforts of the Association. Very soon Wakefield's overbearing interest in colonial land policies and procedures made him *persona non grata* with those in charge of the Crown lands of the united provinces.[70] When in 1845 a bill enlarging the powers of the Association went to Lord Stanley for approval, he turned to Metcalfe in Canada because he had very little authentic information respecting "that Body." And Metcalfe replied that so far as he knew the Association's transactions in the colony had not extended beyond the purchase of the seigniory of Beauharnois.[71]

Believers in Wakefield's theory of systematic colonization professed regret at the haphazard, unplanned method of settling the British American lands. But like Wakefield and theorists generally, the believers were more voluble in words than in deeds. One Wakefieldian, Arthur Mills, did put theory into practice by establishing a little colony at Blenheim, Upper Canada. Mills was already friends with the colonial reformers, Buller, Molesworth, and the radical Godley, when in 1845 he sent a Warwickshire yeoman, Daniel Wakefield, to the colony to buy land, purchase implements, and employ the labourers he sent out. Mills supplied the original £500 of capital, Wakefield chose the land and managed the little pioneer enterprise. Workers who were directed to the colony from time to time by Mills eventually became land purchasers. They were introduced wisely, after preparations for their reception which did much to ensure their ultimate success.

In spite of his responsibilities in England, in Parliament and else-

---

*Settlement, Canals, and Rail Lines. British North America, 1825–1860. Acknowledgments are due to Map Division, Public Archives of Canada, G. P. de T. Glazebrook, *A History of Transportation in Canada* (Toronto, 1938); A. R. M. Lower, *Settlement and the Forest Frontier* (Toronto, 1936), "The Assault on the Laurentian Barrier," *Canadian Historical Review*, X (1929); W. A. D. Jackson, *The Lands Along the Upper St. Lawrence* (College Park, Maryland, 1953, Typescript); W. F. Ganong, "A Monograph of the Origins of Settlements in the Province of New Brunswick," Royal Society of Canada, *Proceedings and Transactions*, Ser. 2, X (1904), Sect. II; F. C. Hamil, *Lake Erie Baron* (Toronto, 1955); D. G. Creighton, *The Empire of the St. Lawrence* (Boston, 1958); and to authors of histories of Canada, D. G. Creighton (1944), J. M. S. Careless (1953), E. McInnis (1959).

where, Mills continued his interest in Blenheim; he visited it in 1846 and again as late as 1881. Proof of the success of his planned colonization was evident from the increase in land values resulting from the labour of the settlers. Seventy-five acres which cost £100 in 1845 were valued at £400 in 1849 and in 1850 at £500.[72]

Thomas Talbot's fame as the greatest individual colonizer is probably matched among colonizing corporations by that of the Canada Company. As might be expected from Galt's wide interests, the company he helped to develop was designed to be more than merely a moneymaker. Though it acquired 2,500,000 acres of fine land in Upper Canada its purpose, according to its prospectus, was "not to encourage or deal with speculators, but to open access to the settlement of lands by a steady, industrious, agricultural population."[73]

Galt began his promotion of the Company with a practical knowledge of both mother country and colony. He understood his Scottish homeland in the years when industrialization and emigration were growing. In 1820 work on the Committee for Revision of the War Claims of 1812 made him a student of Canadian affairs just as sale of Crown and Clergy Reserve lands was suggested. In England companies, including one for colonizing in Australia, were being floated on a ground swell of speculation. Putting all his problems together, Galt came up with one solution: raise funds to pay the war claims by selling the reserve lands to a company, his own.

Though a controversy long delayed the settlement of the war claims, before the end of 1824 the Canada Company had been formed with Charles Bosanquet as chairman and Galt as secretary, and an agreement with the British government had been worked out.[74] After an evaluating commission had set the price of available Canadian lands at 3s. 6d. an acre, the Solicitor-General refused the price and the clergy group obtained the withdrawal of their lands. Though the Company was compelled to negotiate a new contract, it did sufficiently well for itself to raise the cry of favoured monopoly from radicals in the colony.[75] In return for 1,384,413 acres of Crown reserves scattered in almost every township of the province and about 1,100,000 acres of land fronting on Lake Huron,* the Company was to pay in sixteen annual instalments a total of £348,680 sterling. One-third of the payments for the undeveloped Huron Tract lands, however, might be spent on public improvements, and the government was to bear the cost of surveying the Huron lands. With this annual income, Upper Canada prepared to take care of

---

*The Huron Tract ran sixty miles west on Lake Huron and south to the townships of Zorra, Nissouri, London, Lobo, and Wilmot.

the Civil List. The Canada Company was finally chartered on August 19, 1826.[76]

Sales began with the Crown reserves which had been opened across the colony from the Ottawa on the east to the St. Clair River on the west. Payment terms were cash, six instalments in five years, produce, or labour on the roads. For those who paid the first instalment in the mother country or the St. Lawrence ports, the Company eventually provided free transportation inland.[77] Agents were placed in Liverpool, London, Bristol, Hull, Edinburgh, Glasgow, Dublin, Londonderry, Cork, and Limerick. Similar representatives worked actively in Montreal and Quebec, and in Prescott, Cobourg, Kingston, York, and Dundas in Upper Canada. From New York the British consul forwarded newly arrived British emigrants as well as a group of Scottish Highlanders who had suffered in a misguided colonization venture in Venezuela.[78]

Through the work of these agents and by means of an effective prospectus and public notices, the Canada Company wielded a publicity such as no colonizing organization had up to this time. The Company itself claimed that its distribution of maps, pamphlets, and advertisements in every city, market town, village, and hamlet of the United Kingdom made Canada known as a colony fit not only for the poor but suitable for men "of capital, . . . of education and intelligence." During the first two years of its operations, however, the Company paid the Crown £42,500 and spent £35,000 on local improvements while making land sales of some £29,000 on which only £6,000 in cash had been paid.[79] Omitting mention of the current depression, but pleading flaws in the land policy of Upper Canada, the Company petitioned the government for easier terms or an end to its agreement. Lieutenant-Governor Sir John Colborne reported the danger to the Civil List if payments ceased. The imperial government refused the petition and the Company, perhaps sensing the economic upturn ahead, continued its responsibilities. At the end of 1830, 46,063 acres of the Crown reserves had been sold at an increase of about six shillings an acre and in the Huron Tract 4,880 acres for £1,000 more than their cost; the Company had raised £142,240 from its proprietors on 8,890 shares and it held 323,000 acres of land paid for and unsold.[80]

When Guelph was founded in April, 1827, by the felling of a tree and the traditional opening of a flask of whisky, the axe blow echoed through the forest silence. Before the autumn snows fell the essential sawmill and brick kiln, two taverns, stores, and a temporary school were in operation, some score of houses and a road to join the Dundas road had been built, and the prices of town lots and farm land were rising.[81]

Best publicity of all, satisfied emigrants were beginning to write home; in 1832 Robert Fisher assured his parents from his new home in Guelph:

Through all the different townships I passed in my way up the country I give the preference to Guelph; . . . Here is a comfortable little village, . . . public inns, two of which are conducted in quite as fashionable a style as any in Halesworth, and about four times the business carrying on in almost every line. A very fine watermill, which drives three run of stones; and this place was five years since inhabited by bears and wolves. . . . The Guelph mill I am superintending belongs to the Canada Company. . . . Pray keep Anthony to the milling business and get him as forward as you possibly can, for by that in this country he may do well.

I have made every possible enquiry respecting farming; . . . we grind for the settlers from ten to fifteen miles in every direction; many of them have told me, when they reached this country, they had not a cent to help themselves; . . . I was no longer ago than yesterday talking to a farmer who came to this country only one year since; . . . he chopped twenty acres, planted twelve with wheat, which he sold at one dollar per bushel; this he admitted paid him for the land, the chopping of it, and all other expenses, and then had he money to spare. . . . In this country you may do well; I shall advise you by all means to come out next spring, as the prospects for you here are ten to one above what they are in the old country.[82]

On the tenth anniversary of its founding, Guelph's population had reached almost 2,000. Throughout all its lands, the Company had opened more than one hundred miles of road, spent some £87,000 on improvements, and sold about 100,000 acres of land to occupying settlers.[83]

In the more remote Huron Tract where surveys were made by "Dr." William Dunlop, development began in 1828; 100-acre lots on the Maitland Road running from Wilmot to Goderich on Lake Huron were advertised at 7s. 6d. an acre.[84] Here too with assistance of the Company, settlement progressed rapidly. By 1834 about 2,500 persons had entered the area, by the end of 1840 almost 6,000, and cultivated acres numbered 23,000.[85] The value of the land and improvements, including eighteen sawmills, eight gristmills, two taverns, seven distilleries, and other buildings was estimated at £186,206. Company statistics showed similar growth for other regions: on the Otonabee, for example, a summary of the achievements of 635 settlers in 38 townships indicated that the property of 337 emigrants who had begun with no capital whatever was valued in 1840 at £116,228 9s. 6d., and that of 298 who began with £20 each or more at £169,204 1s.[86]

By combining many early recommendations for the speeding up of development by means of public improvements and aid to settlers, the Canada Company pushed settlement on its lands far beyond that on neighbouring properties and, according to some critics, it even delayed progress elsewhere.[87] Though the Company's policy undoubtedly added much to Canadian wealth, at times the Executive Council complained of unwarranted expenditure on steamboats, Goderich harbour, and even roads. In the House of Commons, William Huskisson answered criticism mildly by declaring that though he knew nothing of the Company's profits, he believed its directors had no fear that its "affairs would excite either jealousy or envy."[88] In the first twelve years of its existence, according to a Company defence, the Canada Company raised £25 sterling per share on its 9,000 shares, only 25 of which had been held in Canada. Of that sum and the sum realized from its land sales, a Company agent wrote "not one farthing has been remitted to England. All has been expended in the colony, an expenditure greater than that of the Legislature of the colony during the greater part of that period."[89]

In 1838 when two-thirds of the Company's contract time had elapsed, two-thirds of its purchases had been patented. In the criticism of land policy for the Durham Report, Charles Buller soon wrote that through this "delegation of the powers of Government . . . to a private company," settlement had proceeded with more regularity and rapidity than on the lands "under the control of the officers of the Crown."[90]

In the years following the Rebellion of 1837 when British emigrants were enjoying practically free passage to Australia and the Canada Company had paid £245,000 of the £348,680 due the government, it protested against producing the balance and urged the ministry to spend the same sum on conveyance of emigrants to Canada.[91] This the government refused to do, asserting that the payments had been offered to Upper Canada in return for the Civil List. As usual the storm was weathered; sales for 1842 rose to almost 100,000 acres when credit for Huron Tract lands was extended to twelve years. The Company's optimistic report of 1844 placed capital raised at £410,300 and land paid for but as yet unsold at 1,385,195 acres.[92] Legislation of 1856 provided for the return of capital as well as profits to the shareholders in order that the Company might extinguish itself.[93] But by 1860, the coming of the railroad and the close relationship of the Company's agent, Frederick Widder, with the railroad companies had so increased land values that the Company might have been described as a million-pound corporation. Land sales in 1855 had averaged 44s. 9d. an acre, in 1857 51s. 11d., and in 1859 60s. 5d. The Company was to remain to receive many thousands of British emigrants throughout the nineteenth century.[94]

Though it was not chartered until 1834, the British American Land Company sprang from the same era of optimism and corporate innovation as the Canada Company. When in 1825 a group of Montreal merchants who had subscribed £182,000 to found a land company sent William B. Felton to approach the government in London, he found a similar group of London merchants ahead of him. In May they had promised R. J. Wilmot Horton of the Colonial Office every advantage in colonization dear to his heart: the removal of Great Britain's redundant population, the building of colonial roads and mills, the extension of British economic and political influence, if only they might choose lands in Lower Canada for their purchase. In September with Edward Ellice and later Robert Gillespie in the chair, the London and Montreal groups combined. Felton then offered new proposals to Horton.[95] Lord Dalhousie, governor-general in Canada, opposed the plan as speculative and indeed as impossible under the French land system; then "the disastrous financial events" of 1825 and 1826 intervened. Early in 1832, the project was revived; George R. Robinson became chairman or governor, John Galt honorary secretary. Support for the revival came from a meeting of citizens at Lennoxville, Quebec, a prospectus was issued, and Nathaniel Gould, deputy governor, pointedly described the prosperity of the Canada Company to show that "the comfort of the Emigrants and the improvement of the Province have fully kept pace with the advantage acquired by the shareholders, independent of the benefit arising to the manufacturing and shipping interests of the United Kingdom. . . ."[96]

Even the possibility of such all-embracing advantages failed to move the Colonial Office, and again negotiations lagged. In December Peter McGill told Lord Aylmer in Quebec that the French had no prescriptive right to keep out a company which might develop the Crown's waste lands, so that they could settle them themselves, "proche en proche." Aylmer believed that the government could do all a land company could. But he sent Lord Goderich the report of the Crown Land Commissioner, W. B. Felton, on four thousand square miles of territory south of the St. Lawrence River which was liable to "foreign pillage," and he sent also statistics from the townships of Leeds and Inverness to illustrate the rise in land values resulting from a little effort.[97] At almost the same time, Lord Stanley became secretary of the Colonial Office. Stanley was determined to make the waste lands of the Crown contribute to the Treasury. On December 3, 1833, he signed with G. R. Robinson and Nathaniel Gould as governor and deputy governor of the British American Land Company an agreement for the sale of some 850,000 acres of Crown lands in the Eastern Townships of Lower Canada. The price was £120,000, payable in ten yearly instalments with interest at 4 per cent.

One-half of the purchase money could be expended by the Company, with government approval, on public improvements for the development of the lands purchased.[98]

After obtaining on March 20, 1834, a charter of incorporation which permitted a capital of £300,000 and £50 shares, the British American Land Company set out with high hopes. Peter McGill and George Moffatt, a banker and a merchant of Lower Canada and both members of the colonial legislature, became Company commissioners in Montreal and Samuel Brooks secretary at Lennoxville in the heart of the Company property—some 590,000 acres of unsurveyed Crown lands in Sherbrooke County between Lake Megantic and the St. Francis River and about 250,000 acres surveyed in Shefford, Sherbrooke, and Stanstead counties. Company agents were busy in New York State and the United Kingdom.[99] Gradually the Company provided a few new roads and some shelters for emigrants. Though settlers of means soon bought good lands, special appeals were made to Scottish Highlanders and they arrived in numbers greater than the Company could employ. As late as 1841, the select committee of Parliament which considered the needs of the Highlands received a detailed scheme for placing crofters in the Eastern Townships. From Quebec, the government emigration agent, A. C. Buchanan, tried to induce Moffatt to "screen the poor emigrants from uncertainty" by guaranteeing work and building log huts for them near the older settlements. Moffatt would promise only work at 2s. 6d. per day in the season; after that the emigrant could support himself by hauling timber. Land might be had in 50-acre lots along a sleigh road for £15 12s. 6d., the down payment on which an emigrant could earn in twenty-five days.[100]

Company plans in 1835 and 1836 went far beyond the locating of a few emigrants. Samuel Brooks attended sheriffs' sales and there and elsewhere bought up improved lands, including much of the town site of Sherbrooke. He sold timber from the Company's lands, looked after saw and gristmills, planned the development of Sherbrooke's market place and foundry, and the renovation of its woollen factory; he advised bridging the St. Francis River and acquiring all the reserve lands bordering it. At the end of the year 1836, expenditure in Canada had reached £56,877 sterling, almost the whole amount permissible annually under the charter. The directors warned that emigrants must not depend upon the Company. On April 22, 1837, they demanded "strictest economy." Immediate liabilities were alarming: approximately £7,500 due the government, £8,700 due for Clergy Reserve lands, and £4,500 on private land purchases, £5,400 for provisions, £6,000 on the Sherbrooke bridge and the Victoria and the St. Francis-Richmond roads, £1,350 on mills, factory, and foundry, £600 on the St. Francis wharf, and so on and so on.[101]

Meanwhile as the disturbances of 1837 became acute and the opposition of the French press to the Company grew, the directors stopped payments and requested a modification of their agreement with the government. Lord Durham, at Quebec in 1838, refused the request as inexpedient and injurious. Henry Bruyères of the Company insisted that the directors merely desired the government to spend the Company's instalments on preparing their lands for emigrants "in accordance with the principles and practises of the Colonial Office in . . . other Colonies."[102] Sound argument as it was, it did not bring the government to carry out what it sometimes preached, and the stalemate continued until the arrival of Charles Poulett Thomson as governor-general.

In October, 1840, Thomson ordered the Attorney-General to proceed against the Company for £56,000 sterling, the sum owing. By March the directors had offered to return 400,000 acres of wild lands of the St. Francis territory. Sydenham would have none of it. Criticizing the former government for "granting" the Company 850,000 acres for a mere £120,000, Sydenham went on to tell Lord John Russell of the Company's land purchases, of its expenditure of the improvement moiety for its own good not for the public interest, and of its present position as the "monopolist of almost all the available land in that part of Lower Canada." Two months later with complete confidence, Sydenham reversed himself. He agreed to accept some 500,000 acres of the unsurveyed St. Francis lands in return for the government's abandonment of legal proceedings; it was the best settlement that could be reached. Besides Sydenham had made a discovery. The 500,000 acres in question was the finest land sold to the Company; it adjoined the government land in the Megantic territory where a settlement on the Garrafraxa type was in progress, and the government could run through it a direct road to the Eastern Townships from the port of Quebec.[103]

By the relinquishment of 1841, the proprietors lost 511,237 of the 596,325 unsurveyed acres of Crown lands covered by the agreement of December, 1833. Though that did not cut their 1,000,000-acre monopoly in half because of the large land purchases made after 1834, it did teach them the significance of Sydenham's discovery. The government opened the lands the Company had relinquished and settlers could acquire free, or at a price less than the Company had originally paid, land on which the Company had sometimes made clearings and occasionally built houses. At the same time, the general public expected the Company to sell its more expensive land as cheaply as the newly opened government lands.[104] Inevitably the Company's unpopularity grew and the years following the relinquishment were hard.

A change began in 1844 when Alexander T. Galt became the commissioner. He had worked in the Company office in the beginning days. Now he had broader experience and a vision. He saw a future for the Company's property in the building of the St. Lawrence and Atlantic Railroad from Montreal to Portland, Maine. In 1847, an act of Parliament modified the Company's charter so that capitalization might be increased to £600,000 and the Company might invest up to one-third of its capitalization in railroads, canals, and similar works, provided they were designed to bring advantage to the Company. During Galt's commissionership, $100,000 of stock was bought in the railroad to Portland and another $100,000 loaned to it.[105] Sherbrooke, with convenient markets in both the United States and Canada, was to become an industrial centre.

A new phase of settlement habits in the Eastern Townships, however, was on the way: British emigrants were passing on to Upper Canada, French natives were moving in. Returns from land sales came slowly and from manufacturing slower still. In 1852, the directors appointed Charles Birchoff to survey the Canadian establishment and make recommendations. He examined title deeds in the various regions, found the office system to be efficient but laborious. No "uneasiness need now exist," he wrote, "regarding the heavy investment in the town of Sherbrooke." The cotton and woollen and the pail factories, the paper mill and tannery, the saw and gristmills, the iron foundry and machine shops, all were bound to succeed. The leasing of the immense water power the Company controlled could not but be profitable. As for that essential, the sale of land, Birchoff concluded, if no inducement were held out to purchasers to "commence on the unsettled districts these must remain for many years in the same situation." He advised small sales and a bonus to pioneer settlers.[106]

Galt resigned the year after the report as the long struggle for profits began. In 1871 another act of Parliament was necessary, this time to state that the Company might not borrow on mortgage or bond, and that money received for land or sums outstanding might be divided among the shareholders as return on capital paid up or as dividends, as soon as the debenture debt of £18,500 was eliminated. Twelve years later in 1883, when the debt was gone and capitalization had been reduced to £179,104, the prohibition on borrowing was removed.[107]

Though the sanguine hopes of the founders were not realized fully, some return on the investment was had later in the nineteenth century. By 1895, 463,326 of the 582,825 acres held after the relinquishment had been sold, leasing of water power and also of lands was proceeding, and the closing of the Company office was to be delayed until the second half of the twentieth century.

A third company, the New Brunswick and Nova Scotia Land Company met quite as much opposition from officials in London as the one in Lower Canada. A group which included Samuel Cunard and John Labouchere finally persuaded the Colonial Office to consider their proposals. The New Brunswick Land Company had been formed in 1831 with the encouragement of Lieutenant-Governor Sir Howard Douglas, who wished to stimulate agriculture and, it is said, to counteract the influence of the timber interests.[108] In addition to the usual patriotic promises of land companies these founders averred their intention to sell land only to settlers on it, to provide their emigrants with ocean transport, and to employ able-bodied paupers sent to the colony by English parishes.[109]

Authorizing a capital of £200,000 in stock certificates of £25, the Company early in 1832 applied for some 200,000 acres of New Brunswick lands, with the privilege of buying in the other maritime colonies. Experienced men in the Colonial Office, Lord Howick, R. W. Hay, and others objected to the Company's lack of security and to the sale of large areas to any company.[110] The dickering between the designated promoters, Labouchere and John Bainbridge, and the colonial officials went on for nearly a year while George Baillie, brother of New Brunswick's well-heeled Surveyor-General, Thomas Baillie, became executive officer of the Company and the careful, legal-minded James Stephen advised caution. In the end, as with the British American Land Company, the arrival of Lord Stanley in the Colonial Office and the urging of the colonial executive caused the London officials to capitulate. According to the agreement concluded in November, 1833, the Company promised to pay £56,250 within seven years and £1,000 for surveys in return for 550,000 acres of land situated in York County on the height of land from which the Miramichi, the Nashwaak, and St. John rivers provide transportation to the Gulf of St. Lawrence and the Bay of Fundy. Lands bought from the Cunards were added to this acreage.[111]

The Company's agents went to work in Great Britain along the Tweed and farther north. In Northumberland David Stewart and E. N. Kendall won emigrants easily by promising fifty-year leases of 100-acre farms with five acres in crop, comfortable log houses, and free medical care.

In the north of Scotland an agent, Nicholson, translating into Gaelic somewhat freely no doubt, seemed to promise all this and free transportation too. Consequently in the Company's new town, Stanley on the Nashwaak River near Fredericton, where neither houses nor crops had yet been prepared there were soon problems in plenty. The Scots from the Isle of Skye, being fishermen, found land pioneering irksome; the Company was bringing in cash by selling timber, but the emigrants resisted winter employment at lumbering. When the Lieutenant-Governor visited Stanley, the settlers received him with a petition of grievances. And when this reached the Company, *via* the Colonial Office, the Company replied that it had spent £80,000 in the last three years in converting "a Wilderness into a flourishing Settlement," £8,000 of it on supplies for the people who were complaining.[112] The Company's predicament illustrated forcibly the objections of practical men to many theoretical settlement schemes. As usual the Colonial Office, this time over Grey's and Stephen's signatures, authorized employment for the dissatisfied emigrants on roads or elsewhere. In the end public lands were given to some thirty families who had responded to the Company's promotion.[113]

In London meanwhile the New Brunswick Company, like other companies before it, was begging for an extension of time on its payments. One extension was granted. Thereafter the Company's requests for similar favours because of delays in government surveys or anything else travelled back from London to the colony for reply. But while the Surveyor-General's office described the surveys it had handed over to Company agents, and the colonial government reported that the Company was carrying on a profitable lumbering business and acquiring 10,000-year leases to coal lands,[114] the directors demanded a change in their charter in order to issue additional stock. One-half of the capital stock of £200,000 had been paid up by early 1838, £28,125 had gone to the government, £64,760 had been spent in local improvements and in helping poor emigrants, and Company stocks were selling at 40 per cent discount. This plea brought a reprimand from the office of the Privy Council for Trade on the high impropriety of asking new subscribers to produce what present stockholders would not risk. After the New Brunswick legislature recommended the collection of overdue payments by legal procedure, the Company authorized payment.[115] In the spring of 1840, a committee of the Assembly considered Company pleas, this time for a cash allowance as compensation for delays and changes in the government land sale price. Again the Assembly disallowed the pleas and threatened recourse to the courts if the balance were not forthcoming in three annual instalments in 1840, 1841, and 1842.[116]

In February, 1843, the Company could report that the government had received from it everything due on the purchase price, £60,299 1s. 6d. That was a smaller sum than had been invested in the development of its property for roads, bridges, mills, and aid to settlers. While the Company had sent its agents seeking new settlers in England, while it remitted cash to the colony, so its argument to the Colonial Office ran, the government of New Brunswick had failed to build the promised Royal Road from Fredericton to St. John River falls, and the road from Halifax west was still unbuilt; at the same time, in competition with the Company, the colony had lowered the price of land and terms of settlement for emigrants in such "an extraordinary degree" that the Company felt forced to sell land at prices as low as it had paid for it.[117] By the end of 1843, according to reports in London, it had sold some 18,000 acres, still had more than 500,000 to sell. In 1837 the Colonial Office denied forthrightly that any promise of roads had been made. Seven years later when the roads were still unopened, Lieutenant-Governor Sir William Colebrooke acknowledged that the legislature had not given the encouragement to the building of roads through the Company's domain which it had extended to other parts of the province and to which the Company was entitled in common with others.[118]

The Company's situation with regard to terms of settlement is equally baffling. Before 1830 New Brunswick had tried to develop its waste lands and care for needy arrivals by offering 50-acre lots on easy terms. The Lieutenant-Governor believed that the only settlers fit to open wilderness lands were those least able to pay and, while the Company struggled with discontented settlers, he began to foster government-nurtured settlements, the Harvey, the Cork, and others. The home government, now without interest in New Brunswick's land revenues, let Colebrooke have his way.[119] So the Company's grievances were to continue even into the era when New Brunswick set out on its own responsibility to publicize its advantages and encourage immigration. The winding up of the Company's business began in 1872 and was to continue for many years.

No sufficient explanation for the difficulties of the Canadian land companies can be found without extensive investigation of company records, and records for the purpose are not easy to assemble. Without them, one could jump to the cynical conclusion that British businessmen of the period expected a free hand and favours when operating in the colonies and that the colonial legislators, needing yet resenting "foreign" capital, met the company pleas like fighters with no holds barred. Similarities in the positions of the companies in Lower Canada and New Brunswick are suggestive. Both bought in times of speculative optimism. Both were handicapped by lack of local experience in the emigrants they introduced and in the executives who directed what Colebrooke described as their improvident expenditure. Both they, and the Canada Company as well, pointed out at one time or another that they had spent more on development than the colonial government in a like period. Both accepted generally the colonization and land sale theories then popular in England, and when colonial land prices dropped and the colonial governments flouted English theory by instituting easier settlement terms, both companies proclaimed themselves unable to meet the competition without losing money. Then the contradiction in objectives shrewdly hit upon by Lord Sydenham appeared: in spite of their humanitarian, patriotic pronouncements, directors and stockholders howled as loudly at the losses as if profits had been their sole purpose. The Canada Company, it is true, also began in an era of heavy speculation. But it escaped involvement in impractical theorizing and it enjoyed, besides, the years of Upper Canada's greatest immigration and the prosperity of a railroad-building area. The latter advantage A. T. Galt tried to bring to the British American Land Company in Lower Canada, but his stockholders had to pay heavily for it, as has been seen.

In addition to these influences, local conditions, the timber trade in New Brunswick, the habits of the French settlers in Lower Canada, the skill of some of the farmers imported by the Canada Company, affected the fate of the land companies. But the inexperience of the company administrators and the government's shifting, changing land policy which have been mentioned made up a very large part of the companies' difficulties. By establishing his own settlement rules and sticking to them, Colonel Talbot freed himself from many of these influences and as a planter of colonists he probably achieved the greatest success of all.

The value of the stability provided by leaders like Talbot and Dickson in a pioneer land where government offered no services need not be argued. In later times when farm clearings approached each other and the government land system was better organized, evaluations of the work of individual and corporate leaders will vary pretty largely with the observer's theories regarding systematic colonization.

VII. THE EMIGRANT SHIP AND THE EMIGRANT TRADE,

1815-1860

IN THE CENTURY between the British conquest of New France and the achievement of Confederation, British shipping to the northern colonies grew from a tiny trickle to a great stream carrying thousands of emigrants and thousands of tons of timber, grain, and general merchandise a year. In the same century the controls of the old mercantile system were gradually swept away and materials and men freed to move abroad with the currents of trade and personal advantage. As north Atlantic commerce developed, the shipping interests became one of the most powerful pressure groups at the capital of empire. Together with the theoretical advocates of laissez-faire and with landlords eager to clear their estates, they fought as an invasion of freedom the enactment of humane legislation designed to provide safe conveyance of emigrants at sea. Only in the forties, when the humanitarian influence had become widespread and the arrival of iron and steam promised to transform Atlantic shipping, did the regulation of the emigrant trade win acceptance as a matter of course.

The first legislation on conveyance of passengers, noted above in connection with Scottish emigration, was still in force in 1815 when peace reopened passenger traffic on the north Atlantic.[1] Government officers who supervised the assisted emigrations to Canada soon obtained certain relaxations for their cargoes. Shipping to British American ports gained further favours by enactments in 1816 and 1817 which removed various safeguards and limited vessels to carrying to the United States only one passenger for every five tons burden and authorized British vessels to carry to British colonial ports one adult for every one and a half tons. By 1819, the emigrant traffic had turned almost three to one in favour of British North American ports.[2]

TIMBER: THE OLD EMIGRANT TRADE

A basic change in north Atlantic shipping was already under way. During the struggle with Napoleon, English timber dealers had struck

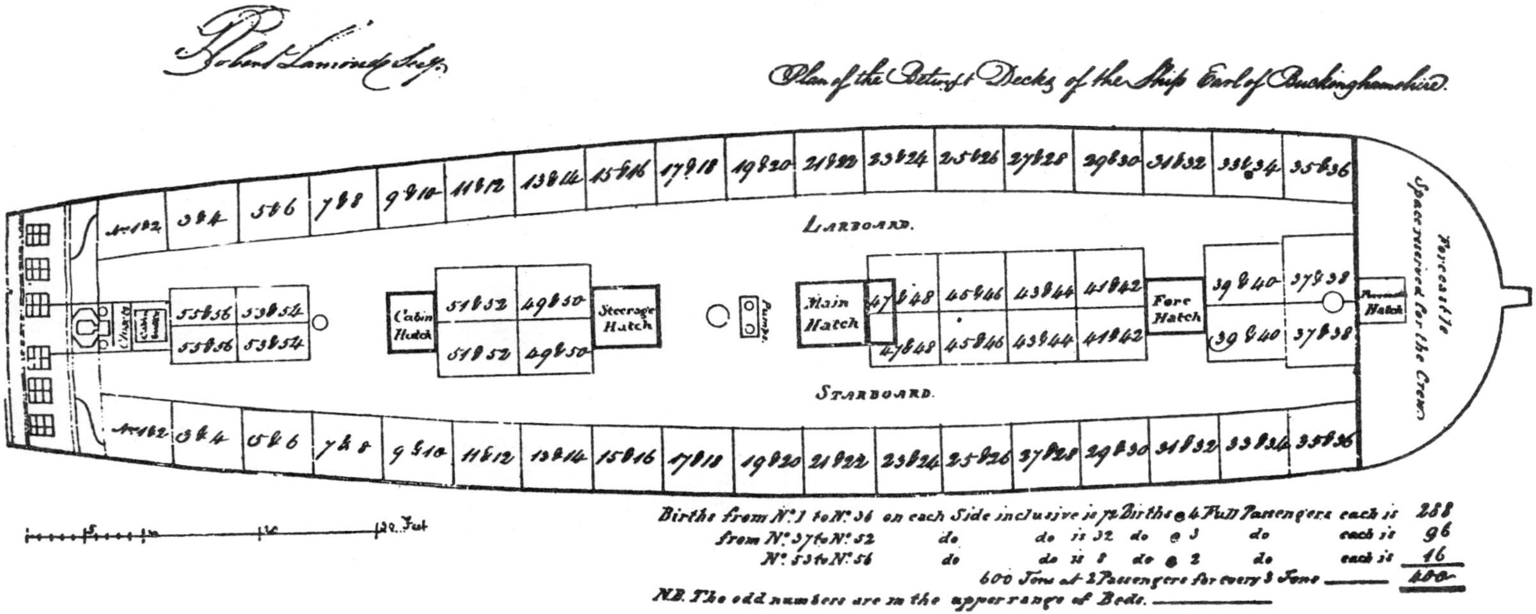

FIGURE 4. Plan of the Betwixt Decks of the Ship, Earl of Buckinghamshire. (Robert Lamond, The Rise and Progress of Emigration, from the Counties of Lanark and Renfrew, Glasgow, 1821.)

some sort of a bargain with their government by which, in return for heavy duties on Baltic timber, they agreed to develop this colonial natural resource. In the years immediately after 1815, timber vessels made up about one-third of all British tonnage, including almost all of the tonnage to New Brunswick, and a large proportion of that to Quebec. In 1819 timber exports from Quebec amounted to some 20,000 tons of oak, 75,000 tons of white pine timber, and 1,236,296 boards and planks. According to Joseph Marryat, the chairman of Lloyd's, in 1820 timber vessels trading to the colonies represented one-seventh of the whole British carrying trade. And according to modern opinion all the battered hulks on the Atlantic drifted into the Canadian timber trade.[3] Their eastbound cargo enjoyed the preference mentioned; once unloaded in Great Britain, a few boards put up in the ship's hold and a few advertisements in local newspapers would guarantee a westbound cargo of emigrants. If the timber preference was threatened, Joseph Marryat could be counted on to oppose change as discouraging to emigration. Even John Richards, examining the colonies in 1830, noted the "reciprocal advantages of the passenger and timber trades" and the benefit "altogether national."

The average timber vessel was little more than a shell; it had no compartments except the captain's quarters aft and the crew's quarters forward, so that on an eastward voyage the whole hulk could be loaded with timber from keel to deck. To prepare for the cargo of emigrants, the shipowner merely laid a temporary deck on the lower beams about five and one-half feet below the upper deck. On a 400-ton vessel this gave a lower deck of perhaps 95 by 25 feet. On it two tiers of rough wooden berths, each six by six feet, were constructed along each side, and sometimes a row down the middle. Under the terms of the Passenger Act of 1803, this space was deemed adequate accommodation for 200 passengers, under the Act of 1835 for 240.[4] There were no port-holes in these vessels nor any means of ventilation beyond the three hatchways. When these were open an eerie half-light and a certain amount of fresh air filtered down. If the vessel met bad weather, the hatches were battened down, and the emigrants were left often in pitch darkness to breathe the stifling air.

Attempts to replace the Acts of 1803, 1816, and 1817 were repeatedly deferred in Parliament. By 1822 the misery and protests caused by the confusion of enforcement and relaxation in the passenger-traffic regulations had convinced the Treasury of the need for more concise legislation. In 1823 a bill prepared by J. C. Herries, financial secretary to the Treasury, was pushed through the House of Commons between June

11 and July 3.[5] It limited passengers to one for every five tons burden and required fifteen square feet of deck space per passenger and a surgeon on vessels carrying more than fifty persons. For Irish emigrants certain provisions were to be remitted. An Act of 1825 added a few refinements to the Act of 1823.[6]

Within a year of the legislation of 1823, the agitation for freedom for labour caused the repeal of the laws prohibiting the combination and emigration of artisans. In 1825 revelations before the select committees on Ireland led many to believe that if population were not permitted to leave the United Kingdom expeditiously the consequence for England as well as Ireland would be disastrous. The following year, while the reviews were urging the need for emigration and cheaper Atlantic fares, the Emigration Committee with R. J. Wilmot Horton, parliamentary under-secretary for the Colonial Office, as chairman began its work. In spite of the evidence of shipowners and colonial officials that the expense of passage was retarding emigration, especially from Ireland, Horton drew up a bill providing moderate safeguards for emigrants. On its presentation in Parliament, it met severe criticism by laissez-faire members. Consequently the committee recommended the repeal of all regulations and the bill was so altered.[7]

The repeal left the whole emigrant trade, for so the conveyance of emigrants may be described, to take care of itself. Shipowners were free to crowd their vessels as they pleased, emigrants to take what provisions they deemed necessary or could afford. When protests were made—and they came within one month of the Act—the government replied over Wilmot Horton's signature that the repeal had been carried on recommendation of a committee of Parliament and presumably was a matter in which the Colonial Office had neither power nor influence. Before the shipping season of 1827 had passed, disasters on the Atlantic proved that the emigrant trade was far from able to take care of itself.[8]

Horton had requested the colonial officials in British America to report upon the operation of the repeal. They complied in full measure. From Halifax, Sir James Kempt described the arrival of the brig *James* from Waterford with over one hundred passengers, all sick of typhus fever. One hundred and sixty had embarked in Ireland; five had died at sea and, the vessel being obliged to put into Newfoundland for food and medical aid, thirty-five had been left behind there, too ill to proceed. Kempt believed that the disease had been caused "solely by their scanty nourishment during the voyage, by the crowded and filthy state of the ship, and by a want of medical assistance." So numerous were the vessels arriving in similar condition that it was necessary to establish a hospital at Halifax for the reception of sick emigrants, and so contagious and serious was the disease that before November of 1827, 800 out of a population of 7,000 had died in the city.[9]

In New Brunswick, 250 passengers arrived from Dublin by the brig *William* without a surgeon or sufficient provisions, and after "dreadful" suffering.[10] The Secretary of the New Brunswick Agricultural and Emigrant Societies believed that "many of the poor Emigrants were deluded from their homes by false but specious statements of Brokers and Ship Masters whose sole object in prosecuting the inhuman traffic appears to be, that of collecting as large cargoes as possible of their unsuspecting fellow subjects." In self-protection the Lieutenant-Governor and citizens suggested that, since the traffic brought profit mainly to the captain of timber vessels, a fund which could be used for the benefit of destitute emigrants might be derived from these men by authorizing officers of the customs to exact a tax of 15*s*. per passenger from every shipmaster carrying emigrants in to New Brunswick.[11] This suggestion was to bear fruit later.

In Nova Scotia the Council, fearing that the province would be overwhelmed "with as many ignorant paupers as the Artful and Unprincipled Men who carry on this Traffic can delude," made a direct request for the re-enactment of the old passenger law.[12] At the same time Nova Scotian legislation, resembling that in effect in New York State, required that two justices of the peace board emigrant ships in the ports and exact from the masters for each emigrant landed a bond of £10 as security that the emigrant would not become chargeable to the local authorities within one year. Moneys taken under the Act were to be paid to the use of poor emigrants.[13] Cape Breton, with its isolated landing spots, was a bootleggers' paradise for merchants in the emigrant trade. But in Halifax the law was enforced under the guns of the fort, and British merchants soon applied to the Colonial Office for redress. For the moment however, that department left the colony to impose regulations which would have been difficult to defend in the Parliament of the day.[14]

Well-intentioned shipowners had protested against the repeal of 1827. "Distress and danger encountered by the Emigrants on the Passage," one of them argued, would "have a greater tendency to prevent" emigration than any clause of the late Act.[15] After an accumulation of these protests had reached William Huskisson, the new secretary for war and the colonies, Wilmot Horton who was still devoted to his subject though now at the Board of Trade brought a motion for a new passenger bill. In the House of Commons, Hume as usual spoke for the principle of perfect freedom as did Sir John Newport, Poulett Thomson, and others representing the shipping and timber interests.[16] Huskisson took the humanitarian and, in this case, the practical attitude. He was "unable to understand the nature of those pure abstract principles which were to prevent them from interfering where the interests of humanity were at stake"; it was the duty of ministers to request power to end such enormities as existed in the emigrant trade; he would do it "even in the teeth of science and philosophy."[17]

The Act of 1828 was a compromise. Possibly because of Huskisson's hurry to get the bill through Parliament, perhaps because of consultations with the shipowners, the original draft requiring two passengers for every three tons was rewritten to read three to every four tons. Space requirements were reduced to nothing but five and one-half feet height between decks and food essentials to only fifty gallons of water and fifty pounds of bread, biscuit, or oatmeal for each emigrant. Shipmasters were to post bond of £1,000 for the performance of the terms of the Act and pay penalties for non-observance of the regulations.[18]

Compromise though it was, the law marked a revolution. It passed the House of Commons in a thin session, after the first full debate on the conveyance of passengers at sea. For the first time, it seemed that responsibility for policy had found a definite location in the Colonial Office, though critics called it a resting place. Under Huskisson that office was exhibiting some of the vigour which would place him among the first imperial statesmen of the nineteenth century. Before the year ended, it instituted a series of measures for the protection of emigrants by appointing an emigrant agent to the port of Quebec. Until his health broke in 1836 the first appointee, Alexander Carlisle Buchanan, kept a close watch on vessels arriving with emigrants and remonstrated personally and through the courts with ship captains whom he detected breaking the passenger vessel law. He aided emigrants in winning redress from such captains.[19] In 1833 in the mother country, Lieutenant Robert Low, R.N. (retired), was appointed as emigrant agent for Liverpool. When in 1834 the Honourable E. G. Stanley, secretary for war and the colonies, won an appropriation of some £1,400 for the purpose, it was possible to send similar agents, all naval officers retired on half pay, to Bristol, Greenock, Leith, Limerick, Cork, Dublin, and Belfast.[20] They undertook the exasperating task of enforcing the passenger vessel law; they became the "appointed poor man's friend," protecting him from fraud if possible, and providing him with reliable information regarding shipping.[21]

Whether the fact should be attributed to over-devotion to duty or to the pestilent state of the emigrants and their vessels, the truth remains that two of the first appointees to these posts, Buchanan and Low, died, worn out before their time, after repeated exposure to typhus and other disease.[22]

Men who worked strenuously for improvement in the regulations, honest shipping merchants well aware of the malpractices of unscrupulous ticket agents, were disgusted with the Act of 1828. On most vessels the law would permit one passenger to every twenty and one-half square inches of deck space.[23] In the "Annals of the Slave Trade," wrote Todhunter from Cork, there was nothing "equal to this." The growth of the colonial timber trade to the United Kingdom from 317,563 loads of squared timber in 1821 to 613,679 in 1841[24] along with a like increase in emigrant passengers was developing a greedy array of middlemen—boarding-house keepers, passage brokers, agents. When proof of imposition upon emigrants reached the newly appointed Commissioners of Emigration whose specific duty it was to provide correct information, they attempted to expose agents who bought up parts of vessels "upon speculation," and then collected passengers by sending out sub-agents to market towns where they deluded the uninformed with expectations of free land, tools, and even temporary support at government expense.[25]

From such agents or from handbills circulated in his parish the would-be emigrant might learn of the early departure of a "fast Sailing Vessel amply supplied with Provisions and Water"; he might pay an agent for passage on a certain vessel to a certain port. But after travelling to the port he was sometimes compelled to sail to another destination, stay weeks in lodging houses, or to return home, his funds exhausted in waiting.[26] Others who arrived in port without previously arranging for passage became the prey of so-called "crimps" or "cads" who surrounded every coach, steamboat, and canal boat, induced the inexperienced countrymen to make deposits on their passage, and then vanished. Frequently it was feared the profits of the port lodging houses which put up delayed emigrants went into the same pockets as the profits of the shipping business. For a time in 1848, the Emigration Commissioners hoped to protect emigrants by sponsoring a reception centre in Liverpool but the project failed, it was alleged, because of opposition of the shipping merchants. In that port, power was finally given to the mayor to proceed against certain impositions and a special police was assigned to the docks.

At best, crossing the Atlantic in the hold of a sailing vessel tried the endurance of the hardiest. Steerage passengers as a rule provided their own sea stores, whatever they could afford packed in wooden chests or bags, together with cooking basins, and vinegar to break the brackish taste of the water supplied by the shipmaster. Foods varied with national origin and the emigrant's means. The Irish took mainly potatoes and no "animal" food. Contemporary references to the emigrants' weakness from lack of food are frequent, but there are also records of quick crossings from which steerage emigrants landed with two weeks' rations to spare. Preparing the food was a physical feat in itself, one which often led to fights for a place at the ship's fires. Cooking if the fires were lit, washing if water could be had, all daily tasks were performed on the deck, open to the gaze of every steerage passenger. The length of voyage varied as much as the food supplies. In 1843, the average voyage of 179 vessels sailing from the British Isles to Quebec lasted 44 days, the shortest 27, the longest 88 days.

False decks, triple tiers of berths, falsification of the age of passengers were among the devices used to deceive the inspectors in order to sail with an excess cargo. Under the Act of 1828, however, a vessel of 400 tons burden could sail with 300 passengers and still be within the law. A diagram from the office of Lieutenant Low, R.N., in Liverpool, shows such a vessel fitted to accommodate 134 passengers in two spaces 36 by 24 and 27 by 24 feet. Crammed with 300 human beings, that space is scarcely imaginable.[27] Moreover the Act did not provide regulations for vessels loaded with passengers and other cargo. Again faithful Lieutenant Low has left the evidence:

I have for several days watched the progress of the British built ship *Cumberland*, Thomas Nicholl, Master, burthen 336 tons register, chartered by Messrs. Robinson Brothers of this place for New York with 86 emigrants, crowded together in the small space of 25 feet by 24 feet 6 inches with their bed places and baggage, stores and provisions.

The remainder of the space of this vessel was taken up with the Cabin, and forecastle for the Crew, besides which she is filled with a Cargo of . . . 126 tons of Iron stowed close to the ceiling, 292 tons of Salt in Cargo, 17 tons of Earthenware and 44 tons of Water, Provisions and Coals, making together 479 tons; with a Crew of 16 men and the Passengers together making a total of 102 Souls, drawing 15 feet 4 inches of Water, built at Whitehaven in the year 1810, and being 23 years old.*

Vessels sailing from Ireland were the worst offenders. Of sixteen entering the port of Quebec between May and July 15, 1831, all carried more passengers than the law allowed and eight more than one person per ton. In a protest against such dangerous practices, the grand jury

*Doubt existed as to the power of the Act of 1828 regarding British vessels sailing to the United States. The Colonial Office wished to have a trial case, but it was not carried through. With the *Cumberland*, however, the emigrant agent was helpless even had it been *en route* to a British colony for the Act did not cover vessels loaded with passengers *and cargo.*

of Quebec handed in the following list of vessels with their tonnage and passengers:[28]

				Tons	Number of emigrants
May	9	Robert Kerr	Belfast	357	370
"	14	Helen	"	305	250
"	15	Thetis	Limerick	276	244
"	16	Breeze	"	321	253
"	17	Earl of Aberdeen	Belfast	278	247
"	19	Sarah	Limerick	223	200
"	20	Agenora	New Ross	250	243
"	23	Jane	Belfast	325	326
"	25	Quiten Leitch	Newry	425	382
"	27	Bolivar	Belfast	399	353
"	31	Eliza Ann	Sligo	229	300
		Jane	"	150	196
June	3	Eliza Ann	Cork	324	362
July	5	Ulster	Londonderry	334	505
"	11	Penelope	Newry	313	346
"	15	Kingston	Waterford	378	447

When complaints reached the government from New Brunswick, Upper and Lower Canada, and Newfoundland, the Colonial Office in December, 1831, took up the suggestion made by New Brunswick three years before. It proposed to appeal to the pecuniary interest of the shipping merchants by having the colonies levy a tax payable on all emigrants arriving and a double tax on all who embarked without the sanction of the officers of the home government, the proceeds of the tax to go to the ports in which the tax was collected.[29] Obviously it was an advantageous arrangement for the colonies, one indeed which might be looked upon as a step towards colonial control of immigration. Obviously too, it relieved the home government of a difficult responsibility, for the fear of overpopulation and the principles of laissez-faire were still strong enough in the House of Commons to render impossible the passage of a strict passenger conveyance law. Nevertheless in cutting down unauthorized departures and overcrowding on shipboard, the effect of the tax was to be slight, as may be seen in Table VIII of Appendix B.

In the winter session of 1832 the Assembly of Lower Canada enacted the tax and New Brunswick and Nova Scotia quickly did the same.[30] Funds so raised would be turned over to the provincial receiver-general and be paid by him to the organizations bearing expense for the care of unfortunate emigrants. After the establishment of the quarantine station at Grosse Isle, the Lower Canadian tax fund was stretched to cover upkeep there. To this fund the imperial government began to contribute a vote, usually of £1,800 currency. During the first four years in which the tax was collected at Quebec, it brought in £13,830 15s.[31] In later years, annual collections there rose to £9,000 and even to £15,000, while expenditures at the quarantine went to £3,000 and more annually.[32] Contrary to expectations, a great part of the money so raised had to be spent, as noted later in chapter IX, on forwarding indigent emigrants to suitable situations inland.

When the British public learned of the colonial emigrant head tax, Highlanders in Scotland and poor in all parts of the kingdom declared that the additional expense would make the price of emigration prohibitive. Advocates of freedom and merchants in the Atlantic trade, including George Moffatt and others in Montreal, protested against this interference with "perfect laissez-faire in emigration."[33] To these Lord Howick, under-secretary in the Colonial Office, replied that the purpose of the law had been to protect emigrants from fraud and build a fund to care for them on arrival.[34] Upper Canada's strong objection to the law caused a bitter quarrel between the two colonies and the London office. Finally the emigration agent at Quebec wrote that the tax was "sapping at the very foundation of British Emigration to the Canadas."[35] In 1833 on the advice of Lord Stanley, the colonial secretary, Lower Canada reserved the act, but only for one season, that of 1834. In one amount or another, the tax was to continue as were the agents and the Grosse Isle station so long as this emigration lasted. And the tide surveyors in the colonial ports, like John Fife in the port of Quebec, continued to board the boats, check the passenger lists, and collect the tax, an "arduous, labourious, and truly unpleasant duty."[36]

The truth was that two forces were at work encouraging laxity in passenger vessel legislation: the shipowners who wanted profits and the poor emigrants who wanted cheap Atlantic fares. Both forces lost out when the government put through the Act of 1823. For a few years, steerage fares rose to £3 and 4 from British ports to St. John and Quebec. Then came the repeal of 1827 and a short heyday for the poorer shippers and the poorest emigrants. The Act of 1828 restored some of the decencies, though not all that humanitarians or even the government desired. By 1831 the cost of the Atlantic steerage crossing from the regular British ports, Liverpool, Belfast, Dublin, Glasgow, varied from 30 to 40 or 50s. without food, and there it stood for a decade.[37] To St. John, the cost was usually higher, and to New York higher still. With food, the price would be doubled, perhaps 80s. This system of pricing seems to have been approved by the Colonial Land and Emigration Commissioners. The emigrant trade could not have been carried on, they wrote, "without creating a competition" and establishing "the modes of conveyance best adapted to the circumstances of those by whom they are to be used."[38] Against this contemporary opinion, one can only place the judgment of modern students of the emigrant trade that no legislation, no rise in fares could have compelled decent conditions with passengers so "filthy" in habits as the Irish.[39]

Before this period ended, however, improvement had been made and the trade paid for it, as in any form of business. By 1846 official estimates recorded average fares to British American ports as 50*s.* and to United States ports as 70*s.* For a time during 1847 when the effects of the repeal of the Corn Laws and the Irish famine were felt, fares fluctuated widely. But thereafter, as will be seen, shipping improved, the business of carrying emigrants became a respectable trade, and passenger fares steadied at about 75*s.* to the United States and 65*s.* to British America.[40] As a rule, rises in costs were now compensated by better sanitation, better food, and seaworthiness as required by the law, and by the arrival of improved boats which provided ventilated quarters and shorter crossings.

Though the cholera epidemic of 1832 was not a fair test of the efficiency of the legislation controlling the emigrant traffic, it drew attention to the subject as nothing else could have done. In 1832 cholera spread like a plague through Scotland in areas from which many of the emigrants including the Irish sailed. In Glasgow mortality rose 20 per cent above the average. Susanna Moodie's ship captain arriving in Quebec August 30 exclaimed, "This cursed Cholera! Left it in Russia—found it on my return to Leith—meets me again in Canada."[41] In Nova Scotia and New Brunswick where a rigid system of inspection by provincial officers had become customary, the ravages of the disease were slighter than in Quebec. When the danger threatened in the spring, Lord Howick had taken the precaution of re-enacting by Order in Council the clauses of the repealed act, 6 Geo. IV, c. 116, which had required vessels to carry a surgeon and medicine chest.[42] But in British ports where a quarantine might have been helpful, vessels were detained only three days; if cholera had not been detected within that time, the Customs had instructions to dispense with regulations of the Order in Council.[43] On June 15, under the title "Melancholy Loss of Life at Sea by Cholera," *The Times* published the following:

The ship *Brutus*, of 384 tons burden, sailed on the 18th of May from Liverpool for Quebec. She had on board 330 emigrants, men, women, and children who, with the crew, made a grand total of 349 souls. Previous to sailing the vessel underwent the usual examinations. . . . She carried an experienced surgeon, who, it is said, was well supplied with medicines. . . . On . . . ninth day out from Liverpool, a healthy man about 30 years of age, was seized with malignant cholera. . . . The next case was that of an old woman, 60 years of age, who died 10 hours after the attack. The ravages of the pestilence then rapidly increased. . . . The greatest number of deaths was 24 in

FIGURE 5. Emigration Vessel, Between Decks. (*Illustrated London News*, May 10, 1851.)

one day. The captain had not, it seems, any intention of returning to port, until the disease began to attack the crew. . . . Under these circumstances, his vessel a lazarhouse, and men, women, and children dying about him, he resolved to put back to Liverpool. The resolution was formed on the 3rd instant and the *Brutus* reached port on Wednesday morning. Up to that date the cases had been 117, the deaths 81, and the recoveries 36. Seven cases remained when the vessel entered the Mersey, two of which proved fatal in the course of the day, making the total number of deaths 83.

The passengers on board the *Brutus* found themselves with provisions. Their stock, however, though the vessel had been but 26 days at sea, was nearly exhausted. . . . The laudanum, too, was exhausted.

Upon the colonial ports fell the severest burden from the epidemic. During the days of the great emigrations which began shortly before 1830, so abominable was the state of vessels entering the Quebec harbour that "the harbour master's boatman had no difficulty, at the distance of a gunshot, either when the wind was favourable or in a dead calm, in distinguishing by the odour alone a crowded emigrant ship." Now day after day in 1832, the emigrant agent described vessels arriving in a loathsome state, the passengers ill and suffering from a shortage of provisions. In 1830 a fever hospital had been set up at Point Lévis on the St. Lawrence opposite Quebec. On the outbreak of cholera in 1831, the government authorized a larger establishment about thirty miles down the river on Grosse Isle. Later as the need for inspection and quarantine continued, the whole island was taken over and permanent quarters were built for the hospital, staff, and for emigrant detention.[44] But in 1832 when the station was new, all the emigrants were put ashore, unwashed, taking their bedding and clothes with them. As sick and well went off together and the quarantine sheds were beside the cholera hospital, the healthy had every opportunity to develop the infection.

More than 25,000 emigrants had disembarked at Quebec by the middle of June, when the ravages of the disease became most serious. The recently appointed Board of Health was active. Tents were pitched on the Plains of Abraham to accommodate 500 persons; a special hospital was opened near the wharves; tar barrels were burned and artillery discharged; and doctors came from New York and Albany to observe and advise. But for a time Quebec was overwhelmed. In the course of a few days, the cholera carried off 1,500 persons, about one in every 28 of the whole population of the city, including emigrants.[45]

Medical officers were placed on board the St. Lawrence River steamboats and, in order to prevent worse congestion in Quebec, emigrants who appeared to be well were sent on up the river. Montreal was soon in a condition similar to Quebec. All who could fled the city. On the river for a few days all movement stopped, as the boatmen deserted their posts to take refuge in the country. In Upper Canada with the aid of Lieutenant-Governor Sir John Colborne, health boards were created at Cornwall, Prescott, and stopping places on the route to the west. Sheds were erected to house the sick and medical attention was provided when possible. In 1831 New Brunswick had enacted legislation to prevent the spread of infectious disease and create boards of health. Special grants of £1,000 from the Treasury were made for the extra expense borne by the colonial ports for quarantine and hospitals. In Upper Canada the burdens were met by the provincial treasury and voluntary contributions.[46]

Though emigrants travelling steerage made up more than 90 per cent of the Atlantic passenger trade until mid-century, regular packets, merchant vessels, and even timber ships often provided well-furnished cabins. Persons of means could engage cabin passage for £15 to 50 and cross the ocean in comfort, as did the Talbots, the Magraths, and the Stricklands. In 1842, the *Pictou Recorder* and the *Observer* reported the arrival in Halifax of emigrants who were "very becoming in manner." Similar arrivals occurred year by year at Quebec. Sometimes passengers thanked the captains of their vessels publicly for their careful attention; one group planned as a reward for theirs "a handsome silver Snuff Box, value Six Guineas." But though many shipowners were trying to transport their passengers in safety, Lieutenant Low at Liverpool watched vessels put to sea in dangerous condition which he was legally unable to prevent. Against overcrowding in the steerage, and mixed cargoes in the hold, against frauds practised on emigrants by brokers and boarding-house keepers he had no means of redress. In the whole matter, the attitude of the Colonial Office was cautious. To hard-working Low, R. W. Hay, for many years under-secretary in the Colonial Office, wrote instructions to remonstrate as he wished with offenders, but he made it clear that the Office was opposed to any further proceedings as merely showing "the non-existence of a power to compel offending Parties to alter their conduct."[47]

In the North American colonies it was seldom possible to prosecute for breach of the regulations which the law did provide. In New Brunswick where procedure was more expeditious than elsewhere, convictions were had, as in the case of the Brig *Billow* of Newry, and fines were laid for presenting an incorrect passenger list and bringing more passengers than the law allowed.* In Quebec the proceedings were so

---

*The brig carried 49 more adults than the passenger list showed and 37 more than the law allowed; the master was fined £30: Minutes of Executive Council of New Brunswick, 1831.

tedious and expensive that a common summons before a justice of peace cost 10*s*. and required as many days to carry through. Emigrants did not often have the means or the knowledge of the world to enable them to remain in Quebec and conduct a prosecution.

The tragic return of the cholera ship *Brutus* to Liverpool has been described. Though the law officers of the government were advised to take action against the master, no evidence could be produced. According to the Act, the *Brutus* of 384 tons was permitted to carry 287 adult passengers; the list showed only 263. As for other regulations, the statement of the tide surveyor certified that all had been complied with.[48] Here the case was dropped and the survivors of the cholera left to recoup their losses by their own devices.

After spending some time in graving dock, another vessel, the *City of Rochester*, had been dismissed as seaworthy. Eight days out from Liverpool a leak was sprung and the vessel, unable to stand the weather, returned. On arrival the passengers were destitute, having exhausted both food and money. Witnesses to substantiate a breach of the bond that the ship was seaworthy could not be found. When the shipowners offered to carry the passengers out again after a second wait for repairs, no action was taken.[49] To Emigration Commissioner Thomas F. Elliot, who was in hopes of forcing the "harpies to return the passage money to their victims," James Stephen, counsel to the Colonial Office, wrote that the passengers might take action against the charterers: "cold comfort you will say for a set of poor wretches whose destination is America, and who could as easily build a ship as defray the costs of an action. I agree with you, but what more can be done for men when they are injured than to give them a legal remedy?"[50] In time, administrative action was to come to the aid of legal remedies.

Recommendations of Nathaniel Gould, Lieutenant Low, and A. C. Buchanan as representatives respectively of merchant interests, of British, and of Canadian feeling regarding the number of passengers, the amount of food permitted, and the enforcement of penalties met varied reception from officials. Under-Secretary Hay was convinced that poor emigrants were "prodigious sufferers from the want of some wholesome regulations to protect them."[51] But Elliot, after confessing that the Act of 1828 was unfitted for others because its computations had been based on the habits of the Irish peasantry, gave his private opinion that the extreme difficulty of passing a new bill through Parliament, where it was sure to be warmly contested "as well by the advocates of conflicting theories in Political Economy as by the Representatives of opposing interests in Commerce," was conclusive objection to further legislation on the emigrant trade.[52] Stephen too reminded those desirous of reform that the old bill had been the work of practical men and the proposers of new terms would be pressed for more reasons and authority than they could hope to produce.[53]

The pessimists reckoned without the new temper of the country and without William E. Gladstone upon whom as under-secretary fell the duty of championing the proposed reforms after the resignation of Stanley. Like Huskisson, Gladstone felt that humanity and good feeling demanded legislative action: as 51,000 had emigrated in 1831, it was clear that "anything which affected the comforts of such a yearly average number was worthy . . . of attention, especially when it was borne in mind that they were of the poorest condition in the community."[54] When Gladstone had finished, members spoke for the first time in Parliament as if they understood the emigrant trade. Alexander Baring knew of seventeen vessels last year and seven hundred emigrants lost by accidents which had "almost all arisen from improvidence or mismanagement." John Roebuck believed precautions were necessary because of proof of lack of food. W. Smith O'Brien realized that vessels set out on the Atlantic that were not fit to cross the channel. Lord Sandon thought that steerage passengers suffered greatly from overcrowding. Others urged the need for clean water containers, not old oil and indigo casks. And the timber merchants, having been consulted beforehand and being busy with their fight against the appointment of a select committee on trade and the timber duties, wasted few words in debate.[55]

The bill as finally approved after the resignation of Peel's cabinet and the departure of Gladstone, though a step forward, was far from being all that the advocates of reform had desired. The quota of passengers to be carried was reduced from three to every four tons to three to every five tons burden, that being, as Gladstone explained, "the mean between the numbers suggested by Mr. Bonham, our Consul in America, and the London Shipowners' Society."[56] Provisions required were raised from fifty to seventy pounds per passenger. Both food and water were to be approved by the port officer. Penalties for improperly landing passengers and for failing to obtain and produce a correct list of passengers were to be summarily recoverable. Finally there were innovations. A table of prices of provisions for sale on shipboard was to be exhibited; spirits were not to be sold and passengers, if detained before sailing or for forty-eight hours after reaching their destination, were to be maintained by the ship's master, not as Gladstone had said "thrust out like beasts of the field."

The years from 1835 to 1842 saw the last great days of the old emigrant trade. One reads of "two-hundred sail riding at anchor" below the heights of Quebec, of 1,100 ships' arrivals and almost 1,200 departures in 1839, nine-tenths of all sailing from or to the British Isles. Eastbound cargoes in 1839 consisted mainly of 19 products of trees: almost 200,000 tons of white pine, over 160,000 tons of red pine, 25,000 barrels of pot and pearl ashes, over 3,000,000 pieces of deals, 3,000,000 puncheon staves, and some 2,000,000 other pieces, and a little flour, beef, and pork. The westbound cargoes were light, small, manufactured articles, more than 1,000,000 gallons of wine and spirits, and of course emigrants.[57] In 1835 revelations which disclosed to Parliament that British ships were carrying Baltic timber across the Atlantic and returning it as Canadian in order to use the colonial tax preference had suggested a good-sized drop in the space available for emigrants. Nevertheless in 1842 while defending the colonial preference in Parliament, Sir Howard Douglas gave the total British tonnage in the British North American trade as 841,348 with about 600,000 tons of this wholly employed in the timber trade. "The outward tonnage, in ballast chiefly," he went on, "makes freight so cheap as to afford great facilities for emigration."[58]

Little improvement followed the Act of 1835. The emigrant agents at the ports made many complaints in 1836. At Quebec Buchanan, the younger, reported "positive infringements of the Passenger Act"; on one vessel the berths were so shakily built that when a number of them fell down, killing two children, the passengers preferred to lie on the deck; on many vessels water casks were poor, tainted with oil or indigo, and water was scanty; on some vessels liquor was sold.[59] Lack of written agreements between master and passengers usually prohibited proceedings against the offenders.[60] In Liverpool in the year 1837 redress for only 894 out of 3,560 complaints could be obtained.[61] Both the newly appointed Colonial Land and Emigration Commissioners and Lord Sydenham now in Canada had reported to Lord John Russell upon the transportation of emigrants. When therefore in February, 1842, Lord Stanley, the secretary, offered a new bill he proposed merely "to legislate upon the experience of eight or nine years"; the only changes required were matters of detail. He wished the bill to pass "after mature discussion but without any opposition from either side."[62]

Stranger than the request is the fact that it was granted, strange that is until one considers the vast number of interests affected by the other subject then under discussion in the House of Commons—the revision downward of hundreds of British tariff schedules. From early March until their defeat in mid-June, the representatives of the timber trade fought for what they insisted was their very existence, the retention of the colonial timber preference at the rate of 56s. 6d. a load tax on Baltic to an 11s. 6d. tax on Canadian timber.[63] They turned in petitions and memorials from citizens of this and that county and from every port in the kingdom; their most impressive defender played up the services of the timber ships as emigrant carriers; but they had little time for the passenger bill. Protests from the trade made to the Colonial Office did not reach the public.[64] So while the shipping merchants lost part of their preference, the passenger bill became law. New terms increased the water ration to three quarts per day per passenger *in sweet casks*; other terms attempted to protect the emigrant by requiring the licensing of dealers and passage brokers, and by stipulating that emigrant carriers must install permanent hold beams for the lower deck with six feet clear height above them and no more than two tiers of berths. Lifeboats must be carried, and inspection of the construction of the vessel was authorized. Undoubtedly the Act amounted to an invasion of the principle of free contract, and it placed an astounding burden upon the port agents.[65]

Iron and Steam: The Revolution at Sea

That the law rarely moves far ahead of material progress is perhaps as true of the passenger traffic as of any other form of business. Whether permanent construction of the emigrant deck would have become obligatory had the old timber vessels been the only ships offering steerage passage, no one can say. As late as 1848 one shipowner, W. Brown, M.P., declared that "the greater part of the ships . . . carrying out emigrants would never return with the weight of cargo they brought from Quebec, if it were not that the cargo carried the ship instead of the ship carrying the cargo"; he recommended therefore stricter port inspection of ship construction. Nevertheless it is true that the passenger business had grown so heavy that *it* paid quite as well as cargoes of cotton or timber, and both packet boats and general cargo vessels were providing accommodation for steerage passengers. This competition as well as the legislation had begun to require ships properly designed for the conveyance of human beings.[66]

In 1819 Alexander Allan of Glasgow had opened a more or less regular service with British America. The service prospered; its ships grew from little 300-ton brigs to 600- and even 1,000-ton ships, built on the St. Lawrence or the Clyde, and well run. By 1838 Samuel Cunard and his new-found associates in England had won a £6,000 Atlantic mail contract, and in 1840 the *Britannia*, the first Cunarder, sailed to

Boston *via* Halifax. From time to time other owners placed ships on the route until the Allan Line, the Anchor Line, and others of recent days permanently entered the Atlantic traffic.[67] The timber merchants did not suffer ruin from the decrease in preference forced on them in 1842 nor even when the demand for railroad ties declined. From 1845 to 1850, British imports of colonial timber never fell below the maximum of one million loads achieved in 1844. But the emigrant trade which the merchants had fostered was becoming profitable enough to stand on its own feet.

In 1843 and 1844 the emigration agents in the mother country and colonies observed an improvement in conditions of the trade. Official placards posted in United Kingdom ports and prosecutions against dishonest brokers protected the emigrants before they sailed. In the colonies the agents found it necessary to impose few fines for scanty, unwholesome food and water or for overloading.[68] An improvement too in the emigrants' health and a coincident drop in the passenger traffic were noticeable. For example, at Quebec in 1843 only 16 out of 279 vessels carried the full complement of passengers permitted under the law.[69] For the time being, the impression prevailed that conditions worsened as the number of steerage passengers increased, no matter what the tonnage of the vessel; and in these years the numbers of passengers per vessel were small, as may be seen from the following:[70]

Number of vessels carrying	*1843*	*1844*	*1845*
Less than 30 passengers	147	109	—
30–100 "	72	48	56
101–150 "	23	31	
151–200 "	19	17	77[a]
201–250 "	8	6	—
251–300 "	6	5	38[b]
301 or more "	4	6	15

[a]Vessels carrying 101 to 200.
[b]201 to 300 passengers.

More succinct proof of improvement may be had from the record of deaths on the Atlantic voyage and in subsequent quarantine. These fell from 265 or 1.02 per cent of the 22,267 embarked in 1840 to 80 or .38 per cent of the 20,555 embarked in 1843. Progress towards better health was interrupted by the Irish famine and disease of 1846 and 1847 when the death rate rose appallingly.

As in the cholera epidemic of 1832, one improvement in transportation had scarcely been recorded before another disaster revealed new inefficiencies. While the size of the human cargo was growing, a change in shipping began to increase the dangers at sea. In 1845 vessels bringing passengers to Quebec had been so small or carried so few emigrants each that but 147 out of 256 ships had been subject to the terms of the Passenger Act. The truth was that the revolution in the British grain trade, caused by the gradual cessation of protection and in 1846 by the repeal of the Corn Laws, was driving grain vessels to compete with the timber carriers for the lucrative emigrant business, and the quality of accommodations was suffering in the competition. Ships were dirty and ill-managed. Deaths at sea were twice as many in 1846 as in 1845. The greatest cause of the new disaster, however, was the Irish potato famine.[71]

Official British records for emigration do not differentiate national origins before 1855, but modern studies of the earlier period indicate unusually large removals of Irish following partial failure of the potato crop in 1822, 1832, and 1845. By August, 1846, the black rot had ruined the potato gardens upon which Irish life depended, and the great flight began. Frequently the fleeing got only to Scotland where the famine fever soon spread, raising the deaths in Glasgow alone from an annual average of 10,000 to 19,000 in 1847.[72] In 1845 the medical superintendent at Grosse Isle, Dr. G. W. Douglas, cared for 465 emigrants in his temporary hospital. In 1846 he inspected 206 ships, bearing 32,753 passengers as is shown in Table VI of Appendix B; over 200 had died at sea, 892 went at once to the Grosse Isle hospital and of these 68 died, as well as Dr. Douglas's nurse. Henceforth the hospital would employ only those who had had typhus, since "from the horrible state of filth in which the sick are brought ashore from the vessels where fever has occurred, it rarely occurs that the hospital attendants, whose duty is to wash and clean them, escape disease." The most horrifying revelations of Dr. Douglas's reports are those that describe the Irish illness of 1846 and 1847 as a "low fever" and bowel complaint "usually caused by want." The Irish poor law unions, he wrote, shipped out emigrants with only one pound of meal per day. Similar unions in England and Germany provided bread, rice, and "animal food" and medical stores; of 902 of the Germans it was necessary to hospitalize only seven.[73]

Though the colonies demanded and the Emigration Commissioners had prepared a more severe passenger bill for 1847,[74] the Secretary of War and the Colonies, Lord Grey, and the parliamentary Under-Secretary, Benjamin Hawes, had agreed that the time for restrictions was ill-chosen; emigration should be facilitated.[75] In Liverpool and the Irish ports, the government emigration agents, hard pressed since 1843, were now in 1847 unable through lack of dock space and personnel to inspect or protect the hordes of departing emigrants. On vessels sailing to Canada from Limerick, Killala, and New Ross in 1847 one emigrant in every forty died; on vessels from Liverpool and Sligo, one in fourteen; on vessels from Cork one in nine.[76]

Early in 1847, foreseeing the result of this transference of a home problem to the new-world ports, Earl Grey had assured Lord Elgin in Canada that he would propose a vote of money as a precautionary aid to the Canadian government. Whatever may be the modern judgment upon a policy which permitted wholesale unassisted emigration as one solution of the perennial Irish disasters, Grey exhibited here an appreciation of Canadian feelings far beyond that of the Lords Commissioners of Her Majesty's Treasury. When Lord Elgin announced the need for an additional £14,738 2s. 10d. currency, the Lords Commissioners expressed surprise that the Canadian Department of Accounts had not anticipated the demand for more emigrant sheds at Grosse Isle. As for "other charges now brought forward under the head of 'Orphans of Emigrants' and 'Clergy Expenses,' " these did not appear to the "Lords to come within the intentions" of the imperial government. Four years and reams of correspondence had passed when, in August, 1853, the objections to the Canadian claims on account of "the Expenses attending the Immigration" of 1847 were finally removed.[77]

Long before the accounts were closed, efforts to correct weaknesses in the passenger legislation had begun. The ineffective amending act pushed through Parliament hurriedly in July, 1847, had forbidden the carriage of dangerous cargoes, gunpowder, green hides.[78] In February, 1848, the Right Honourable Henry Labouchere, president of the Board of Trade, brought in a bill to provide enlarged space and diet for emigrants at sea. When he announced that out of 106,000 emigrants to Canada and New Brunswick in the last year, 6,100 had perished on the voyage, 4,100 immediately on landing, and 5,200 subsequently in hospitals, no one questioned the urgency of the problem. On second reading, M. J. O'Connell hoped that "no mongrel notions of free trade" would stop the progress of the bill; even Hume rose to insist that it was "absolutely imperative" for the House to adopt some such measure. If members needed further education in the realities of the emigrant trade, it was effectively provided by reading into the debates the less painful portions of the description of a crossing to Quebec written by Lord Monteagle's nephew, Stephen de Vere. In the steerage quarters in which de Vere took passage with emigrants from his own part of Ireland, he found meat of the worst quality, water insufficiently dealt out, beds never aired, passengers never washed, liquor sold "producing scenes of unchecked blackguardism," and lights prohibited, undoubtedly wisely, for the vessel "was freighted with Government powder for the garrison at Quebec."[79]

Disturbing as is the extract preserved in the parliamentary *Debates*, it is gentle in contrast with the parts of de Vere's letter which were omitted. Not only did he condemn health regulations as ineffective "notwithstanding the great zeal and high abilities of the Government agents," but he wrote also:

Before the Emigrant has been a Week at Sea he is an altered Man. How can it be otherwise? Hundreds of Poor People, Men, Women, and Children of all Ages, from the drivelling Idiot of Ninety to the Babe just born, huddled together without Light, without Air, wallowing in Filth and breathing a fetid Atmosphere, sick in Body, dispirited in Heart, the fevered Patients lying between the Sound, in sleeping Places so narrow as almost to deny them the Power of indulging, by a Change of Position, the natural Restlessness of the Disease; by their agonizing Ravings disturbing those around, and predisposing them through the Effect of the Imagination, to imbibe the Contagion; living without Food or Medicine, . . . dying without the Voice of Spiritual Consolation, and buried in the Deep without the Rites of the Church. . . . In many ships the filthy Beds, teeming with all Abominations, are never required to be brought on deck and aired; the narrow Space between the sleeping Berths and the Piles of Boxes is never washed or scraped, but breathes up a damp and fetid Stench, until the Day before the Arrival at Quarantine, when all Hands are required to "scrub up" and put on a fair Face for the Doctor and Government Inspector.[80]

By March 28, 1848, less than two months after introduction, another passenger bill to amend the Act of 1842 received Royal assent. Though it too failed to match the hopes of the humanitarians or the specifications drawn up by the Emigration Commissioners, it did limit persons carried to one for every two tons, it increased space per emigrant from ten to twelve feet of deck and, since emigrants could seldom provide enough food themselves, it required a ship's cook, provisions, and cooking apparatus. On the advice of medical associations that doctors could not be obtained, the government "reluctantly" abstained from making it obligatory for shipmasters to engage one. Accompaniments to the change in the law included a slight increase in the number of port emigration agents and an Order in Council for "preserving Order and Securing Cleanliness and Ventilation" on shipboard. However humane, however bold in interfering with freedom in business these regulations were, it must be remarked that measures for their enforcement were lacking. Pushed and pulled, first by practical men who pointed out that in Liverpool alone the passenger business was worth £600,000 a year in fares and employed more than half a million tons of shipping, and second by sensitive humanitarians who demanded correction of every evil exposed, Parliament was replying in a very modern fashion by "wishful" legislation.[81]

In June, 1848, on a surprise visit to Grosse Isle, Lord Elgin found very few emigrants and the hospital sheds and the new military command in excellent shape. In the same year in the United Kingdom, prosecutions for infringements of the terms of the law which in 1846 had brought in £2,000 in Liverpool dropped to two cases. A similar drop occurred in New Brunswick which had fined nine of ten shipmasters in 1846 and even in Quebec where five convictions had been obtained.[82] Early in 1849 the Emigration Commissioners prepared a consolidation of previous law and went a few steps further in humanizing the emigrant trade by inserting regulations for ventilation on shipboard, by increasing the quantity and variety of food, and by including cabin passengers and crew in the formula which permitted two adults per ton of the vessel's registered measurements.[83]

But legislation could not still rumours, rumours of death at sea, of actual neglect in port inspection. Members of the Commons had heard from Sir Aubrey de Vere's brother Stephen; now in 1852 Chisholm Anstey, a protégé of W. Smith O'Brien, assured them that on his voyage to the Cape the passengers were "in fear of plague, pestilence and famine." Despite improvements achieved by the law and the port emigration officers, conditions on emigrant vessels were described as generating "disease and immorality of every sort." As for port inspection, no mention was made of Lieutenant Robert Low who had died in Liverpool in 1839, ill and exhausted after attempting to supervise the sailing of 31,578 emigrants in one season, or of the lone Limerick officer's responsibility for both shores of the Shannon River on its sixty-mile course to the sea. The government might bow to criticism and dismiss Lieutenant Hodder who, it was reported, gave ships clearance as a matter of form, but when thirty vessels with some 8,000 emigrants sailed from four miles of Liverpool's docks on a single tide, what could a few officers do in the way of personal, structural, and technical inspection?[84]

When the select committee which the members demanded had sat under the chairmanship of Sidney Herbert (Wiltshire), the government produced the most explicit bill so far in the history of passenger legislation. Terminology was clearly defined: "passenger vessel" meant a ship carrying more than one person to every twenty-five tons burden; the law applied to any voyage from the United Kingdom outside Europe except to the Mediterranean. Steam vessels might ship two and one-half times more passengers than sailing vessels for which the numbers remained one adult per two tons burden. Decks must be one and a half inches thick, berths six feet long and eighteen inches wide, single men must be berthed apart from other passengers, food must be cooked, and lifeboats, privies, hospital space, passenger stewards, and a medical man (within certain limitations) must be provided. Dock trustees were authorized to pass by-laws to regulate porterage and all aspects of embarkation. Special forms for passage contracts and licensing of passage brokers became obligatory.[85]

Until one considers the revolutionary changes that were transforming British life in the nineteenth century and the slight administration provided for enforcing the Act, it would seem that the legislation of 1852 might have stood for years. A comprehensive memorandum covering the law guided the inspections in thirteen United Kingdom ports of twenty-four officers, all on naval half-pay and all receiving in addition annual salaries ranging from £120 to 400.[86] Year after year, the Colonial Office tried to reward the emigration officers more fully by increasing budgets submitted for approval, like that for 1853-4 which is reproduced in Table XII of Appendix B. Unfortunately these officers were overworked, always in Liverpool, often elsewhere when they had to watch a long coast beyond their regular port. No other of the British ports sent out as many as 3,000 emigrants in one month. On an average winter month Liverpool embarked 7,000 emigrants. There in 1850 one officer with two assistants, one clerk, and three medical aides reported upon 568 sailings and superintended the embarkation of 174,188 passengers.[87] Little wonder they could not carry out fully the multitudinous, technical inspections the law required. Nevertheless the good work of the emigrant agents was mentioned again and again in Parliament and cold figures of losses at sea in the years 1847 to 1853 show one in 1,447 souls lost from ports inspected by the officers and one in 720 from ports not under their supervision.[88]

Meanwhile a revolution in transportation was outmoding the provisions of the law. The better construction of sailing vessels and the use of iron and steam were increasing passenger capacity enormously. Records from 1854 list the departure from the United Kingdom of 55 vessels bearing 300 to 400 adults each, 49 bearing 400 to 500, and 88 carrying more than 500 each, in contrast with only 49 bearing less than 300.[89] In the first years of the Act of 1852, emigrant agents reported exceptional loss of life at sea. What still caused real alarm was of course disease, but now also the use of iron, iron built into the ship and iron as cargo, railway bars from Liverpool, iron pigs from Glasgow. Both deflected the compass, according to contemporary belief; the iron cargoes caused the vessel to labour and spring leaks, and the passengers had to work the pumps and became "hard fagged."[90] From Quebec, Buchanan described two cases: the *Argyle* carrying iron for railroads foundered with a few passengers, and the *Annie Jane* from Liverpool bearing 120 tons of rails, 812 tons of bars etc., and 469 passengers sprang a leak, put back, landed 130 passengers, sailed again, and off the Isle of Barra went down drowning all but 61 of the 334 passengers. Similar reports came from all quarters. Once again an epidemic of cholera, too, ran through Atlantic shipping.[91]

The interest of the House of Commons in passenger vessels was live and persistent. Within a year another select committee set to work, especially appointed "to inquire into the recent cases of extensive Loss of Life aboard Emigrant ships, whether by Sickness, Wreck, or other Causes." After publishing a massive volume of evidence in April the committee, and it was a strong one with John O'Connell in the chair, presented a second set of findings along with its conclusions on July 5, 1854. The evidence of T. W. C. Murdock, chairman of the Emigration Commissioners, of Commander Lean and Captain Schomberg, the port emigration officers at London and Liverpool, of Dr. George Douglas, medical officer from Grosse Isle, and of A. C. Buchanan of Quebec convinced them, first, that in British ports owners and charterers did not take the precautions that were taken in other countries to lighten the strain of an iron cargo and, second, that the emigration officers in the ports lacked the power to alter the load below deck. Interested witnesses protested that legislature should not "fetter mercantile enterprise." But the committee concluded that "security to human life is a paramount consideration to any other"; it therefore strongly recommended the removal of all uncertainty regarding the emigrant officers' right to control outgoing cargo. In November, 1853, in anticipation of this published recommendation, the Emigration Commissioners authorized their port officers to permit no vessel to carry out more deadweight cargo than two-thirds of its registered tonnage.[92]

For the rest, the committee's recommendations for better protection of emigrants from agents on land and hazards at sea, for more space (as advised by Mrs. Caroline Chisholm from her experience in the ports), for better ventilation (*via* the booby hatch), for better navigation instruments, a better diet, and sure-fire legal procedures resulted in the Act of 1855, the Magna Carta of the emigrant.[93] Its 103 clauses of specifications included 11 pages of forms required for passenger lists, licences, and so on, 6 pages on brokers' contracts, 5 pages on passengers' rights. As well as a heavier bond, the master must provide 18 square feet of deck space for each adult steerage passenger, 7 feet height between decks, a doctor if carrying more than 300 passengers, and a multitude of mechanisms and services now listed in stated accord with the number of emigrants carried. Crew and passengers must be certified as well before sailing. However, though the assisted emigrants to Australia were being shipped from government-sponsored depots, all other emigrants were left to fend for themselves prior to embarkation, because the committee's concern over unwholesome port boarding-houses conflicted with the principles of free enterprise.[94]

The severity of the Act of 1855 received plaudits at first. Soon however the emigration officers, trying to inspect the mechanics of ventilation, water closets, the combustibility of coal, and the effect of iron on navigating instruments, met bitter criticism from the shipping trade. Worse than that, the new regulations were raising the price of passage at Irish ports; it was alleged that emigration was being curtailed and that shipowners preferred to forego the traffic rather than conform to the terms of the Act.[95]

The latter contention would be difficult to validate generally for, as ever in the emigrant trade, a new crisis had arisen in shipping. Needs created by the Crimean War had withdrawn many British ships from the Atlantic and, now that the Navigation Acts had been removed, United States ships appeared with emigrant cargoes, making all the more necessary the co-operation with the United States in passenger legislation which the select committees had recommended. In 1853 and 1854 all emigrants to British America from Liverpool sailed in British vessels. In the years from 1856 to 1859 inclusive only 76 per cent of the emigrants to the British American colonies travelled in British vessels. In 1857, 200 of the 247 passenger vessels sailing from Liverpool with 85,837 of the 100,121 emigrants who left that port for North America were United States vessels. When critics of the Act of 1855 contended further that the new severity had not only forced ships out of the traffic but also directed emigrants to the United States, the Emigration Commissioners replied that the Irish famine had deposited in British America thousands more emigrants than those colonies could then absorb; these had moved on to the United States and the drift so established had been increased by the remittances sent home to bring others to join the first.[96]

The Act of 1855 closed an epoch. In the half century since the first passenger law in 1803, the government had tried the revealing experiment in freedom of 1827-8 and then, during a revolution in social outlook and technical progress, the development of regulations to care for every danger the emigrant traveller might encounter. The result was a code of law so complex that the small corps of port agents could not enforce all of it and the Emigration Commissioners were frequently compelled to act in a judicial capacity to settle the controversies that arose. By 1856 the machinery of enforcement was due for an overhaul. None came, for a drop in the emigrant traffic decreased pressure on the agents in the ports. They continued in their devotion to their duties until their work was transferred to the Treasury at the opening of the year 1873. Tributes to their accomplishments followed them into retirement. Even the criticism which they had aroused was often clear evidence of public awareness of problems they themselves had disclosed.

Some legislative reform was accomplished after 1855, though not without the customary protests. The plaint of the timber merchants against interference with free enterprise was replaced by the modern voice of the investor in the new steamship companies. Again members of Parliament rose, as one had in 1852 to report that Mr. Cunard's partner, Mr. M'Iver, had sold out his interest rather than prepare for more costly regulations. But reform went forward, often by means of the power vested in the Emigration Commissioners, to bring more shipping under control, to provide for carrying horses and other animals separately from emigrants as in the Act of 1863, and to care for swifter crossings and other changes that followed the adoption of iron and steam. The record of deaths on the Atlantic crossing and in quarantine gave proof of the value of the reform legislation and the technical progress in shipping. Deaths which had averaged 1.02 per cent of those embarked in 1840 and 16 per cent in the famine year of 1847 dropped to .74 per cent in 1854. Gradually this tragic aspect of emigration disappeared until in 1859 the loss was but .19 per cent.[97]

Steam brought the last great revolution of the period. As early as 1853 the establishment of the Canadian Navigation Company line of steamers from Liverpool to Quebec much enlarged cabin traffic. In 1854, the Company made 9 trips with an average of 246 passengers per trip; by 1858 it carried nearly 18 per cent of all steerage passengers to the St. Lawrence. Weekly schedules began in 1859 when 6 steamships made 28 passages.[98] Gradually steam captured the business. Of 201 vessels to Quebec in 1856, 14 were steamships; of 120 in 1859 there were 35 steamers bringing almost one-half of all that year's passengers.[99] In 1863 some 13,500 emigrants came by steamer, only 1,750 by sail.[100]

Crossings became regular. Unscrupulous agents and port boarding-house keepers had little opportunity to impose upon inexperienced country folk as they hurried to catch their boats. Modern business demanded sanctity of contract. The steamship was thoroughly modern and increasingly efficient. As the Quebec emigrant agent reported, an excellent class of shipowners was now catering for the trade. Through the power of humane-minded legislators, through advances in business and seamanship, and the compassion of a corps of emigrant agents stirred by the sight of suffering, the Atlantic crossing had lost much of its early terror and discomfort and its danger of disease and death.

VIII. THE GREAT EMIGRATIONS,
1830-1860

WHILE THE FIGHT for assisted emigration from the British Isles was still in its early stages, a voluntary emigration began which was to exceed in numbers and variety all that had gone before. Many forces caused this more widespread uprooting of population. Economic, social, and political changes that had been making for upheaval since 1815 and before reached their height in the years following 1825. The depression and disorder of 1819 had been succeeded by a reaction for the better. Order had been preserved by repressive measures, it is true, but prosperity had been encouraged by the commercial reforms of Robinson, Vansittart, and Huskisson in 1822, 1823, and 1824. Poorer householders had been relieved from the exactions of the house and window tax; the manufacturing classes had been encouraged by the reduction of duties on spirits, wines, coffee, and sugar; and with the repeal of the Combination Laws, the workers had for the first time been legally permitted to combine for the purpose of raising wages. Changes of such importance were not suggested for another twenty years.

The result of these reforms was soon apparent in increased consumption and production, the rising prices of agricultural products, and finally in the fever of speculation of 1825. Vivid pictures of the recklessly enthusiastic spirit of the country have been left us: rich and poor, workman and staid spinster, hurried to invest their savings in the phantom companies that sprang up. Soon one company and then another failed. Towns in consternation saw their bank doors close, and the panic came. How weak were the foundations upon which prosperity had been built was soon evident. In the north the weavers voiced their desperation in loud demands for free corn, while they spent their nights in breaking the machines that represented one cause of their ruin. Parliament let in a few hundred thousand quarters of bonded corn, but full repeal did not come. Very slowly the country began to recover, and as it did demands of another sort promised further uneasiness.

THE UPROOTING

The year before the great Reform, Miss Martineau found society in "a discontented and tumultuous state; its most ignorant portion being acted upon at once by hardship at home and example from abroad; and there was every reason to expect a deadly struggle before parliamentary reform could be carried. The ignorant and misled among the peasantry and artisans looked upon the French and other revolutions as showing that men had only to take affairs into their own hands."[1] While the hungry and uninformed thought that parliamentary reform would feed them, the intelligent tradesmen and others, seeing its value in a fairer light, worked patiently for change.

No special recovery followed the Reform Act of 1832. For a time the growth of the factory industries continued to draw workers into the rising towns of the north. Before 1841 about 500,000 natives of agricultural districts had moved to industrial Lancashire. Some of the thousands who were denied relief after the enactment of the Poor Law of 1834 also made their way into the new occupations. By 1837 the textile industry had become the largest single employer in Great Britain with more than 500,000 workers, of whom many (especially in Paisley and Glasgow) were severely upset by the shift from handicraft to machine methods. Metal manufacturing stood next in amount of industrial employment, and then came the potteries. Slightly different in character was railway construction which accounted for the employment of between 200,000 and 300,000. This expansion of industry at first created markets which consumed the produce of English agriculture. But farmers could still suffer from extraordinary overproduction, as in the harvests of the mid-thirties. Everyone suffered when railroad building, the iron and coal, and the textile industries slowed down painfully in the depression years which began in 1836–7 and lasted into the late forties.[2]

As foreign competition grew and the northern occupations could no longer absorb the surplus agricultural labour from the south, emigration of the farming population increased. Stagnation and gloom settled down upon the manufacturing communities. "In all our large towns, Leeds, Manchester, Stockport, Liverpool," wrote the *Manchester Guardian* on November 17, 1841, "those destitute seeking employment are in the tens of thousands." By 1843 Stockport had 1,058 horse power of machinery idle, enough to employ 5,290 operatives, and an office was opened in the town for the sale of tickets to emigrants. Unemployment emptied 1,800 houses in Oldham. Textile workers learned to use the spade, frequented soup kitchens, or sought means to emigrate.[3]

Industrial workers began to adopt the policy of the northern weavers of 1815 and in Carlisle and nearby built up their emigration groups again. So drastically had the weavers' earning power declined that the weekly wage, which in the years 1811 to 1818 would have purchased 131 pounds of food, had provided only 83 pounds since the year 1825.[4]

In their reaction to high prices, decreasing employment, and the introduction of labour-saving machinery, union members readily took up the popular strength-through-scarcity and wage-fund theories with the idea of depleting their numbers for the good of all. The Society of Brush Makers, the Manchester Mechanics and Engineers' Friendly Society, the Amalgamated Society of Engineers, Machinists, Millwrights, Smiths, and Pattern Makers, the Compositors, the Bookbinders, the Journeymen Steam Engine Makers and Millwrights Friendly Society, the Flint Glass Makers, the Potters' Joint Stock Emigration Company, and a host of other groups began in the 1840's to assist their fellows to emigrate and to advocate emigration through their trade publications. In an announcement in the *Potters' Examiner* of June 8, 1844, the call for a meeting to discuss emigration opened with the title "A Home for the Poor" and closed with the admonition "Oh Shame that BREAD should be so dear and HUMAN LIVES so cheap." Independent co-operative loan and later emigration and colonization societies were founded to help the needy to emigrate, one notable group, the Family Colonization Loan Society, being assisted by that friend of emigrants, Mrs. Chisholm.[5]

In Wales where local spirit was strong and the abuses of the old English Poor Law had not developed, the new Poor Law of 1834 along with the commutation of tithes among a nonconformist population brought heavy tax burdens. At the same time an agricultural people felt the disorders of adjustment to a mining economy and became doubly sensitive to shifts in industrial prosperity. Naturally coal mining communities so far away as Nova Scotia and Pennsylvania received profit from this disaster in the accession of experienced miners.

Another group joined the discontented in 1846 when after long discussion and the sudden emergency of the Irish famine the final repeal of the Corn Laws became fact and foreign corn entered Great Britain quite freely. Little by little the protective system had been going down before the victories of Huskisson, Peel, and the other advocates of freer trade. Though the victories eventually built up the wealth of nineteenth-century Britain, for awhile each caused unemployment and often emigration—for example when the department of the Board of Excise at Manchester which had collected the duties on calicoes was abolished,[6] when the malt and candlemaking industries were upset by the removal of the duty on their products, or when the government cut off the duty on barilla and salt and so ended the livelihood of thousands of Scottish kelp workers. But nothing so far had equalled the effect of the loss of the farmers' crops in 1845 and the growing fears that seemed justified by the repeal of the last of the Corn Laws in the spring of 1846. Some

English farmers who had barely survived the ups and downs since 1830 now prepared for removal to other occupations or to the colonies. In Ireland the proprietors felt the loss of advantage in marketing wheat in the new English manufacturing centres; the impulse to enter cattle raising, which rapid transportation to England by steamboat had encouraged for some years past, was greatly strengthened. Competition among the tenant farmers intensified.[7] And with the displaced small farmers there went to the emigration ports many of the small tradesmen whom they had patronized.

Distant from these scenes of change though Scotland seemed to be, it could not escape the same revolutionary adjustments. Highland proprietors, too, converted farmlands to pasturage because the new industrial cities created a demand for meat and the new steamboats provided an easy means of shipping livestock southward. Farm cottages were levelled, whole villages abandoned, and heather grew where the farmer had sowed his corn. A few of the displaced found work in the Lowlands, though opportunities there were limited by the immigration of cheap Irish labour. Some tried the kelp industry while it lasted. When bad weather ruined the potato crop at the same time as the general depression began, many were saved from starvation only by charity or assisted emigration. After considering every means of saving a people from destitution, the parliamentary committee of 1841 recommended emigration, a strange reversal since 1803 when similar investigations brought about the enactment of a passenger vessel law partially designed to stop emigration.[8]

In Ireland political as well as the economic grievances from rents and tithes were growing. The legislation of 1829 which disfranchised the 40-shilling freeholders by raising the qualification to £10 removed the landlord's incentive for retaining a large number of voters on his property and increased the consolidation of farms and the insecurity of small farmers. Some of these travelled north where their lower standards and higher rents enabled them to replace tenants who sold out and emigrated. Others if not assisted to emigrate by their landlords joined the secret orders of White Boys or Peep O'Day Boys who spread the hysteria of the agrarian insurrection. In Ulster the weavers, though troubled by new machines, were still working, but cottage spinning almost ceased in the early 1830's.[9]

Fluctuations in the supply of the basic food, the potato, were usually large, reducing not only the income of the Irish but also their health. When in 1832 the cholera reached Liverpool from Central Europe and then moved across to Belfast and interior Ireland, those Irish who could flee thronged to the ports. New stringent passenger vessel regulations cut down emigration for one year, the following, but only for that one. The poorer Irish never forgot the premonition of doom that settled over their homeland in 1832.[10] Emigration from Ireland between 1830 and 1840 reached probably 650,000 persons, one-third, and that mainly the poorer, going to Great Britain, two-thirds to North America. Sailings from the northwest predominated, particularly from Londonderry and Belfast in Ulster and Sligo in Connaught. Though in some villages in Sligo two-thirds of the population emigrated in three years, Ulster alone accounted for 46 per cent of all Irish emigrants, Munster for 27, and Leinster for 16.[11]

Neither the slight improvement which began after 1835 nor the effect of emigration was uniform throughout the island, yet the Irish population increase dropped from 14 per cent between 1821 and 1831 to less than 6 per cent between 1831 and 1841, and that was a mere beginning. The famine and the final repeal of the Corn Laws being almost coincident gave proprietors additional opportunity for consolidating holdings. So great was distress, emigration, and the loss of young people that between 1841 and 1851 the population of Ireland declined one-fifth.[12] In February, 1846, both Sir Robert Peel and Daniel O'Connell had warned the House of Commons that famine was imminent in Ireland. In March Sir James Graham tried to bring into Parliament a motion for granting temporary aid to the fever-stricken Irish. In May another member described the town of Mallow in County Cork where six thousand in a population of ten thousand were utterly destitute, in want of food. Partial failure of the Irish potato crop had occurred in 1845, as indeed it had in 1839, 1837, 1835, 1832, and various years before. But this time England and Scotland and western Europe too had lost perhaps one-sixth of their yield.

Early summer found the Irish people in debt for food, many without seed for planting, and most of them exhausted, just waiting. One year of shortage had been endured; another would end their world.[13] Almost overnight in July, 1846, the blight hit the potato fields. On July 27 when Father Theobald Matthew, the Irish temperance leader, travelled from Cork to Dublin "the doomed plant bloomed in all the luxuriance of an abundant harvest." When he returned on August 3, he observed with sorrow "one wild waste of putrefying vegetation. In many places the wretched people were seated on the fences of their decaying gardens, wringing their hands and wailing bitterly the destruction that had left them foodless."[14]

Peel's government before it fell had begun to provide food for sale by the local relief committees, though it had done little to touch the basic causes of Irish poverty. As the head of the new government, Lord John Russell promised extensive reforms, then wavered and retracted. In August, quoting from the Poor Law investigation, Lord Devon's commission on land tenure, and the recent census, he illustrated for Parliament the habitual, extreme poverty and the meagre potato diet of the Irish. He read Lord Enniskillen's letter to show the fearful state of Fermoy. Relief would be given, he said, by private traders, made work would be financed by loans to be repaid later. Hastily the government prepared relief projects, mainly the building of roads. For a time these projects employed about one-tenth of the population, paid them less than enough to live on and, while encouraging neglect of farming, also helped to spread the fever among the starved and weakened workers.[15] In October, 1846, Russell was still convinced that the government could not feed the people; by July, 1847, free food rations were being distributed to more than three million.[16]

As realization of the famine spread, Irish ports filled up with vessels bearing cargoes of grain. In one week one hundred vessels brought corn and bread stuffs into the harbour of Cork, but the potato-fed Irish did not know how to bake bread; they lacked ovens for cooking. Before the schooners from the United States and British America were unloaded, they were mobbed by swarms of creatures entreating to be carried away. Escape was the cry of all. At the House of Lords, Thomas Spring Rice, Lord Monteagle, received a petition from the inhabitants of Rattibarren, Barony of Liny in Sligo, begging that the Lords might be "so charitable as to send us to America." Eighty-four persons had signed it, but the signers declared that their names were meaningless, for they could get "as many as would nearly reach across the Channel." But "take us away," they wrote, "and we will bind ourselves to defend the Queen's right in any place we are sent."[17]

Emigrants did not wait as before for the spring fleet; the stream to the ports went on month by month throughout the winter of 1846-7. Thousands rushed to Liverpool even in January. The hysteria for going swept through whole communities, so that some Galway villages lost almost a third of their population in March, and April, 1847.[18] Roads were crowded with would-be emigrants carrying their few possessions and often followed by hundreds of neighbours. They spent the mite of cash they had saved for a final emergency, perhaps for burial, the bit the landlord had given, or the shillings they had begged by the roadside in striking a bargain with the waiting shipmaster. Some thousands of these, it is true, got no farther than English or Scottish ports. By the end of January, 1847, according to Lord Brougham, nineteen-twentieths of the 22,640 paupers receiving relief in Liverpool were Irish. Within the next three months 80,000 to 90,000 more Irish paupers arrived. Many had received a few shillings of "emigration money" from their landlords and less than one-third of all would have means to sail for America.[19] Six years earlier, William Smith O'Brien, M.P., Limerick, had warned the House of Commons that life on potatoes and no milk, with unemployment during thirty weeks of the year for 2,300,000 of the Irish population must inevitably reduce the living standard of labour in England.[20]

For Ireland the first effect of the "disastrous forties" was an enormous swelling of the flood of emigrant labourers and small farmers. Gradually, too, the new Poor Law acted as a stimulus to emigration; large proprietors reduced tenants to avoid a rise in their rates; the position of the smaller landholder was undermined. In 1853 an Irish editor could write, "The Poor Law is the great and permanent depopulator of Ireland."[21]

In addition to such obvious changes as have been noted, developments characteristic of the first half of the nineteenth century quickened the desire for emigration. The increase in the use of the English language, in education, and in printing are influences so old and commonplace today that it is difficult to comprehend their revolutionary effect when new. In Ireland in 1822 some two million of the people spoke only Irish; by 1861 less than 164,000 were so cut off from the progressive Atlantic community. As more and more thousands in the British Isles learned to read they were subjected to the influences of such periodicals as *Chambers's Edinburgh Journal* which generally and *The Times* which mildly favoured emigration to the colonies. Local newspapers in many places took up the topic of emigration when employment failed. Special periodicals devoted almost entirely to emigration were founded, for instance William H. G. Kingston's *Colonist* and the *Emigrants' Penny Magazine*, the *Emigration Gazette*, the *Emigration Record and Colonial Journal*. To the early works descriptive of the British colonies by Adam Hodgson, John MacTaggart, Captain Basil Hall, T. W. Magrath, John Howison, Charles F. Grece, and others, there were now added books deliberately designed to encourage emigrants: Thomas Rolph's *Comparative Advantages between the United States and Canada*, John Robert Godley's *Answer to the Question What is to be Done with the Unemployed Labourers*, John Silk Buckingham's *Canada, Nova Scotia, New Brunswick and the Other British Provinces*, and many more including emigrant guides by the score.[22]

By any but the emigrants desperately fleeing famine, information about the New World was gathered and long-term plans for removal had to be made. Groups of would-be emigrants often met to share information about America. Parishes that wished to encourage emigration tried to have maps available; clergymen and emigrant societies sometimes maintained libraries of emigrant publications. It has been said reasonably enough that "reading families" were oftenest the emigrating families. Of all reading material, letters from friends or relatives in British America undoubtedly were the most influential. Nothing could bear surer proof of the chances for betterment; nothing else could bind up the ties broken by emigration. Letters were often passed from hand to hand or read in assembled gatherings until they literally fell to pieces. If they contained the promise of a prepaid ticket to Quebec or St. John, the receiver was the envy of all.

In the middle of the nineteenth century no form of emigration promotion was more influential than the remittance. Except for evidence from banks and mercantile houses, accurate records of the amounts and places of origin of these remittances, whether the United States or British America, cannot be obtained because of the variety and the privacy of the transactions. As early as 1820 and 1821 when the timber merchants began to fear a drop in the colonial preference on their special cargo, their agents had been selling prepaid passages from Ireland in their offices in Canada and New Brunswick. In the years from 1834 to 1842, four Upper Canada banks alone sent to Great Britain settlers' remittances amounting to more than £20,000. As late as 1857, "large sums of money" were still arriving in northeast Scotland from Upper Canada to enable labourers to emigrate. Year after year, the emigration agent, Buchanan, reported remittances ranging in amount from an estimated £460,000 in 1848 to £957,000 in 1850; about two-thirds of these amounts reached the mother country through Liverpool, one-third through Dublin. The custom had so grown that in 1854 Irish emigrants in British North America probably paid for half the transportation and provided much of the sea stores of their countrymen sailing from the port of Londonderry.[23] The same year the cash contribution from North America struck its all time high, £1,730,000.[24]

Even improving business practices and the advancement of the sciences aided the outward movement. The extension of the banking system to the colonies, on which it will be remembered Edward Gibbon Wakefield and his fellows in the North American Colonial Association of Ireland set much store, and the growing activities of the Bank of Montreal and other companies offered a safer means of transmitting funds and facilitated capital loans. On the Atlantic more frequent sailings, and in the colonies improved transportation, speeded up the postal service and so by bringing colony and mother country closer together made emigration less of an exile. The "mail post from Home" which at first broke York's isolation only annually arrived *via* Halifax or New York almost daily when Mrs. Jameson wintered there soon after the Rebellion. Progress in the construction of steamboats and canals in North America began to open the highway of the St. Lawrence as early as 1809 and the Great Lakes after 1827. In the British Isles greater facility of intercourse and the coming of the railway age rendered more widely accessible the mass of information which was appearing in periodicals, leaflets, and advertisements.

At the same time the very vigour of the emigration movement encouraged subsidiary enterprise, particularly in the sale of transportation and land, which in itself acted as an incentive to emigration. In the early days of the emigrant trade the travellers bought their passage in the port directly from the shipmaster or the shipping company. As the trade assumed the character of big business, the shipowners sold their space outright to agents who roamed the country drumming up emigrants and selling tickets at whatever rates the traffic would bear. The government endeavoured to eliminate graft by licensing the agents but country emigrants were easy to impose upon and the agents sometimes ruthless. By mid-century when reliable passenger companies, usually operating steamboats, had pretty well replaced the old cargo-emigrant shippers the publicity became more trustworthy.

The land business proved as enticing to private agents as the sale of transportation. The activities carried on by the Canada Company, the New Brunswick and Nova Scotia Land Company, the British American Land Company, and the short-lived organizations in which E. G. Wakefield and Thomas Rolph were influential have been mentioned. Individuals too, moved by pecuniary and sometimes magnanimous interests, travelled about the British Isles advocating emigration and of course selling land.[25] It is probable also that United States land agents were effective in familiarizing British residents with New World possibilities even when the Britons were determined to remain under their own flag. Of those agents who acted in the sale of British American lands, James Forest of York appears to have been one of the first. In Belfast in 1820 he chartered a ship and, after visiting market towns in Tyrone, Monaghan, and Armagh, he made contracts with emigrant passengers who were presumably to buy his land. At Londonderry, A. Campbell built up a similar trade in New Brunswick lands.[26]

The sales record of William Cattermole who spent the years 1831 and 1832 in the south of England outstrips that of all others available

FIGURE 6. The Emigration Agent's Office. The Passage Money Paid. (*Illustrated London News*, May 10, 1851.)

today. Apparently he received a commission on emigrants sent out, though he worked during the period with the confidence and approval of the Colonial Office and of Sir John Colborne of Upper Canada. Visiting the parishes in which there was said to be a redundant population, he distributed handbills descriptive of Upper Canada and gave lectures on the province, concerning the capabilities of which he believed the better class of his countrymen were "as ignorant as they [were] about Japan."[27] In the year 1831 he was instrumental in directing over 1,200 persons from Norfolk, Suffolk, Kent, and Essex to Upper Canada. During the same time, according to reports, he sold 100,000 acres of Upper Canadian land to purchasers in Kent, Sussex, and London.

Though neither the home nor the colonial governments gave direct encouragement to emigrants, they did try to provide would-be emigrants with essential information. After 1828 when A. C. Buchanan was appointed at Quebec as the first emigrant agent to any port, the Treasury and the Colonial Office spread a growing band of representatives in the great ports of the mother country and the colonies. As a result of the designation of five commissioners of emigration in June, 1831, the agents in the colonies were required to report upon local opportunities which would interest prospective emigrants. By February, 1832, the government was prepared to distribute "Information published by His Majesty's Commissioners for Emigration respecting the British Colonies in North America." Setting forth the simple facts on land and crop prices, on the means of transmitting funds *via* Smith, Payne and Smiths of Lombard Street, London, to "the bank in Montreal," and on the duties and names of the emigrant agents in the ports (A. C. Buchanan at Quebec, A. Wedderburn at St. John, G. H. Smith at St. Andrews, and J. Cunard at Miramichi), this concise information sheet could be used as a sane corrective to the extravagant promises of private agents. When the Commissioners' office was discontinued in 1832, the work was carried on by their secretary, Thomas Frederick Elliot, a regular employee of the Colonial Office. The government sheet so begun appeared thereafter with current corrections from the colonies, whether emigration details were handled by a Colonial Office employee, an Agent-General for Emigration, or by the Colonial Land and Emigration Commissioners as after 1840.[28]

Almost immediately it became apparent that no amount of information from the government would prevent emigrants starting out insufficiently provided and consequently arriving in the colonies in actual need. Soon after 1815 private groups had organized themselves in the ports to care for the unfortunate landing on their shores and the governments of Canada and New Brunswick incurred annual expenditure for the care of indigent emigrants. Colonial opinion regarded this expenditure as an unjustified imposition and legislatures resisted the vote it required. Therefore as noted above, the assemblies imposed a head tax on emigrants arriving in their ports in order, as the Lower Canada Act stated, "to create a fund for defraying the expense of . . . medical assistance . . . and of enabling indigent persons . . . to proceed to the place of their destination."[29]

Efforts made by the colonies to open their lands for settlement and develop transportation facilities offered employment for the poorer emigrants and inducements for the more well-to-do. The Colonial Office in 1831 authorized the survey of government lands in 100-acre lots and the sale of the lots at 5s. per acre, payable in four instalments within two years; in 1837 the period of credit was reduced to fourteen days.[30] Within the next two decades, as various abuses in the colonies' land systems were eliminated, land terms were developed to meet the needs of practical settlers. In New Brunswick, the lieutenant-governor insisted that, though the price set in 1831 was too high for needy emigrants, it was quite low enough to encourage speculators to create monopolies and ruthless timber men to strip the forests. In Upper Canada in the late 1820's, the government had begun to provide 50-acre lots on easy credit, transportation inland, and first employment on roads or other public works for indigent emigrants. Lieutenant-Governor Sir John Colborne defended the policy enthusiastically for the township of Ops in the Newcastle district, and it was used with some modifications "under the vigilance of Sir James Kempt" when the Scottish settlers were placed in Inverness and Leeds on Craig's Road. Ten years later, after imperial instructions of 1837 had required what amounted to "cash-in-hand" land sales,[31] the Governor of Canada, Charles Poulett Thomson, supposed apostle of Wakefield theory though he was, supported the earlier plan. The land act of Canada in 1841 was to authorize land sales on short-term cash and to provide also for the 50-acre land grants. Without waiting for the act, Thomson in a Minute of Council of June, 1840, made provision for 50-acre land grants bordering a road to be run to Owen Sound on condition that the grantees perform specified road and settlement duties.[32] So the Garrafraxa Road began and others, the Kennebec, the Lambton, the Temiscouata, and various so-called "colonization roads" followed.

New Brunswick and Nova Scotia, too, after early beginnings and disappointments, favoured easier settlement terms for emigrants with little or no capital. In the end, the first opposition of the colonial secretaries, Glenelg, Stanley, Russell, to the experience and plans of the colonists gave way to understanding, and the Emigration Commissioners and that student of the colonies, James Stephen, concluded that in British America the policy of small allotments for poorer emigrants had real value.[33] In Upper Canada after 1830, the new system for placing near-indigent emigrants was pushed with vigour, and news of it encouraged emigration. Colborne had warned the Colonial Secretary, Lord Goderich, that neither parishes nor landlords nor even the mother country's government would produce the funds needed to settle Britain's voluntary emigrants; therefore Canada might have to receive thousands annually who would require immediate support. If any twentieth-century resident of Ontario would enjoy an enlightening view of his province in its beginnings, let him consider how Colborne expended £8,582 10s. 11¾d. on emigrants in 1832: For example, to "John Patton, Agent at Prescott, to defray the expense of forwarding indigent Emigrants to the different Settlements forming in the upper parts of the Province, and also to afford them temporary employment on the road leading from Prescott to the Rideau Canal, £900"; to "Charles Rubidge, for expenses incurred in settling Emigrants in the Newcastle district, £276 11s. 1d."; to "John Bostwick for . . . forwarding Emigrants from Port Stanley to Adelaide, £25 11s. 8¼d."; to "Wellesley Rickey for . . . settling Emigrants in Oro, Medonte, and Orillia, £1,052 6s."; to "Russell [Roswell] Mount, for . . . Settling Emigrants in Adelaide and opening Roads through those townships, £1,844 5s."; to "Francis Hewson [Hudson], for employing Emigrants on a Road leading from Kempenfeldt Bay to Sunnidale, £90 17s. 8½d.". By this means about 400 families were placed in the township of Adelaide in 1832 at a cost to the colony of approximately £6,000; in 1834 Sunnidale township was given a similar addition of population.[34]

Meanwhile the development of necessary highways and waterways employed other new arrivals. In 1836 Sir Francis Bond Head obtained promises from the Upper Canada legislature for the improvement of the Trent and Grand rivers, the construction of harbours, and the completion of the Welland Canal. Three years later Sir George Arthur with the new Governor-General's approval turned to the banks for £37,000 to cover expenditure for the North Toronto, the Dundas and Waterloo, and the Kingston and Napanee roads, for inland navigation in the Newcastle district, and again for the Welland Canal. Soon Lord Sydenham and Lord John Russell arranged Parliament's guarantee of a great loan for public works. In 1829 the Rideau Canal had given work to 2,700; in 1835 Buchanan had estimated that 20,000 labourers would be necessary for public works; now the needs were vastly enlarged.[35]

Even the slight encouragement suggested by the use of these policies in the colonies—the work of the agents and societies in the ports, the aid to poor emigrants in settling—acted as incentives to emigration. Agents who made a living out of the emigrant trade seized upon news of such activities and used it in their promotion. In its regular report of 1819, the Quebec Emigrant Society ventured to insert a few words of advice, meant perhaps as discouragement for emigrants. But the *Londonderry Journal* in January, 1820, carried an advertisement of the *Dominica Packet* which made a contrary use of the fact by asserting that "a society has recently been formed at Quebec for the purpose of affording assistance to poor emigrants who may be without means to support themselves should they not fall into work immediately on landing, or require to go into the interior to meet friends."

THE ARRIVALS

The emigration from the British Isles that followed as a result of these many influences brought to British American shores in the years between 1825 and 1846 more than 600,000 souls. In all but the French colony of Quebec, the influx determined for decades the makeup of the population. It transformed forests into farm lands, frontier villages into rising cities. It more than doubled the population of Upper Canada in less than one-quarter of a century, the total rising from some 150,000 in 1824 to 450,000 in 1841.[36] Toronto which had about 1,600 people in 1825 could record almost 20,000 in 1846, Hamilton had nearly 10,000, Kingston more than 8,000. Galt, Guelph, London in the west, and Cobourg, Port Hope, Brockville, and Bytown in the east, which had been wilderness or little more in 1825, had become promising centres. In Nova Scotia the number of inhabitants had sprung from 75,000 in 1815 to 125,000 by 1835; the Pictou settlement had improved its agricultural lands until it could export wheat in 1837 and its population stood at 2,000. Halifax was a market for some 8,000 people, a commercial *entrepôt* with ties inland and abroad. In New Brunswick population had reached 156,000; close settlements fronted on the St. John River and the county had almost 21,000 inhabitants as early as 1836 and Westmoreland and Northumberland counties some 14,000 each.[37]

Year after year the newcomers made their way inland from St. John and St. Andrews, Quebec and Montreal, leaving few trails behind them but family tales to be dimly recalled by descendants in the twentieth century. Only for the Canadas are records of these pilgrimages available and these merely in numbers which tell nothing of the wonder and dismay of the experience. Nevertheless the numerical summaries compiled annually by the government emigration agents describe roughly at least the tide of population moving into the Eastern Townships, and the Ottawa, Midland, Newcastle, Home, London, and other growing districts.[38]

This growth in the colonies had been achieved by a quarter century of transatlantic movement and adjustment unparalleled in the history of modern free peoples. Sailings from the United Kingdom to British America which, in spite of annual fluctuations from 3,000 to 23,000, had averaged some 10,000 in the ten years from 1816 to 1825, rose to 31,000 in 1830 and in the cholera year of 1832 reached a peak of 66,000. Fifteen years later the potato famine brought an outpouring of almost 110,000 to British America, an annual total not to be surpassed until 1906. In the interval between 1832 and 1847 owing to insurrection in the Canadas and severe agricultural and industrial depression in the mother country, variations in the numbers of emigrants were again wide, ranging from 4,600 in 1838 to 54,000 in 1842.[39] The exact homeland of these shiploads of human beings is difficult to discover. Of approximately 16,000 emigrants arriving in 1829 it has been estimated that 60 per cent came from Ireland, more than 20 per cent from England and the remainder from Scotland. Though the grand total rose and fell and many Irish passed on from British America to the United States, it was not until after 1847 that the proportion of arrivals from Ireland dropped perceptibly.

By that time the numbers of Germans and Scandinavians reaching Quebec on the Liverpool boats had so risen that the published emigration totals badly misrepresented British departures and Canadian accessions. Poor crops along the Rhine River, the potato blight, and changes not greatly different from those in the British Isles were causing a German emigration which reached some 162,000 in 1853 and 200,000 in 1854.[40] Steamboats and railroads made the St. Lawrence cross-Canada route a cheap thoroughfare to the western States. From time to time some Germans remained in Canada; even less frequently a few Norwegians stopped off.[41] Scattered references give German and Scandinavian arrivals in Quebec:[42]

	Total arrivals, all nationalities	German	Scandinavian
1846	[a]	896	[a]
1852	39,000[b]	5,159	2,197
1854	53,183	18,051[c]	—
1857	32,000[b]	4,961	6,470
1861	19,923	10,618[c]	—
1862	22,000[b]	2,516	5,289

[a]Not known. [b]Approximate. [c]Total foreign born.

The emigrant totals measure not only a vast growth inland but a stupendous pressure upon the colonial ports. From 1826 to 1832 for six weeks following the opening of shipping, the St. Lawrence shores stretching a mile and a half from Quebec were crowded with newly landed human beings, "the places of those who might have moved off being constantly supplied by fresh arrivals."[43] Year after year until he died of the effects of the "emigrant fever," the emigration agent Buchanan spent the summer meeting vessels and advising strangers who were sadly harried by dockside agents with unscrupulous suggestions to sell. Later he scouted out over the areas inland, prepared reports upon their possibilities for settlers, and corresponded with the home government, Poor Law Guardians, and private individuals from all parts of the British Isles.

As they went about their duties, the emigration agents in the colonial ports* passed in review every type of the population of the mother country from the humblest labourer to the highly educated and the gently reared. Though they gave most of their time to those emigrants whose removal was financed by charity, emigrants of small means often outnumbered all others. Since 1825 this characteristic had been observable from inquiries received by the Colonial Office and emigration agents in Great Britain. Stories of distress no longer predominated. Pleas for information came from men of every occupation and position in life. Farmers who applied often possessed capital sufficient to buy and cultivate two hundred acres of land. Frequently the applicants were professional men who had been property holders. Two new reasons for removal are evident: the desire to get away before all is lost, and the necessity for taking educated young people from a land in which professions and occupations are already crowded to a colony where openings for them may be found. An example of the first may be seen in the case of an occupier of land in Yorkshire who though at present tolerably comfortable was yet faced "with a certain prospect of ruin . . . should he continue to struggle on much longer in a country where the poor rates" were "absolutely overpowering from a surplus population, the depreciated value of labour and the high price of bread."[44] In Ireland according to Lord Carbury, many farmers impelled by a "spirit of enterprise and speculation" realized that on the small acreages obtainable they had "no prospect of gain beyond their usual subsistence."[45] By

---

*When Alexander Carlisle Buchanan, the first emigrant agent at Quebec, returned home in ill health in 1836 he was succeeded in the port office by his nephew of the same name, a son of James Buchanan, the former British consul in New York.

1849 "strong and opulent farmers," the class that it was most desirable to retain, were emigrating in such numbers that it engaged the attention of the House of Commons. The Lord Lieutenant, Clarendon, believed that the country was losing week after week farmers with as much as £200 in their pockets: "They cut the corn on the Sunday, sell it on Monday morning, and are off to America in the evening, leaving the waste land behind them and the landlords without rent."[46] Evidence of the second new characteristic may be found in the memorial of John Mewburn of Whitby addressed to the Colonial Secretary, as follows:

That your Memorialist forty years of age has practised with much success as a Surgeon and Accoucheur in the town of Whitby for twenty years, that having five Sons and five Daughters whom he has educated at a considerable expense but is unable to place his Sons out in the different professions or trades to which they may be qualified from the number of applicants in similar circumstances and the very extravagant premiums required . . . has determined on removing his family to Upper Canada.[47]

Nothing so representative of all parts and classes of the population of the United Kingdom had ever before left its shores. From Newcastle, Scarborough, and Whitby round the east, south, and west coasts and on up to Whitehaven, thirty-six ports in all sent out shiploads of emigrants to Quebec in 1832; in Scotland sailings took place from eighteen different ports, and in Ireland from twenty-one. The arrival of larger ships and the centralization of the emigrant trade was soon to decrease the number of ports of sail, as may be seen from Table IV of Appendix B, but the emigrations were to increase. Families of moderate means from Yorkshire and Cumberland, from the midland and western counties of England, from the west and south of Ireland, Mayo, Sligo, Dublin, Limerick, and Wexford, and from the Lowlands of Scotland were daily disembarking on the crowded shores of the St. Lawrence at Quebec and setting out on the long route to their final destinations in the Eastern Townships or the far Western District and the Huron Tract.[48]

From the reports of the Quebec and Montreal emigrant societies and officials in the maritime colonies it would seem that the majority of the labouring emigrants became at once an encumbrance to the cities and districts in which they should have received employment. But British America was above all a poor man's country. For those willing to work, there were besides the government settlements, the canals, the roads, mentioned above, and the older settlers to offer employment. In 1831 the immigration of labourers surpassed any before. For a few weeks in June and July the wharves in Quebec and Montreal were seriously congested; by autumn both cities, and indeed all of Canada, were free of unemployed.[49] In 1832 when over 51,000 disembarked on the St. Lawrence, the call for labourers exceeded the supply. So great was the shortage in the London and Western districts that it was necessary to encourage an immigration of workmen from Ohio and Pennsylvania. Officials in London need not have feared that the experience on landing would weaken the "sense of self-reliance in the poor."[50] During their first years, all but those possessing a few hundred pounds capital cast about for employment by the day. But as soon as a little ready money was obtained, the labourer himself became a proprietor, and within a few years an employer. So exactly in proportion as the emigrants succeeded in establishing themselves did the demand for labour grow.

Opportunities for obtaining employment were increased by the arrival of thousands of settlers of means whose departure from the United Kingdom has been noted. Though a poor emigrant could cross the Atlantic, travel inland, and take up his residence on a fifty-acre lot at an expense of about £60, for a man travelling with his family in the ship's cabin and settling in a colony with any degree of comfort, capital amounting to at least £500 was necessary. F. W. Magrath of Erindale near Toronto estimated that his father and family of eight accomplished their settlement in Upper Canada for £421.17.0, the items of expenditure being:[51]

	£	s.	d.
Total cost from Liverpool to the settlement	135	0	0
Articles of furniture	12	0	0
Purchases of land	100	0	0
Seed wheat	3	5	0
Building houses and offices	85	0	0
Two cows	6	0	0
Clearing ten acres	35	0	0
One horse	13	0	0
Oxen, waggon, yoke, and chains	27	0	0
Tools	5	12	0

Two of the most serious needs of the early colony were here supplied by the emigrant of means. First settlers had suffered from the lack of a market for their produce, but after 1832 emigrants passing through the older settlements to the new lands beyond took all the farmers could supply at a full price. In the second place, deposits of capital made in the Bank of Upper Canada after 1825 raised the interest on bank stock to 8 per cent and in 1832 to 16 per cent, when a bonus of 8 was given in consequence of the "country rising into such rapid prosperity." As similar returns could not be obtained in the United Kingdom, the rate acted as an inducement in bringing capital into the colony. In 1831 it was estimated that £250,000 entered through the port of Quebec; in

1832, £600,000, one emigrant alone depositing £16,000 in a Quebec bank.[52]

In 1837 as disorder in the Canadas began to limit the movement to the St. Lawrence River ports, the total of arrivals fell to about 22,000. Many of these were described as "wealthy and respectable," and quickly moved on to take up lands near Toronto. Others less well-equipped found immediate work on the river improvements which employed some 1,500 in that year, or on government projects at Kingston and Cornwall. Though the immigration total dropped to about 4,000 to Canada in 1838 and rose irregularly thereafter, the character of the immigrants changed little until the famine. In 1839 most "came out" to friends and some brought plentiful funds.[53] The pick-up afer the Rebellion arrived swiftly, the numbers tripling in 1839 and doubling again in 1840. In New Brunswick where no rebellion had cut down the influx, the increase was equally great. More than 3,000 emigrants arrived in 1839, though there had been but 900 in 1838.[54]

In four days in the early summer of 1841 when some 8,600 emigrants landed at Quebec, almost half of whom had received assistance to emigrate, A. C. Buchanan, the younger, again found all well provided. The Atlantic crossing had been so short that even the assisted emigrants started off to the west with two days' rations. Some of these probably met disappointment, for reports of good opportunities and high wages at Toronto were so alluring that Buchanan could retain only five hundred to work at 3s. 6d. and 3s. 1½d. per day respectively on roads and government projects near Quebec and Montreal.[55]

For 1842 prospects were promising. On the advice of Sir Charles Bagot, colonial officials in the British Isles spread the report. Unfortunately for the hordes of labourers who responded in that year, work on the Lachine and Grenville canals was soon finished and that on the Welland Canal and some of the roads did not develop. For a while the streets of Quebec were filled with the destitute. Then what some have called the "pathetic procession" moved on to Kingston, to Niagara, and even across to Rochester, Utica, Albany, and New York. As a result the winter of 1842–3 witnessed one of the early backwater movements in the history of emigration, for from New York some of the disenchanted managed to ship back to the mother country along with a few hundred British sailors who had been discharged from United States ships. Evidence of the true character of these unfortunates however is confusing because the emigration agent at Quebec believed that few of those who were "industriously disposed" remained without employment at the end of the year 1842.[56] Nevertheless, however unusual a phenomenon the emigrant turning about and going home may have seemed in 1842, it became commonplace in the 1850's. Commercial crisis was then spreading from the United States to the British American colonies, and in Great Britain certain industries and army recruiting were expanding. In 1857 for instance 18,839 British emigrants went back, a number equal to almost 9 per cent of the total departures of that year; some had come from Australia and many from the United States and British America.[57]

In New Brunswick, too, the immigration of 1842, amounting there to about 8,300 souls, turned out to be more than could be employed. By August the government's warning was posted in the Dublin Customs House: "too many emigrants have arrived there [in New Brunswick] already." Emigrants of means would have aided the colony materially because the fascination of lumbering had led New Brunswick farmers to mortgage their lands to merchants in return for lumbering licences and supplies; consequently partially cleared farms were available cheap. Moreover fine undeveloped lands were plentiful. But in New Brunswick, as in Nova Scotia, the emigrants who arrived only added to the misfortunes already "heavily pressing on the community." By the "timorous intervention" of the Lieutenant-Governor, Sir William Colebrooke, the "accumulating torrent" was stayed in 1843.[58]

At the same time emigration totals to Canada fell off one-half because of the bad reports of 1842. But cabin passengers, emigrants with some cash such as farmers apprehensive of a change in the Corn Laws, had begun to increase, their numbers rising from 614 in 1842 to 803 in 1843. Many too in 1843 had come to meet friends and were thus at once removed from uncertainty.[59] The 1844 season again brought emigrants of superior quality; some carried with them, it was believed, from £500 to £1,500 each. Those without capital, if willing to work, were soon occupied, for crops were good and employment on public projects plentiful. Remarkable among the arrivals of 1844 were the number of women whose way obviously had been paid by relatives already in the colonies. Two hundred and forty-five wives arrived at Quebec to join husbands and brought 713 children with them; 173 widows with 488 children came out to live with sons or daughters.[60]

An indication of the calamitous emigration to come appeared with the arrivals of 1845. Many were still small farmers, but the great bulk were agricultural labourers, all quite penniless. Landings at Quebec which had been some 25,000 in 1845 rose to almost 33,000 in 1846. Though there were 600 cabin passengers among the hordes, some with capital of £100 to 500, about half of all were totally unskilled, less than

1,000 were artisans or mechanics. The Irish made up two-thirds of the 33,000. Small farmers were now many times outnumbered by mobs of untrained, inexperienced labourers, often ignorant of the English language and as lost in the New World as children in a maze.[61] Probably it should be noted here as is evident in Table XIII of Appendix B that these proportions were not characteristic of later years. In 1857 and 1859 for example, some 30 per cent of male arrivals were listed as farmers, and about 40 per cent as labourers, including mechanics. In the latter year a new category, "clerks," which accounted for one-tenth of all males, bears the significant notation, "not likely to succeed."[62]

In the mid-forties, the general debilitation in which emigrants finished the Atlantic voyage became markedly noticeable in Quebec and the maritime ports. In 1846 mortality at sea and after landing was high, a result possibly of the weakened condition of the poor and of smallpox and fever contracted at home or in unwholesome boarding-houses before embarkation. On arrival at Quebec, 1,325 passengers had to go at once into quarantine, and of these 105 died. Sickness followed the emigrants inland, where government agents cared for another 1,200 and local charities for unknown numbers.[63] Colonial government officials did what they could to prepare for the throngs of famine emigrants who were already fleeing Ireland.

A special medical board was appointed at Quebec, an efficient steamboat provided for the port health officer. At Halifax, the Board of Health struggled to improve Richmond hospital and develop quarantine and sick quarters on Melville Island. Extra provisions were laid in at Quebec, additional sheds were thrown up, and ten thousand tents were taken over from the ordnance department. But from May 8 when the *Urania* of Cork, the first plague ship of 1847, reached the quarantine at Grosse Isle, every dire expectation was exceeded by far. In the last three weeks of May a strong east wind drove in eighty-four vessels, "each heavily laden with disease and death." All brought famine fever, hunger, and typhus; all exuded the "intolerable stench of dying creatures who had existed for weeks in the most abject squalor, crowded past decency, and too weak, ignorant, and dispairful to exert themselves for their own good." Bewildered orphans and the feeble and decrepit mingled with the weaklings of the famine and the victims of typhus. By the end of May, twelve hundred sick had been placed in hospital or tents, and thirty-five vessels were waiting to unload their ailing. Ten times as many as were under cover had to live on the Island on damp ground, on the stones of the beaches, dying under the sky, until the new hospital was finished late in August.[64]

At Grosse Isle scarcely anyone escaped infection for longer than three weeks. Inland every orphanage was soon filled. In Montreal a whole congregation of nursing nuns went down with the fever. The Halifax Board of Health faced bills not only for "Ferriage of the Sick" but also for "Truckage of Coffins." In Ireland government officers were ordered to land all emigrants affected with disease; but fever, even when latent at sailing, soon developed on shipboard. Lord Grey promoted the use of M. Ledoyen's disinfecting fluid, then offered M. Ledoyen £1,000 to go out with Colonel Calvert to superintend its use at Grosse Isle. Later the government provided emigrant vessels with supplies of Sir W. Burnett's somewhat similar prophylactic liquid for use on the voyage.[65]

Emigration to Quebec amounted to well nigh 90,000 in 1847, and in all British America the totals climbed from 45,000 in 1846 to about 110,000 in 1847. Of these in 1847 the loss by death was more than 16 per cent. When the Emigration Commissioners assembled the figures for the year, the tragic totals stood:[66]

	For Canada	For New Brunswick	Total
Numbers embarked	89,738	17,074	106,812
Died in passage	5,293	823	6,116
Died in quarantine	3,452	697	4,149
Died in hospitals	6,585	595	7,180
TOTAL DEATHS	15,330	2,115	17,445

For Canadians, the summer of 1847 marked the nadir of the emigrants' misery and the height of colonial charity. In the spring, Canadians had collected £20,000 for the starving in Ireland and a commensurate contribution had gone from New Brunswick. In June Governor-General Lord Elgin forwarded to London the Executive Council's protests against the arrival of the destitute and fever-stricken. By November, the Quebec emigrant agent was "at the point of death from fever caught in the discharge of his duties," and provincial expenditures on emigrants had become so heavy that Lord Elgin was compelled to request new arrangements for the interest due on the British guaranteed loan. Because of the congestion on Grosse Isle, which is apparent from Table VII of Appendix B, thousands of emigrants had been shipped upriver too soon. They carried inland "the seeds of this fearful pestilence," until there was no town in Canada from Quebec to Niagara, or in New Brunswick from St. John to the province line, in which it did not exist. It was impossible, according to the Emigration Commissioners in London, "to do justice to the humanity and self-sacrifice with which the inhabitants of these towns and the clergy of all denominations devoted themselves to the succour of the unfortunate emigrants."[67]

While the government clerks added up the emigration totals and the cost in human lives, members of Parliament counted the cost in pounds, shillings, and pence. Early in 1847, Earl Grey had been grieved to report that tales of great suffering among emigrants in British America were entirely true. In anticipation of the disaster, the Colonial Office had allowed the government of Canada £10,000.[68] Now in the spring of 1848, Grey told the House of Lords that the Canadian government had been compelled to spend £114,000 for relief of the sick and destitute; £55,000 had been provided by Parliament and the Military Chest; the emigrant head tax had brought in only £15,000. That tax would be doubled. But Grey pointed out that though the colonial government had to pay £44,000 of the costs itself, what Canadians most objected to was the calamity these diseased emigrants carried with them into the colonial settlements.[69]

In spite of the overwhelming numbers of the arrivals in 1847, Canada experienced a labour shortage. Six-sevenths of all emigrants were destitute Irish, wholly unskilled. Besides employers feared their disease. After the loss of some 10,000 by death and the departure of many to the United States, able-bodied workers remaining were so few that wages in the ports rose steeply. In New Brunswick practically all of about 11,000 emigrants in 1847 were penniless and the problem of care correspondingly heavy.[70]

The year 1848 brought an amazing drop in emigration. Arrivals in Canada fell to about 28,000, in New Brunswick to some 4,000. A miraculous decline in the death rate lowered casualties to but 1 per cent. This tremendous change was not so much the result of a weakening of the emigrant stream as of a shift in direction. In 1848 British emigration to the United States increased by about 46,000, largely Irish, and that to Australia and New Zealand by 19,000—a change which almost accounted for the decrease to British North America. Buchanan believed that the improvement at his port of Quebec was due to the new colonial law which raised the emigrant head tax to 10s. and imposed penalties for being detained in quarantine. New Brunswick and Nova Scotia passed similar legislation which brought similar results.[71] In one sense modern control of immigration by the Canadian government may be traced to the experience and legislation of the famine years. The Canadian act was so severe, however, requiring as it did physical detail in the passengers lists and other minutiae, that the Colonial Office recommended softening it. Both Canada and New Brunswick in the following year reduced the tax, that for Canada falling first to 7s. 6d. and then to 5s.[72]

The decrease in the tax had little effect on the trend of arrivals. For the seven years following the famine, the numbers removing from the British Isles to British North America varied only between 31,000 and 43,000 annually, and in 1855 returning prosperity in Great Britain, the gold rush to Australia, commercial crisis in North America, and the influence of the Crimean War cut them down to 18,000. In the years from 1830 to 1839, the British Isles had sent 321,000 emigrants to British North America and 292,000 to the United States; but from 1840 to 1849 the tide turned, 428,000 going to British America and 912,000 to the United States. In this shift the preference of the Irish for the United States, the change in British commercial policy, as well as the colonial head tax, played a part. In 1849, 73 per cent of all British emigrants to North America ended up in the United States; in 1850 the percentage rose to 79.[73]

Apparently, too, the drain of British emigrants from the colonies to the south would continue. From both the maritime colonies and Canada, the route was well worn. More British emigrants followed it from New Brunswick and Nova Scotia than remained in those provinces. In 1832 the loss amounted to 7,000 out of 9,000; in 1851 "nearly all" of the 3,470 new arrivals in New Brunswick passed on to the south. Year after year until 1862, while annual landings in New Brunswick ranged from 500 to 1,000, the emigration agent at St. John reported somewhat similar departures.[74] Many reshipped at St. John to the steamer which plied to Eastport; others went by ferry from St. Andrews to the nearest United States harbour. Nevertheless by 1851 the population of New Brunswick had risen to 193,800; this was an increase of about 40,000 in the last decade, a greater growth proportionately than that in the adjoining New England states. To Nova Scotia the emigration was small, perhaps less than 14,000 between 1838 and 1851, and in the next few years the Customs House showed little familiarity with the movement. From Government House in December, 1852, came the report that since the influx of 1,621 emigrants during the famine season of 1847, emigrants arriving at Halifax had been only 72 in 1849, 21 in 1850, and 101 in 1851. This bit of information was closed with the dismal addendum that during the same years the Nova Scotia legislature had been compelled to spend £3,884 15s. 2d. sterling on needy emigrants.[75] Assuredly it was not a record to encourage further emigration.

From Quebec between the years 1825 and 1832 probably one-third of all who landed travelled up the St. Lawrence to Upper Canada, only to cross Lake Ontario or Lake Erie to the United States. After 1832, according to contemporary reports, the proportions increased. In 1849,

FIGURE 7. The Embarkation, Waterloo Docks, Liverpool. (*Illustrated London News*, July 6, 1850.)

THE GREAT EMIGRATIONS, 1830–1860

with total emigration to Canada at 38,000, removals to the South were still more than 10,000.[76] When the completion of the Great Western Railroad soon after 1850 enabled the emigrant to travel from Hamilton on Lake Ontario to Chicago in Illinois for £2, the St. Lawrence River and Canadian steamboats and railroads became a popular route to the United States and attracted many emigrants both British and foreign born who might otherwise have been added to the population of Canada. In earlier days emigration from the United States to Canada partially balanced this loss of British emigrants, but the arrival of the railroad and the development of the western states before the prairie provinces upset this exchange of population. By 1856 Grand Trunk railway agents were selling through tickets in the British Isles not only to Canada but to the United States West,* and the tendency to pass by Canadian opportunities grew stronger.[77] At the same time as this revolution in transportation tied Hamilton and Toronto to Chicago, it crossed the Niagara River with the famous Suspension Bridge, and improved canal and railroad routes from New York City to Lake Ontario. Emigrant traffic *via* the Suspension Bridge entered Canada mainly in transit to the western United States. In Canada the determination of the year's accession of immigrant population became more complicated. A. C. Buchanan, the senior emigration agent in the colony, deprecated the accuracy of figures showing the number of emigrants settled in Canada, but just the same attempted to draw up tables from "the best resources" at his command. From 1856 to 1858 he and his agents reported:[78]

	1856	1857	1858
Arrivals at Quebec	22,118	30,257	11,114
Arrivals *via* railway from Portland	—	2,871	—
Arrivals *via* Suspension Bridge and Hamilton	4,229	35,943	24,840
Arrivals *via* Rochester, Oswego, St. Lawrence River	6,500	3,180	2,060
Total arrivals	32,907	72,251	38,014
Departures to United States *via* Great Western Railroad, St. Lawrence River, etc.	8,227	37,034	25,675
Departures to Eastern United States	—	685	—
Returned to United Kingdom and lost in burning of steamer *Montreal*	—	869	—
Settled in Canada	24,680	33,663	12,339

Efforts were made to inform emigrants regarding the advantages of the British American colonies. The emigrant agents in the ports had

*Even before 1850, Canadian merchants whose profits came from transportation publicized the completion of 66 miles of canals fit for 300- to 400-ton boats which would make the St. Lawrence River a shorter route to the United States mid-West than the route *via* New York.

Buchanan's and Perley's pamphlets and later the Information Sheets and the Colonization Circulars of the Colonial Land and Emigration Commissioners to hand out. Though the land regulations were gradually liberalized as control came more and more into local colonial hands, the complicated, changing terms which the information sheets contained sadly puzzled land-seeking emigrants. In general in the early forties, the emigrant was told that he could acquire the better lands in Canada West at 8s. currency per acre, payable at once, and poorer lands there and in Canada East at lower prices; for Nova Scotia, prices were listed as fixed at about 1s. 9d. per acre; and in New Brunswick at auction sales prices ranged from 4s. 6d. to 10s. currency. After 1841 too, Clergy Reserve lands were thrown on the market. Good government land, however, was growing scarce and the real farmer settlers were obtaining too little of it. Free granting of lands persisted. Between 1802 and 1824, Upper Canada had disposed of some 3,500,000 acres and only one-third of that to emigrant settlers. From the inception of land sales in 1831 to the time of the Durham mission in 1838, all the British North American colonies had sold little more than 1,300,000 acres, Upper Canada only about 100,000, though it had granted free nearly 2,000,000 acres. In 1846 a Commission of Enquiry into the Crown Lands Department of Canada examined the hard facts arising from emigration to the United States, the scarcity of good lands, and the demand for easy credit on land purchases. Though twenty-five of twenty-nine persons questioned by the Commission favoured easy credit, nothing came of the Commission's work until after 1849 when the colony assumed the full powers implied in responsible government. Then at one stroke in July, 1852, the Council opened 95 per cent of the remaining Crown lands for sale on ten-year terms, conditional of course on performance of settlement duties.[79]

Neither these policies nor others greatly changed the current of emigration to the colonies or from the colonies to the United States. In Canada, it is true, the northward thrust of the land seekers was being halted by that outcropping of rocks, the Laurentian Barrier, which runs across the country one hundred miles or more north of the lake shore at Toronto. As advancing settlers came face to face with the Canadian Shield, even the enticements of the 50-acre land grants on the roads authorized by the Act of 1841 (three of them were run in the Lake Huron-Georgian Bay region, two in the rear of settlements on Lake Ontario) failed to hold them. New settlers slipped away from the rocks and pines as fast as they were placed on their land. This influence of geography was not clearly discerned at the time, except by a few land surveyors, and the emigrants continued to move on to the south.[80]

After watching the phenomenon for some time, the Land and Emigration Commissioners concluded that the great bulk of emigrants must settle in the United States since "Canada does not possess a tithe of the capital necessary for their employment." By 1851 they regarded the loss as a matter of course. To employ the exodus in British America would require an expenditure by the British Treasury which was not justified as "a relief from surplus population so long as the labour market of the United States is sufficient to employ all who want to resort to it." As it was, emigration proceeded at small public cost, for out of an estimated £1,743,500 expended on it in 1849 only some £228,000 had been public funds. According to the Commissioners, the privately supported was "a very healthy emigration."[81] Much of this private support of course had been provided by emigrants in North America in the form of remittances sent home which amounted in 1852 alone to the sum of almost £1,500,000. Since these great annual contributions came mainly from the United States, especially from emigrants from Ireland where every family already had "one leg over the Atlantic," the effect would be permanent. In accord with colonization theories, the Commissioners believed that the drift to the United States might have been corrected earlier if the Treasury had advanced to the North American colonies a wage fund of £400,000 annually, plus incidentals for housing and the like. Nevertheless the conclusion was obvious: so far as emigration was a relief to the mother country, the relief was the same "whether the emigrants went to the United States or the British colonies." Finally it was thought that the present emigration of 35,000 to 40,000 was quite sufficient to supply Canadian needs.[82]

On the latter point opinion fluctuated, perhaps inevitably. The emigration of 1852 met all Buchanan's hopes. The new arrivals were healthy, well-clothed, and completely lacking in the "squalid misery" of recent years. Canada had never presented "a more favourable opening for the reception of all classes of Her Majesty's subjects or such others as desire to seek a comfortable home." New Brunswick had had a prosperous year. Acreage of land cleared had increased 50 per cent since 1840. The colony's feeling towards British emigrants could be seen from its reduction of the emigrant head tax to 2s. 6d. and the welcome given emigrants in the succeeding years.[83] In 1853 with wages for common labour running at $1.00 a day, and for bricklayers at $2.00, new-world optimism revived. A high degree of material prosperity, according to Sir Edmund Head, was producing contentment and patriotism. "For the emigrant no country offers better guarantees for the successful pursuit of competence and happiness" than this, went the report from the

St. Lawrence. From St. John the tune was the same: sawmills, shipbuilding, agriculture—all were prospering.[84] And in Nova Scotia, dismal discouragement over population growth was giving way before prosperity. Then in 1854 wage rates fell as the commercial crisis began to spread from the United States and the economic improvement in the mother country, mentioned above, decreased the need for removal. The annual average of emigration from the British Isles during the years 1847 to 1854 inclusive had been about 300,000 and to British North America some 46,000. In 1855 the comparable figures were some 177,000 and 18,000.[85] The decline continued irregularly until 1863. The gain in population for Canada fell to approximately 23,500 in 1856, 12,000 in 1858, 6,300 in 1859, and 7,000 in 1860.[86]

A New World

Colonial optimists refused to accept such numbers as sufficient supply for their labour markets. In 1856 as he watched the Norwegian emigrants travel through Canada to the United States, the emigration agent at Quebec was moved to suggest the despatch of a judicious British emissary to Europe to induce such "steady, industrious" folk to come to Canada, and the Secretary for the Colonies, Henry Labouchere, approved the suggestion. Since little emigration could be expected from the United Kingdom, he wrote August 26, 1856, would the Canadian government send him a memo which he could forward to British ministers and consuls in Europe. Pamphlets for the same purpose had already been used by railroad and other agents. In 1856 growing vigour in the Canadian Bureau of Agriculture which now assumed supervision of immigration brought a new piece devised by William Hutton for use in Europe.[87] At the same time the emigration agents, M. H. Perley of New Brunswick and A. B. Hawke from Canada, crossed to England to encourage emigration, and the Canadian land surveyor, William Wagner, went to Germany, and Helge Haugen from the Eastern Townships to Norway. By 1861 A. C. Buchanan, the "celebrated" emigration agent from Quebec, was in Liverpool taking over Hawke's work and placing sub-agents in Scotland and Ireland. In 1863 following a change of policy in the Bureau of Agriculture, Buchanan again reorganized the immigration agencies abroad.[88] A revolutionary change, indeed, since 1828 when William Huskisson had sent Buchanan's uncle to supervise British arrivals in the far-away St. Lawrence port of Quebec! It signalled the victory of the principles of laissez-faire in the mother country and of responsibility for their own government in the colonies.

Though the colonists would not agree with the Emigration Commissioners that immigration to the colonies was achieving a balance with opportunities there, great changes on all sides heralded a new era. British capital which had early sought rich returns in the United States, in spite of the need for it in the British American colonies, was now arriving to carry through large projects. Before Confederation the government of Canada had spent about $31 million and other sources more than $116 million on railroads. At first only tiny links in gaps in the water transportation system, the railroads by 1860 had become gigantic lines, measuring 1,888 miles in Canada and 266 miles in the maritime colonies and capable of employing thousands of workers in their building and upkeep.[89] Some slight diversification of industry had begun;* mechanics had not as before to seek employment in the United States. Public works provided occupation even in winter. In both Canada and New Brunswick farmers needed male and female servants, and in the towns opportunities for newcomers were increasing. Some of the little settlements of 1840 and before had become cities: Montreal had in 1861 a population of 90,000, Quebec 60,000, Toronto almost 45,000, St. John 27,000, Halifax 25,000, and Hamilton 19,000. The people of the British American colonies who numbered less than one and a half million souls in 1840 were to enter Confederation with a population of almost three and one-half million.

Though it was a new world, its roots were quite plainly in the old. Families descended from the United Empire Loyalists were now far outnumbered by new arrivals whose relatives were still in Scotland, Ireland, and England. Yet from 1847 onward, the arriving emigrants were not newcomers in the old sense, for they came to meet friends and family members who had prepared for them.[90] The heterogeneous appearance of the inhabitants of the colonies noted by John Robert Godley in 1844 had not greatly changed. There were still the Irish with the brogue, the Scots with the broad Scots accent, the English with the undeniable accent of Yorkshire, and the French with their red caps and sashes and distinctive language. Godley's warning was becoming a reality, nevertheless: a national character with definite traits was forming.

In short, it seemed that British emigration was entering a new phase. Growing employment opportunities in England and even in Ireland were reducing the forces driving British subjects outward. On the high seas

---

*Parliamentary Paper, 1852, LXVIII (1650), 18, illustrates the growing diversification of industry by listing among the emigrant arrivals in 1852: 133 plumbers, bricklayers, and masons; 222 cabinet makers and joiners; 91 coopers, dyers, engineers, hatters, and weavers; small numbers of painters, tailors, watchmakers; some 5,000 farm labourers; and more than 6,000 common labourers.

better shipping and more regular sailings offered safer, dependable transport. Before the fifties the amount of emigration fluctuated widely because it depended upon the changing circumstances of what was then known as "the labouring classes." It rose and fell in pretty near accord with the greater or less pressure upon those classes because they were driven to the colonies no matter what the conditions there, no matter what the shipping available, by the "fear of destitution." Now such Britons were not in quite the same way forced to emigrate, but instead were induced to remove mainly by the hope of advancement.[91] And in the colonies a commercial and also a political revolution were providing opportunities for that advancement in almost every occupation and profession.

IX. HELP FOR
THE NEEDY EMIGRANT

DURING THE YEARS of agitation for government aid to emigration, assisted emigration was being carried on by various means. Parishes and local organizations, until 1834 unauthorized by act of Parliament, shipped away to British North America or the United States at their own expense persons who were chargeable to the parish. Private individuals, proprietors wishing to clear their estates, landowners trying to relieve themselves of the pressing weight of the poor rates, and a few organizations, with a philanthropic interest in improving the opportunities of those in need, gave help in the removal of emigrants. And, though the government did not again after 1825 attempt to give civilians direct assistance to emigrate to the American colonies, special terms of settlement were given to military pensioners.

Assisted emigration of this sort does not imply colonization. In the absence of such a system, certain provisions for the welfare of the emigrants were made by the Colonial Office and the governments of the colonies. Emigration agents who Wilmot Horton believed necessary for the regulation of emigration were appointed to the port of Quebec in 1828 and to United Kingdom ports in 1833 and 1834, as has been noted.[1] The Emigration Commissioners, the Agent-General for Emigration and the Colonial Land and Emigration Commissioners, also referred to above, took over in turn part of the responsibility for the emigration movement. In 1834 when the Poor Law Act provided for emigration by parish aid an agent, J. D. Pinnock, was named to form the link between the Colonial Office and the organizations carrying on emigration.[2] From this skeleton force, there developed the machinery which supervised both the systematic colonization movement to Australia and the sporadic assisted emigrations to British North America in the mid-nineteenth century.

Parish-aided emigration had been discussed in England as early as 1821. In 1822 and 1823, the parishes of Smarden, Headcorn near Maidstone, and others about Hemstead in Kent had begun to send emigrants to the United States where they could be set ashore, landing fees paid, and left with "two sovereigns in pocket," for £13 10s. per person.[3]

After 1823 as the state of agricultural and manufacturing labourers failed to improve, 800 out of a population of 1,600 in Maidstone were receiving relief. There the assessment for relief amounted to 15s. on the pound, throughout the whole country to 10s., on every man, woman, and child of the population. Frome, Somerset, a weaving town for three centuries, found its unemployed tethered to the spot by the law of settlement when its manufacture of blue cloth for the Navy ceased in 1815. Cobbett visiting it in 1826 described a small Manchester; its population had increased one-third in the last seven years and, to his regret, the weavers of former days were now at work on the roads, supported by parish relief. In 1831, 557 able-bodied men were receiving assistance and the parish was endeavouring to remove 250 by emigration. In Wiltshire, Gloucestershire, and other areas of the early woollen industry, unemployment was also severe.[4]

When the year 1828 passed without the promised emigration act, many parishes went ahead unassisted. In Pennsylvania authorities, "much exasperated" by English paupers, imposed a tax of two dollars a head on passengers arriving, in addition to the dollar required of all immigrants as hospital money, and New York adopted regulations by which it could send back to England all immigrants arriving "helpless, old, and useless." Though the United States Supreme Court in 1848 held all state legislation imposing taxes on foreign arrivals unconstitutional, the bond demanded of shipmasters to prevent the landing of paupers could be commuted by a cash payment and the court action had little practical effect.[5] In the North American colonies at the same time, the colonial governments and private organizations were caring for emigrants in need.

Until 1834 local organizations conducted these emigrations according to their own ideas of fitness. Parishes raised their own funds, often by borrowing from a well-disposed resident. They engaged ocean passage and despatched the emigrants usually with a parting gift in lieu of relief. At times, the emigrants met good fortune. Again as in the case of the Dorking emigrants to Upper Canada in 1832, food was short and passengers were badly treated by the ship's officers. In Dorking, subscriptions amounting to £415 17s. 6d. had been collected by the local emigration society; the parish had furnished clothing and tools which would have been supplied had the emigrants remained "on the parish," and forty-seven adults and fifteen children had been shipped to Montreal together with a superintendent at an average expense of £10. The parish reaped the benefit of the removals. In 1833 the eighty persons formerly chargeable to the parish were reduced to forty and a contemporary states that emigration was the relieving factor.[6]

A substantial emigration took place in the years 1831 and 1832 and again after 1837 from Wiltshire, chiefly from the estates of Lord Heytesbury of Heytesbury. Ten years earlier, passing through Wiltshire William Cobbett had written, "In my whole life I never saw human wretchedness equal to this."[7] The condition in 1831 may be imagined. A campaign for assisted emigration had been opened in Wiltshire in 1830 by John Silcox, a returned minister from Canada, and some sixty-five persons were helped to return with Silcox. Now both private subscription and parish aid were used. A relative of Lord Heytesbury, Colonel E. H. A'Court, M.P., was untiring in providing for the emigrants of 1831. They were furnished with letters to the emigration agent at Quebec, sent out on the ship *Euphrosyne* under a good master, and given between £2 and 3 each on arrival at Quebec. Nevertheless when they reached York, their resources were badly depleted. It was only through the foresight of Sir John Colborne in preparing the townships of Oro, Dummer, and Douro that these settlers from Wiltshire, together with a similar group from Yorkshire, in all 430 families of more than 3,000 persons were safely placed before the coming of winter.[8]

The best example of a well-conducted emigration during these years is that from Sussex where unemployment and the philanthropic interests of the Earl of Egremont, lord lieutenant of the county from 1819 to 1833, brought about the formation of the Petworth Emigration Committee in 1832. The purpose of the committee was not to shovel out paupers but "to remove from the minds of persons of all classes the notion that emigration to Canada is banishment, and to cherish the idea, that it is only a *removal* from a part of the British empire, where there are more workmen than there is work to be performed, to another, a fertile, healthful, and every way delightful portion of the same empire, where the contrary is the case."[9] In the five years from 1832 to 1836 more than sixteen hundred emigrants were sent to Quebec from Petworth and nearby parishes and from Portsmouth, Chichester, and the Isle of Wight. The Earl of Egremont bore the entire expense of the emigration from Petworth and districts where his holdings were large; elsewhere he was assisted by landlords and the parishes. Usually the outfit for the emigrant was prepared by the parish and so provided work for those who remained at home.[10] Two business men of Petworth and the Rev. T. R. Sockett bargained with the shipping agents, Carter and Bonus, for ships to sail from Portsmouth which would provide food, proper personal accommodations, and free landing at Quebec for about £6 per adult. Superintendents accompanied the Petworth emigrants until they found occupation as labourers or settlers on land of their own.[11]

The Sussex emigrants of 1832 and 1833, 769 in the former year and 200 in the latter, went to Adelaide and Galt. Those of 1834, 1835, and 1836 were supervised by James Marr Brydone. In Adelaide they formed such a gathering of Sussex people that a request was made to change the name of their district to Petworth or Egremont. In 1837 the Petworth Committee, still active, was proposing to buy a block of land north of the Canada Company on Lake Huron, where Lord Egremont hoped "to extend his aid more effectually to a class of Emigrants rather above the common labourer."[12]

Emigration from other counties was meanwhile being carried on in less efficient fashion. By 1832 parishes in Somersetshire, Suffolk, Northamptonshire, Kent, Lincolnshire, Norfolk, Gloucestershire, and Hampshire were raising money to enable those dependent upon the parish to emigrate. In each of the years 1831 and 1832 there landed at Quebec some forty-nine hundred whose way had been paid by parochial and, to a smaller extent, by private funds. Even when sufficient provision had been made by the parishes, money given for use on arrival in the colony—landing money—was often spent on shipboard so that many arrived in Quebec or St. John destitute and then frittered away their time in importuning charitable agencies. Though parishes were advised to transmit their contributions directly to Quebec, as late as 1836 two years after the appointment of a special general agent for emigration, one of whose duties was to arrange parish emigration, paupers from Hampshire were landed in a deplorable condition.[13] Observing similar arrivals in 1840, Lord Sydenham was to ask, "Is their condition bettered by sending them to starve under the Rock at Quebec."[14]

Methods did not alter greatly after the new Poor Law clauses providing for emigration came into force in 1835. When the funds required could be raised by subscription or any means other than that of borrowing, the parish carried out the removal as before without appeal to the new Commissioners of the Poor Law. When it was necessary to borrow on the security of the poor rates under clauses LXII and LXIII of the amending Act of 1834,[15] all arrangements for raising the money, as well as all contracts for the conveyance of the emigrants, were submitted to the Commissioners. According to the Act, funds so raised were not to exceed one-half of the yearly average rate for the last three years and were to be returned within five years. The Poor Law Commissioners specially stipulated that none of the money could be spent on emigration to the United States, though it appears that some was so spent in 1835. Working with J. D. Pinnock, on the whole the Commissioners provided efficient, though complicated, machinery for conducting parish emigrations.

At Quebec the emigration agent, A. C. Buchanan, was compelled to develop a busy correspondence with parish officers and private individuals, especially from Wiltshire, Yorkshire, Berkshire, Hampshire, Sussex, and Norfolk, who interested themselves in the welfare of English emigrants they had helped to forward to Canada. Attached to the agent's report for 1836, then printed on legal-size paper, are ten closely filled pages of letters of that year. John Matteaux of Beachamwell Hall, Norfolk, a magistrate and landowner, wrote to thank Buchanan for directing the emigrants sent by the parish of Swaffham and to announce the departure of some of his own tenants for whom he had given the captain of the *Shannon* half crowns to distribute on shipboard. They were to go to Port Hope and a letter of credit from W. E. Chapman of London to William Patton of Quebec would provide for their transportation and an additional two pounds each on their arrival in Port Hope. From North Runcton, Norfolk, David Gurney sent his advice regarding the emigrants from his parish. A year later John Matteaux reported that the success of the Gurney emigrants had excited throughout the whole district a great desire to move to Canada.

In Hampshire the same sequence was proceeding. John Harrison, the vicar of Sherborne St. John, sent out in 1835 at a cost of £6 each a group of promising young agricultural labourers who were eager to settle near friends in Canada. The following year Harrison interested himself in the emigration of forty-six emigrants who were aided by neighbouring parishes. Again, the Earl of Stradbroke at Henham Hall, Suffolk, on April 18, 1836, warned Buchanan that the Board of Guardians in charge of the local emigrants now on their way to Toronto insisted that their charges should be shipped straight through. And on June 12, Buchanan assured the Earl that he had the river steamboat "go alongside" the *Allandale*, take his parish emigrants aboard, and sail at once for Montreal.[16]

In spite of the idea popular at the time that some stigma attached to parish-aided emigration, one cannot but feel on reading Buchanan's correspondence for this and later years that the emigrant who arrived so advised and guarded was fortunate indeed. Those going out under the sanction of the Poor Law Commissioners enjoyed as well as free passage, an outfit of clothing for the colony and one pound in cash to be paid on their arrival. Cases of distress occurred of course, but among parish emigrants they were probably less numerous than among emigrants who received private aid or came alone insufficiently provided.

By 1837 and 1838 when disturbances in the Canadas temporarily stalled economic life there, the great day of English parish emigration to British North America had ended. At Quebec in 1837, Buchanan noted down the arrival of some 1,500 pauper emigrants, dividing them into good and bad by his own standard—whether or not their landing money was paid in the colony. Only 378 received this payment, in their case £447 18s., in Quebec; all the others from Yarmouth, London, Bristol, Hull, and Portsmouth had taken this final favour from their mother country before sailing and arrived in Quebec prepared to depend upon the colony. Year after year the little groups reported to Buchanan: in 1841 some 4,000 in all, 116 assisted from Lord Portman's estates in Dorset and Kent, other hundreds from Scotland and Ireland, 15 men sent out by the Poor Law Commissioners in London, 59 from the House of Industry, Isle of Wight, some from Salethurst and Readcourt and other parishes; in 1851 some 3,500 (Table X of Appendix B); and in 1858 and 1859 a few hundred from the New Ross, the Chatham, Clonmel, Wexford, Cork, and Londonderry Poor Law unions, some from the London and Glasgow reformatory schools, and a few sent out by Lord Erskine, the Marquis of Lansdowne, and other landed proprietors.[17] But the total number of parish-aided under the Poor Law of 1834 was only some 800 in 1841 and 659 in 1843, and thereafter that movement declined swiftly to a very few hundred in the 1850's and in 1860 to only 55. Returning prosperity accounts partially but not wholly for the decline. In 1857 when a committee of gentlemen in London, including Thomas Baring, contributed to the Wellington Fund in order to assist unemployed artisans in the building trades, the numbers swelled to more than 1,000.[18]

The Poor Law Amendment Act was in one way a test of the soundness of Wilmot Horton's emigration theories. He had worked for emigration on the assumption that pauperism was due to the pressure of population upon the available means of subsistence. All had agreed that relief to the able-bodied must be discontinued. Horton himself had been convinced that emigration would be necessary to absorb the unemployed when that relief ceased. Experience proved that England had unsuspected powers of absorption within her own shores.

Relief to the able-bodied ended in 1835 when parish-aided emigration became effective. Yet no increase in emigration followed. In the first year of operation under the new system, some 5,000 parish-aided emigrants left England for all the British colonies.[19] In the following decade from July, 1836, to the end of 1847 only 9,476 were assisted to emigrate. In one district where there had been 30,000 recipients of out-door relief before 1834 there was afterwards great difficulty, notwithstanding the exertions of two agents, in filling two emigrant ships and that with people who were slightly above the type for whom the

Act was intended.[20] After two centuries of stagnation, as has been said, the end of this relief at last set the rural population in motion. For various reasons parish emigration was unpopular. For one class of persons there was the shame somehow connected with relief. Compared with the flattering remittances from friends in the New World who wanted them to come, this handout from strangers who wanted them to go was humiliating. There were the opportunities now created by Great Britain's industrial expansion. For another class, contemporary opinion held, there was the fact that they naturally preferred "an idle but certain dependence on the parish at home, to an uncertain independence abroad, to be procured by industry and good conduct." The evidence of three-quarters of a century did not change the truth of these conclusions. In 1909 the Poor Law Commissioners, having pointed out that emigration was "a means of dealing with a certain class of cases, which are likely to make a fresh start under new conditions," virtually agreed with an early Poor Law Commissioner, George Nicholls, that at no time had "the distribution of the population been largely affected by this means."[21]

In Scotland where there was in existence no system of parish relief on the English model, the assistance of landlords or of weavers' societies and public subscription were the only forms of emigration aid practised. For a time after 1825 the strongest pressure brought to bear upon the government came from the Scottish and northern emigration societies then organized as they had been in 1820 to demand help during a depression in the weaving industry. Between June and October, 1826, more than thirty Scottish societies with membership ranging from fifty to six hundred each laid their petitions before the Colonial Office. One society wrote that the labour to which the handloom weavers were now subjected was brutifying in the extreme, the fruits of it "poverty and disease, mental and physical." Meetings were held, northern members were active in London, until a return of prosperity finally cancelled the recommendations for government aid. The weavers' petitions continued however, dropping off in 1828, only to increase again in 1829 and 1830. Even Hume in the latter year spoke in favour of the pleas of the workers of Irvine. He believed, of course, that the best method of assuring relief was by letting in foreign corn and increasing production, but if such measures were impossible emigration was better than no remedy at all.[22]

The weavers had asked for transportation to Canada, free grants of land, and rations for the payment of which the societies were willing to bind themselves. In the winter of 1829-30 the Secretary in the Colonial Office, Sir George Murray, so far departed from regulations as to promise free grants of fifty acres to each head of family, larger grants to leaders, and the service of an agent of government in placing the emigrants. An appeal was made "unto the Benevolent and Wealthy Inhabitants of Glasgow" and, with the help of the Established Presbytery of the city, means were obtained for equipping two parties. Two leaders, James Tudhope and Alexander Shanks, carried to the governors of Upper and Lower Canada instructions for free land for their parties. Once again in 1832, the same privilege was accorded to the Glasgow Emigration Society and a group under Daniel McIntyre went out to Upper Canada on the terms of 1830.[23] Privilege or no privilege, the Perth Emigration Society and other Scottish weavers' groups persisted. As late as 1864, 813 of the 991 assisted emigrants reaching Quebec were Scottish handloom weavers sent by their societies.[24]

In the Highlands and Islands of Scotland the building of roads and canals and the encouragement of the kelp industry, which followed the agitation of the Highland Society at the beginning of the century, for a time gave occupation to many. Population continued to increase. But after the removal of the tax on salt, the price of kelp had fallen from £10 a ton to about £2 and, when many manufacturers gave up its sale altogether, the Highlanders who had removed to the coasts were again without means of subsistence. On the Isles of Mull, Tyree, Coll, and Skye, according to a report made to the Treasury, the inhabitants were in "a state of unexampled destitution." At the same time, the profitableness of the fisheries began to wane and bad weather destroyed the main support of life, the potato crop. In 1836 and 1837 some £70,000 had to be raised by local and governmental contributions for the relief of the starving. Emigration was the natural expedient but, since it could not be undertaken on the enormous scale really necessary, the Agent-General could only hope that the smaller arrangements for emigration to Australia might be of help to the Highlanders. For a time, while Alexander Macgregor outlined the advantages of a government grant-in-aid for emigration in the *Quarterly Journal of Agriculture*,[25] and Dr. Thomas Rolph made his sorties through Scotland, encouraging landlords to look to government for help in removing tenants, some Scots may have expected government action. But after Rolph's friend, Henry James Baillie, M.P. (Inverness), interrogated witnesses before the Select Committee on Emigration for Scotland in 1841, the government made its refusal undeniably clear.

From 1826 onward, petitions for assistance had come to the Colonial Office in large numbers from all the western islands. In 1826 alone over a dozen, one of which bears six hundred signatures, were received. Another requests aid for these "poor, Loyal, Peaceable and Industrious

TO THE
BENEVOLENT FRIENDS OF DISTRESSED MANUFACTURERS,
THE PETITION OF THE NORTH-QUARTER GLASGOW-EMIGRATION SOCIETY,

HUMBLY SHEWETH,

That your Petitioners are above three hundred individuals, chiefly hand-loom weavers, whose genius and industry, for many years, constituted a principal part of the splendour and opulence of this once happy land, and diffused wealth through every rank of society; but owing to their trade coming in contact with the machinery of the power-loom, and the consequent reduction of their wages, they have now to deplore the want of the commonest necessaries of life, being only able to lengthen out a miserable existence; their children without education, obliged to work at their own employment in comparative infancy, and by that means perpetuate their miserable trade. Want, absolute want, with all its baneful appendages, has long been familiar in their dwellings, so as to place them in the degrading position of becoming a useless weight on the wealthier part of the community, with every vestige of hope destroyed in their native land, and their unfortunate situation acknowledged by all. They have many friends in Upper Canada comfortably situated; and the Colonial Government of that country has offered fifty acres of land to each family arriving there from Scotland. They therefore consider it more honourable to make this humble and last appeal to the humane gentlemen of their country, for a subscription to enable them to freight a vessel, and provision them to Upper Canada in April, than to remain a useless weight on the charitable institutions of their country. Gentlemen favouring the Society with their signatures, will pay their subscriptions to JOHN HUNTER, Jun. Esq. W.S. of Lockhart, Hunter, and Whitehead, W.S. 5 Fettes Row, their Treasurer in Edinburgh; and all communications respecting the Society, will be kindly received by him.

DANIEL M'ANDREW, *Preses.*
JAMES LITTLE, *Secretary.*

COMMITTEE.

The Rev. D. MACFARLAN, D.D. Principal of the University of Glasgow.
The Rev. WILLIAM BLACK, D.D.
The Rev. MICHAEL WILLIS, D.D.
The Rev. J. HENDERSON, D.D.
The Rev. J. FORBES, D.D.

HUGH TENNENT, Esq. Wellpark.
ROBERT KERR, Jun., Esq.
WILLIAM M'LEAN, Esq. of Plantation.
CHARLES J. TENNENT, Esq. of St Rollox, Treasurer, 49 Cochrane Street.

W. P. PATON, Esq.
The Rev. PETER NAPIER, 40 Buccleugh Street, Sub-Treasurer.
JOHN HUNTER, Jun. Esq. 5 Fettes Row, Treasurer to the Society in Edinburgh.

CERTIFICATE.

GLASGOW, *28th August,* 1840:—The Case of the NORTH QUARTER HAND-LOOM WEAVERS' SOCIETY, for obtaining assistance in Emigrating to Upper Canada, is most earnestly and anxiously recommended to encouragement and support by the

Rev. D. M'FARLAN, D.D. Principal of Glasgow College.
Rev. Dr WILLIAM BLACK, Minister, Barony.
A. ALISON, Sheriff, Lanarkshire.
Rev. PETER NAPIER, Minister, St Georges in the Fields.
Rev. ROBERT WILSON, Minister, Maryhill.
J. W. DICKSON, Sheriff, Falkirk.

THOMAS AITKIN, Provost, Falkirk.
Rev. WILLIAM BEGG, Minister, Falkirk.
CHARLES TENNENT, Esq. St Rollox; Office, 49 Cochrane Street, Glasgow, our Treasurer. All Remittances and Communications to him will be gratefully received.

COPY OF OUR SUBSCRIPTION BOOK.

Name	£ s d	Name	£ s d	Name	£ s d	Name	£ s d
Charles Tennent, Esq. St Rollox,	£10 10 0	William Brown, Esq.	£2 2 0	Messrs Higgenbottom & Co.	£5 0 0	James Ewing, Esq.	£1 0 0
J. Campbell, Esq. Lord Provost	5 0 0	Alexander Dennistoun, Esq.	1 0 0	William Kidston, Esq.	2 2 0	Corbett, Alexander, & Co.	1 1 0
Rev. D. M'Farlan, Principal, Glasgow College,	2 0 0	A. Alison, Esq. Sheriff.	1 1 0	Henry Monteith & Co.	5 0 0	Rev. William Begg, Falkirk.	1 1 0
Rev. Dr Black,	2 0 0	Rev. Dr Willis.	1 1 0	Robert Brand, Esq.	1 1 0	Thomas Aitkin, Esq.	0 10 6
Hugh Tennent, Esq.	5 5 0	Alexander M'Gregor, Esq.	2 2 0	Donald Cuthbertson, Esq.	1 1 0	Wm. Forbes, Esq. Callander.	5 0 0
James Dunlop & Sons,	2 2 0	John M'Farlane, Esq.	1 1 0	Lord Belhaven,	3 0 0	Messrs Ure & Crawford, Esqs.	1 1 0
James Lumsden, Esq.	2 2 0	William Paton, Esq.	1 1 0	Marquis of Breadalbane,	5 0 0	Archibald Smith, Esq.	1 1 0
William Dunn, Esq.	10 10 0	A. S. D.	1 1 0	Duke of Argyle,	2 0 0	John King, Esq.	1 1 0
William Graham, Esq.	2 2 0	James Black, Esq.	1 1 0	William Stirling, Esq.	2 0 0	J. M'Intyre, Esq.	1 1 0
Robert Dalglish, Esq.	2 2 0	William Middleton, Esq.	2 2 0	John Dennistoun, Esq. M.P.	5 0 0	Thomas Kennedy, Esq.	1 1 0
Robert Gourlay, Esq.	1 1 0	John Cogan, Esq.	1 1 0	Andrew Mitchell, Esq.	1 1 0	Samuel Wilson, Esq.	1 1 0
James Fleming, Esq.	1 1 0	John M'Lean, Esq.	1 1 0	John Mitchell, Esq.	1 1 0	Duncan M'Lean, Esq.	1 1 0
A. M'Farlane, Esq.	0 10 6	William Gilmour, Esq.	1 1 0	James Watson, Esq.	1 1 0	A. B. C.	2 2 0
A. Bell, Falkirk.	0 10 6	David Sandiman, Esq.	1 1 0	Archibald Campbell, Esq.	1 0 0	Rev. Robert Muter, D.D.	1 0 0
Thos. Aitkin, Esq. Falkirk.	1 1 0	William Campbell, Esq. Dunoon Castle,	10 0 0	J. C. Colquhoun, Esq.	1 0 0	Neil Caw, Esq.	1 1 0
James Watson, Esq.	1 1 0	Kirkman Finlay, Esq. Castle Toward,	1 0 0	A. Turner, Esq.	1 0 0	William M'Lean, Esq.	1 1 0
				Thomas Edington, Esq.	1 0 0	R. Bard, Esq.	1 0 0
				R. & J. Alexander, Esqs.	5 0 0	Wingate & Son,	1 1 0

SUBSCRIBERS IN EDINBURGH.

Name	£ s d	Name	£ s d	Name	£ s d	Name	£ s d
Lockhart, Hunter, & Whitehead,	2 2 0	John Jeffrey, Esq.	1 1 0	Miss Campbell,	1 0 0	Right Rev. Bishop Walker,	1 0 0
Roger Aytoun, Esq. W.S.	1 1 0	Right Hon. A. Rutherfurd, M.P.	1 1 0	John Murray, Esq.	1 0 0	Rev. R. Candlish,	0 10 6
James Adam, Esq. W.S.	1 1 0	Lord Advocate of Scotland,	1 1 0	R. Downie, Esq.	1 0 0	W. Blackwood & Son,	1 1 0
Lord Jeffrey,	1 1 0	Lord Mackenzie,	1 1 0	Sir James Stewart,	0 10 6	Rev. J. Sym,	0 10 6
Lord Provost of Edinburgh,	1 1 0	Lord Cockburn,	1 1 0	Dr J. Davidson, Esq.	1 1 0	Rev. Archd. Bennie,	0 10 6
Mark Sprot, Esq.	1 1 0	Jas. Mackenzie, Esq. W.S.	1 0 0	Alexander Campbell, Esq.	1 0 0	Jas. Balfour, Esq. W.S.	1 1 0
Rev. Dr Chalmers,	2 2 0	Rev. Dr David Welsh, Professor,	1 1 0	A. Dyrbrough, Esq.	0 10 6	W. Whitehead, Esq.	0 10 6
Dr Alison, Professor,	1 1 0	Lord Gillies,	1 1 0	John Aitchison, Esq.	0 10 6	Robt. Thomson, Esq.	0 10 6
Lord Cuningham,	1 1 0	Dr Abercrombie,	1 1 0	Donald Horne, Esq. W.S.	1 0 0	W. & M. Johnson, Esqs.	0 10 6
A. Wood, Esq. Advocate,	1 1 0	Alex. Cowan & Sons,	1 0 0	Alexander Berwick, Esq.	0 10 6	J. Dalmahoy, Esq. W.S.	0 10 6
Dn. M'Neill, Esq. Advocate,	1 1 0	Sir A. C. Maitland Gibson, Bart.	1 1 0	James M'Kenzie, Esq. W.S.	1 1 0	Jas. Creighton, Surgeon,	0 5 0
James Renton, Esq. Accountant,	1 1 0	Rt. Grieve, Esq. 77 South Bridge	1 1 0	D. J. Thompson, Esq.	1 0 0	Mrs Blackburn,	1 0 0
John S. More, Esq. Advocate,	1 1 0	Lord Fullerton,	1 1 0	Geo. Ritchie, Esq.	0 10 6	Thos. W. Baird, Esq. Advocate,	1 1 0
G. Speirs, Esq. Sheriff of Edin.	1 1 0	Lord Glasgow,	1 1 0	Wm. Robertson, Esq.	1 1 0	T. Robertson, Esq. Accountant,	1 0 0
J. Macgregor, Esq. Advocate,	1 1 0	Thos. Sprot, Esq.	0 10 6	John Muir, Esq.	0 10 6	Alexr. Gifford, Esq. S.S.C.	0 10 6
J. P. Bertram, Esq. W.S.	1 1 0	Rev. Dr Dickson,	1 1 0	Dr Baildon,	1 0 0	Rev. R. Elder,	0 5 0
Lord Ivory,	1 1 0	Rev. Dr W. Muir,	1 1 0	Alexr. Morton, Esq.	0 10 6	A. Connell, Esq.	0 10 6
A. Dunlop, Esq. Advocate,	1 1 0	Robt. Hunter, Esq. Advocate,	1 1 0	John Anderson, Esq. W.S.	0 10 6	John Geddes, Esq.	0 10 6
John Cowan, Esq. Advocate,	1 1 0	W. & R. Chambers, Esqs.	1 1 0	Fras. Anderson, Esq. W.S.	0 10 6	A. Campbell, Esq.	1 0 0
Lord Moncreiff,	1 1 0	Dr M'Lagan,	1 1 0	W. D.	0 10 6	John Ramsay, M.D.	1 0 0

FIGURE 8. The Petition of the North-Quarter Glasgow Emigration Society. To the Benevolent Friends of Distressed Manufacturers. 1841. (Public Archives of Canada, R G 7, G 20, vol. 2.)

People" similar to that given to "the unruly and riotous Manufacturers."[26] To all but one in these years was sent the uniform reply—that as no funds were available for emigration and land was no longer granted free, the Colonial Office could not extend the assistance requested.

The exception made to this general rule was the petition of the Duke of Hamilton who had used his influence for the weavers in 1820, and in 1828 had interested himself in the northern and western emigrations. The tenants on his property on the Isle of Arran had increased in the last few years from three to eight thousand; many of them wished to move to Perth in Canada, but they demanded not only free land but also seed and implements. The latter favours were denied at once, but 100-acre grants of land being promised "free of any charge except the fees upon the grant," the Duke prepared to send out at his own expense, probably about £1,440, a trial party of twenty-six families. The party, under the leadership of Archibald McKillop, reached Quebec in July 1829 and there, discouraged, they requested permission to settle in the lower colony. The emigration agent and the land board accordingly promised the Arran emigrants the remission of the fees on their land grants, if they would cross the St. Lawrence River to the new townships of Leeds and Inverness.[27] In 1830 a small band also from the Duke's estates joined the first group on the same terms. When a third party arrived however, changed land regulations were in force which required high fees, and further relaxation of rules for the Duke's Arran tenants was refused as "partial and unjust."[28]

Assisted emigration of the Scots continued, but under different arrangements. As early as 1825, the proprietor of the Island of Rum in the Hebrides had cancelled the debts of his overcrowded tenants, divided £600 among them, and paid their passage to Canada. In 1842, one year after the Duke of Argyll told the Select Committee on Emigration that he had permitted subdivision by the crofters on the Isle of Tyree until emigration was the only solution possible, 946 Scottish emigrants who had received private aid landed at Quebec. In 1843 the numbers rose to 1,051; of these the Duke of Sutherland had sent 36, emigrant societies the remainder.[29] At the same time, many were being assisted to remove to Cape Breton and Prince Edward Island—in 1840 about 700 emigrants from the Isle of Skye. The Duke of Sutherland's shipments continued; in 1848 the *Ellen*, which he had chartered, brought a cargo of Scots into Pictou on their way to Prince Edward Island. Year after year until the fifties, Cape Breton received "a dreadful inundation" of needy, displaced Scots, the lieutenant governor authorized help, and the magistrates doled out meal and potatoes. By 1849 landlords far and wide had taken up the idea of clearing their estates by the emigration of tenants. That year some 1,000 were sent out from Harris, Uist, and Benbicula where Macdonald of Clanronald had been supporting his tenantry off and on since 1826.[30] Before the end of 1851, Colonel Gordon of Cluny had prepared and shipped to British North America about 1,500 souls from his estates on the Isles of Barra and Uist South, and Sir James Mathewson some 1,000 of his tenants from Lewis. In 1852 alone 435 of the 606 assisted Scottish emigrants who landed at Quebec had passage paid and rations provided by Sir James.[31]

Though the large immigration of penniless Scots aroused indignation in British North American ports where the emigrant societies were overwhelmed, in 1853 another heavy inundation swept in, mainly from the Glengarry district of Inverness-shire which had been "cleared." In the following years this type of Highland emigration to the British American colonies fell off markedly, partly because the Highlands and Islands had actually decreased in population, the decrease being recorded for Inverness after 1841 and for Kirkcudbright, Cromarty, Ross, and Sutherland after 1851, and partly because the Highlands and Islands Emigration Society in which Sir Charles Trevelyan had been active had begun to encourage emigration to Australia.[32] The difficulty of redirecting an established train of emigration may be realized when it is understood that Australia had been recommended as a destination for the Scots years before in 1837. By 1851 the Emigration Advances Act, previously mentioned, permitted landlords to borrow funds for assisting tenants to move to the colonies. The effect of the legislation was slight, for the numbers of those so aided reaching Quebec had almost totally dwindled away by 1857, the year of maximum emigration of the late 1850's.[33]

In Ireland the need for emigration was probably more urgent than in Scotland; from the north, south, and west petitions reciting misfortune of every sort found their way to the Colonial Office. Labourers in Coleraine who had long been supported by the liberality of landowners asked for free passage to Canada. Weavers in Belfast suffering from the same depression as was noted in Scotland begged a similar favour. Informers in Clare, Tipperary, and neighbouring counties, tormented by the "turbulent and obnoxious Peasantry" whose activities they had revealed, got Dublin Castle to intercede for them at the Colonial Office. From proprietors in Limerick, Sligo, Roscommon, and the south came requests for aid such as had been given to Cork in 1825 or to the Duke of Hamilton in 1829.[34]

In a few cases where distress was particularly great and the counties in consequence were burdened with heavy contributions, organizations formed by the county officers—in Kildare by the magistrates assembled in petit sessions—called for subscriptions and removed a portion of the population. In 1830 Kildare sent to Quebec a group of 155, "all bred to the same branch of the Woolen Manufacture." They arrived in the port "perfect paupers," and were sent on to the townships opening above Montreal, expenses being paid by the charity of the boatmen who conveyed them. Sir James Kempt, the governor at Quebec, objected strongly to the policy of sending emigrants "destitute among strangers," and the Colonial Office ordered an inquiry into the deportation, as Stanley was to do a decade later when he protested the "transferring of persons in entirely destitute circumstances from this country to the colonies." When paupers from one English parish turned up in another, they could be returned but, if they were removed to the colonies, the Colonial Office could only inquire and protest. If counties such as Kildare chose to "emigrate" their redundant labourers and the regulations of the Passenger Act could be avoided or obeyed, there was nothing to hinder them depositing any number of paupers in any state of destitution on the shores of British America.[35]

As the practice of large farming spread, proprietors and Irish witnesses before parliamentary committees were unanimously in favour of emigration, especially if the state would provide the funds for it. When the government failed to give this assistance, many landholders in the south and west undertook the expense of emigration themselves. In the year 1835, 47 of 60 parishes widely scattered through Ireland reported in returns to the Poor Law Commissioners that landlords had given direct aid to emigrants; in 23 others emigrants had received public assistance, probably from general contributions.[36]

A typical emigration of the early years was that managed by one Clendenning in the spring of 1831 from the estates of St. George Caulfield in county Roscommon. The object of the undertaking, according to Clendenning, was to carry on depletion of population until plans for the reorganization of the estate could be embarked upon. Once committed to this plan of "political plebotomy"—the phrase is Clendenning's—the promoters of the emigration permitted tenants who were willing to remove to sell their crops to adjoining farmers, their rents in arrears were retained from the sale price, and a loan for emigration was advanced by Caulfield on the security given by the new occupiers. By this inducement 36 heads of families, occupying 50 acres of land and paying in all only £45 17s. 2d. yearly rent, were enabled to emigrate. Two-thirds of the whole party, it was believed, would have been in a state of starvation by June. Caulfield therefore considered himself well rid of such an encumbrance at the price of £723 2s. 9d., the total sum advanced by him in loan and grant.

The emigration agent at Quebec felt that the encumbrance had merely been transferred to Canada. Clendenning had dubbed his party "a set of Ragamuffins in appearance, but with wit, bone and sinew worthy of better fortune" and, perhaps because of these qualities, the agent found it difficult to discover how genuine were the pleas of distress they raised on arrival. When he offered them location tickets in the district of Newcastle or employment near Quebec, Patrick Bly and his fellows assured the agent that they had had nothing but their passage from Clendenning. Investigation being made, the proprietor gave proof that from the three principal tenants who had complained he had retained only about £14 for arrears in rent and that the advances made had been over £60.[37] Another landlord in Roscommon did not fare so well as Caulfield. In 1848 the 2,400 people on Major Mahon's 2,000 acres were producing only one-third of the food needed for their own support; rents and rates were three years behind and the workhouse overflowing. Mahon offered free ocean transport, free provisions, and permission to sell stock and effects; he spent, he claimed, £14,000 on the emigration. Yet 25 per cent of his emigrants died at sea, others reached Quebec in a most wretched condition, and within months Mahon was murdered by agrarian agitators. Though Mahon's case is unusual, it is true that a Roscommon fund for shooting "oppressors" appears to have received contributions from overseas.

The introduction of the Poor Law of 1838 which authorized assistance to emigrants, made little change in the habits of proprietors who wished to reorganize their lands unless perhaps to increase the removals of lesser tenantry in order to escape heavy poor rates. Eviction is an unpleasant business at best; nevertheless some investigators have concluded that the Irish evictions of the 1840's were carried out with due regard to legal forms, to the advantage of the estate and the tenant, and often with real care for the suffering of the evicted.[38]

From the estates of the Earl of Egremont in County Clare, the Earl's son, Colonel George Wyndham, shipped away to Quebec in 1839 about 180 persons, the members of the Ennis Emigration Society. The emigration agent, Buchanan, and Dr. Thomas Rolph wrote flatteringly of the perfect health of the group and their settlement under Captain Rubidge, R.N. But stories that spread from the Newcastle district where the emigrants were placed increased Canadian opposition to this type of emigrant. Nothing however could stop the emigrations. Colonel Wyndham continued his shipments in 1841 and was joined by Lord Charlemont of Armagh and other proprietors. More than five hundred Irish emigrants who had received private assistance sailed into the port of Quebec in 1841 and 1842. From the colony the Governor-General, Sydenham, assured Lord John Russell that he had forwarded Wyndham's emigrants at Wyndham's expense, since his motive was said to be benevolent. It might be convenient, he wrote, for gentlemen to ship off crowded tenantry, but "the last thing to which they can lay claim in doing so is Benevolence."[39]

After 1844 when Francis Spaight, a timber merchant who carried staves to Shannon and brought emigrants back, bought the property of Derry Castle on the Shannon in Tipperary, the "worst overpopulated district in Great Britain," larger clearances began. Spaight at once offered free passage on his ships and landing money to tenants on his new estates provided they would move to Canada and level or destroy their homes on departure. In 1846 Spaight gave £2 clear to each adult of 20 families he embarked. The following year he sent off 710 more to join the first group, this lot at a cost of £3 10s. per adult head. As usual the better sort of tenants emigrated. Perhaps also as usual, Spaight's tax rate did not go down for a less well-managed neighbouring estate in Temple Kelly could not raise its own rates.[40]

In 1845 when the Devon Commission took evidence, fifteen of the witnesses appearing stated that they had already aided emigration directly, among them Lords Clanicarde (who had spent £551 for the purpose in 1841 and 1842), Fitzwilliam, Palmerston, Stanley, and Midleton, Sir Lucius O'Brien and William Stuart Trench. Ten other witnesses had given money which was used for emigrating. By 1846 Colonel Wandesford of Kilkenny had shipped to America three thousand tenants at a cost of £5 each. Though protests against his economical methods soon reached the Colonial Office from Canada, Wandesford considered them a good investment. His farmers, once in Canada or Pennsylvania, soon sent back remittances which carried on the movement, and Lord Darnley and other landlords took up the practice.[41] Two-thirds of the proprietors providing direct aid in these years held lands in the area stretching across from Galway to Cork where the famine was soon to cause great loss of life.

At the end of the period, one of the most controversial clearances and emigrations of many took place from the estates of Lord Palmerston and Sir Robert Gore Booth in County Sligo. Though the rundale system with its clusters of peasant huts and scattered lands had been eliminated in 1837, Palmerston's Cliffony property was still so overcrowded in 1848 that the agent, Kincaid, was authorized to aid those tenants who would give up their rights and emigrate. Kincaid opened an application list and sent off 894 persons at a cost of £4 10s. per head. Gore Booth and his wife had a reputation of kindness and liberality; they equipped their tenants generously and their shipmasters, co-operating with merchants in New Brunswick, found employment for many of the 1,500 tenants they brought. Yet when the first of these tenants landed in New Brunswick, the emigration agent at St. John, M. H. Perley, accused Gore Booth of shovelling out the old and infirm and asserted that Lord Palmerston's emigrants wore the foulest rags and the children appeared stark naked. Some of the emigrants at once became public charges, and the citizens of St. John protested in shocked surprise that a minister of the Crown would permit such heartless treatment. When a large cargo of Cliffony tenants reached Quebec in early November as the winter closed in, the Quebecois rose in "righteous indignation." Whatever may have been the fate of the individuals in the New World, Palmerston's property enjoyed the benefit of the removal. Within the year its tenants were described as prosperous in contrast with the "multitudes . . . suffering in most acute misery" on the neighbouring Ballina estate where no emigration had occurred. Through the little Cliffony post office, Palmerston's former tenants had already sent back to friends and relatives almost £2,000.[42]

When Lord Grey, now colonial secretary, had the Sligo County landlords questioned regarding the accusations from the colonies, Palmerston's agent acknowledged that he had sent near paupers and Gore Booth that the emigration had removed "what might be termed bad characters." But Grey's careful inquiries, his patience with colonial objections and landlords' explanations revealed an impossible impasse: landlords insisted that they had spent large sums on emigration, Gore Booth £6,000, Wyndham £700, and actually on the tenants who the colonists described as arriving destitute.[43] The difference in point of view was perhaps inevitable. The colonies needed sound, working citizens; so did the Irish landlords. A year later the emigration agent at St. Andrews reported as follows on the emigrants sent to his port by the Poor Law Commissioners from Ireland: Patrick Driscoll, "aged, infirm, and very drunken"; Thomas Leary, "aged, consumptive, now dead"; Hannah Leary, "aged, very drunken, worthless"; Mary Murphy, "aged, infirm, incorrigible termagent, sore eyes, now stone blind"; Eliza Magner, "aged, infirm, drunken, worthless"; Patrick Coughlan, "insane, now dead"; Ellen Daly, "subject to fits," and so on, name after name.[44]

The famine finally broke the tenant's attachment to his soil. Instead of meeting resistance to their offers of emigration, landlords resembled

E. S. Roche, M.P. (Cork) who felt like a man "in a Garrison infested by the enemy" as soon as he promised his tenants assistance to emigrate. In the spring of 1847, the number of assisted emigrants sailing from Dublin rose to 2,000, from Limerick to 1,400, and from various other ports to 2,000. In that year, one shipper carried out 8,000 assisted emigrants. Quebec received about 5,000 of these in 1847 and New Brunswick was also inundated by penniless Irish.[45] Though Lord Lansdowne spent £15,000 in 1851 in sending overseas every pauper chargeable on his Kerry estate, this was an exception, for after 1850 landlord-aided emigration declined. In 1852 the total number disembarking at Quebec was less than 3,000 and in 1854 the decline continued, so that during the decade the average number was scarcely 500 annually.[46]

That parish-aided as distinct from proprietor-aided emigration did not reach larger proportions when the Irish need was obviously great puzzled some members of Parliament and irritated others. According to Sir George Grey, the home secretary, legislation for the purpose had been practically inoperative, only 27 persons having been sent to the colonies in 1848 under the Acts 1 and 2 Vic. c. 56, a mere seven under the next Act, though each Act had provided means for the parish to raise money for emigration.* Parishes had been raising money by other means; in 1849 when the guardians of Limerick Union had advertised for tenders for £6,000, all that could be raised on the security offered was £500. With that amount, 91 persons were "sent out" at an average cost of £5 10s. each and 15s. as landing money. Since every one of the emigrants had already been supported at a cost of £14, the union would have saved money by promoting emigration sooner.[47]

After 1848 as economic conditions in Western Europe more and more resembled conditions in Ireland and canal and railroad transportation across England improved, Liverpool shipping merchants began to promote the European emigrant trade. So in Quebec the busy emigrant agent struggled not only with Highland Scots who knew no English but also with Germans and Scandinavians who had been sent to the New World by their parishes or central governments. As with the Irish, the numbers arriving in Canada fluctuated; the Bavarian government sponsored 172 in 1852, other agencies in Prussia, Weimar, and Sweden sent 31 in 1853, 408 in 1855, and 104 and 194 in 1856 and 1857 respectively. Of 90 paupers shipped to New Brunswick by Württemberg in

---

*The Act of 1847, 10 and 11 Vic., c. 31, authorized the parish to aid the emigration of dispossessed tenants whose proprietors would pay two-thirds of the cost of the emigration and cancel rents in arrears.

1855, none could speak English and 87 had to be lodged in the almshouse.[48]

Sometimes it was necessary for the emigrant agent at Quebec to hire an interpreter, sometimes to provide employment at Canadian expense or transportation to the west for the foreign-born emigrants. In 1854 Buchanan recommended the imposition of regulations to forbid such emigrants using British shipping and British ports. These foreign paupers, he believed, were "supplied with aid, not because they were fitted to succeed as settlers in America, but because they are burthensome at home; and it was evident . . . that the same disability which had rendered them valueless to the community in their own country would affect them here in an increased degree." Loyal civil servants though the Buchanans were, A. C. Buchanan the younger did not hesitate to complain in 1859 that in this the foreign paupers resembled some sent out by parishes in the United Kingdom. And the Emigration Commissioners, reading Buchanan's suggestions sympathetically and sending them on to the Poor Law Commissioners in Ireland, advised that the Foreign Secretary do the same with the Court of Baden and other German governments.[49]

Official efforts to assist retired and discharged military men brought problems of another colour, some success, and considerable failure. A general order from the Horse Guards of July 18, 1829, authorizing free land grants of 1,200 acres for lieutenant colonels and decreasing amounts down to 500 acres for subalterns had scarcely gone into effect when the Colonial Office adopted the policy of sales rather than free grants of land. The government then provided that officers could buy land at the regular colonial land sales and receive from the Military Chest refunds graduated according to rank and length of service. In most cases the officers who accepted these terms were, as the colonial authorities intended they should be, valuable additions to the back settlements of the maritime colonies and Canada. But as for the military pensioners of Chelsea Hospital, the purpose of the assisted emigration was to enable soldiers existing in the British Isles on meagre allotments to establish themselves in the colonies at small cost to the government; the results of the efforts were in accord with the limitations of the purpose.

Under terms of a War Office memo of October, 1830, non-commissioned officers or privates entitled to out-pension from Chelsea Hospital might commute their pensions for cash, up to a total of four years' pension, and receive from 100 to 200 acres of land free in the colonies, in return for remission of all future claims upon the government.[50] Though there were in 1831 over 80,000 pensioners in the

British Isles, only 1,745 accepted the offer made by Chelsea Hospital. Of these 1,392 went to the American colonies, some 1,000 pensioners numbering with their families 3,500 souls landing at Quebec in the season of 1831.[51] Before the end of the year, complaints from the colonies caused the colonial officials to request suspension of the regulations for commutation. But the War Office professed to be prepared to certify that all men permitted to commute would be able to maintain themselves by labour.[52] Consequently during 1832 a further small emigration was conducted on the principles of 1831.

Faulty administration of the plan as well as the habits of the beneficiaries explain the failure. As a rule the pensioners received part of their money from the Chelsea Board before embarkation; some "drank themselves to death, or squandered it, and then refused to leave the country." Others who were to receive part of their sum in the colonies turned up without their instruction papers. When written for, the papers had to be obtained by the Chelsea Board from the War Office, which had to apply to the Treasury, and the papers, "after being bandied about from office to office, from clerk to secretary, from secretary to clerk, were sent, at length, after a lapse of eight or ten months, during which the poor men, worn out with suspense, had taken to begging, or to drinking, in utter despondency; and when the order for their money *did* at last arrive, they had become useless, abandoned creatures." Even then some pensioners who had received their final payment only at Quebec reached Montreal penniless and had to be sent forward by the emigration agent at the expense of the colony. In the second place, no provision was made for placing the pensioners on land. In Upper Canada, Lieutenant-Governor Sir John Colborne had them conveyed at provincial expense to districts where both land and employment could be found. There those who were strong, healthy, and industrious ultimately made good. But there, too, the third outstanding fault of the scheme appeared. Pensioners who were infirm or indifferent soon abandoned their locations and became a burden to the community. Too little care had been taken in selecting men fit for emigration. One-half of the pensioners, Mrs. Anna Jameson wrote, presented "a list of all the miseries and diseases incident to humanity," some with one arm, some with one leg, bent, lame, halt, blind.[53]

From New Brunswick came the complaint that the majority of the pensioners were "totally unfit to become Settlers, many of them being worn out and incapable of labour." To the great annoyance of the Lords of the Treasury in London, Lieut. Governor Campbell of Nova Scotia sent back to England at British expense 29 widows and orphans of pensioners and as many pensioners who had already spent their commutation money. Colborne in Upper Canada thought it cruel to tempt old soldiers to a hard pioneer life by £40 or 50 in place of regular pension.[54] He gathered 68 of the most helpless from the hovels of Toronto in 1835 and placed them in huts at Penetanguishene, in the hope of saving their families. In 1836 the Upper Canada Assembly begged the Colonial Office to have the men put back on the pension list; Sir Francis Bond Head requested the government to relinquish "the hard advantageous bargain it made with these brave but improvident veterans." The War Office blamed the failure on the methods of aid practised in the colonies; the pensioners had received all that was due them from their country—their commutation. Of the 850 settled in Upper Canada only 450 were living in 1837; 300 on their land grants, 150 living on the charity of government. When after 1840 the list of recipients of British government aid was checked by Chelsea Hospital, it contained names which had never been on the Chelsea rolls.[55]

As the factory system spread and the employment of children and juvenile delinquency both increased in the new centres of population, concern over child welfare was aroused. Emigration of destitute children had been advocated in 1830 by different private agencies which were inspired by the humanitarian motives of the age. In that year the Society for the Suppression of Juvenile Vagrancy, later the Children's Friendly Society, gave some few children training in their homes and removed them to apprenticeship in the colonies. When a group organized in London for the care of unfortunate children approached the Treasury with proposals for emigration, the suggestion was immediately laid before Lord Aylmer at Quebec. Doubting that an organization for receiving and apprenticing the children could be founded in the colony, Lord Aylmer recommended that the children should be apprenticed to emigrants who were about to leave England for the colonies. The Colonial Office opposed this plan and for more than two years seems to have been influential enough to hold the efforts of the Children's Friendly Society and other emissaries of Exeter Hall at a standstill.[56]

Early in the spring of 1835, one band of twenty boys sponsored by the society sailed on the *Eleutheria*. They were received at Quebec by A. C. Buchanan and sent on to Toronto in the care of an agent, Orrock, who placed them as apprentices in Upper Canada. Three months later a second party arrived and were successfully apprenticed by the same agent. Small groups from the West Kirk Workhouse in Edinburgh were also arriving, with their "opportunities" in Canada carefully stipulated by W. Gray of the workhouse. The boys were to be apprenticed until they were twenty-one and the girls until eighteen years of age, on condition that they be properly fed, clothed, and lodged. Buchanan found situations for them at Port Stanley. On August 4, 1835, he advised his assistant to give every protection to "these young travellers; the name of the oldest boy is R. Danier," he wrote, "and the oldest girl Jane Allen."[57]

The problem of the juvenile, meanwhile, was repeatedly brought before Parliament. In 1838 the Secretary for War and the Colonies, Lord Glenelg, went so far as to suggest that young British criminals might find reformation with freedom from the temptation of old world cities by removal to the Canadian wilderness. Fortunately this proposal was dropped at the time and again later.[58] During the same years, the humane-minded Lord Ashley, M.P. (Bath) began to present the cause of child welfare. After painting a painful picture of strays, waifs, and delinquents in the metropolis in June, 1848, after eulogizing the work of the Poor Law Ragged Schools, and insisting that witnesses for Australia thought that the colonies could absorb great numbers of children, Ashley outlined an emigration plan which the Commissioners of Emigration believed to be perfectly practicable. Nevertheless when he brought in a motion to provide for an annual emigration from the Ragged Schools to the British colonies, that motion like others before and after it was dropped.[59]

Though emigration from the Poor Law Schools to Australia rose to 150 children in that year and was to continue, the abstinence of Parliament in 1848 may have been lucky for the American colonies. Before two years passed, twelve boys who were given transportation to Canada by the Ragged School of Smithfield found life in the colony so unattractive that their story became a warning for a select committee of Parliament. Landing in Quebec in 1850, two of the boys went "up country" and neglected to report their fate to their benefactors; ten used their landing money to go into lodgings in the port. By August, four had returned to England and the remaining six were awaiting means to do the same.[60] In England efforts were being made to equip poor children for useful lives by providing industrial training in the schools on the plan developed by the Norwood Training School. The Limehouse School was soon turning out excellent boys. By 1852 almost 34,000 children were attending the workhouse schools and industrial training had greatly improved. Employment for them was easily found. In 1858 and 1859 the London Ragged School was shipping children to Quebec with apparent success;[61] sixty-five reformatory boys arrived in each of the years 1861 and 1862.[62] In spite of the disapproval with which the central authorities in the British Isles viewed the parish-aided emigration of children, various unions managed to circumvent their government; some Irish unions used legislation which enabled them to enforce a rate of six pence on the pound to send to the colonies not the adults the law intended but destitute children from their workhouses.[63]

From the colonies the demand for children grew. In 1852 Moses H. Perley, the emigration agent at St. John, New Brunswick, applied directly for 100 male and 100 female children from the Poor Law unions. Later he obtained definite lists of needs: for King's County 62 male and 43 female children, for Carleton County 58 male and 47 female, and so on to a total of 249 male and 176 female children. Presently however, the Poor Law Board developed scruples and formulated legal demands which Perley and his counties could not meet.[64] It was not until after Confederation that the emigration of children was so conducted as to win the assistance and approval of the board.

Years before the Emigration Commissioners announced their belief that "for the permanent growth of a colonial population every single man who is sent out in excess of the number of single women is absolutely useless," benevolent societies and Poor Law unions began to promote the emigration of women to the British American colonies. The need for domestic servants and other female helpers and for wives was well nigh insatiable and, according to some Poor Law officers, the supply was equally inexhaustible. In Ireland girls were so willing to endure the discipline of the workhouse in a "sort of distant hope that some day or another they may be sent out of the country," that the Earl of Donoughmore opposed any further emigration whatever at public expense.[65]

Poor Law unions seized the opportunity of ridding themselves of a troublesome burden. Early in 1841, in spite of publicity in the London *Observer* and the opposition of the Poor Law Commissioners, the guardians of the locally controlled Marylebone parish shipped to South Australia "some of the most vicious paupers." Later in the decade, the Irish unions began to "emigrate" pauper women and after the Poor Law Acts which permitted the removal of workhouse inmates, mentioned above, the practice gained popularity. At times the agent on the St. Lawrence had some success in placing Irish workhouse girls in domestic service in Bytown and elsewhere.[66] At times he could report that the girls from one county were highly recommended, others not. Again in 1858 and 1859 when unions sent out helpless widows and children and in 1863 when the Irish girls landed knew nothing about domestic work, the agent protested sturdily.[67]

Better success with choice of emigrants and placements in the colonies was attained by a benevolent society, the London Female Emigration Society, which itself paid the passage of the women and arranged for their reception in the New World. The first group of emigrants, eighteen in number, all working women, made the trip from London to Toronto in the spring of 1850. As their services were well received, the system so established continued year after year. In 1862, the Female Emigration Society had two matrons travelling in charge of women on the way to Quebec. Passage was still free and clothing had been provided, but the women bound themselves to repay one-half the expenditure upon them.[68]

The system for assisting the needy which developed as this emigration progressed belies the assertion that British North American colonization was characterized only by the virtues of individualistic, free enterprise. The emigration agents at Quebec and St. John, A. C. Buchanan and M. H. Perley, were in constant touch with the Colonial Office and the Emigration Commissioners in London as well as with the executives in the colonies. As shipping improved, the agents received weekly reports upon the emigrants to be expected and reported back weekly on the condition of those arriving. They compiled information on opportunities in the colonies which was used by officials in the mother country in directing or restraining emigrants. One of Buchanan's pamphlets for the season of 1853 warns emigrants against parting with their tickets or refusing employment. (See Appendix A.) It lists the Montreal and Portland and the Quebec and Richmond railroads, the Great Western and the Toronto and Simcoe as in need of labourers, and it gives detail on the routes and rates of passage to many parts of Canada. The agents personally directed emigrants to employment and available land in the colonies. Since they provided the transportation of thousands of emigrants annually, they determined in co-operation with colonial planners like Colborne and Colebrooke the routes the emigrants followed inland and the areas in which they were placed. For New Brunswick, Perley became an authority upon whom the home government relied.[69] So efficient and influential in settlement policy did Buchanan become in Canada that Colonel Thomas Talbot openly resented the power the government gave "that Beast."

Financial support for this assistance to emigrants came from both mother country and colony. The itemized budget for the emigration agents in United Kingdom ports and the large establishment of the Emigration Commissioners was placed before Parliament annually for vote. The Quebec emigration agent's salary beginning in 1828 was drawn from the land and timber fund; the colonies themselves cared for the additional local agents as they were appointed. Theoretically the costs of the emigration agents' offices in the colonies were to be borne from the proceeds of the emigrant head taxes levied in the ports following instructions of December 11, 1831. In Canada, the Quebec agent's returns for the tax collected in 1853 stood as given below:[70]

> 23,741 adults at 5s.
> 10,260 children at 3s. 9d.
> 364 uncertified at 7s. 6d.
> 53 penalized at 40s.
>
> Less expense ....
> £7,953 7s. 6d.

In New Brunswick in contrast with Canada, the income from the tax was paid directly to the colonial government, and the Assembly then allocated *via* the commissioners of the parochial poor a sum, usually insufficient, to the emigration agent's office. In 1846 though the tax brought in £1,362, the Assembly appropriated for the agent's work only £300 and carried the residue of £1,062 to general purposes.[71]

In Quebec enormous though the numbers of emigrants were, the head tax produced a sum too small to cover the costs of aid. Lord John Russell developed the plan already noted for assisting emigration by having the home government finance the head tax of indigent emigrants, provided they could be approved before sailing as suitable settlers. But opposition to even this limited form of assistance was strong and the plan failed to mature. Occasionally before and regularly after 1840, the Colonial Office obtained by parliamentary vote £1,500 sterling, about £1,800 currency, for the Quebec agency. Since this did not meet expenditures, an extra vote became customary. In 1842 the extra amounted to £5,000, in 1843 to £2,244, and in 1844, as Lord Stanley began to suspect undue liberality in Canadian assistance, to only £1,000.[72] In seasons of cholera, typhus, and famine, the greater part of the funds from these sources went to furnish medical service, and the home government therefore increased its contributions. In Canada in normal years the heaviest expense was contracted for transportation of emigrants who often arrived to all appearances totally indigent. The London offices believed that the indigence was often feigned because emigrants had learned of the Canadian custom of giving free transportation. As a rule, port agents disagreed with that point of view, and no one had a closer acquaintance with the arriving emigrants than they. In 1853, the Quebec agency spent £2,379 8s. 3d. for transporting 4,698 adults. Of these, 2,368 went to Montreal at a cost of 2s. 4½d. each,

1,069 to Toronto at 11*s*. 11¼*d*. each, and 965 to Buffalo, Milwaukee, and Chicago at 25*s*. each, and 295 by the Champlain route, also to the United States, at 19*s*. each. In much the same way, the agents at Montreal and Toronto expended £1,551 17*s*. 6*d*. and £132 17*s*. 8*d*. respectively. Calculating the total expenditure against the total emigration, the Quebec agent found that in 1848 costs were 14*s*. 7½*d*. per head, in 1849 6*s*. 2½*d*., and in 1850 only 4*s*. 10*d*.[73]

Accounts kept in the emigration agent's office in Quebec present a view of the operation of the aid given to emigrants. They show also, for the fairly normal years summarized in Table IX of Appendix B, the extent to which the aid was paid for by the emigrants themselves through the tax and to what extent by the British government which had disavowed all intention of assisting British subjects in their removal to North America. In the years 1842 and 1843 the tax evidently provided less than half the sum necessary for the assistance given; in 1852 and 1855, on the other hand, the tax made up a good proportion of the funds used.

Early in 1854 the Colonial Office decided that Parliament would no longer approve annual appropriations for the British American emigration agencies. The Secretary of State for the Colonies took pains to explain the British Treasury's large expenditures in assuring the safe transportation of emigrants to British America and his own belief that the Canadian government would "feel it only fitting to maintain on its own side of the water the establishments requisite for the proper reception and distribution of the people who arrive in Canada." After the year ending March 31, 1855, therefore, no further application on this account would be submitted to Parliament by the Colonial Office.[74]

It was inevitable that many colonists should view pauper emigration with eyes inclined towards disapproval. If such emigrations did nothing but shift misery from one part of the empire to another without working the transformation Wilmot Horton had promised, the colonies were bound to complain and the home government—the only body interested in conditions in both colonies and mother country—would be forced to take up an inactive, non-committal policy.

Of those who saw the dangers which might arise from an unrestricted immigration of helpless settlers Sir Howard Douglas, lieutenant-governor of New Brunswick, was among the most far-seeing. If it were forced too abundantly upon the colonies, he believed it would "defeat more or less the measures of relief contemplated." In Canada, Lord Aylmer could not say what would happen if the idea were to get abroad that it was intended "to relieve the United Kingdom of indigent and disorderly persons who [were] . . . troublesome to Society, by sending them to Canada"; restrictive measures might be adopted "to check the progress of Emigration generally." However, legislation enacted by Nova Scotia in 1828 to restrict the immigration of paupers found in the Colonial Office only James Stephen to defend it. In Montreal in 1840 the local emigrant committee had to raise £497 to supply food to emigrants for whom the government provided free transportation to Upper Canada. Five years later the Bishop of Toronto protested against the arrival of indigent emigrants, who were often ill, lame, and blind, and always in need of funds. He found them "a heavy item of expense."[75] The French press too criticized the government "qui a l'injustice de nous envoyer un surcroît de population pauvre et denuée . . . et que l'humanité nous porte à secourir . . . lorsqu'ils sont jetés pour ainsi dire au milieu de nous."

Certain colonial officials representing the British government, it is true, and landowners in need of labour were openly in favour of inducing the immigration of the poor. Buchanan used his influence again and again to counteract the propaganda of the Quebec Emigrant Society and the French press, reiterating his conviction that the French objection was political and the Society benevolent but misguided. The opinion of Lieutenant-Governor Sir John Colborne of Upper Canada was equally strong and his advice of a practical nature. Feeling that the province generally was so desirous of new population that no opposition would be made to receiving the bad with the good, he developed the schemes for the reception of poor emigrants which have already been mentioned. With the permission of the Colonial Office, a provincial fund was set aside, and when the great emigrations almost overwhelmed the colony, Colborne was able to place satisfactorily many who must otherwise have passed on to the labour market of the United States.

These first steps taken by the colonies in receiving and caring for their immigrants began a new phase of development. In the early schemes of assisted emigration, settlement had been directed mainly from London. Such a system was suitable so long as the local legislatures were immature and the settlements sparse. Now thirty years of growth had produced in the colonies both the experience and the income necessary for managing that most troublesome portion of their incoming population, the needy.

X. THE TRIUMPH OF LAISSEZ-FAIRE

IN THE CENTURY between 1765 and 1865 one and a half million emigrants sailed from the British Isles to the British North American colonies. This immense immigration transformed the colonies won from the French in 1763 into growing nations which by 1865 were on the whole British in tradition and outlook. Of three and one-half million souls recorded in 1871 in the first census of the newly federated Dominion of the four eastern colonies, only one-third were of French stock; the remainder traced their origin to the few United Empire Loyalists of revolutionary days and later emigrants from the south, or to the British emigrants of the last fifty or seventy-five years. By the same time, practically all of the available agricultural land in the four original provinces had been taken up and the main outline of the economic system, which was to serve throughout the remainder of the nineteenth century, had been drawn.

The pioneers' wilderness of 1765 and 1815 had been opened by roads and canals. Railroads spread their smoke and carried their cargoes from deep sea ports into the Maritime Provinces and through the countryside all the way from Rivière du Loup on the lower St. Lawrence River to Montreal and Toronto and Hamilton and on to the United States boundary in western Canada. On the coasts fishing and wooden ship-building were becoming important industries. Inland the lumbermen exploited the forest resources. In central Canada, the farmlands were closely scattered and the towns busy and thriving. Everywhere small industries were rising, shoes, woollens, furniture, and implements. Exports of unfinished products were growing and so enlarging the market for British imports. British capitalists had begun to come in, hesitantly and without reward at first, but with eyes on the future.

In Great Britain emigration had become a common topic; in Ireland it touched almost every family personally. Newspapers recorded sailings to North America as they did the wars; magazine editors, converted to the "new" economic theories or opposed to them, found space to print their views on emigration. Publishers of travellers' tales and emigrant guides did such a rushing business in new books that large compendiums have been put out in recent years merely to summarize the best of them. It must have been an isolated British subject, indeed, who after 1830 or 1840 had not had opportunity to form his own opinion upon the advantages and disadvantages of emigration.

To believe that this transformation was accomplished in absence of mind or haphazard indifference is to misunderstand the discussions of Parliament and the activities of government ministers. In 1843 when members of the House called for more detail on colonial affairs, the Secretary for the Colonies reminded them that in 1842 the government had presented 43 papers on the colonies, in all 2,700 large printed pages. It is also to ignore the voice of the people expressed in their own correspondence and publications. The *Illustrated London News*, publishing its sketch of the emigrants on their way to the port, found similar scenes of bravery, hope, and sorrow so numerous as to be commonplace in the British countryside. It is possible that few events in the century, with the exception of the political and industrial revolutions, had a greater effect upon the mother country than this outpouring of population and founding of new communities of British subjects.

Though informed opinion regarding emigration was never fully united in support of any one policy at any one time during the century, in general it may be said to have passed roughly through three different phases. At first, in spite of the lesson of the American Revolution and the supposed indifference towards matters colonial prevailing at the turn of the century, the principles of the old mercantile system still governed those administering colonial affairs. Discharged soldiers and merchants as before followed the advance of the British outposts into the newly acquired territories and, as before, any further removal of population was regarded by those who thought at all upon the subject as loss of power to the mother country.

With the peace of 1815 and the alarming state of unemployment then revealed, a period began during which emigration was advocated by one group of publicists and opposed by various other interests. Many thoughtful men in different party groups agreed with Malthus that any vacuum created by the removal of population would speedily fill up and thus forbid the achievement of relief by means of emigration. Similarly many free traders of the Manchester School fought systematic colonization though they were closely associated in other matters with free traders among the colonial reformers who supported emigration. In the final analysis, the majority of the old Tory and the old Whig party members were generally opposed to government participation in an activity so startlingly different from customary procedure as the removal of population. On government-assisted emigration they argued, as did the Colonial Land and Emigration Commissioners more than once, that the cost would be prohibitive. The argument proved doubly agreeable to a growing business community which considered the world its market and believed that a British emigrant would be as useful to British industry in the United States or South America as in the British colonies.

The third and longest phase of public opinion thus arrived naturally. Laissez-faire England was consistent in this: free trade in goods was matched by free export of capital and population. In an era of freedom for industry and free competition for employment, free voluntary emigration became a permanent phenomenon. Though the propertied classes of Victorian England enjoyed ease and comfort, three-quarters of the people were often so insecurely established that a decline in national prosperity sent them overseas in search of a better living. Contrary to the axioms of the economists and the expectations of business this phenomenon of emigration was to maintain the empire. In line with the growing humanitarian influence in the country, the government gradually moved to provide safe transportation for emigrants, at their own expense if they planned only the short Atlantic crossing, with some assistance on Wakefieldian principles if they were moving to the Australian colonies. But in the encouragement of emigration, in the individual's decision to emigrate or not to emigrate, the government announced again and again it would have no part.

The original impetus for emigration came, irrespective of party, from the courageous British subjects themselves. By the thousands, they applied to their government, their landlords, and their members of Parliament for information and assistance for emigration. Faced with the call for immediate action, Parliament acted democratically; it inquired and discussed and let the rush of emigration carry it along. The appeals from the people were the force that pushed governments, Whig or Tory, to provide, first, assistance in emigration and, later, information and protection. Wilmot Horton's scheme for a great government-aided emigration was matured under a Tory government, in which it is true that Robert Peel could appreciate the theories of Jeremy Bentham and the philosophical radicals; the scheme was lost under that Tory government and the following Whig ministry. Powerful speeches by Henry George Ward, W. Smith O'Brien, Colonel Robert Torrens, and others including the master Charles Buller himself, as well as the recommendations for an emigration system made by committees which investigated the state of the poor in Ireland and in the Highlands of Scotland, all failed to convert the same ministry to action. In the succeeding Tory and Whig governments, as conditions in Ireland and Scotland continued to worsen and parliamentary committees continued to recommend assisted emigration, the policy of laissez-faire did not change. When the Whig ministry fell in 1852 and prosperity for Great Britain was on the horizon and responsible government and free trade were changing the colonies, the day for vigorous imperial action on emigration to British America had passed. The colonies meanwhile were taking over control of immigration for themselves.

In spite of the plausibility of the arguments offered by the free traders of the Manchester School and the non-believers in the value of emigration, voluntary or assisted, events proved that the supporters of the movement had the greater vision. Huskisson, Horton, Wakefield, Gladstone, Russell, Durham, Grey believed in the empire. They saw how one part of the British possessions might supply another in material resources and population and generally they believed that the colonists would show attachment to the mother country. However that might be, if the tie was to be broken, it was for the colonists not the British Parliament to break it. Huskisson early realized the need for advising emigrants; at present "our duty" was to imbue them with British feelings and traditions. Grey may have had moments of doubt but on the whole his conviction was firm; free trade and colonial interests were not incompatible; the empire was a trust and possibly a source of power. Russell believed that the Australian colonies would combine their independent progress with "the zealous maintenance of ties . . . cemented alike by feeling and principle." And Gladstone, when confronted later in life with the rumour that he had been a Little Englander, expressed surprise: never at any time, he replied, had he favoured such views. As for Durham, holding the colonies and trying to govern them well should be tried, he advised, before giving in to the pessimists and abandoning the vast dominion "which might supply the wants of our surplus population, and raise up millions of fresh consumers of our manufactures and producers of a supply for our wants." Almost while he wrote, James Stephen was working in the Colonial Office on the famous circular despatch of October, 1839, which, in spite of Lord Sydenham's doubts and his own concentration on administration rather than policy, was to initiate the experiment in responsible government in troubled Canada and become the charter of responsible government for all the colonies.[1]

Then followed the years of real crisis for the North American colonies —the effects of the repeal of the Corn Laws, the final collapse of the Old Colonial System, as preference and the Navigation Laws, the whole delicately balanced creation of generations, all went down together.

The long-expected separation did not follow. In London, Lord Grey looked into the future as he wrote in a Minute for the Cabinet: "It seems to me that it would be no ordinary calamity if the British Empire were to lose and the United States were to gain this extensive territory [the North American colonies], having already a population of two millions, which is increasing with unexampled rapidity, and to the future amount of which it would be difficult to set a limit."

In Canada, Lord Elgin, practising what the colonial reformers had taught and adopting responsible government generously had begun to show the colonists that colonial existence was not provisional, that bonds with Britain need not be broken, and that under the system he was installing the colonies might attain the social and political development "to which organized communities of free men have a right to aspire." Responsible government was not, as its opponents and some of its friends had said, a half-way house on the road to independence and separation. This support was what the colonists needed. In spite of the loss of the old economic favours, their natural ties with the only land they knew would do the rest. Even while laissez-faire principles grew stronger in Britain, while the attractions of the United States appealed and family differences developed, the colonists would cling to the empire. The art of colonization had not been lost. This age of marvels produced nothing more truly marvellous, one contemporary said in 1858, "than the recent growth of our colonial empire." Canadians who arrived as emigrants but yesterday were now, he continued, "the constituents of a legislature unrivalled in dignity or power by any legislature on earth except the Parliament of this kingdom and the Congress of the United States."[2]

The great emigrations had spread their influence farther than has been heretofore understood, for this free movement of people, more than theories of trade or government policy, assured the continuance of British colonization and indeed the life of the whole colonial community of nations. Though the talk of emigration seemed endless, there were few in Parliament to describe the little groups of British people voluntarily planting settlements in the North American wilds; there were more than a few to explain that nothing could be gained by maintaining colonial lands. In Parliament Huskisson, Horton, Gladstone, and later Grey and Russell bowed to the will of the majority, gave up their generous bills and compromised on ineffective passenger vessel laws and a watch-dog emigration policy.

So it was with the struggle between the theoretical advocates of assisted systematic colonization and the believers in free, voluntary emigration.

There were many to announce, as did *Chambers's Edinburgh Journal* in 1850, that left to itself emigration was wasteful, conducted on no plan:

Crowds of people in struggling circumstances ship themselves off anywhere, and anyhow; when they arrive in the country of their choice, they scatter themselves abroad in forests and wastes; buy land at a few shillings an acre; toil like slaves for years. . . . They seldom fail to obtain plenty of food; their animal wants are fully satisfied; but an intelligent man aims at something besides mere food and shelter. And yet the mass of emigrants get nothing else. The consequence of such undirected plans is a very slow social progress—often a protracted barbarism.[3]

There were few to explain that before Confederation the British American colonies had lost part of the characteristics which some have extolled as frontier virtues and had taken on in their place the appearance of more fully organized life. Official correspondence reflected the change: its main concern was no longer pleas for land and patronage but railroad building, canal improvement, the electro-magnetic telegraph, devices for better navigation at sea, the development of natural resources, public works. Professional men, lawyers, doctors, ministers, artisans of every description formed a goodly proportion of the mid-century emigration. In New Brunswick smuggling from the United States declined perceptibly because the skills of new arrivals supplied necessaries of life hitherto unobtainable. In Upper Canada, the founding of a college and an increased number of school teachers began to remove anxiety from the minds of many parents who had been forced to take young families from the educational advantages of the mother country. Changes which came with conquest of early dangers and growth and expansion created an atmosphere of hope and confidence that impressed the emigrant and inspired in him a new attitude of assurance and even ease of mind. Visiting travellers and business men felt the same influence and acted upon it.

In other spheres and later times when emigration was taken as a matter of course, the work of the emigrants and of men of wide experience was also overshadowed by the prominence given to theory and propaganda. Because the adoption of the system of sale of colonial land appeared to follow the agitation of Edward Gibbon Wakefield, the whole credit for the change has often been given to that theorist. But a plan for the sale of colonial lands was drawn up in the Colonial Office as early as 1825 and portions of it were in effect in British North America before Wakefield's followers were organized or his ideas fully stated.[4] As for the Wakefield theory that the labourer should not be made a proprietor on first arrival in the colony, this was not the discovery of a new principle, but the statement of the method by which the voluntary, penniless emigrant had long been making his way in the American colonies.

The efforts of able, hard-working men in colonial affairs sometimes met a similar fate from the theorists. The systematic colonizers announced their satisfaction at the failure and withdrawal of Wilmot Horton after a decade of concentration on colonial problems. Charles Buller, one of the most vocal of the colonial reformers, characterized James Stephen as Mr. Mother Country, a relic of the Old Colonial System, in whose "Sighing Rooms" honest, well-deserving colonial petitioners often grew grey in waiting, their cases unheard or undecided. Yet James Stephen was no last ditch defender of the old system but rather its severe critic, with his conclusions based on lessons learned through thirty-four years of experience as counsel to the Treasury and the Colonial Office and as assistant and permanent under-secretary in the latter. He disapproved of the Treasury's colonial patronage by which the British office might appoint to a colonial post a favourite for whom the colony must pay though he might never visit the colony. He disapproved of the British veto of colonial laws: he would not "attempt to prescribe to the Gov. [sic] any line of policy on any internal question whatever." "A hundred and thirty thousand Englishmen," he wrote of New South Wales in 1842, "will never be at a loss to manage a large proportion of the details of Governm[en]t for themselves, if invited or permitted to do so."[5]

Administering colonies from the centre of empire involved cumbersome and risky procedures even in recent times. In the days of communication by sailing vessel, when colonial and imperial offices were sometimes filled by privileged appointees, the difficulties of efficient administration were immeasurably multiplied. In spite of them, the extent of co-operation between London and the outposts and the vigour with which many colonial officers executed their tasks is impressive. The wisdom and devotion of James Stephen and Earl Carey are traditional. Stephen organized the Colonial Office and reformed the administration of the colonial empire; Earl Grey, handicapped as he was by brilliant predecessors in office and his own incisive and impatient mind, carried his despatch boxes to the country, recalled the lessons from his long interest in colonial affairs (longer than that of any member of Parliament), and supported progressive policies. Criticism of colonial administration became so habitual after the publicity achieved by the systematic colonizers that it is difficult to realize the effort and consideration given the problems recounted in the mass of correspondence that came and went between colony and mother country. Let him who has doubts study the comments by secretaries and under-secretaries which remain on that correspondence and then follow the writer as he answers queries in the House of Commons. Some decisions may have been unwise, some office holders unfit, as they are today, but probably not more so.

In the particular story of emigration no better example of vigour and co-operation in administration is now available than the work of the Agent-General for Emigration, Thomas Frederick Elliot, who was appointed in 1837, and that of the Colonial Land and Emigration Commissioners (of whom Elliot was one) who succeeded him in 1840. While the general public and members of Parliament berated government administrators for tragic conditions and calamities in port and at sea, these officers, struggling as they were with insufficient staff and growingly complex legislation (and handling the emigrations to Australia with which this story is not concerned), wisely guided their far-flung corps of agents throughout the British Isles and the colonies. They co-ordinated their agents' practices, gave them uniform interpretations of the passenger vessel legislation they were to enforce, and gathered evidence from which better legislation could be drawn. When this co-operation was no longer necessary, because the colonies had taken over their own land revenues and begun to manage their own immigration, the Commissioners' work declined and disappeared.[6] It is an interesting commentary on the age that while freedom in trade, employment, and emigration was preached as a gospel, freedom in each of these areas was being limited more and more by the ideals of the humanitarians and the efficiency of business agents who, like the Emigration Commissioners, made it their duty to regulate and improve the operations for which they were responsible.

Before as well as after the policy of laissez-faire became the rule in the British economy, controversy over the ultimate value of the emigration of population was widespread. Though emigration has been a movement congenial and customary to the British people, whether in times of prosperity or adversity, it has never been established that as a remedy for unemployment and depression in business the mere removal of population has proved entirely satisfactory. Its efficacy may be measured by two standards: its value in alleviating the discomforts of those remaining in the mother country, and of the emigrants themselves.

Wilmot Horton, some of the early parliamentary committees which considered home problems, and many of the critics of the government before 1847 emphasized the value of emigration in the first sense.

Theoretically, it would seem that their arguments were plausible. It should be possible to balance effective capital and labour and so relieve unemployment by the planned removal of labour as well as by the introduction of capital. Practically, in most of the nineteenth century in England and parts of Scotland, the theory did not operate. The condition of the weavers was worse in 1821 than in 1820, though twelve hundred had been shipped out in the interval. When improvements came it was not from emigration but from a revival of trade. After depression had continued until Parliament and the Manufacturers' Committee in 1827 were about to vote an unprecedented sum for aiding emigration, suddenly the necessity for assistance was eliminated by improving conditions in the industry. Evidence from similar schemes of assistance leads to the same conclusion. As a means of alleviating misery in the home country, assisted emigration has been ineffective.

Explanation is not wanting. In the first place, assisted emigration did not remove those most burdensome to the community. As early as 1826 the colonists signified their unwillingness to receive the "refuse" population of great Britain; as late as 1847 when the unfit arrived, protests were loud and strong. No matter how excellent the plans of assistance prepared, there must be left in the homeland those most likely to be in need of employment or other aid. Again, the colonies could at first give work to agriculturalists mainly and many of the needy had been employed in industry. Therefore it was impossible without systems for training the emigrants to transform "the redundant labour and curse of the mother country" into the "active labour and blessing" of the colonies. In the third place, assisted emigration was costly. Neither the government in the period of small experiments nor the parishes and proprietors in the time of the great emigrations provided sufficient funds to remove an effective part of the unemployed from any large district suffering from a surfeit of labour.

Of the value of the free, voluntary movement of emigration it is difficult to make a just estimate. In 1913, Toynbee pointed out that 8,500,000 departed from the United Kingdom between 1815 and 1880; he believed that this large emigration had materially lightened the labour market. But the fact must not be overlooked that this total placed the yearly average at something over 100,000, a figure commensurate with the total of 1832, an emigration which had little or no effect upon conditions in the British Isles and was followed by a number of years of severe unemployment and distress.[7]

The whole question of the effect of emigration upon the home country is beclouded by the lack of reliable emigration figures not only for departures as a whole but for national origins in particular. For the years of the great emigrations of the forties and the early fifties it has been calculated, for example, that nine-tenths of the sailings from Liverpool, much the largest British port, and one-third of those from the Clyde were Irish in origin.[8] This estimate, if correct, greatly reduces the supposed number of English and Scottish departures and enlarges the Irish. And in Ireland and the north of Scotland, emigration does appear to have brought some relief to the population remaining. But here too, the issue is confused by the scarcity of sound statistics and by still another controversy, that over the relative influence of the "pull" and the "push" in causing emigration. After 1853, war and returning prosperity in Great Britain reduced the force of the "push" upon the British worker. At the same time, commercial crisis in North America lowered the power of the "pull." The two forces working together, not against each other as sometimes, reduced the emigration from the British Isles to the level of the years before 1845. And this in itself would affect the workhouse load and the wage rate, those early means of measuring depression and the need for emigration upon which the studies of the effect of emigration have been partially based.

Whatever the conclusion regarding that controversy, population did decrease in certain Scottish counties from which emigration was heavy, and in Ireland land use altered after the forties, apparently because of the departure of small tenants.[9] The great decline in Irish population, previously noted and detailed in Table XI of Appendix B, may have made possible the Irish agricultural revolution of later years. The decrease in the supply of farm labourers seems to have provided employment for the remaining home labour force most of the year, instead of a few months or weeks. In 1867, Lord Dufferin rejoiced that emigration had forced him to pay higher wages. The Poor Law Commissioners too, using the old formula, noted the depletion of numbers in the workhouses from 2.6 per cent of the population in 1852 to .8 per cent in 1857, and laid the improvement to the drain of labour produced by emigration. And John Locke in his *Ireland's Recovery or Excessive Emigration and its Reparative Agencies in Ireland* went so far as to announce that emigration "blesses him that stays and him that goes."[10]

On the latter point, the benefit to "him that goes," there has been little or no disagreement. This was the second standard mentioned above for measuring the efficacy of emigration. No matter what it may have failed to do for the mother country, it undoubtedly brought an improvement in the way of life of the emigrants. One can do no better than offer as proof the lesson to be learned from every chapter in this work.

Whether it be the weavers of 1820, the Irish of 1823, the later parish-aided, or the voluntary emigrants, the testimony is the same. Emigration meant much that was trying—hard work, severe exposure—but it brought rude comfort, hope for the future.

Between 1765 and 1865, the British people passed through a crucial period. Great events shook belief in the old order and, resulting for a time in uncertainty and upheaval, finally roused new activity in every sphere of life. The effect was to be seen in political and humanitarian reforms, in unprecedented economic growth, and the greatest outward movement of population the world had yet known. Gigantic forces at work at the beginning of the century had led men from the old idea of guarding population on the principles of the mercantile system to an acceptance of emigration as a natural development in the life of a great nation. The contribution to this end of the advocates of laissez-faire who fought humanitarian passenger vessel legislation and expenditure on colonial establishments was exactly the opposite of that intended, for the pessimism that their teachings engendered meant a negation of policy which left the colonial officials often unhampered and the people free to follow their own devices. While the economists preached the doctrine of wealth founded on trade returns in no way dependent on national boundaries, the people themselves went out in their need and set up a new empire on the surer foundations of faith and hope.

It was the task of the theorists to interpret this phase of imperialism, but not to create it. That part was the work of the men and women who sailed in the emigrant ships and step by step cut their way through the dark forest to safety and security. The virtue of the British colonial system in the first half of the nineteenth century was that it produced a few men who could see what lay beneath the early crudities of colonial life: the conquering energy of a host of nameless men and women who went out to live in strange places and bear their children, that through them the men of the future might subdue nature and inherit the earth.[11]

NOTES AND APPENDIXES

NOTES

CHAPTER ONE

1. E. A. C. Belcher and J. A. Williamson, *Migration within the Empire* (London, 1924), 7–8, 26–7; J. H. Rose, A. P. Newton, and E. A. Benians, eds., *Cambridge History of the British Empire* (7 vols., Cambridge, 1929–40), I, 235–6.
2. Public Archives of Canada, *Report*, 1894, I, 3ff.; J. Bouchette, *The British Dominions in North America* (2 vols., London, 1831), II, 3.
3. T. B. Akins, "History of Halifax City," Nova Scotia Historical Society, *Collections*, VIII (1892–4), 4.
4. C.O. 5/753, Shirley to Board of Trade, July 10, 1745; W. S. McNutt, "Why Halifax Was Founded," *Dalhousie Review*, XII (1933), 529–30.
5. W. A. Carrothers, *Emigration from the British Isles* (London, 1929), 4–5; J. B. Brebner, *New England's Outpost: Acadia before the Conquest of Canada* (New York, 1927), 167–84.
6. M. L. Hansen and J. B. Brebner, *The Mingling of the Canadian and American Peoples* (New Haven, 1940), 29–33.
7. W. O. Raymond, "Colonel Alexander McNutt and the pre-Loyalist Settlements of Nova Scotia," Royal Society of Canada, *Transactions*, Ser. 3, V (1911), sect. II, 25–115.
8. P.A.C., *Report*, 1894, I, 225, 228, 232, Reports of Lords of Trade, March 5, 1761, Lords of Trade to King, April 8, 1761; B. Rand, "New England Settlements in Acadia," American Historical Association, *Report*, 1890, 42.
9. Calendar of Home Office Papers, 1760–5, no. 1036, Halifax to Attorney-General, Oct. 13, 1763; C. W. Alvord, *The Mississippi Valley in British Politics* (2 vols., Cleveland, 1917), II, 186.
10. S. C. Johnson, *A History of Emigration from the United Kingdom to North America, 1763–1912* (London, 1913), 192.
11. D. Allison, "Notes on a General Return of the Several Townships," Nova Scotia Historical Society, *Collections*, VII (1889–91), table opposite p. 56.
12. W. F. Ganong, "A Monograph of the Origins of Settlements in New Brunswick," Royal Society of Canada, *Transactions*, Ser. 2, II (1904), sect. II, 43–4.
13. N. Macdonald, *Canada, 1763–1841: Immigration and Settlement* (London, 1939), 103.
14. A. Shortt and A. Doughty, *Documents Relating to the Constitutional History of Canada, 1759–1791* (Ottawa, 1907), 132–49, Instructions to Murray, Dec. 7, 1763.
15. A. L. Burt, *The Old Province of Quebec* (Toronto, 1933), 79–82; G. Patterson, "Land Settlement in Upper Canada, 1783–1840," Ontario Department of Public Records and Archives, *Report*, 1921, 19.

242 NOTES: CHAPTER ONE

16. Macdonald, *Canada, 1763–1841*, 43; R. England, "Disbanded and Discharged Soldiers in Canada prior to 1914," *Canadian Historical Review*, XXVII (1946), 3–4.

17. Burt, *The Old Province*, 93.

18. Haldimand Papers, B.M. Add. MSS 710, War Office to Haldimand, June 9, 1783, North to Haldimand, Aug. 8, 1783; 698, Germaine to Carleton, March 26, 1777; 708, War Office to Haldimand, April 5, 1779; Burt, *The Old Province*, 214, 295.

19. W. S. Wallace, *The United Empire Loyalists* (Toronto, 1914), 100; Burt, *The Old Province*, 279–80, 366–70.

20. Burt, *The Old Province*, 370–3; Patterson, "Land Settlement," 21–3; England, "Disbanded and Discharged Soldiers," 5.

21. Macdonald, *Canada, 1763–1841*, 55–6.

22. *Ibid.*, 103, 469; Burt, *The Old Province*, 395.

23. E. A. Cruikshank, ed., *The Correspondence of Lieut. Governor John Graves Simcoe* (4 vols., Toronto, 1923–6), II (1924), 104.

24. S. R. Mealing, "The Enthusiasms of John Graves Simcoe," Canadian Historical Association, *Report*, 1958, 57–8.

25. D. G. Creighton, *Dominion of the North* (Toronto, 1944), 187.

26. Burt, *The Old Province*, 396; Macdonald, *Canada, 1763–1841*, 50.

27. Hansen and Brebner, *The Mingling*, 52–4; Wallace, *The Loyalists*, 63.

28. J. B. Brebner, *The North Atlantic Triangle* (Toronto, 1945), 65; Hansen and Brebner, *The Mingling*, 55–6; Ganong, "A Monograph," 55.

29. Josiah Tucker, *The True Interest of Britain, Set Forth in Regard to the Colonies* (Philadelphia, 1776); John Cartwright, *American Independence, the Interest and Glory of Great Britain* (London, 1774).

30. C.O. 42/19, Finlay to Nepean, Dec. 10, 1787.

31. C.O. 42/11, Reports of Committees, Feb. 13, 1787.

32. C.O. 42/87, memo by Dorchester, Feb. 20, 1786.

33. C.O. 42/19, Smith to Nepean, Aug. 18, 1787.

34. C.O. 42/88, note found with "Considerations upon the Government of Lower Canada, to be settled under the late Act of Parliament, 1791."

35. C.O. 42/82, Report of Council, Jan. 11, 1791.

36. C.O. 42/83, Dundas to Dorchester, Sept. 16, 1791.

37. C.O. 42/316, Dundas to Simcoe, July 12, 1792; Cruikshank, *Correspondence of Simcoe*, I (1923), 178–9.

38. Mealing, "Enthusiasms of Simcoe," 54–6.

39. C.O. 42/83, meeting of Quebec Agricultural Society, Sept. 5, 1791; C.O. 42/82, Nov. 1, 1790; D. G. Creighton, *The Commercial Empire of the St. Lawrence* (Toronto, 1937), 89.

40. C.O. 42/319, Simcoe to Privy Council Committee for Trade, Dec. 20, 1794; Cruikshank, *Correspondence of Simcoe*, III, 228.

41. C.O. 217/121, memorial of Ranna Cossetis to Hobart; notes by J. T. Desbarres; C.O. 217/80, memorial of Feb. 18, 1806.

42. *Hansard's Parliamentary Debates*, XXXVI (1802), 854; C.O. 42/120, Pitt to (?), Dec. 27, 1802; C.O. 42/327, Hunter to Colonial Office, acknowledging Portland's circular of Dec. 18, 1800; Upper Canada Committee on Hemp, June 18; C.O. 217/75, Wentworth to Portland, Nov. 25, 1801.

43. C.O. 42/120, Banks to Lord Glenbervie, July 30, 1802; C.O. 42/339,

Camden to Hunter, Sept. 5, 1805; N. Macdonald, "Hemp and Imperial Defence," *Canadian Historical Review*, XVII (1936), 385–98.

44. C.O. 42/121, Milne to Sullivan, May 31, 1803; C.O. 42/340, Sturges Bourne to Camden, Oct. 11, 1805.

45. John Bristed, *The Resources of the British Empire* (New York, 1811), 136; Creighton, *Commercial Empire*, 149–50.

46. *Parl. Deb.*, VI (1806), 835; H. W. Temperley, *Life of Canning* (London, 1905), 81, from F.O. 56.

47. Hugh Gray, *Letters from Canada; Written during a Residence there in the Years 1806, 1807, and 1808; Shewing the present State of Canada* (London, 1809); John Lambert, *Travels through Canada and the United States of North America, in the Years 1806, 1807, and 1808* (2 vols., London, 1813); George Chalmers, *An Estimate of the Comparative Strength of Great Britain* (London, 1782, 1786, 1794, 1802, 1810); Patrick Colquhoun, *A Treatise on the Wealth, Power, and Resources of the British Empire* (London, 1814).

CHAPTER TWO

1. S. Johnson, *A Journey to the Western Islands of Scotland* (London, 1775), 334–8.

2. T. Douglas, Earl of Selkirk, *Observations on the Present State of the Highlands of Scotland with a View to the Causes and Probable Consequences of Emigration* (London, 1805), 10–13.

3. 19 Geo. II, c. 39; 20 Geo. II, c. 43, 50; 21 Geo. II, c. 21.

4. M. I. Adam, "The Highland Emigration of 1770," *Scottish Historical Review*, XVI (1919), 283–91. Miss Adam gives five possible causes for the emigration of 1760–70 and of these marks the last as most important: (1) the union of farms for the introduction of sheep; (2) redundancy of population; (3) the effect of the Jacobite Rebellion; (4) the influence of returned Highland soldiers; (5) the rise in rents. See also N. Macdonald, *Canada, 1763–1841: Immigration and Settlement* (London, 1939), 6–7; D. F. Macdonald, *Scotland's Shifting Population, 1770–1850* (Glasgow, 1937), 142–4.

5. M. I. Adam, "The Causes of the Highland Emigrations of 1783–1803," *Scottish Historical Review*, XVII (1920), 77.

6. *Caledonian Mercury*, March 1, 1786.

7. *Ibid.*, May 31.

8. C.O. 42/82, Hope to Macdonnell, Sept. 25, 1786; *supra*, 11.

9. C.O. 42/82, Council Minutes, Jan. 11, 1791; see also D. F. Macdonald, *Scotland's Shifting Population*, 144.

10. Douglas, *Observations*, 143–5; Adam, "The Causes," 76.

11. C.O. 217/63, late 1791.

12. G. Patterson, *Memoir of Rev. James Macgregor, D. D., Missionary* (Edinburgh and Philadelphia, 1859), 256–8.

13. G. Patterson, *A History of the County of Pictou, Nova Scotia* (Montreal, 1877), 226–8.

14. C.O. 42/12, Information from Lord Dorchester, Dec. 17, 1791.

15. *Caledonian Mercury*, Aug. to Oct., 1792.

16. C.O. 42/94, Land Committee Report, Nov. 19, 1792; C.O. 42/93, Ogden to Clarke.
17. *Caledonian Mercury*, Dec. 22, 1791; *Edinburgh Evening Courant*, Aug. 16, Oct. 23.
18. A. Irvine, *An Inquiry into the Causes and Effects of Emigration from the Highlands and Western Islands of Scotland, with Observations on the Means to be Employed for Preventing It* (Edinburgh, 1802), 9.
19. Douglas, *Observations*, 50; *Edinburgh Review*, VII (1805), 185–202.
20. Adam, "The Causes," 83–9.
21. Highland Society of Scotland, *Transactions*, Ser. 1, I (1799), viii.
22. *Caledonian Mercury*, Aug. 3, 1789.
23. Highland Society of Scotland, *Transactions*, Ser. 1, II (1803), viii–ix.
24. *Parliamentary Report*, 1802–3, IV (45), 7–8.
25. K. A. Walpole, "The Humanitarian Movement of the Early Nineteenth Century to Remedy Abuses on Emigrant Vessels to America," Royal Historical Society, *Transactions*, Ser. 4, XIV (1931), 197–224.
26. *Edinburgh Evening Courant*, July 1, 1802.
27. *Parl. Rep.*, 1802–3, IV (45), 16.
28. *Journals of the House of Commons*, LVIII (1803), 471, 478.
29. 43 Geo. III, c. 56.
30. *Journals of the House of Commons*, LVIII (1803), 471, 478.
31. Highland Society of Scotland, *Transactions*, Ser. 1, III (1807), xix.
32. R. Brown, *Strictures and Remarks on the Earl of Selkirk's Observations* (Edinburgh, 1806), 7–8; N. Macdonald, *Canada, 1763–1841*, 480.
33. D. Wordsworth, *Recollections of a Tour Made in Scotland, A.D. 1803* (Edinburgh, 1874), 92–7.
34. *Caledonian Mercury*, July 8, 1801.
35. C.O. 42/360, Macdonell's memorial, 1817; J. A. Macdonell, *A Sketch of the Life of the Honourable and Right Reverend Alexander Macdonell* (Alexandria, 1890), 15; Q 157, Macdonell to Dalhousie, Dec. 16, 1820, and enclosure in Dalhousie to Bathurst, Jan. 18, 1821, "An Account of the Fencibles"; P.A.C., Upper Canada Sundries, statement of Rev. A. Macdonell in a letter to Bathurst, Dec. 20, 1814.
36. C.O. 42/330, Proposal tending to . . . Security of Ireland, by Selkirk, March 31.
37. C.O. 42/330, note with Pelham note to Hobart, May 27, 1802.
38. C.O. 42/330, Selkirk to Colonial Office, Nov. 30, 1802.
39. Douglas, *Observations*, 176.
40. H. I. Cowan, "Selkirk's Work in Canada: An Early Chapter," *Canadian Historical Review*, IX (1928), 299–308.
41. C.O. 42/331, Hobart to Hunter, Feb. 15, 1803.
42. C.O. 42/330, note on Selkirk's proposal of March 31, 1802.
43. C. Martin, *Lord Selkirk's Work in Canada* (Oxford, 1916), 31.
44. *Ibid.*, 44.
45. *Caledonian Mercury*, March 27, 1800, April 2, 1801.
46. Highland Society of Scotland, *Transactions*, Ser. 1, II (1803), 469.
47. S. Johnson, *A Journey*, 336.
48. *The Times*, Nov. 9, 1810.
49. *Parliamentary Paper*, 1821, XVII (718), 289.

NOTES: CHAPTER TWO

50. J. A. Williamson, *The Evolution of England* (Oxford, 1931), 341.
51. A. H. Johnson, *The Disappearance of the Small Landowner* (Oxford, 1909), 90.
52. W. H. R. Curtler, *The Enclosure and Redistribution of Our Land* (Oxford, 1920), 240; T. S. Ashton, *An Economic History of England: The Eighteenth Century* (London, 1955), 46.
53. J. H. Rose, *Pitt and the Great War* (London, 1911), 291–8; Curtler, *The Enclosure*, 265–77.
54. Williamson, *Evolution of England*, 343; Curtler, *The Enclosure*, 240.
55. 36 Geo. III, c. 23 of 1796 made general the practice of giving outdoor relief; see also Curtler, *The Enclosure*, 241, and Ashton, *An Economic History*, 46.
56. *Parliamentary Debates*, N.S., XXXV (1817), 907; J. L. Hammond, *The Village Labourer, 1760–1832* (London, 1911), 150; A. H. Johnson, *Small Landowner*, 145.
57. C.O. 384/1, Matthenson to Colonial Office.
58. *Parl. Rep.*, 1820, II (255); 1821, IX (668); 1822, V (165, 236, 346); 1823, VI (561).
59. *Parl. Rep.*, 1819, II (529), 249.
60. J. L. and B. Hammond, *The Skilled Labourer, 1760–1832* (London, 1919), 8.
61. J. Galt, *Annals of the Parish* (2 vols., Edinburgh, 1936), II, 57.
62. Hammond, *Skilled Labourer*, 70, quoting from Report of Committee on Hand Loom Weavers, *Parl. Rep.*, 1835, XIII (341).
63. J. B. Holroyd, Earl of Sheffield, *Letter on the Corn Laws* (London, 1815), 3.
64. Hammond, *Skilled Labourer*, 83.
65. *Parl. Deb.*, N.S., XX (1811), 608, 744; XIX (1811), 1017.
66. Robert Thomas Malthus (1766–1834), *An Essay on the Principle of Population* (London, 1798, 1803); Graham Wallas, *The Life of Francis Place* (London, 1898).
67. *The Times*, March 31, 1818; *Edinburgh Review*, XCII (1850), 492–3.
68. 5 Geo. IV, c. 97; A. Redford, *Labour Migration in England, 1800–50* (Manchester, 1926), 154.
69. C.O. 42/347; *The Times*, Oct. 9, 1811, Feb. 21, 1812.
70. *Parl. Deb.*, N.S., VIII (1807), 865 *et seq.*; XXXII (1816), 831–2.
71. *Parl. Pap.*, 1817, VI (462), 20; 1818, V (358).
72. *Parl. Pap.*, 1819, II (529), 249, 269–75.
73. F. Morehouse, "The Irish Migration of the 'Forties," *American Historical Review*, XXXIII (1928), 579.
74. T. Newenham, *Population of Ireland* (London, 1805), 46–9, 137, 183.
75. E. Wakefield, *An Account of Ireland, Statistical and Political* (2 vols., London, 1812), II, 723–4.
76. In R. D. Edwards and T. D. Williams, eds., *The Great Famine* (Dublin, 1956), see "Ireland on the Eve of the Famine," by R. B. McDowell, 4, quoting K. H. Connell, *The Population of Ireland* (Oxford, 1950).
77. W. F. Adams, *Ireland and Irish Emigration to the New World* (New Haven, 1932), 3–7.

78. Wakefield, *Account of Ireland*, I, 253, 299, 304; Adams, *Ireland and Irish Emigration*, 13–14.
79. *Parl. Pap.*, 1819, VIII (314), 52; 1818, VII (285, 359).
80. Adams, *Ireland and Irish Emigration*, 16–34, 11, quoting *Digest of Evidence*, Devon Commission, II, 828.
81. 1 and 2 Vic. c. 56; Adams, *Ireland and Irish Emigration*, 303, 312, 318.
82. Morehouse, "The Irish Migration," 580; *Parl. Pap.*, 1827, V (550), 460.
83. C.O. 42/93, Despatches and enclosures; *supra*, 15, 26.
84. A Young, *A Tour in Ireland*, edited by A. W. Hutton (2 vols., London, 1892), II, 57.
85. Wakefield, *Account of Ireland*, II, 713; C. S. Parker, *Robert Peel* (3 vols., London, 1891–9), I, 234.
86. *Niles Register*, Oct. 7, 1820, 93; Adams, *Ireland and Irish Emigration*, 63, 107–8, 118–24, quoting local Irish newspapers.
87. 58 Geo. III, c. 89.

CHAPTER THREE

1. C.O. 42/90, Lower Canada Land Committee Report, 1792; C.O. 217/93, Council and Assembly of Nova Scotia to Prince of Wales, 1814; C.O. 43/23, Bathurst to Prevost, Oct. 29, 1813; *Parliamentary Debates*, XXXI (1815), 917.
2. C.O. 42/355, Drummond to Prevost, Feb. 19, 1814.
3. C.O. 42/164, Young to Transport Board, April 25, 1814.
4. *Parl. Deb.*, XXXI (1815), 917 *et seq.*
5. *Bathurst Papers*, Roy. Hist. MSS Comm., 324, Liverpool to Bathurst, Jan. 16, 1815; C.O. 42/164, Peel to Goulburn, April 10, 26, 1815.
6. C.O. 42/164, Transport Office to Goulburn, April 11; C.O. 42/54–6, Goulburn to Treasury, Dec. 23, 1816.
7. *Caledonian Mercury*, March 6, 8, 1815.
8. C.O. 384/2, John Campbell's list of settlers, 1815.
9. *Caledonian Mercury*, Feb. 25, 1815.
10. C.O. 42/164, Transport Office to Goulburn, May 6, 1815. The *Atlas* sailed on July 11 with 242 emigrants; the *Dorothy* July 12 with 194; the *Baltic Merchant* July 14 with 140; and the *Eliza* Aug. 3 with 123.
11. C.O. 42/164, Admiralty to Colonial Office, June 30, 1815; Transport Office to Goulburn, June 23, 24, and Goulburn's note.
12. 57 Geo. III, c. 10.
13. C.O. 42/163, Drummond to Bathurst, Dec. 26, 1816.
14. C.O. 42/357, Gore to Drummond, Feb. 23, Gore to Bathurst, Feb. 23, 1816; Upper Canada Council, Nov. 4, 1815; C.O. 42/359, Gore to Bathurst, 150 pages; C.O. 42/163, Drummond to Bathurst, Oct. 30, 1815; R. Gourlay, *Statistical Account of Upper Canada* (2 vols., London, 1822), I, 539–40.
15. *Quebec Mercury*, Oct. 29, 1816; for this and succeeding military settlements, see G. F. Playter, "An Account of the Founding of Three Military Settlements," with notes by E. A. Cruickshank, Ontario Historical Society, *Papers and Records*, XX (1923), 98–104.

NOTES: CHAPTER THREE

16. C.O. 42/357, Gore to Bathurst, Nov. 20, 1816; Gourlay, *Statistical Account*, I, 524.

17. C.O. 42/164, Treasury to Goulburn, Dec. 5, 1815; Storekeeper's office to Colonial Office, Sept. 5, 1815; C.O. 42/162-3, Drummond to Bathurst, May 20, June 10, 29, 1815; T 28/48, Treasury to Goulburn, April 10, 1818, Sept. 4, 1816; C.O. 43/24; Bathurst to Sherbrooke, Oct. 3, 1816.

18. C.O. 43/24, Bathurst to Sherbrooke, Feb. 14, 1816; C.O. 43/53, Goulburn to Campbell, April 15, 1816; P.A.C., Upper Canada Sundries, 47, Lieut. Colonel Cockburn's abstract of June 9, 1820, showed 2,330 men, in all 5,830 young and old already placed in the Rideau military settlements.

19. C.O. 217/99, Dalhousie to Lord Bathurst, Jan. 2 and enclosure.

20. C.O. 43/56, Goulburn to Treasury, Dec. 6, 1817.

21. C.O. 42/22, Feb. 23, 1818, and succeeding dates.

22. C.O. 42/183, account rendered by the Navy for expense of passage to Canada: from Greenock, £2,032 2s. 4d.; from Whitehaven, £597 1s. 9d.; and from Cork, £1,270 12s. 7d.

23. C.O. 384/3, Navy Office to Goulburn, May 7, 1818. The party included the Millburn and the Hutchison families.

24. C.O. 384/4, Burnwell to Bathurst, March 6, 1819; B. Hall, *Travels in North America in the Years 1827 and 1828* (3 vols., Edinburgh, 1829), I, 293.

25. C.O. 384/1, Campbell to Colonial Office, Jan. 11, 1817; McDermid to Bathurst, March 18, 1817.

26. *Caledonian Mercury*, June 28, 1819; *The Times*, quoted from *Inverness Journal*, July 1, 1819.

27. C.O. 384/3, enclosure in Navy Office to Goulburn, July 10.

28. C.O. 43/24, Bathurst to Richmond, July 4, 1818.

29. C.O. 226/36, enclosure in Smith to Bathurst, March 15, 1820; C.O. 43/70, Stanley to Treasury, Dec. 20, 1827; C.O. 226/45, Ready to Huskisson, June 2, 1828; *Quebec Mercury*, some arriving as late as Sept. 9.

30. C.O. 384/3, Talbot to Bathurst, May 28, 1818; C.O. 43/56, Goulburn to Commissioners of Navy, April 2, 8; W. A. Carrothers, *Emigration from the British Isles* (London, 1929), 63.

31. E. A. Talbot, *Five Years' Residence in the Canadas* (2 vols., London, 1824), I, 17, 27.

32. *Ibid.*, I, 80.

33. *Ibid.*, I, 83.

34. T. Campbell, "The Beginning of London," Ontario Historical Society, *Records and Papers*, IX (1910), 68; Talbot, *Five Years' Residence*, I, 95, 106; II, 198.

35. *Parl. Deb.*, XL (1819), 1544; C. D. Yonge, *Life and Administration of Robert Bankes, Second Earl of Liverpool* (3 vols., London, 1868), II, 438.

36. C.O. 384/2-3, notes on petitions; C.O. 384/4, printed form sent to Michael Butler, April 6, 1819; C.O. 43/60, Goulburn to Broke, Feb. 28, 1821; C.O. 384/7, Goulburn's note on petitions; *The Times*, Jan. 18, 1822.

37. C.O. 42/206, summary of land regulations.

38. *Scots Magazine*, N.S., III (1818), 231.

39. *Cambridge Chronicle and Journal and Huntingdonshire Gazette*, March 1, 1816.

NOTES: CHAPTER THREE

40. *Parl. Deb.*, XXXIII (1816), 34, 671.
41. J. W. E. Conybeare, *A History of Cambridgeshire* (London, 1897), 257; *Parl. Deb.*, XXXIII (1816), 186.
42. *The Times*, June 26, 1816.
43. *Cambridge Chronicle*, May 16, 23, for notice of sailings.
44. W. Cobbett, *Rural Rides* (2 vols., London, 1885), I, 3.
45. H.O. 42/170, Sept. 28; *Parl. Deb.*, XXXV (1817), 322.
46. H.O. 79/3, Oct. 12.
47. *The Times*, June 13, 1817.
48. *Parl. Deb.*, XL (1819), 1549–50, for vote of £50,000; *Parl. Pap.*, 1827, V (550), 400–1.
49. *Parl. Deb.*, XL (1819), 672.
50. C.O. 384/1–2–3–4–5.
51. C.O. 384/5.
52. C.O. 384/4, 2.
53. *Parl. Deb.*, XL (1819), 1550; *supra*, 33–4.
54. M. L. Hansen, *The Atlantic Migration* (Cambridge, 1940), 99; W. S. Shepperson, *British Emigration to North America* (Minneapolis, 1957), 31.
55. H. B. Fearon, *Sketches of America* (London, 1818); M. Birkbeck, *Letters from Illinois* (London and Boston, 1818); F. Hall, *Travels in Canada and the United States in 1816 and 1817* (London and Boston, 1818).
56. Hansen, *Atlantic Migration*, 100.
57. C. F. Grece, *Facts and Observations Respecting Canada and the United States of America* (London, 1819), 3.
58. C. Martin, *Lord Selkirk's Work in Canada* (Oxford, 1916), 187.
59. *Parliamentary Paper*, 1821, XVII (718), 289.
60. *Annual Register*, 1815, Chron., 15; *Inverness Journal*, June 28, 1816.
61. *Caledonian Mercury*, Aug. 28, 1819.
62. C.O. 42/202, Cameron to Colonial Office, April 3 and to House of Commons.
63. C.O. 384/4, petition of Gordon, Jan. 12; *The Times*, July 1, 1819.
64. C.O. 384/5, Brown to Home Office, April 1819; *Scots Magazine*, N.S. IV (1819), 465; W. F. Ganong, "A Monograph of the Origins of Settlements in the Province of New Brunswick," Royal Society of Canada, *Transactions*, Ser. 2, X (1904), Sect. II, 75.
65. C.O. 384/9, McNab to Colonial Office, 1823; C.O. 42/370, Maitland to Bathurst, March 13, McLean to Bathurst, Oct. 5, 1823; *Edinburgh Review*, XLVII (1828), 221.
66. C.O. 43/63, Horton to McLean, Dec. 23, 1823.
67. *Parl. Pap.*, 1825, VIII (129), 12; 1826, IV (404), 79.
68. *Scots Magazine*, N.S., V (1819), 74.
69. *Quebec Mercury*, Aug. 8, 1820.
70. J. M'Donald, *Emigration to Canada: Narrative of a Voyage to Quebec and Journey thence to New Lanark* (Edinburgh, 1823), 3–6.
71. A. Jameson, *Winter Studies and Summer Rambles* (New York, 1839), 322–3.
72. J. Howison, *Sketches of Upper Canada* (Edinburgh, 2nd ed., 1825), 61; G. E. Hart, "The Halifax Poor Man's Friend Society, 1820–27," *Canadian Historical Review*, XXXIV (1953), 109.

NOTES: CHAPTER THREE

73. T 28/48, Lushington to Goulburn, March 23, 1819.
74. C.O. 217/99, Dalhousie to Bathurst, July 6, 1817; C.O. 42/179, Richmond to Bathurst, Aug. 11, 1818; Hart, "Halifax Poor Man's Friend Society," 109–22; *Parl. Pap.*, 1842, XXXI (301), 292.
75. C.O. 384/4, Quebec Emigrant Society meeting, Oct. 11, 1819.
76. C.O. 42/196, Dalhousie to Bathurst, April 28, 1823, on grant of £750; S. C. Johnson, *A History of Emigration from the United Kingdom to North America, 1763–1912* (London, 1913), 159.
77. T 28/50, Harrison to Horton, Sept. 2, 1823.
78. C.O. 42/204, Quebec Emigrant Society Report, 1824.
79. A. Hodgson, *Letters from North America* (2 vols., London, 1824), II, 45; English Farmer, *A Few Plain Directions* (London, 1820), 41–6.
80. C. Stuart, *The Emigrant's Guide to Upper Canada* (London, 1820), 18–19.
81. J. Mactaggart, *Three Years in Canada* (2 vols., London, 1829), II, 85.
82. C.O. 188/39, Baillie's MSS Report on New Brunswick Crown Lands, March 1, 1827.
83. C.O. 188/30, Douglas to Bathurst, Oct. 21, 1824. For Fredericton Emigrant Society organized in 1819, and its successor, see *Parl. Pap.*, 1842, XXXI (301), 292–3; 1826, IV (404), 38. Ganong, "A Monograph," 73; D. C. Harvey, "Scottish Immigration to Cape Breton," *Dalhousie Review*, XXI (1941), 315–16; Carrothers, *Emigration*, 78–9, quoting R. J. Uniacke, 1826.
84. Talbot, *Five Years' Residence*, II, 177–8.
85. *Ibid.*, II, 171–2; Howison, *Sketches of Upper Canada*, 243.
86. *Scots Magazine*, July 1816, 549.
87. *Parl. Deb.*, XLI (1819), 891–3.
88. J. Williamson, *The Evolution of England* (Oxford, 1931), 377–8.
89. J. L. and B. Hammond, *The Skilled Labourer, 1760–1832* (London, 1919), 119.
90. *Caledonian Mercury*, June 21, 1819.
91. C.O. 384/6, Townsend Emigration Society to Lord Blantyre.
92. *Parl. Deb.*, XL (1819), 671.
93. *Glasgow Herald*, May 8, 1820; C.O. 43/41, Bathurst to Maitland, May 6, 1820.
94. *Caledonian Mercury*, May 22, 1820; T 17/30, Lushington to Finlay, July 31, the Treasury paid Finlay £766 7s. 4d.
95. *Glasgow Herald*, April 3, 1820; C. S. Terry, *A History of Scotland* (Cambridge, 1920), 606–7.
96. *Caledonian Mercury*, July 8, 1820.
97. C.O. 384/6, Hopetoun to Colonial Office, June 6; C.O. 43/60, Goulburn to Finlay, Sept. 4; C.O. 384/7, Finlay to Goulburn, Feb. 7, 1821.
98. C.O. 42/191, Finlay to Goulburn, March 2; C.O. 43/60, Goulburn to Finlay, Sept. 4; C.O. 384/7, Campbell to Goulburn, March 13, 1821.
99. *Scots Magazine*, N.S., IX (1821), 81; R. Lamond, *A Narrative of the Rise and Progress of Emigration from the Counties of Lanark and Renfrew* (Glasgow, 1821).
100. *Quebec Mercury*, June 12, 1821; M'Donald, *Emigration to Canada*, 3–6.

101. M'Donald, *Emigration to Canada*, 6–8.

102. C.O. 42/187, Cockburn to Dalhousie, May 28, 1821; C. 626, for requisition; N. Macdonald, *Canada, 1763–1841: Immigration and Settlement* (London, 1939), 250.

103. J. M'Donald, *Emigration to Canada*, 16, 24; N. Macdonald, *Canada, 1763–1841*, 351.

104. C.O. 42/187, enclosure in Dalhousie to Bathurst, June 14, 1821; C. 626, Cockburn to Dalhousie, May 22, 1821.

105. C.O. 42/382, letters on British settlers.

106. C.O. 43/41, Bathurst to Maitland, Dec. 7, 1822; C.O. 42/222, Kempt to Murray, March 24, 1829; C. 627, Military Secretary to Cockburn, Sept. 10, 1822; C.O. 42/191, Dalhousie to Bathurst, April 22; C.O. 43/42, Murray to Colborne, June 20, 1829, states the task of collecting was left to Canadians.

107. P.A.C., Dalhousie Papers, XVI, Marshall to Darling, June 7, 1828; Bathurst to Dalhousie in 1826 and settlers' petition of 1828; C.O. 42/393, petition signed by W. Gordon, John McLaren, Thomas Scott, *et al.*, 1831; C.O. 43/75, Hay to Treasury, Aug. 23, 1831; C. 631, Superintendent Marshall's opinion; C.O. 43/45, enclosure in Glenelg to Head, Feb. 4, 1836.

108. C.O. 42/204, Dalhousie to Bathurst, March 27, 1825; C.O. 42/205, Report of Committee of Inquiries Appointed in April to Proceed to His Majesty's Dominions in North America, presented Dec. 6.

109. C. 627, population of Perth, Lanark, and Richmond.

110. R. J. Wilmot Horton, *Lecture* I (II), delivered at London Mechanics Institute (London, 1831), 28; C.O. 42/382, Letters on British settlers.

111. N. Macdonald, *Canada, 1763–1841*, 251–4.

112. *Parl. Pap.*, 1831-2, XXXII (334), 21–48; T. Rolph, *A Descriptive and Statistical Account of Canada* (London, 2nd ed., 1841), 152. For growth of settlements, see also, W. A. D. Jackson, "The Lands along the Upper St. Lawrence" (University of Maryland dissertation, 1953), 116.

CHAPTER FOUR

1. *Parliamentary Paper*, 1819, VIII (314), 52; 1818, VII (285, 359).

2. *Parliamentary Debates*, N.S., IX (1823), 1157.

3. Peel Papers, British Museum Add. MSS 40328, Goulburn to Peel, Jan. 18, 30, 1822, Peel to Goulburn, Nov. 6, 1822; *Parl. Deb.*, N.S., VIII (1823), 790–9.

4. W. F. Adams, *Ireland and Irish Emigration to the New World* (New Haven, 1932), 247–8; *Parl. Deb.*, XXXIII (1816), 814–5, XXXV (1817), 1079, XXXVIII (1818), 289–90.

5. Peel Papers, 40328, Peel to Goulburn, Nov. 6, 27, 1822; 40329, Peel to Goulburn, April 30, 1823; 40330, Peel to Goulburn, Aug. 4, 1824.

6. *The Times*, July 24, 1815; Adams, *Ireland and Irish Emigration*, 72, 86–7.

7. 56 Geo. III, c. 83; 57 Geo. III, c. 10; G. R. Porter, *Progress of the Nation* (London, 1851), 374.

8. Adams, *Ireland and Irish Emigration*, 89, 97.

9. *Ibid.*, 104, 113, 118, 120.

10. C.O. 42/264, Buchanan's emigration report.
11. C.O. 43/24, Bathurst to Sherbrooke, Jan. 10, 1817, no. 61.
12. C.O. 42/357, Buchanan to Gore, July 8, 1816, Gore to Buchanan, July 31, 1816; Adams, *Ireland and Irish Emigration*, 264, quoting F.O. 5/116, Buchanan to Castlereagh, Nov. 12, 1816; F.O. 5/119, Goulburn to Hamilton, Nov. 21, 1816.
13. *Parl. Pap.*, 1826, IV (404), 168.
14. Adams, *Ireland and Irish Emigration*, 126, 129.
15. *The Times*, Nov. 5, 1816; C.O. 384/1, 2, 3, etc.
16. C.O. 384/11, Limerick County petition; C.O. 384/9, Brady petition, March 21, 1823, Sligo petition, 1823.
17. C.O. 42/206, Buchanan to Bathurst, March 10; C.O. 42/371, Astle to Horton, Sept. 11, 1823.
18. *Parl. Pap.*, 1825, VIII (129), 12; C. 630, Archdeacon Mountain to Major General Darling, Nov. 29, 1826, agreed with the colonial under-secretary.
19. C. S. Parker, *Sir Robert Peel* (3 vols., London, 1891–9), I, 234, Peel to Liverpool, June 24, 1816.
20. C.O. 384/1, Russell to Colonial Office, April 22, 1817, and others in same.
21. *Parl. Pap.*, 1823, VI (561), 11, 172–3.
22. *Ibid.*, 1825, VIII (129), 5.
23. C.O. 43/62, Bathurst to Lord Kingston, June 29, 1822.
24. C.O. 42/371, statement of terms; C. 628, enclosure in Bathurst to Dalhousie, June 5, 1823.
25. *Parl. Pap.*, 1825, VII (200), 249; C.O. 384/12, Ennismore to Horton, May 30, 1823, Robinson to Horton, April 2, 1824.
26. C.O. 384/12 Robinson to Horton, June 9; *Parl. Pap.*, 1823, VI (561), 178.
27. C.O. 384/12, Robinson to Horton. This part of the correspondence was omitted from *Parl. Pap.*, 1825, VII (200).
28. C.O. 384/12, Robinson to Horton, June 14, 9, 29, July 1, 1823.
29. *Ibid.*, June 19, July 8, 1823.
30. C.O. 42/197, Robinson to Horton, Sept. 2.
31. C.O. 43/25, Bathurst to Dalhousie, June 5, 1823.
32. C. 629, Commissary of Accounts Office, Quebec, to Colonel Darling, May 10, 21, 1824; N. Macdonald, *Canada, 1763–1841: Immigration and Settlement* (London, 1939), 255.
33. C.O. 384/12, Robinson to Horton, July 20, 1824, stating that the issue of blankets was absolutely necessary as the settlers were quite uncovered; Feb. 19, 1824.
34. C.O. 324/95, Horton's private correspondence, 1824.
35. C.O. 42/196, Dalhousie to Bathurst, Dec. 20, 1823; C.O. 42/200, Dalhousie to Bathurst, May 18, 1824, with enclosure of Marshall, May 5, 1824.
36. C.O. 42/372, Maitland to Bathurst, Feb. 23, 1824; C.O. 42/373, enclosure in Maitland to Bathurst, July 27.
37. C.O. 42/377, enclosure in Maitland to Bathurst, May 12; C.O. 384/87, Robinson's report to Horton on limited emigration in 1823.
38. C.O. 384/12, from statement of expenditure which was later than

that given in *Parl. Pap.*, 1825, VII (200); Robinson to Horton, Jan. 1, 1825.

39. Adams, *Ireland and Irish Emigration*, 141, 143, and Appendix for various estimates.

40. 4 Geo. IV, c. 84; Adams, *Ireland and Irish Emigration*, 145, 154.

41. *Parl. Pap.*, 1825, VIII (129), 12.

42. C.O. 42/372, Maitland to Bathurst, Feb. 23, 1824.

43. C.O. 43/64, Horton to Robinson, Feb. 25, 1824; C.O. 384/13, Robinson to Horton, May 22, 1824.

44. C.O. 43/64, Bathurst to Goulburn, July 30.

45. *Parl. Deb.*, N.S., XII (1825), 1358.

46. *Parl. Pap.*, 1825, VII (200), 191.

47. *Parl. Deb.*, N.S., XII (1825), 1360.

48. *Acc. & Pap.*, 1825, XVIII (131), 358.

49. C.O. 384/13, Beecher to Robinson, Oct. 2, Mount Cashell to Robinson, Oct. 20, Doneraile to Robinson, Nov. 23, 1824.

50. E. C. Guillet, ed., *The Valley of the Trent* (Toronto, 1957), 87–9.

51. C.O. 324/95, Horton to Robinson, April 16, 1825.

52. *Ibid.*, May 4, 1825.

53. C.O. 384/13, Robinson to Horton, April 12, May 8, 1825.

54. C.O. 384/13 and C. 630, Commissary General's Office report of arrivals, July 8, 1825:

Total emigration 2,024—385 men   325 women
                  267 male children above 14   199 female above 14
                  459 male children below 14   389 female below 14
                                                              ─────
                                                              2,024

Resolution Transport, sailed May	5	Passengers	227
Albion " " "	5	"	191
Brunswick " " "	5	"	343
Fortitude " " "	5	"	282
Star " " "	10	"	214
Amity " " "	13	"	147
Regulus " " "	13	"	157
Elizabeth " " "	16	"	210
John Barry " " "	21	"	253

2,024

55. C.O. 384/13, Navy Office to Horton, March 7, Robinson to Horton, May 31, Ordnance Office to Horton, May 4.

56. C.O. 384/17, Dr. Reade's report, March 13, 1827.

57. C.O. 42/380, enclosure in B. Robinson to Horton, Jan. 22.

58. *Parl. Pap.*, 1827, V (237, 550), Report of Select Committee on Emigration, 345–7; Guillet, *Valley of the Trent*, 116–25.

59. F. Stewart, *Our Forest Home* (Toronto, 1889), 47; Guillet, *Valley of the Trent*, 109–10, 124, quoting Robinson's letter to his brother, Oct. 6, 1825, and Robinson's report, May 4, 1827.

60. Guillet, *Valley of the Trent*, 109, 116, for Robinson's report and memo of John Thomson, Surgeon.

61. *Ibid.*, 110, 353.

62. C.O. 42/380, enclosure in B. Robinson to Horton, Jan. 22; *Colonial Advocate*, Dec. 8, 1825.

NOTES: CHAPTER FIVE

63. C.O. 42/204, Dalhousie to Horton, Nov. 12, 1825.
64. C.O. 42/377, Maitland to Bathurst, March 31, 1826; Q 340, pt. 2, 412–8.
65. Guillet, *Valley of the Trent*, 112, quoting Stewart's letter, Jan. 20, 1826.
66. R. J. W. Horton, *Inquiry into the Causes and Remedies of Pauperism*, Third Series (London, 1831), 79–80.
67. C.O. 384/27, Audit Office to Treasury, March 11 and Feb. 21, 1831; C.O. 42/415, Robinson to Colonial Office, Dec. 21, 1833; *Acc. & Pap.*, 1826–7, XV (160), 277.
68. *Parl. Pap.*, 1827, V (550), 350; 1828, XXI (148), 443; Cockburn gave two estimates, £56 and £66.
69. C.O. 384/13, Robinson to Horton, May 31, Doneraile to Horton recd. July 6, 1825.
70. Guillet, V*alley of the Trent*, xlii, 350.
71. A. Picken, *The Canadas* (London, 1832), 153–66, from an inspection made by John Smith, Jr., deputy provincial surveyor, 1827; *supra*, 44.
72. J. R. Hale, ed., *Settlers* (London, 1950), 37–50; Guillet, *Valley of the Trent*, 350–8.
73. Stewart, *Our Forest Home*, 47; C. R. Weld, *A Vacation Tour in the United States and Canada* (London, 1855), 98–110; R. J. W. Horton, *Ireland and Canada* (London, 1839), 56; S. Strickland, *Twenty-seven Years in Canada West* (2 vols., London, 1853), II, 139; *Parl. Pap.*, 1831–2, XXXII (334), John Richards in 1830 describing Peterborough, with saw, flour, and carding mills, tannery in "regular work," about 60 houses and 22 framed buildings erected in the last 11 months.
74. Macdonald, *Canada, 1763–1841*, 493–4; Guillet, *Valley of the Trent*, 33; G. M. Craig, ed., *Early Travellers in Canada* (Toronto, 1955), 208.
75. Hale, *Settlers*, 37–50, 72–98; Guillet, *Valley of the Trent*, 361–7, 400
76. Q 351, Colborne to R. W. Hay, April 2, 1829; Q 192, Buchanan reporting May 25; *Parl. Pap.*, 1831–2, XXXII (334), 4, 17, 24; F. C. Hamil, *Lake Erie Baron* (Toronto, 1955), 145–8.
77. Q 357, Colborne to Goderich, Sept. 5, 1831; Hamil, *Lake Erie Baron*, 147, quoting Kingston *Chronicle*, May 14, 28, July 23, Aug. 20, Sept. 3, 17, 1831.
78. Macdonald, *Canada, 1763–1841*, 497.
79. *Parl. Pap.*, 1847–8, XLVII (368), 11, Elgin to Grey, March 15, 1848.
80. C.O. 384/6, Easton to Bathurst, May 19, 1820.
81. Hale, *Settlers*, 39, 44; J. W. Bannister, *Sketch of a Plan for Settling in Upper Canada, a Portion of the Unemployed Labourers of England* (London, 1821).

CHAPTER FIVE

1. *Edinburgh Review*, XLV (1826), 67.
2. C.O. 384/15, Edmund Worlthorp to Horton, July 1, 1827.
3. R. J. W. Horton, *An Inquiry into the Causes and Remedies of Pauperism*. First Series. Correspondence with C. Poulett Thomson (London, 1830), 33–4.

NOTES: CHAPTER FIVE

4. *Parliamentary Debates*, N.S., XIX (1828), 315.
5. R. J. W. Horton, *A Letter* [to Sir F. Burdett . . .] (London, 1826), 2–3.
6. Horton, *An Inquiry into the Causes and Remedies of Pauperism. Fourth Series. Explanation of Mr. Wilmot Horton's Bill in a Letter and Queries addressed to N.W. Senior* (London, 1830), 3.
7. *Parliamentary Report*, 1823, VI (561), 7, 11; 1825, VIII (129), 208; 1825, IX (181), 59.
8. *Edinburgh Review*, XLIII (1825), 494, XLV (1826), 54; *Parl. Rep.*, 1825, VIII (129), 691, 835. Between 1841 and 1861, the Irish-born in England and Wales rose from 289,000 to 602,000, and in Scotland from 126,000 to 204,000.
9. *Parl. Rep.*, 1823, VI (561), 170; C.O. 384/12.
10. Peel Papers, Br.Mus. Add. MSS 40329, Peel to Goulburn, April 30, 1823.
11. *Parl. Rep.*, 1823, VI (561), 498–510.
12. *Ibid.*, 1825, VIII (129), 17–8, 820.
13. *Ibid.*; *Edinburgh Review*, XXXVII (1822), 252; XXXIX (1824), 343.
14. C.O. 324/95–6–7, Horton's private correspondence.
15. C.O. 43/70, Horton to Robinson, Nov. 17, 1827.
16. Horton, *A Letter*, 24–5; *Parl. Rep.*, 1827, V (550), 237, 240, 798 et seq.; *Journals of the House of Commons*, June 4, 1829.
17. Horton, *An Inquiry*. Fourth Series, 17; *Parl. Rep.*, 1827, V (550), 257.
18. *Parl. Deb.*, N.S., XVI (1826–7), 475.
19. Horton, *An Inquiry*. First Series, 27.
20. *Parl. Rep.*, 1826, IV (404), 137–9, 191, 195, 197–8; 1827, V (550), 232, 440–53; 1827, V (237), 144–5, 233–5.
21. *Parl. Rep.*, 1826, IV (404), 79; C.O. 384/14–15, petitions from the Glasgow emigration societies and William S. Northhouse representing 4,653 petitioners. *Parl. Deb.*, N.S., XVII (1827), 929; *Parl. Rep.*, 1827, V (237), 3–7; 1827, V (550), 237.
22. *Parl. Rep.*, 1826, IV (404), 49–50, 147–55.
23. C.O. 217/33, Douglas to Horton, Nov. 16, 1826.
24. *Parl. Rep.*, 1826, IV (404), 124; 1827, V (237), 154–5; 1827, V (550), 256–7, 559–60, 610–12.
25. *Ibid.*, 1827, V (550), 18–34, 242–4; *Parl. Deb.*, N.S., XIX (1828), 1515.
26. *Parl. Rep.*, 1826, IV (404), 38–40, 133, 172, 395; 1827, V (550), 287.
27. 6 Geo. IV, c. 97.
28. C.O. 42/214, Todhunter to Horton, June 8, 1827; *Parl. Deb.*, N.S., XVIII (1828), 939, 1208–19.
29. *Parl. Rep.*, 1827, V (550), 242–3, 256.
30. C.O. 384/96, Horton to Peel, July 15, 1826; R. J. W. Horton, *The Causes and Remedies of Pauperism in the United Kingdom Considered: Part I* (London, 1829), 16–20; *An Inquiry*. Fourth Series, 3.
31. Wellesley, Arthur, 1st Duke of Wellington, *Despatches, Correspon-*

NOTES: CHAPTER FIVE

dence, and Memoranda of Field Marshall Arthur, Duke of Wellington (8 vols., London, 1867–80), III, 432–7; R. Russell, ed., *Early Correspondence of Lord John Russell* (2 vols., London, 1913), I, 253.

32. C.O. 43/69, Horton to Cockburn, June 25, 1827; J. S. Martell, *Immigration to and Emigration from Nova Scotia* (N.S. Archives, no. 6, 1942), 22.

33. *Westminster Review*, VI (1826), 344; *Edinburgh Review*, XLV (1826–7), 57; XLVII (1828), 242; N. W. Senior, *Two Lectures on Colonization* (London, 1829), 80–9.

34. M. Sadler, *Ireland, Its Evils and Their Remedies: Being a Refutation of the Errors of the Emigration Committee* (London, 1829), *The Law of Population* (London, 1830); Horton, *The Causes and Remedies of Pauperism: Part I*.

35. W. Cobbett, *Rural Rides* (2 vols., London, 1885), II, 81; C.O. 384/17, Francisco to Horton; R. J. W. Horton, *Lecture II*, delivered at the London Mechanics Institute (London, 1831).

36. C.O. 43/70, Horton to Robinson, Nov. 17, 1827; *Parl. Deb.*, N.S., XVIII (1828), 1553; XIX (1828), 1517; XIV (1826), 1364.

37. Wellington, *Despatches*, IV, 455, 476–7; *Parl. Deb.*, N.S., XVIII (1828), 1547.

38. *Parl. Deb.*, N.S., XVIII (1828), 961, 1553–6; XIX (1828), 1501, 1514–18.

39. *Journals of the House of Commons*, June 4, 1829; *Parl. Deb.*, N.S., XXIII (1830), 26, 53, 782.

40. *Spectator*, Feb. 26, 1831; *Parl. Deb.*, Ser. 3, II (1830–1), 875–80.

41. E. G. Wakefield, *A View of the Art of Colonization* (London, 1849), 39–40.

42. *Ibid.*, 138; E. G. Wakefield, *Statement of the Principles and Objects of a Preposed National Society, for the Cure and Prevention of Pauperism, by Means of Systematic Colonization* (London, 1830), 1, 26.

43. C. Tennant, *Letters Forming Part of a Correspondence with Nassau William Senior, Esq.* (London, 1831), 36; Wakefield, *A View*, 39.

44. *Parl. Pap.*, 1837–8, XL (388), 3.

45. Wakefield, *A View*, 42.

46. *Parl. Deb.*, N.S., XVII (1827–8), 142–3, for Gourlay's petition presented by Joseph Hume, Nov. 27, 1826, for a select committee to consider Poor Law reform and emigration. While Wakefield was in Canada with the Durham mission, Gourlay talked with him at Quebec and Wakefield then, apparently, acknowledged his indebtedness to Gourlay (F. Bradshaw, *Self-government in Canada* (London, 1909), 167). For Gourlay's criticism of the land practices of the government of Upper Canada, see W. S. Wallace, *The Family Compact* (Toronto, 1915), 28–31; also J. H. Rose, A. P. Newton, and E. A. Benians, eds., *Cambridge History of the British Empire*, II, 442, 463.

47. C.O. 188/88, Report of Committee of Council on Land Regulations, July 25, 1844; C. Lucas, ed., *Lord Durham's Report* (3 vols., Oxford 1912), II, 229–30.

48. Horton, *An Inquiry*. Third and Fourth Series, 90, 96; R. Garnett, *Edward Gibbon Wakefield* (London, 1897), 91; Wakefield, *A View*, 40–1.

49. *Parl. Deb.*, Ser. 3, II (1830–1), 875–905.
50. H. T. Manning, "The Colonial Policy of the Whig Ministers, 1830–37," *Canadian Historical Review*, XXXIII (1952), 203–8.
51. *Gazette*, June 24, 1831.
52. *Parl. Pap.*, 1831–2, XXXII (724), 6, 9; F. H. Hitchins, *The Colonial Land and Emigration Commission* (Philadelphia, 1931), 13; Manning, "Colonial Policy of Whig Ministers," 208.
53. Hitchins, *Colonial Land and Emigration Commission*, 13, quoting C.O. 384/27, Goderich to Commissioners, Aug. 4, 1832, printed in *Parl. Pap.*, 1831–2, XXXII (724).
54. D. J. McDougall, "Lord John Russell and the Canadian Crisis, 1837–1841," *Canadian Historical Review*, XXII (1941), 373–4; W. F. Adams, *Ireland and Irish Emigration to the New World* (New Haven, 1932), 307; R. B. McDowell, "Ireland on the Eve of the Famine," in R. D. Edwards and T. D. Williams, eds., *The Great Famine* (Dublin, 1956), 42–50.
55. Adams, *Ireland and Irish Emigration*, 312–13, quoting *Parl. Pap.*, 1836, no. 43, 8, 25–9.
56. *Parl. Deb.*, Ser. 3, XXXI (1836), 429; XXXIII (1836), 590, 598; W. T. M. Torrens, *Memoirs of the Right Honourable Second Viscount Melbourne* (2 vols., London, 1878), II, 243–4; C. S. Parker, ed., *Sir Robert Peel* (3 vols., London, 1899), II, 326.
57. *Parl. Deb.*, Ser. 3, XXXVI (1837), 459–78, 496–7; McDowell, "Ireland on the Eve of the Famine," 45; Torrens, *Memoirs of Melbourne*, II, 243; *Parl. Deb.*, Ser. 3, XCVIII (1848), 1313.
58. 1 and 2 Vic., c. 56; *Parl. Deb.*, Ser. 3, XXXVIII (1837), 370; McDowell, "Ireland on the Eve of the Famine," 46–7.
59. Garnett, *Wakefield*, 243–4; *Parl. Pap.*, 1836, XI (512), iii; H. E. Egerton, *A Short History of British Colonial Policy* (London, 1897), 283–4; W. P. Morrell, *British Colonial Policy in the Age of Peel and Russell* (Oxford, 1930), 9.
60. P. Knaplund, *James Stephen and the British Colonial System, 1813–1847* (Madison, 1953), 93–4; Morrell, *British Colonial Policy*, 41–2, 201.
61. Hitchins, *Colonial Land and Emigration Commission*, 21–4; *Parl. Pap.*, 1838, XL (388), Report to the Colonial Office from the Agent General for Emigration.
62. Lucas, *Lord Durham's Report*, II, 242, 259, III, 34–130, "Sketch of Lord Durham's Mission to Canada," by Charles Buller; Morrell, *British Colonial Policy*, 17.
63. 3 and 4 Vic., c. 35; W. G. Ormsby, "The Civil List Question in the Province of Canada," *Canadian Historical Review*, XXXV (1954), 97–102.
64. P.A.C., G 1, vol. 97, Russell to Sydenham, May 3, 1841; O. A. Kinchen, *Lord John Russell's Canadian Policy* (Lubbock, 1945), 149.
65. Kinchen, *Lord John Russell's Canadian Policy*, 106–7; McDougall, "Lord John Russell and the Canadian Crisis," 369–88.
66. G 1, vol. 102, Hope to Bagot, Aug. 18, 1842; G 12, vol. 60, Bagot to Colonial Office, April 1, 1842 (confidential); D. G. Creighton, *Dominion of the North* (Toronto, 1957), 254; *Cambridge History of the British Empire*, VI, 375.

NOTES: CHAPTER FIVE

67. *Parl. Deb.*, Ser. 3, XLVIII (1839), 841–95, 919; *Parl. Pap.*, 1840, VII (30).

68. Hitchins, *Colonial Land and Emigration Commission*, 306; *Parl. Pap.*, 1852–3, LXII (1004).

69. *Parl. Pap.*, 1840, VII (30), XXXIII (613), 104–5, 108.

70. C.O. 384/61, Emigration Commissioners to Russell, April 21, 1840, and Report, April 25, 1840; G 2, vol. 4, Stanley to Bagot, Feb. 4, 1843; Adams, *Ireland and Irish Emigration*, 325, quoting Report of an Extraordinary Meeting of the Shareholders of the North American Colonial Association of Ireland (1844).

71. L. C. Sanders, ed., *Lord Melbourne's Papers* (London, 1889), 376.

72. J. C. Hobhouse (Lord Broughton), *Recollections* (6 vols., London, 1910–11), V, 136; R. J. W. Horton, *Ireland and Canada: Supported by Local Evidence* (London, 1839).

73. *Journals of the House of Commons*, 1839, XCIV, 429.

74. *Parl. Deb.*, Ser. 3, LIV (1840), 832–70, 878ff.

75. *Ibid.*, LVI (1841), 515–18, 524–6; *infra*, 175.

76. *Parl. Pap.*, 1841, VI (333), iii–iv for recommendations, VI (182) for committee; XXVII (60), 2–3; W. S. Shepperson, *British Emigration to North America* (Minneapolis, 1957), 237, using C.O. 384/61.

77. 14 and 15 Vic., c. 91; *Parl. Deb.*, Ser. 3, CXVIII (1851), 1303, 1389, 1549–50, 1929.

78. Morrell, *British Colonial Policy*, 29–30.

79. *Parl. Deb.*, Ser. 3, LXIII (1842), 482; LXII (1842), 815; LX (1842), 77.

80. *Parl. Deb.*, Ser. 3, LX (1842), 57, 76; *infra*, 125.

81. J. S. Buckingham, *Canada, Nova Scotia, New Brunswick, and the Other British Provinces in North America* (London, [1843]), 439–55; *Parl. Deb.*, Ser. 3, LXVIII (1843), 554; *infra*, 210.

82. "Emigration and Colonization," in *Fisher's Colonial Magazine and Commercial Maritime Journal*, III (1843), 118, 171; *Parl. Deb.*, Ser. 3, LXVIII, 484–531; LXXI, 762–92.

83. F. Hincks, *Reminiscences of His Public Life* (Montreal, 1884), 109; Morrell, *British Colonial Policy*, 63–4.

84. P. Knaplund, "Some Letters of Peel and Stanley on Canadian Problems, 1841–1844," *Canadian Historical Review*, XII (1931), 53–4; *Parl. Deb.*, Ser. 3, LXVIII (1843), 544–69.

85. *Parl. Pap.*, 1845, XXVII (624), 273, 23; 1841, XI (327), 494–9; 1843, XXI (468), 32–3, 37–8, quoted by McDowell, "Ireland on the Eve of the Famine," 51, 54.

86. McDowell, "Ireland on the Eve of the Famine," 75, 79, quoting W. E. Hudson, *A Treatise on the Elective Franchise and the Registration of Electors in Ireland under the Reform Act of 1832* (Dublin).

87. *Parl. Pap.*, 1845, XIX (605), 28–9. The report quoted four previous select committees as favourable to emigration, those of 1826–7, 1830, 1832, 1835.

88. *Parl. Deb.*, LXXXI (1845), 212–13; McDowell, "Ireland on the Eve of the Famine," 80.

89. O. MacDonagh, "Emigration during the Famine," in *The Great Famine*, 343, quoting Monteagle MSS, N. L. I., Monteagle to Grey, Oct. 9, 1846.

90. G 1, vol. 114, Grey to Elgin, Dec. 31, 1846; MacDonagh, "Emigration during the Famine," 344, quoting Monteagle MSS, N. L. I., Grey to Monteagle, Oct. 14, Monteagle to Grey, Oct. 22, 1846; *Parl. Pap.*, 1847, XXXIX (824), 6–9; XXXIII (809), 56–7.

91. C.O. 384/79, Emigration Commissioners to J. Stephen, March 27, 1847; *Parl. Pap.*, 1847, XXXIX (777), 3–6.

92. C.O. 384/79, Commissioners to Stephen, Jan. 28, 1847, Canada Company to Commissioners, Jan. 28, 1847, with note by Grey "G/28"; G 1, vol. 115, New Brunswick Land Company to Commissioners, Jan. 29, 1847; Grey to Elgin, Feb. 3, 1847, no. 25; Morrell, *British Colonial Policy*, 472–3, quoting Howick Papers; MacDonagh, "Emigration during the Famine," 343, 346.

93. G 1, vol. 115, Grey to Elgin, Jan. 29, 1847, no. 20; *Parl. Pap.*, 1847, XXXIII (809), 58–9.

94. *Parl. Pap.*, 1847, VI (737 II), 203–16; P.A.C., Elgin-Grey Correspondence, Elgin to Grey, May 7, 1847.

95. *Parl. Deb.*, Ser. 3, XCIII (1847), 97–108; MacDonagh, "Emigration during the Famine," 348.

96. *Parl. Deb.*, Ser. 3, XCIII (1847), 108–17; CI (1848), 20–5; *Parl. Pap.*, 1847, VI (737), iii–iv. Lord Monteagle had Aubrey de Vere recount Lord John Russell's speech of Feb. 13, 1837, Grey's of Feb. 22, 1831, and Lord Fitzgerald's of June 13, 1838, as favouring emigration, *ibid.*, 530.

97. M. A. Ormsby, *British Columbia: A History* (Toronto, 1958), 96–8; Shepperson, *British Emigration*, 228–31; G 1, vol. 116, Grey to Elgin, April 17, 1848; *Elgin-Grey Papers, 1846–1852* (4 vols., Ottawa, 1937), I, Elgin to Grey, May 7, 1847, Grey to Elgin, Nov. 16.

98. *Elgin-Grey Papers, 1846–1852*, I, Grey to Elgin, Dec. 1 (private), Dec. 15, 1848, Jan. 12, Feb. 23, 1849, Minute of Council, Dec. 1848, Elgin to Grey, Dec. 19, 1848, Feb. 14, 1849.

99. *Parl. Deb.*, Ser. 3, XCVIII (1848), 73–80.

100. S. Walpole, *Life of Lord John Russell* (2 vols., London, 1889), II, 74; *Parl. Deb.*, Ser. 3, CV (1849), 667–70; *Illustrated London News*, XIII (1848), 219–21, 229–30.

101. G. P. Gooch, ed., *The Later Correspondence of Lord John Russell* (2 vols., London, 1925), I, 168.

102. Walpole, *Russell*, II, 75–80; MacDonagh, "Emigration during the Famine," 351, quoting Monteagle MSS, N. L. I., Clarendon to Monteagle, Jan. 28, 1849, and Russell Papers, G. D. 7, Wood to Russell, June 1, 1849.

103. H. G. Grey, *The Colonial Policy of Lord John Russell's Administration* (2 vols., London, 1853), I, 239–45; *Parl. Pap.*, 1852, XVIII (1499), 10–11. For decline of population 1841–51, heaviest in western and southern counties, see map in *The Great Famine*, 260; A. Schrier, *Ireland and the American Emigration* (Minneapolis, 1958), 3.

104. *Parl. Deb.*, Ser. 3, XC (1847), 859–60; Morrell, *British Colonial Policy*, 433, quoting Howick Papers, and C. Buller, *Thoughts on the Irish Measures of the Government*.

105. Knaplund, *James Stephen and the British Colonial System*, Appendix for Stephen's address of Oct. 13, 1858; "Sir James Stephen and British North American Problems," *Journal of Modern History*, I (1929), 40–6; Morrell, *British Colonial Policy*, quoting Howick Papers, Stephen to Grey, Jan. 15, 1850, Note on Lord Grey's Minute, Jan. 1850.
106. MacDonagh, "Emigration during the Famine," 480; *Cambridge History of the British Empire*, II, 446–9.
107. *Parl. Deb.*, Ser. 3, CI (1848), 46–7; CII (1849), 458–9.
108. Knaplund, *James Stephen and the British Colonial System*, 260–1.
109. N. Gash, "Peel and the Party System, 1830–50," Royal Historical Society, *Transactions*, Ser. 5, V (1951), 66.
110. *Parl. Deb.*, Ser. 3, CI (1847), 38–50.
111. Grey, *The Colonial Policy*, I, 244–5; *Cambridge History of the British Empire*, II, 456.

CHAPTER SIX

1. *Parliamentary Debates*, N.S., XVIII (1828), 1355.
2. A. G. Doughty and D. McArthur, eds., *Documents Relating to the Constitutional History of Canada, 1791–1818* (Ottawa, 1914), 60–2.
3. E. A. Cruikshank, "An Experiment in Colonization in Upper Canada," Ontario Historical Society, *Papers and Records*, XXV (1929), 32–77; G. C. Patterson, "Land Settlement in Upper Canada, 1783–1840," Ontario Archives, *Report* (Toronto, 1921), 43.
4. H. I. Cowan, *Charles Williamson, Genesee Promoter* (Rochester, 1941), 30, 73–81.
5. A. J. H. Richardson and H. I. Cowan, eds., *William Berczy's Williamsburgh Documents* (Rochester, 1942), 144–7.
6. P.A.C., Berczy Papers, *passim*; *Parliamentary Paper*, 1831–2, XXXII (334), 5, for John Richard's report on New Market, "a very flourishing village," about thirty years old.
7. M. G. Hutt, "Abbé P. J. L. Desjardins and the Scheme for the Settlement of French Priests in Canada, 1792–1802," *Canadian Historical Review*, XXXIX (1958), 93–124.
8. J. Carnochan, "Count Joseph de Puisaye," Ontario Historical Society, *Papers and Records*, V (1904), 36–52; L. Textor, *A Colony of Emigrés in Canada* (Toronto, 1905), 35, 62–3.
9. C.O. 42/330, Talbot to Sullivan, Oct. 27, 1803; Q 291, 514–7, Kent to Hobart, Oct. 11, 1801; Q 294, 37, Colonial Office to Hunter, Feb. 13, 1802, 54, Hunter to Colonial Office, May 15, 1803; F. C. Hamil, *Lake Erie Baron* (Toronto, 1955), 56–8, quoting Land Book G, 43, 331, Land Petitions T 8, nos. 1, 29. For Talbot's life and work, see besides Hamil, E. D. Ermatinger, *Life of Colonel Talbot and the Talbot Settlement* (St. Thomas, 1859), J. H. Coyne, ed., *Talbot Papers, 1806–1852*, Royal Society of Canada, *Transactions*, Ser. 3, II (1907, 1909).
10. N. Macdonald, *Canada, 1763–1841: Immigration and Settlement* (London, 1939), 131–2; Hamil, *Lake Erie Baron*, 93, quoting Q 358, Pt. 3, 685–6 and State Papers, Talbot portfolio; Q 358, 674–9, Talbot to Goderich,

July 29, 1831, 680–4, to Colborne, explaining the origin of his superintendence, Gore's part in it and his fees, and Bathurst's authorization of Feb. 26, 1818.

11. Q 352, 228–30, Colborne to Murray, Nov. 10, 1829; Patterson, "Land Settlement in Upper Canada," 190; A. Jameson, *Winter Studies and Summer Rambles* (2 vols., New York, 1839), II, 7; Hamil, *Lake Erie Baron*, chapter v, describes Talbot's plans and difficulties in acquiring the power he desired for the roads and the settlements bordering them.

12. *Parl. Pap.*, 1831–2, XXXII (334), 6; Macdonald, *Canada, 1763–1841*, 136; Hamil, *Lake Erie Baron*, 100 ff.

13. C. O. Ermatinger, *The Talbot Regime* (Toronto, 1904), 99–100, 123; Land Book K, 357, Jan. 20, 1820, Land Book L, 35–40; Jameson, *Winter Studies*, I, 316, 335.

14. Q 332, 533 ff.; Hamil, *Lake Erie Baron*, 116, quoting Q 359, 75–6; A. Picken, *The Canadas* (London, 1832), 300–1. Talbot was appointed a member of the Legislative Council but appears not to have attended its meetings, for which see Hamil, *Lake Erie Baron*, 60, C. O. Ermatinger, *Talbot Regime*, 107, and also E. A. Talbot, *Five Years' Residence in the Canadas* (2 vols., London, 1824), I, 105, who disagrees.

15. Q 322, 371 ff., Talbot celebration, March 8, 1817, 359–60, Gore to Talbot, March 20, 1817, requesting him to remit fees; 348, Talbot to Upper Canadian government, Nov. 6, 1817, that he is going to England because Upper Canada Council report shows misunderstanding of Hobart's authorization; 361–8, Council on Nov. 9, 1817, advises payment of fees on threat of opening lands; Q 332, 515–18, Talbot to Hillier, Oct. 6, 1820; Q 352, 228–30, 242–3, Colborne to Talbot, Oct. 28, 1829, Colborne to Murray, Nov. 10, 1829.

16. Q 398, 37–47, Bond Head to Glenelg, Sept. 20, 1837; G 83, 56–8, Glenelg to Bond Head, Nov. 10, 1837, requesting Talbot to "wind up affairs."

17. G. Patterson, "The Professional Settler in Upper Canada," Ontario Historical Society, *Papers and Records*, XXVIII (1932), 122; Q 352, 228–30, Colborne to Murray, Nov. 10, 1829; P.A.C., Upper Canada, Sundries, Dec. 1834, Remarks of the Chief Justice; J. Bouchette, *The British Dominions in North America* (2 vols., London, 1832), I, 104 ff.; Hamil, *Lake Erie Baron*, 122.

18. H. I. Cowan, "Lork Selkirk's Work in Canada: An Early Chapter," *Canadian Historical Review*, IX (1928), 299–308.

19. Q 293, 167, Selkirk to Hobart, Aug. 21, 1802, 219 ff., King's Memo of May 27, 1802; P.A.C., Selkirk Papers, LXXVI, 26, 2–3, 18–20, Aug. 3, 1802, for terms to Skye settlers; LIII, Selkirk to Burns, March 12, 1804; P. C. T. White, ed., *Lord Selkirk's Diary, 1803–4* (Toronto, 1958), xiv–xviii.

20. Macdonald, *Canada, 1763–1841*, 153–5, quoting Selkirk Papers, LII, Hobart to Selkirk, Feb. 12, 1803, Q 293, 201, Selkirk to Hobart, July 6, 1802.

21. Thomas Douglas, Earl of Selkirk, *Observations on the Present State of the Highlands of Scotland* (2nd ed., London, 1806), 198–215.

22. Selkirk Papers, LXXIII, Colville to Selkirk's heirs, April 7, 1838.

23. C.O. 42/331, Hobart to Hunter, Feb. 15, 1803; F. C. Hamil, "Lord

NOTES: CHAPTER SIX

Selkirk in Upper Canada," Ontario Historical Society, *Papers and Records*, XXXVII (1945), 35–48, and *The Valley of the Lower Thames* (Toronto, 1951), chapter IV.

24. Macdonald, *Canada, 1763–1841*, 158–60.

25. Q 293, 201, Selkirk to Hobart, July 6, 1802; C.O. 42/330, Note on Selkirk's proposal of March 31, 1802; C. Martin, *Lord Selkirk's Work in Canada* (Oxford, 1916), 31.

26. Martin, *Lord Selkirk's Work*, 38; W. Kingsford, *History of Canada* (10 vols., London, 1888–98), IX, 113–15; John Halkett, *A Statement Respecting the Earl of Selkirk's Settlement* (London, 1817), 2–3; D. Mackay, *The Honourable Company* (New York, 1936), 133–6; Hist. MSS Comm., *Report of the Laing Manuscripts* (1925), II, 716 ff., giving Selkirk's correspondence on obtaining settlers from the Highlands.

27. C.O. 384/9, McNab to Colonial Office, 1823; C.O. 42/370, Maitland to Bathurst, March 13; Macdonald, *Canada, 1763–1841*, 186–200; for McNab's inheritance, family, debts, and flight see R. Wild, *McNab, the Last Laird* (London, 1938).

28. Q 335, 383–5, Executive Council to Maitland, Nov. 5, 1823; Patterson, *Land Settlement in Upper Canada*, 193.

29. Wild, *McNab, the Last Laird*, 46–9, 78–82; A. Fraser, *The Last Laird of McNab* (Toronto, 1899), 17–18; M. J. H. Fraser, "Feudalism in Upper Canada," Ontario Historical Society, *Papers and Records*, XII (1914), 145.

30. P.A.C., Upper Canada, Sundries, April 20, 1825; State Book M, land petitions, McNab to Executive Council, March 16, 1831; A. Fraser, *Last Laird of McNab*, 20–5.

31. Upper Canada, Sundries, Peter Ferguson to Sir George Arthur, June 29, 1840: "Archibald McNab told your Memorialist that the township of McNab was his own private property."

32. J. MacTaggart, *Three Years in Canada* (2 vols., London, 1829), I, 277–8; A. Fraser, *Last Laird of McNab*, 27–40, 48, 74–8, 90; P.A.C., McNab Papers, A. Macdonald's report to Attorney-General Robinson, June 25, 1830; Macdonald, *Canada, 1763–1841*, 191–3.

33. Upper Canada, Land Book T, 49, 330, Aug. 11, 1837, June 29, 1838; Macdonald, *Canada, 1763–1841*, 196.

34. MacTaggart, *Three Years in Canada*, I, 278; Land Book T, 511–13, Executive Council report, Feb. 8, 1839, 525–6, Attorney-General on the case, read, Feb. 14, 1839; Upper Canada, State Book M, 185–8, Executive Council report on McNab township, Sept. 17, 1839, McNab's agreement and accounts.

35. A. Fraser, *Last Laird of McNab*, 119–20, 165–8, 177; Macdonald, *Canada, 1763–1841*, 200–1.

36. C.O. 42/202, Cameron to Colonial Office, April 3, and to House of Commons; Q 334, 140, Cameron to Colonial Office, June 5, 1823, with verification by Lieut. Colonel P. Cameron, and D. MacIntyre, Minister of Kilmalie; Q 386, 278–92, Executive Council to Colborne, Nov. 26, 1830.

37. Q 337 A, 123, Horton to Maitland, June 24, 1823; Q 170, 249–52, April 3, 1824; Patterson, *Land Settlement in Upper Canada*, 196.

38. Upper Canada, Land Book M, 462–3, Nov. 21, 1825, 566–7, March 8, 1826; Upper Canada, Sundries, Cameron to Hillier, Nov. 21, 1825.

39. Upper Canada, Sundries, Oct. 15, 1830; Q 356, 73–84, Executive Council report, Nov. 26, 1830, reviewing Cameron's case, and giving decision following Smalley's report.

40. Q 390, 400 ff., Report of Executive Council to Bond Head, May 9, 1836.

41. Q 358, 120 ff., Petition to the Throne, March 12, 1831, attacking Judge John B. Robinson and his brother; Upper Canada, Sundries, Cameron to Bond Head, April 28, 1836, and by date for settlers' petitions; Q 424, 173, Cameron to Colonial Office, Feb. 17, 1839.

42. Q 386, 262–4, Colonial Office to Colborne, Nov. 30, 1835, for inquiry regarding delay of Executive Council in handling Cameron's case; Upper Canada, Sundries, 169, Cameron to Bond Head, Aug. 18, 1836, marked "Put by"; Q 390, 400 ff., report of Council, May 9, 1836, 410, Feb. 27, 1837; Q 419, 139–43, report of Select Committee on petition, April 12, 1836.

43. Upper Canada, Land Book C, 389–90, Committee of Executive Council, Dec. 31, 1845; Land Book E, 14–16, Aug. 30, 1848, report of Executive Council Committee, finally disposing of the case by refusing Cameron's petition, 281, Council on June 9, 1849, repeating final disposal of Aug. 30, 1848.

44. James Young, *Reminiscences of the Early History of Galt and Settlement of Dumfries* (Toronto, 1890), 15–18; 40–4; A. Fergusson, *Practical Notes Made during a Tour in Canada* (Edinburgh, 2nd ed., 1834), 128–9, 283–4; Macdonald, *Canada, 1763–1841*, 495–6.

45. J. Galt, *Autobiography* (2 vols., London, 1833), I, 364; Fergusson, *Practical Notes*, 284; Young, *Reminiscences*, 51–2; T. Rolph, *A Brief Account, Together with Observations Made During a Visit to the West Indies, and a Tour through the United States of America, in Parts of the Years 1823–4; Together with a Statistical Account of Upper Canada* (Dundas, Upper Canada, 1836), 229; T. Rolph, *Canada v. United States* (London, 1842), 23.

46. The second edition, London, 1841, of Rolph's *Brief Account*, was entitled, *A Descriptive and Statistical Account of Canada: Shewing its Great Adaptation for British Emigration. Preceded by an Account of a Tour through Portions of the West Indies and the United States.* The preface to the Dundas edition of 1836 states: "Although I am free to confess that my object in appending a Statistical account of Upper Canada, to my notes of the West Indies and the United States, is to induce that portion of the British population, whose prospects at home are gloomy and indifferent, to examine into the actual resources of a Province that would prove a blessing to emigrants, and be improved by emigration; yet I have carefully endeavoured to give only such statistics as I can fully and entirely substantiate."

47. T. Rolph, *Canada vs. Australia: Their Relative Merits Considered in an Answer to a Pamphlet by Thornton Leigh Hunt* (London, 1839); Galt, *Autobiography*, I, 294; Macdonald, *Canada, 1763–1841*, 270.

48. W. Canniff, *The Medical Profession in Upper Canada* (Toronto, 1894), 604; W. S. Shepperson, *British Emigration to North America* (Minneapolis, 1957), 41–2.

49. T. Rolph, *Emigration and Colonization* (London, 1844), 20–2;

Simmond's Colonial Magazine and Foreign Miscellany, II (1844), 420, on systematic emigration and colonization.

50. Rolph, *Emigration and Colonization*, 23, 35; C.O. 384/61, for Rolph's petitions; *Parl. Pap.*, 1842, XXXI (301), 239–48, Sydenham to Russell, April 6, 1841, Colonial Land and Emigration Commissioners to Stephen, Aug. 17, 1841, and Petitions of Colonial Society, North American Committee of London, and of the British American Land and the Canada Companies, the North American Colonial Association of Ireland, etc.

51. Canniff, *Medical Profession in Upper Canada*, 604; Rolph, *Emigration and Colonization*, 74, 79; *Colonial Magazine and Commercial Maritime Journal*, IV (1841), 258, VIII (1842), 115–16, quoting *Toronto Patriot*, Nov. 9, 1841.

52. G 12, vol. 56, Sydenham to Russell, Dec. 23, 1840, no. 207, T. W. C. Murdock to Rolph, Nov. 25, Dec. 22, 1840; Rolph, *Emigration and Colonization*, 81–2; P. W. Gates, "Official Encouragement to Immigration by the Province of Canada," *Canadian Historical Review*, XV (1934), 25; *Colonial Magazine and Commercial Maritime Journal*, III (1840), 375, IV (1841), 258–61.

53. *Parl. Pap.*, 1841, VI (182), 133–43, First Report from the Select Committee on Emigration: Scotland.

54. Rolph, *Emigration and Colonization*, 114; petitions mentioned in note 50; *Simmond's Colonial Magazine and Foreign Miscellany*, II (1844) 420–35 and 342–50 for review of Rolph's book.

55. G 20, vol. 1, Association Memorial, signed by Mountcashell, Argyll, G. P. Scrope, W. S. O'Brien, G. R. Robinson, C. Franks, T. Rolph et al., Rolph to Murdock, April 23, May 3, 17, June 3, 1841; G 12, vol. 56, Sydenham to Russell, April 6, 1841, no. 41, Murdock to Rolph, April 3, 1841; Rolph, *Emigration and Colonization*, 113, 156–69, 249–55.

56. C.O. 384/74, "British American Association for Emigration and Colonization" [a pamphlet, 28 pp.]; *Parl. Pap.*, 1840, XXXIII (613), 102–3; for McNab's reception by the "Men of Gore," see *Colonial Magazine and Commercial Maritime Journal*, I, (1842), 510.

57. *Parl. Pap.*, 1843, XXXIV (269), ship *Barbadoes*; Rolph, *Emigration and Colonization*, 252–4.

58. C.O. 384/74, for pamphlet by Sir Richard Broun; *Parl. Deb.*, Ser. 3, LXVIII (1843), 873–6.

59. G 12, vol. 62, Bagot to Stanley, Feb. 17, 1842, no. 33; vol. 64, Metcalfe to Stanley, Dec. 17, 1843, no. 148; G 1, vol. 106, Stanley to Metcalfe, Oct. 31, 1843, no. 109; *Parl. Pap.*, 1842, XXXI (301), 239, 246–8; Gates, "Official Encouragement to Immigration," 29 ff.; *Parl. Deb.*, Ser. 3, LXXVII (1843), 444–5.

60. Q 219, 322–4, H. W. Hobhouse to (?), Aug. 7, 1834; P.A.C., *Report*, 1900, xvii–xviii.

61. P.A.C., *Report*, 1900, xvii; Q 387, 251–8, Brydone to Civil Secretary, Upper Canada, Sept. 12, 1835, Brydone to Commissioner of Crown Lands, Sept. 14, Oct. 1, 1835.

62. Q 219, Pt. 2, Coghill to Stanley, Sept. 28, 1833; Palliser to Spring Rice, July 29, Singer to same, Sept. 8, 1834; Q 383, Colborne to Spring Rice,

Dec. 2, 1834, no. 72, same to same, same date (confidential); Q 224, Pt. 2, Coghill to Colonial Office, Feb. 23, 1835, Henchey to Hay, March 2, 1835. Prospectus of Feb. 14, 1835, and financial statement of Feb. 15, 1835.

63. U. Macdonell, "Gibbon Wakefield and Canada," *Queens Quarterly*, XXXII (1924–5), 119 ff., 285 ff.; Prospectus of Association.

64. G 1, vol. 96, Russell to Sydenham, March 26, 1841, no. 344. Though Russell remarked that the group included persons "of considerable wealth and commercial eminence," he believed that he could explain their purpose better than they.

65. G 12, vol. 57, Sydenham to Russell, July 26, 1841, no. 97, and C.O. 384/67.

66. C.O. 188/68, New Brunswick Act 1257, March 31, 1840, Russell to Harvey, June 30, 1840; *Parl. Deb.*, Ser. 3, LXI (1842), 837, LXII (1842), 1178, LXIII (1842), 1238, 1316, LXIV (1842), 858; *Parl. Pap.*, 1840, XXXIII (613), 59; for Stephen's objection to the sale see, P. Knaplund, *James Stephen and the British Colonial System, 1813–1847* (Madison, 1953), 75.

67. C.O. 42/495, also G 12, vol. 63, Bagot to Stanley, July 19, no. 157, July 19, Private, Aug. 6, Oct. 11, 20, 1842; *Colonial Magazine and Commercial Maritime Journal*, I (1842), 380; A. R. M. Lower, ed., "Notes and Documents: Edward Gibbon Wakefield and the Beauharnois Canal," *Canadian Historical Review*, XIII (1932), 38–44.

68. Macdonell, "Gibbon Wakefield," 286–7.

69. J. C. Dent, *The Last Forty Years* (2 vols., Toronto, 1881), I, 310; *supra*, 105.

70. G 14, vol. 52, Crown Land Commissioner to Civil Secretary, Jan. 13, 1844.

71. G 1, vol. 109, Stanley to Metcalfe, Aug. 18, 1845; G 12, vol. 64, Metcalfe to Stanley, Sept. 27, 1845 (private).

72. P. Knaplund, "Arthur Mills' Experiment in Colonization," *Canadian Historical Review*, XXIV (1953), 139–50.

73. *Parl. Pap.*, 1827, V (550), 461–3, for prospectus handed in to the Emigration Committee by Simon M'Gillivray as "Prospectus of terms upon which the Canada Company propose to dispose of their lands."

74. R. K. Gordon, *John Galt* (Toronto, 1920), 55–8; Macdonald, *Canada, 1763–1841*, 271, quoting Dalhousie Papers, IX, Dalhousie to Cockburn, Nov. 9, and to Galt Nov. 23, 1824; Q 359—I, Galt to Bathurst, July 31, 1824.

75. Galt, *Autobiography*, I, 305–6; 6 Geo. IV, c. 75; Bouchette, *British Dominions*, I, 113–14; MacTaggart, *Three Years in Canada*, II, 272, 275–6.

76. Ontario Archives, Canada Company Papers, Minutes of the Court of Directors, May 30, 1826, An Agreement between Lord Bathurst and the Directors of the Canada Company, May 23, 1826, amending the terms of the contract of Nov. 26, 1824; Patterson, *Land Settlement in Upper Canada*, 200; H. M. Morrison, *The Crown Land Policies of the Canadian Government* (Clark University, MSS, 1933), 50. The body of the Canada Company papers is in the Ontario Archives and those papers, together with papers of other Canadian land companies in Ottawa and elsewhere, await the study the subject deserves.

77. Q 373, 124–35, for lands to be disposed of by the Canada Company; Fergusson, *Practical Notes*, 272; Montreal *Gazette*, Aug. 28, 1828; S. Strickland, *Twenty-five Years in Canada West* (2 vols., London, 1853), I, 281.

78. C.O. 384/27, Canada Company Circular; Canada Company Prospectus, 1833; Galt, *Autobiography*, II, 93–7, 331; J. W. Bannister, *Emigration to Upper Canada* (London, 1831), 44; Q 371, Galt to Horton, April 7, 1827, with Way Card.

79. Upper Canada, Sundries, May–Oct. 1829, Bosanquet to Hay, May 21, Oct. 29, 1829; Q 373, statement on assets and expenditures.

80. Q 351, 385–7, Colborne to Colonial Office, May 23, 1829; Q 373, 85–117, report of June 1830 and April 1831.

81. Galt, *Autobiography*, II, 56 ff.; MacTaggart, *Three Years in Canada*, II, 271–5.

82. Patterson, *Land Settlement in Upper Canada*, xii–xiii; see also Q 373, 70–85, 147–58, for letters to relatives in Yorkshire by Richard Beilby, in Ireland by James Mayes, and in Scotland by John Inglis.

83. "Canada Land Company, 1824–35," "Statement of Sales and Results, 1841," in volume of Canada Company pamphlets in Colonial Office Library.

84. C.O. 384/27, *Canada Company*, a circular with maps of the Huron Tract; *Quebec Mercury*, Dec. 1, 1827; Strickland, *Twenty-seven Years in Canada West*, I, 196, 274, 281.

85. Q 383, p. 251, Colborne to Colonial Office, Dec. 2, 1834.

86. *Parl. Pap.*, 1841, VI (333), 41; Macdonald, *Canada, 1763–1841*, 278, quoting T. M. Jones, a statement by the company of the progress made in the Huron Tract.

87. R. L. Jones, *History of Agriculture in Ontario* (Toronto, 1946), 69, for W. L. Mackenzie's attack on the Company as "one of the greatest drawbacks upon . . . the Colony," from Journal of Legislative Assembly of Upper Canada, 1835, Appendix 11, iii; *Parl. Pap.*, 1831–2, XXXII (334), 3–4, Richard's report: H. Merivale, *Lectures on Colonization* (London, 1861), 441; L. F. Gates, "The Decided Policy of William Lyon Mackenzie," *Canadian Historical Review*, XL (1959), 188.

88. W. Huskisson, *Speeches* (3 vols., London, 1831), III, 247–8; Macdonald, *Canada, 1763–1841*, 278–9.

89. R. and K. M. Lizars, *In the Days of the Canada Company, 1825–1850: The Story of the Settlement of the Huron Tract and a View of the Social Life of the Period* (Toronto, 1896), 137.

90. Patterson, *Land Settlement in Upper Canada*, 204; C. Lucas, ed., *Lord Durham's Report* (3 vols., Oxford, 1912), III, 55.

91. Imperial Blue Book Relating to Canada, 1840, paper 317, C. Franks to Russell, Jan. 9, 1840, R. V. Smith to Franks, Jan. 18, 1840.

92. Canada Company, *Report of the Court of Directors . . . to the Proprietors, 1844*; G 14, vol. 51, Widder to Upper Canada Executive, Feb. 4, 1843; *Fisher's Colonial Magazine and Commercial Maritime Journal*, II (1843), 250, 382.

93. G 1, vol. 138, Canada Company to Colonial Office, Feb. 11, 1856; Labouchere to Head, Feb. 15, 1856.

94. Canada Company, *Report of the Court of Directors . . . to the*

Proprietors, 1861; *Simmond's Colonial Magazine and Foreign Miscellany*, XI (1847), 476.

95. P.A.C., British American Land Company Papers (hereinafter B.A.L.C.P.), "Letters"; Q 173, G. H. Markland to Horton, May 13, C. Dalrymple to Bathurst, May 20, 1825, Felton to Horton, Sept. 10, 1825.

96. P.A.C., Dalhousie Papers, XI, Dalhousie to Bathurst, June 19, 1826; Q 176, 499–505, Dalhousie to Bathurst, same date, enclosing report of committee of Council, May 3, 1826; B.A.L.C.P.: "Letters" and R. W. Heneker, "Sketch."

97. Q 203, McGill to Aylmer, Dec. 5, 1832; Q 206, Aylmer to Goderich, Jan. 16, 1833, W. B. Felton's report of Jan. 10, 1833.

98. B.A.L.C.P., "Letters," agreement of Dec. 3, 1833, supplementary article of Aug. 6, 1834; H. T. Manning, "The Colonial Policy of the Whig Ministers, 1830–37," *Canadian Historical Review*, XXXIII (1952), 342.

99. B.A.L.C.P., Letter Book, 1834–6; Royal Charter of March 20, 1834; Morrison, *Crown Land Policies*, 50.

100. Lower Canada, Sundries, 1838, A. C. Buchanan's report; Montreal *Gazette*, July 2, 1836; *Parl. Pap.*, 1836, XI (76), 19–20, 1839, XXXIX (536, I), 31, 1841, VI (182), 222–3, Bruyères to Duke of Argyll, Marquis of Northampton, *et al.*

101. B.A.L.C.P., Letter Book, 1834–6; extracts from Instructions to Directors, Dec. 21, 1836, Feb. 14, April 22, 1837.

102. B.A.L.C.P., Correspondence, 1835–59, Durham to Glenelg, July 31, 1838, Grey to Bruyères, Oct. 17, 1838, Bruyères to Grey, Nov. 8, 1838.

103. B.A.L.C.P., Attorney-General's case filed, Feb. 18, 1841; Correspondence, 1835–59, claim Feb. 1840; G 12, vol. 56, Sydenham to Russell, May 10, 1841, no. 59, July 5, 1841; G 20, vol. 1, G. R. Robinson to Colonial Office, March 13, 1841, *infra*, 183.

104. B.A.L.C.P., Correspondence, 1835–59, Report of Charles Birchoff, Nov. 28, 1853.

105. 10. Vic., c. 56; Heneker, "Sketch."

106. For British American Land Company advertisement of land on credit "under the patronage of the Church" (*La Minerve*, Sept. 4, 1848), see Morrison, *Crown Land Policies*, 59–60; B.A.L.C.P., Correspondence, 1835–59, Report of Charles Birchoff.

107. B.A.L.C.P., collection of charters, by-laws, acts, 1834–95, Acts of 1871 and 1883.

108. C.O. 188/42, 68–72, for meetings in summer of 1831 to organize the company, 84–114, for proposals and prospectus of 1831; C.O. 188/41, Douglas to Colonial Office, June 24, 1831.

109. C.O. 188/41–42, as in note 108; H. Merivale, *Lectures on Colonization and Colonies Delivered before the University of Oxford in 1839, 1840, and 1841* (2 vols., London, 1841–2), II, 145.

110. C.O. 188/42, 97–114 for minutes on Company proposals by "RWH" [Hay], "JS" [Stephen], rehearsing previous experience and advising wariness, and for apparent refusal by "G*h" [Goderich]; C.O. 188/44, 85–136 for resolutions of Provisional Committee, March 2, 1832, John Labouchere in chair and subsequent correspondence of John Bainbridge and Colonial Secretary, March 22, 31, 1832; Manning, "Colonial Policy of the Whig Ministers," 234.

111. Macdonald, *Canada, 1763–1841*, 307, quoting C.O. 188 (198), vol. 6, Nov. 7, 1835 (Deed of Conveyance), etc.; J. Hannay, *History of New Brunswick* (2 vols., St. John, 1909), II, 70; *Cambridge History of the British Empire* (7 vols., Cambridge, 1929–40), VI, 278, for Stanley; W. F. Ganong, "A Monograph of the Origins of Settlements . . . in New Brunswick," Royal Society of Canada, *Transactions*, Ser. 2, X (1904), sect. II, 82.

112. C.O. 188/61, Grey to Company, May 3, 1838, Bainbridge to Howick, May 18, 1838; C.O. 188/60, Harvey to Colonial Office, Sept. 30, 1838, Hayne to Colonial Office, Sept. 27, 1838.

113. C.O. 188/61, Grey to Stephen, May 15, 1838; *Parl. Pap.*, 1841, VI (182), 40; Hannay, *History of New Brunswick*, II, 70–1.

114. C.O. 188/54, Campbell to Glenelg, Feb. 5, 1836, no. 3, with notes thereon by Murdock and Stephen, Surveyor-General Baillie's explanations of Feb. 3, 1836; C.O. 188/59, Baillie on May 15, 1838; C.O. 188/60, Harvey to Glenelg, June 18, 1838.

115. C.O. 188/59, Harvey to Glenelg, May 16, Baillie to Harvey, May 15, 1838; C.O. 188/61, Bainbridge to Colonial Office, Feb. 10, 13, 1838, Glenelg to Bainbridge, Feb. 16, 1838, Privy Council for Trade to Stephen, April 7, 1838; C.O. 188/63, Report from House of Assembly, March 13, 1839; C.O. 188/64, Harvey to Normanby, May 7, June 22, 1839; C.O. 188/65–66, Baillie to Lieut.-Governor, Sept. 5, 1839, Harvey to Colonial Office, Nov. 27, 1839.

116. C.O. 188/68, select committee report, March 21, 1840, Harvey to Colonial Office, May 11, 1840.

117. M.G. 10, vol. 106 (New Brunswick Executive Council Papers), Stanley to Colebrooke, Feb. 9, 1843, no. 131, enclosing Company to Stanley, Feb. 1, 1843; Ganong, "A Monograph," 82.

118. C.O. 188/62, Colonial Office to Harvey, Oct. 21, 1837; C.O. 188/88, Colebrooke to Colonial Office, July 30, 1844, no. 63.

119. C.O. 188/88, Report of Committee of Council on Land Regulations, July 25, 1844, Colebrooke to Colonial Office, July 30, 1844; C.O. 188/86, Colebrooke to Colonial Office, Feb. 27, 1844; C.O. 188/100, same to same, May 13, Aug. 13, 1847; C.O. 188/89, Emigration Commissioners to Colonial Office, Sept. 12, 1844. For Harvey and Teetotal settlements, see *Edinburgh Review*, XCI (1850), 50–1, *Simmond's Colonial Magazine and Foreign Miscellany*, I (1844), 505.

CHAPTER SEVEN

1. 43 Geo. III, c. 56; *supra*, 24.
2. 56 Geo. III, c. 114; 57 Geo. III, c. 10; *supra*, 39, 51–2.
3. *Parliamentary Debates*, N.S., I (1820), 856–8; D. G. Creighton, *The Commercial Empire of the St. Lawrence* (Toronto, 1937), 187; A.R.M. Lower, *Colony to Nation* (Toronto, 1946), 97–8; C. Wright and C. E. Fayle, *A History of Lloyd's* (London, 1928), 243, 293.
4. K. A. Walpole, "Emigration to British North America under the Early Passenger Acts, 1803–1842," Institute of Historical Research, *Bulletin*, VII (1929–30), 189.

5. *Journals of the House of Commons*, LXXVIII (1823), 386–449; 4 Geo. IV, c. 84.

6. 6 Geo. IV, c. 116; *Journals of the House of Commons*, LXXX (1825–6), 485–626.

7. K. A. Walpole, "The Humanitarian Movement of the Early Nineteenth Century to Remedy Abuses on Emigrant Vessels to America," Royal Historical Society, *Transactions*, XIV (1931), 204–5; *The Times*, March 27, Dec. 29, 1827; 7 and 8 Geo. IV, c. 19; *Journals of the House of Commons*, LXXXII (1826–8), 336–85, 391, 395, 401, 429.

8. C.O. 42/214, Todhunter to Colonial Office, June 8, 19, 1827; C.O. 43/70, Horton to Todhunter, June 27, 1827; *Southern Reporter*, June 7, 1827.

9. C.O. 217/147, Kempt to Goderich, Sept. 7, 1827, Kempt to Huskisson, Nov. 25, 1827; *Parl. Deb.*, N.S., XVIII (1828), 962.

10. C.O. 188/35, enclosure in Douglas to Secretary of State, Aug. 1, 1827.

11. C.O. 188/35, enclosure in Douglas to Goderich, Sept. 14, Oct. 16, 1827.

12. C.O. 217/147, enclosure in Kempt to Huskisson, Nov. 25, 1827.

13. C.O. 217/148, Kempt to Huskisson, May 22, 1828; C.O. 217/152, Kempt to Colonial Office, Dec. 10, 1831; C.O. 226/46, Prince Edward Island Act.

14. C.O. 217/149, Young to Murray, April 2, 1829; C.O. 43/72, Hay to Young, April 2, 1829; D. C. Harvey, "Scottish Immigration to Cape Breton," *Dalhousie Review*, XXI (1941), 314.

15. C.O. 384/17, Todhunter to Horton, Dec. 22, 1827; Fitzhugh to Stanley, Nov. 24, 1827.

16. *Parl. Deb.*, N.S., XVIII (1828), 1214–15, 1219.

17. *Ibid.*, 962; W. Huskisson, *Speeches* (3 vols., London, 1831), III, 234.

18. 9 Geo. IV, c. 21.

19. Walpole, "The Humanitarian Movement," 210; *infra*, 153, 158, 168, 182.

20. Walpole, "The Humanitarian Movement," 214–15.

21. *Parliamentary Paper*, 1837–8, XL (388), 9.

22. Walpole, "The Humanitarian Movement," 219.

23. C.O. 384/20, Todhunter to Huskisson, April 1, 1828.

24. G. R. Porter, *Progress of the Nation* (London, 1851), 579.

25. *Parl. Pap.*, 1831–2, XXXII (724), 3.

26. C.O. 42/394, enclosure in Colborne to Colonial Office, Nov. 24, 1831; C.O. 384/28, Galindo to Howick, March 2, 1831.

27. C.O. 384/32, diagram by Lieut. Low; others in C.O. 384/35.

28. C.O. 42/233, enclosure in Aylmer to Goderich, Oct. 12, 1831.

29. *Acc. & Pap.*, 1832, XXXII (730), 3, circular despatch to Governors, Dec. 11, 1831.

30. *Ibid.*, 3–6.

31. C.O. 42/258, Emigrant Agent Buchanan's report, 1835; *Parl. Pap.*, 1840, XXIII (613), 81, Stephen to Emigration Commissioners, May 29, 1840.

32. *Infra*, Tables VI and IX in Appendix B.

33. C.O. 217/154, McIver to Colonial Office, April 5, 1832, and note on

it: "Same answer as that which has been given to many similar letters." C.O. 42/236, enclosure in Aylmer to Goderich, March 21, 1832.

34. C.O. 43/76, Howick to Lambert, April 10, 1832; C.O. 42/236, Aylmer to Goderich, March 21, 1832.

35. C.O. 384/35, Buchanan to Colonial Office, May 1, 1834, April 21; C.O. 384/38, Buchanan to Hay, Jan. 22, 1835.

36. C.O. 43/29, Stanley to Aylmer, Aug. 4, 1833; C.O. 42/251, Aylmer to Stanley, April 4, 1834; Walpole, "The Humanitarian Movement," 212. Opponents of the tax claimed that shipmasters sold emigrant's bedding and clothing to raise the tax money. In later years, even the Emigration Commissioners objected, G 1, vol. 100, Commissioners to Stephen, Feb. 2, 1842.

37. *Parl. Pap.*, 1831-2, XXXII (334), 6, 24; 1836, no. 550, Part I, 18, 77; *Parl. Pap.*, 1842, no. 301, 206-7.

38. *Parl. Pap.*, 1831-2, XXXII (724), 6.

39. Walpole, "Emigration to British North America under the Early Passenger Acts, 1803-1842"; O. MacDonagh, "Irish Emigration during the Famine," in R. D. Edwards and T. D. Williams, eds., *The Great Famine* (Dublin, 1956), 365.

40. *Parl. Pap.*, 1854, XIII (163), 78, First Report . . . Emigrant Ships.

41. D. F. Macdonald, *Scotland's Shifting Population* (Glasgow, 1937), 92; S. Moodie, *Roughing It In the Bush* (2 vols., New York, 1853), I, 20.

42. C.O. 43/75, Howick to Committee of Privy Council for Trade, March 26, 1832; C.O. 384/30, Lack to Howick, March 14; *Gazette*, March 28; C.O. 217/156, Act "To prevent spreading of contagious diseases," and for performance of quarantine.

43. C.O. 385/6, Elliot to Sockett, April 25, 1832.

44. C.O. 42/241, Buchanan's emigration report, 1832; S. C. Johnson, *A History of Emigration from the United Kingdom to North America* (London, 1913), 160-1.

45. C.O. 42/237, Aylmer to Goderich, June 30, 1832 (private), and enclosure.

46. C.O. 42/411, Colborne to Hay, July 5, 1832 (private and confidential); C.O. 43/75, Howick to Treasury, March 2, 1832; C.O. 42/414, giving acts; C.O. 217/156, Campbell to Spring Rice, Nov. 12, 1834; J. Hannay, *History of New Brunswick* (2 vols., St. John, 1909), II, 21; F. C. Hamil, *Lake Erie Baron* (Toronto, 1955), 148-9, quoting Upper Canada *Gazette*, July 12, 1832, Kingston *Patriot*, June 19, 1832.

47. C.O. 385/8, Hay to Low, May 22, 1834; E. C. Guillet, *The Great Migration* (Toronto, 1937), 110; R. G. Flewwelling, "Immigration to and Emigration from Nova Scotia, 1839-1851," Nova Scotia Historical Society, *Collections*, XXVIII (1949), 79.

48. C.O. 384/30, Elliot's memo for Stephen, June 19, 1832; enclosure in Law Officers to Colonial Office, June 28, 1832.

49. *Ibid.*, letters from passengers to Howick, received June 28, 1832; Bourchière to Howick, Aug. 13, 1832.

50. *Ibid.*, Stephen to Elliot, July 31, 1832; O. MacDonagh, "The Regulation of the Emigrant Traffic from the United Kingdom, 1842-1855," *Irish Historical Studies*, IX (1954-5), 162-89, and "Emigration and the State, 1833-1855," Royal Historical Society, *Transactions*, Ser. 5, V (1955),

133–59, show that in spite of, partly because of, increasingly complex legislation demanded for the passenger traffic, the Emigration Commissioners seemed compelled to act more and more as zealous agents, by acquiring discretionary powers and taking the law into their own hands.

51. C.O. 43/80, Hay to Baring, Feb. 12, 1835.
52. C.O. 42/239, memo by Elliot on Gould's letter of Feb. 17, 1832.
53. C.O. 384/35, Stephen to Colonial Office, no date except 1835.
54. Walpole, "The Humanitarian Movement," 216; *Parl. Deb.*, Ser. 3, XXVI (1835), 1235.
55. *Parl. Deb.*, Ser. 3, XXVIII (1835), 857–8, XXVI (1835), 1238; W. F. Adams, *Ireland and Irish Emigration to the New World* (New Haven, 1932), 308.
56. 5 and 6 Wm. IV, c. 53; *Parl. Deb.*, Ser. 3, XXVI (1835), 1236.
57. J. S. Buckingham, *Canada, Nova Scotia, New Brunswick and the Other British Provinces* (London, 1843), 239, 241.
58. *Parl. Deb.*, Ser. 3, XXVII (1835), 214; LXIII (1842), 1282.
59. *Parl. Pap.*, 1837, XLII (132), 4.
60. C.O. 42/162, Buchanan to Pinnock, July 25, 1836; C.O. 384/41, Low to Stephen, Sept. 7; C.O. 42/263, enclosure in Gosford, July 25, 1836.
61. C.O. 384/43, letter to Lieutenant Low, R.N., with supplementary remarks.
62. *Parl. Deb.*, Ser. 3, LX (1842), 77–8; *Parl. Pap.*, 1842, XXV (355), 3, 6, 7, Sydenham to Russell, Jan. 26, 1841.
63. G 1, vol. 126, Office of Privy Council for Trade to Merivale, May 27, 1851; Porter, *Progress of the Nation*, 374.
64. *Parl. Deb.*, Ser. 3, LXI, LXII, LXIII, March to June 1842. For protests which reached the Colonial Office, see MacDonagh, "The Regulation of the Emigrant Traffic," 165, quoting C.O. 384/73; G. Tucker, *The Canadian Commercial Revolution, 1845–1851* (London, 1936), 169–71.
65. 5 and 6 Vic., c. 107. The Act of 1842 did not require passenger vessels to carry a surgeon, but 7 and 8 Vic., c. 112 removed the exemption; in May 1845, however, 8 Vic., c. 14, again enacted the exemption; see C.O. 384/75.
66. *Parl. Deb.*, Ser. 3, XCVI (1848), 1034; F. Morehouse, "The Irish Migrations of the 'Forties," *American Historical Review*, XXXIII (1928), 592.
67. G 12, vol. 62, for Cunard's claim for £500 for conveying Bagot from Halifax to Quebec in the *Unicorn* in October 1841, following Sydenham's death.
68. G 1, vol. 101, Stanley to Bagot, April 24, 1842; *Parl. Pap.*, 1844, XXXV (181), 27; 1846, XXIV (706), 19; 1847–8, XXVI (961), 18.
69. *Parl. Pap.*, 1844, XXXV (181), 27; 1845, XXVII (617), 361.
70. *Ibid.*, 1854, XLVI (1763), 17; XXXV (181), 27.
71. *Ibid.*, 1844, XXXI (178), 10; 1859, XIV (2555), Sess. II, 13; *Parl. Pap.*, 1846, XXIV (706), 14; F. Morehouse, "Canadian Migration in the Forties," *Canadian Historical Review*, IX (1928), 317–19.
72. Macdonald, *Scotland's Shifting Population*, 93.
73. *Parl. Pap.*, 1847, XXXIX (777), 30–1.
74. *Ibid.*; G 12, vol. 65, Elgin to Grey, May 28, June 28, Nov. 20, 1847; G 1, vol. 117, Grey to Elgin, Dec. 1, 1847, no. 142.

NOTES: CHAPTER SEVEN

75. C.O. 384/80, Emigration Commissioners to Stephen, Jan. 15, 1847, favouring a severe bill; Grey and Hawes to Commissioners, Jan. 28, opposing the same; *Parl. Pap.*, 1847, XXXIX (777), 9-10.

76. *Parl. Pap.*, 1847-8, XLVII (964), 23-31; MacDonagh, "Emigration and the State," 151.

77. G 1, vol. 126, Grey to Elgin, Jan. 4, 1851, with enclosures from the Treasury and the Commissariat; *Parl. Pap.*, 1849, XXXVIII (593 II), 11, Lords Commissioners of Treasury to Grey, March 6, 1849; Grey to Elgin, March 10, 1849; 1854, XLVI (1763), 9, Treasury Statement, Aug. 20, 1853.

78. 10 and 11 Vic., c. 103.

79. *Parl. Deb.*, Ser. 3, XCVI (1848), 540, 1024, 1029-30; CXIX (1852), 476; W. Ward, *Aubrey de Vere: A Memoir* (London, 1904), 184, note. C.O. 384/79, for Stephen de Vere's letter to Monteagle; Monteagle sent it to Grey, for which see, MacDonagh, "The Regulation of the Emigrant Traffic," 169.

80. *Parl. Pap.*, 1847-8, XVII (415), 45, First Report from the Select Committee of the House of Lords on Colonization from Ireland, giving evidence of Thomas Frederick Elliot before Lord Monteagle who was an uncle of de Vere. Elliot had asked de Vere to report to him. For Stephen de Vere as M.P. (County Limerick), see *Illustrated London News*, June 13, 1857.

81. C.O. 384/89, April 17, 1852, and following correspondence from Liverpool Shipowners' Association; G 1, vol. 118, Grey to Elgin, April 7, 1848, no. 194; 11 and 12 Vic., c. 6; *Parl. Pap.*, 1847-8, XXVI (961), 58.

82. C.O. 384/81, G 12, vol. 65, Elgin to Grey, June 28, 1848, no. 85; *Parl. Pap.*, 1847, XXXIII (809), 19; 1849, XXII (1082), 18.

83. 12 and 13 Vic., c. 33; G 1, vol. 122.

84. G 1, vol. 121, Grey to Elgin, March 1, 1849, no. 337; C.O. 384/86, Hodder to Emigration Commissioners, June 28, Grey to Commissioners, July 5, 1851; *Parl. Deb.*, Ser. 3, CXIV (1851), 769, 1165; CXIX (1852), 476.

85. 15 and 16 Vic., c. 44, June 30, 1852; *Parl. Deb.*, Ser. 3, CXIX (1852), 475.

86. *Parl. Pap.*, 1854, XLVI (255), 3. All salaries given below are in addition to naval half-pay and *without* special bonuses at London for handling emigrants to Australia and at Liverpool for pressure of work: at London, Commander J. S. Lean, £358 5s., with four assistants, 150 to 170; at Liverpool, Captain C. F. Schomberg, 400, with six assistants, 200; at Plymouth, Lieut. T. Carew, 208 5s.; at Southampton, Lieut. E. A. Smith, 208 5s.; at Glasgow and Greenock, Captain C. Keel, 208 5s.; at Belfast, Commander M. de Courcy, 208 5s.; at Londonderry, K. L. Sutherland, 208 5s.; at Sligo and outposts, Commander J. L. R. Stoll, 208 5s.; at Limerick and Tarbert, Commander Ellis, 208 5s., and Captain Fitzgerald, 100; at Queenstown, Commander Friend, 208 5s.; at Waterford and New Ross, Lieut. Griffith, 120; at Galway, Lieut. Saunders, 120.

87. C.O. 384/86, Lieut. Hodder's account of the growth at Liverpool; Morehouse, "The Irish Migrations of the 'Forties," 590; Johnson, *History of Emigration*, 118.

88. *Parl. Pap.*, 1854, XXVIII (1), 4. Swift mail packets now hurried the British port agent's reports across the Atlantic to the colonial port agents.

89. *Ibid.*, 1854–5, XVII, 14.

90. C.O. 384/88 and 90, Emigration Commissioners to Stanley, August 1851, regarding iron cargo; *Parl. Pap.*, 1854, XIII (349), iv–v.

91. *Parl. Pap.*, 1854, XLVI (178), 2–9; MacDonagh, "The Regulation of the Emigrant Traffic," 185; C.O. 384/75, April 24, July 17, Sept. 28, 1854.

92. C.O. 384/75, for House of Commons; G 1 vols. for 1853–5 for shipwrecks; *Parl. Pap.*, 1854, XIII (163, 349); F. H. Hitchins, *Colonial Land and Emigration Commission* (Philadelphia, 1931), 147.

93. 18 and 19 Vic., c. 119, contains 103 sections, and has 15 schedules and an abstract; see G 1, vol. 137; *Parl. Pap.*, 1854, XIII (163), 162–3.

94. Hitchins, *Colonial Land and Emigration Commission*, 149–51; C.O. 384/81, 1694, Aug. 30, 1848.

95. C.O. 384/94, Emigration Commissioners on coal, Jan. 13, 1855; *Parl. Pap.*, 1857, XXVI (125), Sess. II, VII; MacDonagh, "Emigration and the State," 156–7.

96. *Parl. Pap.*, 1857–8, XXIV (2395), 16–17; 1860, XXIX (2696), 22–5.

97. *Parl. Deb.*, Ser. 3, CXXII (1852), 101; 26 and 27 Vic., c. 51, the first amendment to follow the Act of 1855; *Parl Pap.*, 1859, XIV (2555), Sess. II, 13.

98. *Parl. Pap.*, 1854–5, XXXIX (464), 13; 1859, XXII (218), Sess. II, X; 1860, XLIV (606), 12.

99. *Ibid.*, 1860, XLIV (606), 3; 1857, XXVIII (125), Sess. II, IV.

100. *Ibid.*, 1864, XVI (3341), 36.

CHAPTER EIGHT

1. H. Martineau, *History of England during the Thirty Years' Peace, 1816–1846* (2 vols., London, 1849–50), II, 24.

2. M. L. Hansen, *The Atlantic Migration* (Cambridge, 1940), 130, 144, from *Liverpool Mercury*, 1840–2, *passim*; W. S. Shepperson, *British Emigration to North America* (Minneapolis, 1957), 77.

3. A. Redford, *Labour Migration in England* (Manchester, 1926), 102–7.

4. *Parliamentary Paper*, 1835, XIII (341), xiii, Report on Hand-loom Weavers.

5. C.O. 384/91 and 92, for "Rules and Tables for the Formation of Emigration and Colonization Societies . . . ," sent to the Colonial Office, 1853; Redford, *Labour Migration*, 156; S. and B. Webb, *The History of Trade Unionism* (New York, 1920), 201–2; *Chambers's Edinburgh Journal*, XIII (1850), 366.

6. C.O. 384/25, Reader to Colonial Office, Aug. 1, 1831; Hansen, *Atlantic Migration*, 141–3.

7. W. F. Adams, *Ireland and Irish Emigration* (New Haven, 1932), 163–4, 168, from *Belfast News Letter*, June 4, 1930; Hansen, *Atlantic Migration*, 266–7.

8. *Parl. Pap.*, 1841, VI (182, 333), 66–72, 197–206.

9. 10 Geo. IV, c. 8; Hansen, *Atlantic Migration*, 132–4.

10. Adams, *Ireland and Irish Emigration*, 183–6, again from local newspapers.

NOTES: CHAPTER EIGHT

11. *Ibid.*, 188, and map opposite p. 158.
12. A. Schrier, *Ireland and the American Emigration* (Minneapolis, 1958), 67; Adams, *Ireland and Irish Emigration*, 211.
13. *Parliamentary Debates*, 1846, LXXXIV, 980 ff.; 1846, LXXXVI, 913; LXXXIII, 1050–1, 1078–9, 1263; Hansen, *Atlantic Migration*, 245.
14. W. P. O'Brien, *The Great Famine* (London, 1896), 67, quoted by W. A. Carrothers, in *Emigration from the British Isles* (London, 1929), 187.
15. *Parl. Deb.*, LXXXVIII (1846), 767; 8 and 9 Vic., c. 107; Hansen, *Atlantic Migration*, 248–9.
16. *Parl. Pap.*, 1847–8, XXXIII (963), 4; *Parl. Deb.*, LXXXVIII (1846), 768; K. B. Nowlan, "The Political Background," in R. D. Edwards and T. D. Williams, eds., *The Great Famine* (Dublin, 1956), 143; for map showing the numbers receiving rations in 1847, ranging from 90 to 100 per cent of the population in the west to 20 per cent in the northeast, see 242.
17. Carrothers, *Emigration from the British Isles*, 188, quoting Report of the Select Committee of the House of Lords on Colonization from Ireland, 1847, App. 25: though they thought it useless "to be relating our distress, . . . for none could describe it; it can only be known by the suffering themselves."
18. *Parl. Deb.*, LXXXIX (1847), 1324; O. MacDonagh, "Emigration during the Famine," in *The Great Famine*, 320–21.
19. MacDonagh, "Emigration during the Famine," 320; *Parl. Deb.*, LXXXIX (1847), 598–9; XCI (1847), 544–5.
20. *Parl. Deb.*, LIV (1840), 837–8; CV (1849), 669–70.
21. Hansen, *Atlantic Migration*, 281, quoting *King's County Chronicle* (Parsontown), Oct. 26, 1853.
22. Thomas Rolph, *Comparative Advantages between the United States and Canada for British Settlers Considered in a Letter to Allardyce Barclay* (London, 1842); John Silk Buckingham, *Canada, Nova Scotia, New Brunswick and the other British Provinces in North America* (London, 1843).
23. Adams, *Ireland and Irish Emigration*, 149, 181; *Parl. Pap.*, 1836, no. 35, Part I, 77; 1851, XXII (1383), 35; *London Illustrated News*, April 25, 1857.
24. *Parl. Pap.*, 1854 (308), II, 232; *Colonial Magazine and Commercial Maritime Journal*, I (1842), 119; Schrier, *Ireland and the American Emigration*, 167, quoting *Parl. Pap.*, 1873, XVIII (768), 78.
25. *Supra*, 124–42; Shepperson, *British Emigration*, 49–63.
26. Adams, *Ireland and Irish Emigration*, 148, again quoting *Belfast News Letter*, April 14, 1820, and also *Londonderry Journal*, March 7, 1820.
27. C.O. 384/28, Cattermole to Howick, April 23, 1831; C.O. 385/13, Elliot to Twopeny, Feb. 14, 1832.
28. G 12, vol. 62, Bagot to Colonial Office, April 16, 1842, no. 84, on new information pamphlet; G 12, vol. 64, Metcalfe to Stanley, Dec. 21, 1843, on same; *Parl. Pap.*, 1831–2, XXXII (724), 8–12, 30.
29. *Parl. Pap.*, 1831–2, XXXII (730), 4.
30. R. G. Riddell, "A Study in the Land Policy of the Colonial Office, 1763–1855," *Canadian Historical Review*, XVIII (1937), 395, quoting C.O. 43/43, Goderich to Colborne, Nov. 21, 1831.
31. Q 198, pp. 142–4, Aylmer to Goderich, July 14, 1831; Lower Canada, Sundries, A. C. Buchanan's report, June 12, 1839.

32. Q 351, Colborne to Hay, April 2, 1829, Private; Q 192, Notice for emigrants, June 12, 1829; C.O. 42/394, Colborne to Goderich, Nov. 24, 1831; *Parl. Pap.*, 1831–2, XXXII (334), 12–13; H. M. Morrison, "The Principle of Free Grants in the Land Act of 1841," *Canadian Historical Review*, XIV (1933), 394; C.O. 384/67, C. Poulett Thomson to Russell, Jan. 14, 1841, no. 25, and same to same, May 26, 1840; Upper Canada Land Book, M, 448–50; G 1, vol. 100, Stanley to Bagot, March 3, 1842, enclosing Emigration Commissioners to Stephen, Feb. 19, 1842, and Thomson's of June 22, 1840, no. 124; G 12, vol. 57, Sydenham to Russell, July 5, 1841; G 12, vol. 62, Bagot to Stanley, Feb. 17, 1842, no. 34; G 14, vol. 51, Crown Land Department, June 8, 1842; P.A.C., Elgin-Grey Papers, I, Elgin to Grey, March 26, 1847. For map of colonization roads, see H. M. Morrison, *Crown Land Policies of the Canadian Government* (Clark University, 1933), 83–4.

33. C.O. 188/88, Report of Committee of Council on Land Regulations, July 25, 1844, with a history of land policy from 1827; C.O. 188/86, Colebrooke to Colonial Office, Feb. 27, 1844, with a report on special settlements; C.O. 188/99, same to same, Feb. 26, 1847, no. 16; C.O. 188/62, Glenelg to New Brunswick, "May 1837"; C.O. 188/103, Emigration Commissioners to Stephen, June 28, 1847; G 1, vol. 100, Stanley to Bagot, March 3, 1842; C.O. 217/178, Stephen's Minute on Falkland to Stanley, Dec. 21, 1841, quoted by P. Knaplund, *James Stephen and the British Colonial System* (Madison, 1953), 74; C.O. 42/541, T.W.C.M. [Murdock] to Stephen, April 20, 1847.

34. *Parl. Pap.*, 1833, XXVI (141), 25, Colborne to Goderich, Jan. 10, 1833; C.O. 42/415, enclosure in Colborne to Stanley, Sept. 14, 1832; C.O. 42/426, Hawke to Rowan, June 8, 1833. For Adelaide, Warwick, and Sunnidale, see F. C. Hamil, *Lake Erie Baron* (Toronto, 1955), 148, quoting Sandwich, *Canadian Emigrant*, Sept. 29, 1832, and 154 for government expenditure of £7,558 in Adelaide and Warwick.

35. Q 427, Thomson to Arthur, May 20, June 30, 1840, Arthur to Thomson, June 20, 1840, Arthur to Russell, July 14, 1840, and related correspondence; G 1, vol. 97, Russell to Sydenham, May 3, 1841, no. 369.

36. Q 378, III, Colborne to Stanley, Oct. 2, 1833; C.O. 42/476, report of W. Macaulay to Lieut.-Governor Sir George Arthur, March 2, 1841.

37. C.O. 188/86, Colebrooke to Colonial Office, April 24, 1844, no. 28; Carrothers, *Emigration from the British Isles*, 169; J. S. Martell, *Immigration to and Emigration from Nova Scotia, 1815–1838* (Public Archives of Nova Scotia, no. 6, Halifax, 1942), 8.

38. Appendix B, Table V.

39. Official British emigration statistics, as in Appendix B, Table I.

40. C.O. 384/95, British representative at Leipzig to Foreign Office, Feb. 1855, at the same time as the Colonial Office refused to send an emigration agent to Germany; *Parl. Pap.*, 1847, XXXIX (777), 8; Hansen, *Atlantic Migration*, chap. XI.

41. *Parl. Pap.*, 1854, XLVI (1763), 22; XLIV (606), 9.

42. *Parl. Pap.*, 1847, XXXIX (777), 8; 1852–3, XL (1647), 44; 1854–5, XXXIX (464), 12; 1857–8, XXIV (2395), 42; 1857–8, XLI (165), 19; 1862, XXII (3010), 35; 1863, XV (3199), 34.

43. C. P. Lucas, ed., *Lord Durham's Report* (3 vols., Oxford, 1912), II, 244.
44. C.O. 384/15, Alderson to Colonial Office, April 1, 1827; C.O. 384/24, Corah to Howick, Jan. 17, 1831, Henwood to Howick, Feb. 14, 1831; C.O. 384/30, Cattermole to Howick, March 19, 1832.
45. *Bathurst Papers*, Historical Manuscripts Commission, 601, Carbury to Bathurst, April 27, 1826; *Cork Herald*, April 4, 1834.
46. *Parl. Deb.*, N.S., CV (1849), 506; O. MacDonagh, "Emigration during the Famine," in *The Great Famine*, 326.
47. C.O. 384/29, Mewburn to Colonial Office, 1832; Hamil, *Lake Erie Baron*, 150, quoting *Kingston Chronicle*, May 26, June 2, 9, 16, 1832, for the *Caroline* from London, bearing emigrants with £15,000 to £20,000 among them, and also cattle, seed, and tools.
48. C.O. 42/241, A. C. Buchanan's emigration report for 1832. See also Table IV in Appendix B for emigration from British ports.
49. S. Moodie, *Roughing It In the Bush; or Life in Canada* (2 vols., New York, 1852), I, 101, II, 221; B. Hall, *Travels in North America* (3 vols., Edinburgh, 1829), I, 298; W. Moorsom, *Letters from Nova Scotia* (London, 1830), 175; C.O. 42/233, Buchanan's emigration report for 1831.
50. *Parl. Pap.*, 1833, XXVI (141), 22, Goderich to Aylmer, March 8, 1833.
51. T. W. Magrath, *Authentic Letters from Upper Canada* (Dublin, 1833), 24.
52. *Ibid.*, 128; C.O. 42/233, Buchanan's report for 1831, and C.O. 42/241 for 1832; Hamil, *Lake Erie Baron*, 152, for Talbot's sale of beef cattle.
53. *Parl. Pap.*, 1837-8, XL (389), 5; 1839, XXXIX (536), I, 31, for reports of A. C. Buchanan, the younger.
54. J. Hannay, *History of New Brunswick* (2 vols., St. John, 1909), II, 70.
55. R. Bonnycastle, *The Canadas in 1841* (2 vols., London, 1842), II, 332.
56. F. Morehouse, "Canadian Migration in the Forties," *Canadian Historical Review*, IX (1928), 310-11; *Parl. Pap.*, 1847, XXXIII (809), 41.
57. *Parl. Pap.*, 1857-8, XXIV (2395), 15.
58. C.O. 188/79, Colebrooke to Colonial Office, Nov. 14, 1842; G 1, vol. 103, Report of Emigration Commissioners for 1842; *Parl. Pap.*, 1843, XXXIV (109), 33-4; *Colonial Magazine and Commercial Maritime Journal*, I (1842), 244.
59. See C.O. 384/74 or *Parl. Pap.*, 1844, XXXI (178), for Buchanan's report.
60. *Parl. Pap.*, 1845, XXVI (617), 36; 1847, XXXIII (809), 41.
61. Morehouse, "Canadian Migration," 318; *Parl. Pap.*, 1846, XXIV (706), 14; Adams, *Ireland and Irish Emigration*, 238-9.
62. *Parl. Pap.*, 1857-8, XXIV (2395), 42; 1857-8, XLI (165), 5; 1860, XXIX (2696), 39.
63. *Ibid.*, 1846, XXIV (706), 14; Morehouse, "Canadian Migration," 317-19.
64. R. G. Flewwelling, "Immigration to and Emigration from Nova Scotia, 1839-1851," Nova Scotia Historical Society, *Collections*, XXVIII

(1949), 91; MacDonagh, "Emigration during the Famine," 370; Morehouse, "Canadian Migration," 319.

65. G 1, vol. 117, Grey to Elgin, July 19, Aug. 3, 1847; *Parl. Pap.*, 1847-8, XXVI (961), 14.

66. *Parl. Pap.*, XXVI (961), 15.

67. G 12, vol. 65, Elgin to Grey, May 28, June 28, Nov. 20, 1847; G 1, vol. 117, Dec. 1, 1847, no. 142; C.O. 188/101, Colebrooke to Colonial Office, Sept. 14, 28, 1847.

68. *Parl. Deb.*, XCIV (1847), 181; *Parl. Pap.*, 1847-8, XXVI (961), 14; 1847, XXXIX (824), 11, Grey to Elgin, April 1, 1847.

69. G 1, vol. 117, Grey to Elgin, Dec. 1, 1847; *Parl. Deb.*, XCVII (1848), 1200.

70. *Parl. Pap.*, 1847-8, XXVI (961), 17.

71. *Ibid.*, 1850, XXII (1082), I, 16-17.

72. *Ibid.*, 1847-8, XXVI (961), 16; 1850, XXIII (1024), 2, 24; 1850, XXII (1082), 16; 1852, XVII (1499), 1.

73. *Ibid.*, 1857, XVI (33), 10; 1850, XXIII (1024), 1; 1851, XXII (1383), 7.

74. *Ibid.*, 1852, XVIII (1499), 50; 1851, XXII (1383), 19; 1857, XVI (33), 41; 1857-8, XXIV (2395), 39; 1862, XXII (3010), 36.

75. C.O. 188/45, Campbell to Goderich, April 8, 1833; C.O. 188/117, for population statistics; J. Hannay, *History of New Brunswick*, II, 155; *Parl. Pap.*, 1852-3, LXVIII (1650), 54; Flewwelling, "Immigration to and Emigration from Nova Scotia," 76.

76. C.O. 42/264, Buchanan's report; *Parl. Pap.*, 1850, XXIII (1204), 71.

77. Committee of Executive Council, Feb. 5, 1850, quoted in *Parl. Pap.*, 1850, XXIII (1204), 71. See also *Parl. Pap.*, 1854-5, XXXIX (464), 13; 1857, XVI (33), 39.

78. Almost all of the traffic over the Suspension Bridge in these years was in transit through Canada to the United States West; *Parl. Pap.*, 1857, XXVIII (125, Sess. 2), 13; 1859, XXII (218, Sess. 2), 7.

79. *Simmond's Colonial Magazine and Foreign Miscellany*, II (1844), 306; G. C. Patterson, "Land Settlement in Upper Canada, 1783-1840," Ontario Archives, *Report, 1920* (Toronto, 1921), 178-9; N. Macdonald, *Canada, 1763-1841: Immigration and Settlement* (London, 1939), 352, table; H. M. Morrison, *Crown Land Policies of the Canadian Government 1838-1872* (Clark University, 1933, MSS), 5, 71-2; *Gazette*, Aug. 7, 1852; Council Minute, July 23, 1852, Journal of Assembly, 1854-5.

80. Morrison, *Crown Land Policies*, 84-5, 92; A. R. M. Lower, "The Assault on the Laurentian Barrier," *Canadian Historical Review*, X (1929), 300-01.

81. *Parl. Pap.*, 1850, XXII (1082), 3; 1850, XXIII (1204), 3-4.

82. Select Committee on Poor Removal, *Parl. Pap.*, 1854, no. 308, II, 232; *Parl. Pap.*, 1852, XVIII (1499), 15.

83. C.O. 188/124, M. H. Perley to Emigration Commissioners, June 20, 1855; *Parl. Pap.*, 1852-3, XL (1647), 46-7.

84. G 12, vol. 66, E. Head to Molesworth, Oct. 22, 1855, no. 139; *Parl. Pap.*, 1854, XXVIII (1833), 59-60; D. C. Harvey, "Scottish Immigration to Cape Breton," *Dalhousie Review*, XXI (1941), 324.

85. O. MacDonagh, "Emigration and the State, 1833–1855," *Royal Historical Society, Transactions*, Ser. 5, V (1955), 158; *Parl. Pap.*, 1854–5, XVII (1953), 46; 1856, XXIV (2089), 34.

86. *Parl. Pap.*, 1857, XVI (33), 38; 1859, XXII (208, Sess. 2), 7; 1860, XXII (2696), 39; 1861, XXII (2842), 12.

87. *Ibid.*, 1857, XXVIII (125, Sess. 2), 26.

88. G 14, vol. 55, memo of Minister of Agriculture; G. R. C. Keep, "A Canadian Emigration Commissioner in Northern Ireland," *Canadian Historical Review*, XXXIV (1953), 151–7; P. W. Gates, "Official Encouragement to Immigration by the Province of Canada," *ibid.*, XV (1934), 24–38.

89. J. J. Talman, "The Development of the Railway Network of Southwestern Ontario," *Canadian Historical Association, Report*, 1953, 55 ff., notes that 17 bills for railroads in the area were presented between 1825 and 1840, that the Great Western Railway Company began construction in 1851 and was opened to Detroit in 1854, and that Grand Trunk Railroad trains were running from Montreal to Toronto in 1856. See also [E. B. Biggar], *Canada: A Memorial Volume* (Montreal, 1889), 84.

90. For remittances sent home, see *Parl. Pap.*, 1860, XLIV (606), 12; 1863, XV (3199), 12.

91. *Ibid.*, 1854, XXVIII (1833), 10.

CHAPTER NINE

1. C.O. 384/20, Buchanan to Hay, April 24, 1828; C.O. 43/27, Huskisson to Dalhousie, May 8, 1828, no. 29; C.O. 384/33, Mayor of Liverpool to Goderich, Jan. 4, 1833, Stanley to Althorp, April 20, 1833; C.O. 384/36, Treasury to Hay, Jan. 27, 1834.

2. *Gazette*, June 24, 1831; C.O. 384/27, Instructions and Warrant issued by Goderich, July 1, 1831. The Instructions explained that the commissioners were to take the place of the commissioners contemplated in the emigration bill of 1831. C.O. 43/74, Hay to Cosway, March 4, 1832; *Acc. and Pap.*, 1832, XXXII (724), 29; C.O. 384/27, Sheets no. 1 and 11; *supra*, 97.

3. *Parliamentary Paper*, 1826, IV (404), 133.

4. W. Cobbett, *Rural Rides* (2 vols., London, 1885), II, 103–4; R. J. W. Horton, *Lecture I: Delivered at the London Mechanics Institute* (London, 1831), 14; W. S. Shepperson, *British Emigration to North America* (Minneapolis, 1957), 78.

5. C.O. 42/220, Buchanan to Hay, Aug. 14, 1828; C.O. 384/39, J. Buchanan to Foreign Office, March 21, 1835; M. L. Hansen, *The Atlantic Migration* (Cambridge, 1940), 257–60.

6. C. Barclay, ed., *Letters from the Dorking Emigrants Who Went to Upper Canada in the Spring of 1832* (London, 1833), 12–13, 61.

7. Cobbett, *Rural Rides*, I, 21; Shepperson, *British Emigration*, 40, 72.

8. C.O. 384/28, A 'Court to Hay, March 15, 1831; C.O. 42/394, Colborne to Goderich, Sept. 5, 1831, no. 36; F. C. Hamil, *Lake Erie Baron* (Toronto, 1955), 147.

9. T. Sockett, *Emigration: A Letter to a Member of Parliament* (Petworth, 1833), 21.

10. C.O. 384/41, printed sheet; C.O. 384/30, information to Emigrants,

Petworth, March 1, 1832, advising emigrants to take with them bedding, tools, cutlery, metal dishes, and recommending a fur cap, duck and canvas frock and trousers, shirts, stockings, shoes, "Flushing Jacket and Trowsers," Bible, and Prayer Book.

11. C.O. 384/30, Sockett to Colonial Office, Feb. 22, 1832; C.O. 385/13, Elliot to Baring, no date; Sockett, *Emigration*, 5.

12. C.O. 43/44, Stanley to Colborne, Sept. 15, 1834; Hamil, *Lake Erie Baron*, 151; C.O. 42/427, enclosure in Colborne to Glenelg, Oct. 3, 1835, no. 59.

13. C.O. 42/233, Buchanan's emigration report, 1831; C.O. 42/241, Buchanan's report, 1832; C.O. 42/264, Buchanan's report, 1836.

14. G 20, vol. 2, Sydenham to Russell, Oct. 1, 1840, no. 166.

15. 4 and 5 Wm. IV, c. 76.

16. *Parl. Pap.*, 1836, XL (76), 16–17; 1837, XLII (132), 15–28.

17. *Parl. Pap.*, 1837–8, XL (389), 12; 1843, XXXIV (291), 47–8; 1859, XXII (218, Sess. 2) and 1860, XLIV (606); R. H. Bonnycastle, *The Canadas in 1841* (2 vols., London, 1842), II, 331.

18. *Parl. Pap.*, 1857–8, XLI (165), 3, 21, 28–9, correspondence on the care of assisted emigrants, etc.

19. *Parl. Pap.*, 1909, XXXVII (4499), 206.

20. W. A. Carrothers, *Emigration from the British Isles* (London, 1929), 182, quoting "Account of persons assisted to emigrate from England and Wales under the Poor Law Amendment Act," *Acc. and Pap.*, 1848; Nicholls and Harvey, *History of the English Poor Law* (3 vols., London, 1898–99), III, 202.

21. Hansen, *Atlantic Migration*, 281; *Parl. Pap.*, 1834, XXVI (44), 205; 1909, XXXVII (4499), 663, 365.

22. C.O. 384/14, petition of Nov. 13, 1826; *Parliamentary Debates*, N.S., XXIII (1830), 379.

23. C.O. 43/73, Hay to Tudhope, April 24, and to Clarke, Dec. 23, 1829; C.O. 43/43, Hay to Colborne, April 23, 1831.

24. C.O. 384/74 and G 12, vol. 64, Perth Society's request for land on the Garrafraxa Road; C.O. 43/43, Howick to Colborne, March 1; *Parl. Pap.*, 1865, XVIII (3526), 50.

25. C.O. 384/43, Robert Graham's report to the Treasury; Hansen, *Atlantic Migration*, 330, quoting *Quarterly Journal of Agriculture*, IX (1840–1), 257–97.

26. C.O. 384/14, petition of Neil Macleod, April 2, 1827.

27. C.O. 384/22, Richardson to Secretary of State, April 8, 1829, with notes; Memo for Arran emigrants, March 6, 1829; C.O. 42/224, Kempt to Murray, July 10, 1829, no. 80; *supra*, 183.

28. C.O. 384/23, Richardson to Murray, March 11, and Murray's note on it; C.O. 43/75, Hay to Richardson, July 29, 1831; C.O. 43/29, Howick to Aylmer, Nov. 2; C.O. 42/241, Felton's report in Aylmer to Goderich, Feb. 8, 1833.

29. *Parl. Pap.*, 1843, XXXIV (109), 13; 1844, XXXV (181), 13.

30. *Ibid.*, 1827, V (550), 287–91; 1852, XXXIII (1474), 8–10; R. G. Flewwelling, "Immigration to and Emigration from Nova Scotia, 1839–1851," Nova Scotia Historical Society, *Collections*, XXVIII (1949), 95;

D. C. Harvey, "Scottish Immigration to Cape Breton," *Dalhousie Review*, XXI (1941), 321–2.

31. G 12, vol. 66, Elgin to Grey, Nov. 27, 1851, no. 136, on Mathewson's benevolence; G 1, vol. 105, Stanley to Metcalfe, Aug. 3, and G. W. Hope to same, Aug. 1, 1843; C.O. 384/74, for full correspondence; G 1, vol. 127, Grey to Elgin, Nov. 4, 1851, inquiring *in re* the "destitute condition" of Gordon's emigrants; *Parl. Pap.*, 1852–3, LXVIII (1650), 9; Carrothers, *Emigration from the British Isles*, 17, quoting *Dundas Warden*, Oct. 2, 1851.

32. *Parl. Pap.*, 1857, X (14), 23; 1857, XXVIII (165, Sess. 2), 19; W. S. Shepperson, "Agrarian Aspects of Early Victorian Emigration to North America," *Canadian Historical Review*, XXXIII (1952), 261; *London Illustrated News*, Jan. 15, 1853.

33. 14 and 15 Vic., c. 91; *Parl. Pap.*, 1857–8, XLI (165), 21; 1862, XXII (3010), 35; 1863, XV (3199), 36.

34. C.O. 384/23, petition of Aug. 31, 1830; C.O. 42/392, petition of Nov. 6, 1830; C.O. 384/29, Hodgson and Clarke to Colonial Office, no date; Dublin Castle to Colonial Office, May 28, 1832.

35. G 1, vol. 105, Hope to the Lord Provost, May 15, 1843; C.O. 42/230, Colonial Office to Emigration Agent, Quebec, June 21, 1830; R. J. W. Horton, *The Causes and Remedies of Pauperism* (London, 1829), 98.

36. W. F. Adams, *Ireland and Irish Emigration to the New World* (New Haven, 1932), 167, quoting *Parl. Pap.*, 1836, no. 38, supplement.

37. C.O. 384/28, Clendenning to Caulfield, March 20, 1831, Buchanan to Howick, June 25, 1831; C.O. 42/233, Clendenning to Buchanan, Sept. 20, 1831.

38. 1 and 2 Vic., c. 56; F. Morehouse, "The Irish Migrations of the 'Forties," *American Historical Review*, XXXIII (1927–8), 582; O. MacDonagh, "Irish Emigration during the Famine," in R. D. Edwards and T. D. Williams, eds., *The Great Famine*, (Dublin, 1956), 337, 476.

39. G 20, vol. 2, Sydenham to Russell, Oct. 1, 1840, no. 66; *Parl. Pap.*, 1842, XXXI (373), 6; 1843, no. 109, 13; Bonnycastle, *The Canadas in 1841*, II, 332; T. Rolph, *Canada v. Australia* (London, 1839), vi.

40. Morehouse, "The Irish Migrations of the 'Forties," 585.

41. G 12, vol. 64, Metcalfe to Stanley, June 12, 1845, no. 292; *Parl. Pap.*, 1847, VI (737), 189–93; *Parl. Deb.*, Ser. 3, CV (1849), 503, 531.

42. *Parl. Pap.*, 1847–8, XVII (593), 255–82, Second Report from the Select Committee on Colonization, Ireland, giving evidence of Sir Robert Gore Booth, with details of those emigrated, his own expenditure of £5,599 on emigration and of £15,994 on relief in Ireland; *Parl. Pap.*, 1847–8, XLVII (50), 150; Morehouse, "The Irish Migrations of the 'Forties," 584; MacDonagh, "Irish Emigration," 338–9, 477.

43. *Parl. Pap.*, 1847–8, XLVII (50), 162–4; 1847–8, XVII (593), 266–7; C.O. 188/107, Colonial Office to Head, April 22, 1848, no. 15; Gore Booth to Emigration Commission, March 16, 1848; C.O. 188/103, Poor Law Commissioners to Colonial Office, Jan. 9, 1847, Emigration Commissioners to Hawes, Aug. 18, 1847; C.O. 188/105, Head to Grey, June 19, 1848, no. 49; C.O. 188/109, Head to Grey, May 17, 1849, no. 51; G 1, vol. 117, Grey to Elgin, Dec. 20, 1847, no. 147, same to same, Dec. 27, 1847, no. 149.

44. *Parl. Pap.*, 1852, XXXIII (1474), 51.

NOTES: CHAPTER NINE

45. C.O. 384/80, March 6, 1847, Roche to Hawes, that he is performing a more urgent and painful duty by remaining at home than going to Parliament; *Parl. Pap.*, 1847–8, XLVI (964), 23–4.

46. *Parl. Pap.*, 1851, XL (348), 16; 1852, XXXIII (1474), 20, 30–1; 1852–3, LXVIII (1650), 9; 1854, LXVI (1763), 19; 1854–5, XXXIX (464), 20; 1857, X (14), 7, 23; 1857–8, XLI (165), 21.

47. *Parl. Deb.*, Ser., 3, CXI (1850), 440; CV (1849), 523.

48. C.O. 188/126, Emigration Commissioners to Colonial Office, Nov. 23, 1855; note 46.

49. G 1, vol. 135, Emigration Commissioners to Merivale, March 30, 1855; *Parl. Pap.*, 1860, XLIV (606), 10; 1854–5, XXXIX (464), 32; A. Jameson, *Winter Studies and Summer Rambles* (2 vols., New York, 1839), I, 287.

50. C.O. 43/75, Hay to Somerset, July 4, 1831, giving full range of refunds and stating they did not apply to militia officers; 1 Wm. IV, c. 41; C.O. 384/27, memo forwarded to War Office, Oct. 11, 1830, War Office to Colonial Office, Aug. 9, 1831.

51. C.O. 42/233, Buchanan's emigration report, 1831. Of those who landed in Canada, about 100 "whom no example could stimulate to industry" returned at once to the United Kingdom; *Parl. Pap.*, 1833, XXVI (141), 6.

52. C.O. 384/30, Sullivan to Hay, Jan. 25, 1832; C.O. 384/27, Howick's note of Dec. 28, 1831.

53. C.O. 42/237, Commissary General Routh to Treasury, June 25, 1832; C.O. 42/426, Colborne to Aberdeen, June 1, 1835; A. Jameson, *Winter Studies and Summer Rambles*, II, 330–3.

54. C.O. 42/394, Colborne to Hay, Oct. 27, 1831; C.O. 43/76, Howick to Sullivan, Aug. 25, 1832; J. S. Martell, *Immigration to and Emigration from Nova Scotia* (Public Archives of Nova Scotia, no. 6, Halifax, 1942), 29.

55. C.O. 42/431, Head to Glenelg, Oct. 19, 1836; C.O. 42/428, Sullivan to Grey, July 28, 1835; C.O. 42/438, enclosure in Head to Glenelg, May 5, 1837, no. 56; G 1, vol. 105, Stanley to Metcalfe, July 19, 1843, indicates that British relief was given to the pensioners in Canada and that men who had never been on the Chelsea Hospital list were making claims for it.

56. C.O. 42/238, enclosure in Aylmer to Goderich, Dec. 10, 1832; C.O. 384/33, note on Gouger to Colonial Office, April 2, 1833; C.O. 43/79, Hay to Lemon, June 18, 1834; S. C. Johnson, *A History of Emigration from the United Kingdom to North America, 1763–1912* (London, 1913), 274, quoting E. M. Hance, *Reformatories and Industrial Schools* (Liverpool, 1883), 9.

57. C.O. 42/258, Wood of Exeter Hall to Buchanan, March 28, 1835, and Buchanan to Hawke, in Buchanan's emigration report, 1835; *Parl. Pap.*, 1836, XL (76), 22.

58. F. Morehouse, "Canadian Migration in the Forties," *Canadian Historical Review*, IX (1928), 316, quoting Select Committee Report, Criminal and Destitute Children, 1852–3, 19–159, and *Acc. & Pap.*, 1851, XL, 8.

59. *Parl. Deb.*, Ser. 3, LVII (1841), 677; LX (1842), 101; XCIX (1848), 455, 470; CXXII (1852), 1328–31. For advocacy of juvenile emigration to New South Wales by J. Denham Pinnock, see *Parl. Pap.*, 1839, no. 536, II, 15–16.

NOTES: CHAPTER TEN 281

60. *Parl. Pap.*, 1851, XL (348), 8.
61. *Ibid.*, 1859, XXII (218 Sess. 2); 1860, XLIV (606); XXIX (2696); *Edinburgh Review*, XCII (1850), 497, 503.
62. *Parl. Pap.*, 1862, XXII (3010), 35; 1863, XV (3199), 36.
63. *Parl. Deb.*, Ser. 3, CV (1849), 523.
64. C.O. 188/19, Head to Colonial Office, Jan. 10, 29, 1853, nos. 5 and 10; *Parl. Pap.*, 1852, XXXIII (1474), 48; 1852-3, LXVIII (1650), 48.
65. Johnson, *A History of Emigration*, 256; *Parl. Pap.*, 1854, no. 396, Select Committee on Poor Removal, I, 161.
66. *Parl. Deb.*, Ser. 3, LVII (1841), 597; Morehouse, "Canadian Migration," 316.
67. *Parl. Pap.*, 1859, XIV (2555, Sess. 2), 37; 1860, XXIX (2696), 39; 1864, XVI (3341), 37; *Illustrated London News*, XXII (1853), 204, S. Herbert's fund.
68. *Parl. Pap.*, 1863, XV (3199), 36; Johnson, *A History of Emigration*, 255.
69. *Parl. Pap.*, 1854, XLVI (1763), 33-5; *supra*, 197-8, 200.
70. *Parl. Pap.*, 1854, XLVI (1763), 23.
71. *Ibid.*, 1847, XXXIII (809), 17-18.
72. G 1, vol. 107, Stanley to Bagot, March 29, April 31, 1844, nos. 191 and 204; *Parl. Pap.*, 1847, XXXIX (777), 14.
73. G 20, vol. 20, Murdock to Buchanan, June 12, 1841; C.O. 384/75, Emigration Commission to Stephen, March 21, 1844; *Parl. Pap.*, 1851, XL (348), 20-1; 1854, XLVI (1763), 23.
74. G 1, vol. 133, Newcastle's despatch, Feb. 15, 1854, no. 73, also in *Parl. Pap.*, 1854, XLVI (1763), 41-2.
75. C.O. 188/33, Douglas to Horton, Nov. 16, 1826, Private; C.O. 42/233, Aylmer to Goderich, Nov. 11, 1831, no. 80; P. Knaplund, *James Stephen and the British Colonial System* (Madison, 1953), 27; *Colonial Magazine and Commercial Maritime Journal*, IV (1841), 257; *Simmond's Colonial Magazine and Foreign Miscellany*, VII (1846), 483. For English opinion see *Parl. Pap.* 1850, XXIII (1204), 62.

CHAPTER TEN

1. J. H. Rose, A. P. Newton, and E. A. Benians, eds., *Cambridge History of the British Empire* (Cambridge, 1929-40), II, 369, 406, 441, VI, 285; K. N. Bell and W. P. Morrell, *Select Documents on British Colonial Policy, 1830-1860* (Oxford, 1928), xxiv; H. E. Egerton, *A Short History of British Colonial Policy* (London, 1897), 301, quoting *Parl. Pap.*, 1855; P. Knaplund, "Sir James Stephen and British North American Problems, 1840-1847," *Canadian Historical Review*, V (1924), 27, with relevant notes. In his position as under-secretary, Stephen seemed careful to deal only with administration, leaving broader problems to policy-makers, Lord John Russell and others, for which see: P. Knaplund, *James Stephen and the British Colonial System, 1813-1847* (Madison, 1953), 273, quoting J. R. M. Butler, "Note on the Origin of Lord John Russell's Despatch of October 16, 1839," *Cambridge Historical Journal*, II, 248-51.
2. W. P. Morrell, *British Colonial Policy in the Age of Peel and Russell*

(Oxford, 1930), 251, quoting Cabinet Minute, Feb. 8, 1849 in Howick Papers; Knaplund, *James Stephen and the British Colonial System*, 297, Stephen's address, Oct. 13, 1858.

3. *Chambers's Edinburgh Journal*, XIV (1850), 61.

4. C.O. 42/206, 378, summary of new land regulations; C.O. 188/88, report of Committee of Council on Land Regulations, July 25, 1844.

5. Knaplund, *James Stephen and the British Colonial System*, 258; Knaplund, "Sir James Stephen and British North American Problems," 34, 28, quoting C.O. 42/514, Stephen to Hope, Nov. 15, 1844.

6. Even a select committee of the House of Commons which had every opportunity to hear the worst about the passenger system could not close its report without expressing "their sense of the zeal and discretion" with which the regulations of the Passenger Act had been carried out "under circumstances of considerable difficulty." See K. A. Walpole, "The Humanitarian Movement of the Early Nineteenth Century to Remedy Abuses on Emigrant Vessels to America," Royal Historical Society, *Transactions*, XIV (1931), 224. A contrary view is given by O. MacDonagh, "Emigration and the State: An Essay in Administrative History," Royal Historical Society, *Transactions*, Ser. 5, V (1955), 133–59.

7. A. Toynbee, *Lectures on the Industrial Revolution* (London, 1913), 13.

8. *Parl. Pap.*, 1852–3, LXVIII (1650), 62; 1854, XLVI (1763), 17.

9. W. S. Shepperson, "Agrarian Aspects of Early Victorian Emigration to North America," *Canadian Historical Review*, XXXIII (1952), 261.

10. A. Schrier, *Ireland and the American Emigration* (Minneapolis, 1958), 67–70, 73–4, 76, quoting John Locke, *Ireland's Recovery or Excessive Emigration and its Reparative Agencies in Ireland* (London, 1853), 10, etc.

11. Bell and Morrell, *Select Documents on British Colonial Policy*, xlix.

APPENDIX A

For the Information of Emigrants. Notice to Captains of Passenger Vessels. Caution Against Refusing Employment. Routes, Distances, and Rates of Passage from Quebec. A. C. Buchanan, Chief Agent, Emigration Department, Quebec, 27th July, 1853. (*Parliamentary Paper*, 1854, XLVI (1763), 33–5.)

APPENDIX A

For the Information of Emigrants.

Passengers are particularly cautioned on no account to part with their contract tickets to the Master or any other party whatsoever, without communicating with the Emigrant Office.

There is nothing of more importance to emigrants, on arrival at Quebec, than correct information on the leading points connected with their future pursuits. Many, especially single females and unprotected persons in general, have suffered much from a want of caution, and from listening to the opinions of interested and designing characters, who frequently offer their advice unsolicited. To guard emigrants from falling into such errors, they should, immediately on their arrival at Quebec, proceed to the office of the chief agent for emigrants, where persons desirous of proceeding to any part of Canada will receive every information relative to the lands open for settlement, routes, distances, and expenses of conveyance; where also labourers, artizans, or mechanics will be furnished, on application, with the best directions in respect to employment, the places at which it is to be had, and the rates of wages.

Emigrants are entitled by law to remain on board the ship forty-eight hours after arrival; nor can they be deprived of any of their usual accommodations and berthing during that period, and the master of the ship is bound to disembark them and their baggage free of expense, at the usual landing place, and at reasonable hours, as may be seen in the following extract from the Provincial Passenger Act:—

Notice to Captains of Passenger Vessels.

"And whereas inconvenience and expense are occasioned by the practice of masters of ships carrying passengers, anchoring at great distances from the usual landing places in the port of Quebec, and landing their passengers at unreasonable hours: Be it therefore enacted, That all masters of ships having passengers on board shall be held, and they are hereby required to land their passengers and their baggage free of expense to the said passengers, at the usual public landing places in the said port of Quebec, and at reasonable hours, not earlier than six of the clock in the morning, and not later than four of the clock in the afternoon; and such ships shall, for the purpose of landing their passengers and baggage, be anchored within the following limits in the said port, to wit: the whole space of the River St. Lawrence, from the mouth of the River St. Charles to a line drawn across the said River St. Lawrence, from the flag-staff on the citadel on Cape Diamond at right angles to the course of the said river, under a penalty of 10*l.* currency, for any offence against the provisions of this section."

Any offence against this section will be rigidly enforced.

Small capitalists in search of cleared farms are invited to call at this office, where they will be furnished with the descriptions of a number of farms in various stages of improvement, situated in different sections of the province, many of which combine the advantages of being in the neighbourhood of churches, schools, post offices, grist and saw mills; and, from their vicinity to Quebec and Montreal, the highest market-price may always be obtained for any surplus produce.

On the route from Quebec to their destination, they will find many plans and schemes offered to their consideration; but they should disregard such statements, unless well satisfied of their correctness. On all occasions when emigrants stand in need of advice, application should be made to the Government agents, who will gratuitously furnish every requisite information.

Ample notice having now been given, as well in Great Britain and Ireland as in Canada, that an Act has been passed by the Legislature, in which it is expressly stipulated that the emigrant tax levied under its authority should be applied *only* to the relief of destitute sick emigrants, all parties are therefore distinctly informed that no relief whatever will be afforded out of this fund, unless in cases of sickness.

Agents have been stationed at the following ports:—Quebec, Montreal, Toronto, and Hamilton,—who will furnish emigrants with advice as to routes, distances, and rates of conveyance, and give them information respecting the Crown and other lands for sale in their respective districts, as well as direct emigrants in want of employment to places where they will be most likely to obtain it.

Caution against Refusing Employment.

It is of the greatest importance that emigrants should be disabused of the very erroneous ideas which they almost all entertain as to the remuneration they will receive for their labour on arrival in this country. They should bear in mind that for the first season, and until they become acquainted with the labour of the country, their services are worth little more than one-half of those rendered by experienced labourers. Many have been offered advantageous engagements and permanent employment on their first arrival, which they refused, preferring to proceed, in hopes of better wages; but in this very many are disappointed. Six dollars to eight dollars per month, with board and lodging, is as much as farmers will or can afford to give to newly arrived emigrants. Good hands, after a year's residence, will generally command from ten dollars to fourteen dollars per month.

A large number of labourers are now required on the several railroads in course of construction in this province, viz.:—

The Quebec and Richmond Railroad	100 miles.
The Montreal and Portland Railroad	31 ,,
The Prescott and Bytown Railroad	54 ,,
The Toronto and Simcoe Railroad	66 ,,
The Great Western, from Hamilton to Windsor	180 ,,

Wages from 4s. 6d. to one dollar per day.

Wanted at Toronto 5,000 men on the Toronto and Sarnia section of the Grand Trunk of Railway. The highest wages will be given to masons, bricklayers, and labourers.

Emigrants proceeding to the Eastern Townships, especially the populous and flourishing villages—Drummondville, Kingsey, Shipton, and Melbourne, and the county-town of Sherbrooke—will proceed by the regular steamer to Montreal, and thence by the St. Lawrence and Atlantic Railroad from Longueuil to Sherbrooke, 103 miles. This district, for its healthfulness, cheapness of land, facility of access, and manufacturing, agricultural, and commercial capabilities, is particularly deserving of the notice of emigrants of every class; and where there is a constant demand for mechanics and labourers of every description, especially farm servants.

Mr. S. M. Taylor, the agent of the British American Land Company, Montreal, will furnish intending settlers with full information, and to whom emigrants proceeding to this section of the province are recommended to apply.

BYTOWN AND THE OTTAWA RIVER SETTLEMENTS.
To Emigrants requiring Employment or seeking Locations for Settlement.

Owing to the diversion of the route of emigrants proceeding to the west from the Ottawa and Rideau Canal route to that of the St. Lawrence, but a few emigrants have proceeded during late years to that section of the country; consequently, labourers are now much wanted, and the rates of wages have consequently increased.

The lumber trade of the Ottawa, which annually requires from 25,000 to 30,000 men, is now, owing to the increased demand for that great staple of the country, about to be much extended; and as almost all those who transact this business are largely engaged in farming, a most favourable opportunity is now offered to emigrants to proceed to that section of the country: good, active men will get, the first year, from 2l. to 3l. per month, with their board; and, after they have become acquainted with the work of the country, and acquired the necessary skill, they will be competent to earn the highest wages, from 3l. 10s. to 4l. per month, or from 35l. to 40l. per annum.

Crown lands, and those belonging to private individuals, can be obtained on more reasonable terms than in any other section of the province; and farmers receive the highest cash prices for all the surplus produce they may have to dispose of.

Route from Montreal to Bytown, by steamer daily, 129 miles; Bytown to Aylmer, by land, 9 miles; Aylmer to Sand Point, by steamer, 45 miles; Sand Point to Castleford, by steamer, 8 miles; Castleford to Portage-du-Fort, 9 miles; Portage-du-Fort to Pembroke, by land and water, 33 miles.

Emigrants should remain about the towns as short a time as possible after arrival. By their proceeding *at once* into the agricultural districts, they will be certain of meeting with employment more suitable to their habits; those with families will also more easily procure the necessaries of life, and avoid the hardships and distress which are experienced by a large portion of the poor inhabitants in our large cities during the winter season. The Chief Agent will consider such persons as may loiter about the ports of landing to have no further claims on the protection of Her Majesty's agents, unless they have been detained by sickness or some other satisfactory cause.

Mr. Conlan, the sub-agent at Montreal, will furnish the best advice and information as to the routes, rates of passage, &c. from that port; also as to the demand for employment existing in the district.

ROUTES, DISTANCES, AND RATES OF PASSAGE FROM QUEBEC.

From Quebec to Montreal, 180 miles, by Steamers, Every Day, at Five o'Clock; through in 14 Hours.

	Stg.	Cy.
By the Royal Mail Packets	2s. 0d.	2s. 6d.
By Tait's Line	1 6	1 10½

From Montreal to Toronto, Hamilton, Buffalo, and other Ports on Lakes Erie and Michigan.
Daily by the Royal Mail Line at 9 o'clock A.M.

		Distances. Miles.	Deck Fare in Stg. Cy.
From Montreal to	Cornwall	78	4s. 5s. 0d.
„ „	Williamsburg	104	
„ „	Matilda	112	
„ „	Prescott	127	6s. 7s. 6d.
„ „	Brockville	139	
„ „	Kingston	189	8s. 10s. 0d.
„ „	Cobourg	292	
„ „	Port Hope	298	
„ „	Bond Head	313	
„ „	Darlington	317	12s. 15s. 0d.
„ „	Whitby	337	
„ „	Toronto	367	
„ „	Hamilton	410	
„ „	Niagara and Lewiston	437	14s. 17s. 6d.
„ „	Buffalo, by railroad	489	18s. 22s. 6d.

Passengers by this line tranship at Prescott to the Lake steamers.

Daily by the American Line, at 1 o'clock P.M.

		Miles.	Stg. Cy.
From Montreal to	Ogdensburg	138	6s. 7s. 6d.
„ „	Cape Vincent	190	8s. 10s. 0d.
„ „	Sacket's Harbour	242	12s. 15s. 0d.
„ „	Oswego	286	12s. 15s. 0d.
„ „	Rochester	349	16s. 20s. 0d.
„ „	Lewiston	436	14s. 17s. 6d.
„ „	Buffalo	467	18s. 22s. 6d.

Passengers by this line tranship at Ogdensburg to the Lake steamers for Oswego and Buffalo, and at Cape Vincent to the steamer for Toronto and Hamilton.

The passengers for both lines embark at the Canal Basin, Montreal, and arrive at Hamilton and Buffalo in 48 hours.

| Passage from Quebec to Hamilton | 17s. 6d. |
| „ „ Buffalo | 25s. 0d. |

From Buffalo to Ports on Lakes Erie, Michigan, &c., Every Evening, at Nine o'Clock, by the Michigan Central Railroad Line.

		Miles.	Stg. Cy.
From Buffalo to	Cleveland, on Lake Erie, by steamer	194	4s. 5s. 0d.
„ „	Sandusky, do.	254	4s. 5s. 0d.
„ „	Detroit, direct, do.	260	8s. 10s. 0d.
„ „	Chicago, by railroad	530	12s. 15s. 0d.
„ „	Do. by steamer, via Lake Huron and Michigan	1,075	12s. 15s. 0d.

Passage from Quebec to Chicago, 32s. sterling, or 8 dol. Passengers for Cincinnati or St. Louis land at Sandusky, and proceed by railroad.

Steamers leave Kingston daily for the Bay of Quinte and the River Trent, calling at Picton, Adolphustown, Belleville, and other landing places in the Bay.

From Toronto steamers leave daily for Port Dalhousie, the entrance of the Welland Canal, and for Hamilton, calling at Port Credit, 15 miles; Oakville, 25 miles; Wellington Square, 37 miles; and Hamilton, 43 miles.

Steamers leave Toronto daily for Niagara, Queenston, and Lewiston; passage, 3s. 9d. At Lewiston the rail cars leave twice a day for Buffalo; fare, 5s.

Freight steamers carry passengers from Montreal to Kingston for 5s. each adult. To Toronto and Hamilton, 10s. cy., or 8s. stg.

OTTAWA RIVER AND RIDEAU CANAL.

From Montreal to Bytown and Places on the Rideau Canal, by Steam daily, through to Bytown in 12 hours.
Leaves Montreal every morning at 8 o'clock.

		Distance. Miles.	Deck Passengers. Stg. Cy.
From Montreal to	Carillon	54	3s. 3s. 9d.
„ „	Grenville	66	4s. 5s. 0d.
„ „	L'Original	73	
„ „	Bytown	129	6s. 7s. 6d.
„ „	Kemptville	157	
„ „	Merrickville	175	
„ „	Smith's Falls	190	8s. 10s. 0d.
„ „	Oliver's Ferry	199	
„ „	Isthmus	210	
„ „	Jones' Falls	226	

Passengers proceeding to Perth, Lanark, or any of the adjoining settlements should land at Oliver's Ferry, 7 miles from Perth.

ROUTE TO THE UNITED STATES.

Emigrants proceeding to any of the following States of the American Union, viz.—Maine, New Hampshire, Massachusetts, Connecticut, Vermont, New York, and Pennsylvania.

By the Champlain and St. Lawrence Railroad Company.—Mr. W. A. Merry, Secretary.

Office on the Wharf, opposite the Steamboat Landing, Montreal.

	Stg.	Cy.
To Boston	16s. sterling	20s. currency.
To New York	12s. „	15s.

Montreal and New York Railroad Company.— Mr. J. Farrow, Secretary.

Office at the Railroad Terminus, St. Antoine Suburbs; and Mr. Holt, Agent—Office, Great St. James Street.

	Stg.	Cy.
To Boston	16s. sterling	20s. currency.
To New York	12s. „	15s.

Trains of the above company leave Montreal daily for New York and Boston, through in 14 hours.

100 lbs. of luggage allowed each passenger free; all over that quantity will be charged extra.

NEW BRUNSWICK.

The best and most expeditious route is by the St. Lawrence and Atlantic Railroad, from Montreal to Portland; thence by steamer which leaves for St. John's, New Brunswick, every Monday and Wednesday evening, at 8 o'clock.

	Route.	Stg.	Cy.
From Quebec to Montreal, by steamer		2s.	2s. 6d.
„ Montreal to Portland, by railroad		16s.	20s. 0d.
„ Portland to St. John's, by steamer		16s.	20s. 0d.
		34s.	42s. 6d.

Throughout these passages children under twelve years of age are charged half-price, and those under three years are free.

The gold sovereign is at present worth 24s. 4d. cy.; the English shilling, 1s. 3d.; and the English crown-piece, 6s. 1d.

CAUTION TO EMIGRANTS.

Emigrants should exercise caution when paying their passage, and, when in any doubt, apply at once to this Office, where they will receive every advice and protection.

The agents now in Quebec authorized to book passengers are—

For the Royal Mail Line . . . . Mr. A. Samuels, } Office—on Napoleon
„ American Line . . . . Mr. G. H. Church, } Wharf.

Emigrants only proceeding to Montreal will find it better not to take tickets, but pay their passage to the captain of the steamer they proceed by, as it will save trouble and prevent mistakes.

Emigrants on arriving at Buffalo, if proceeding further, will, on application to Mr. J. Movius, agent of the Michigan Central Railroad Company, receive correct advice and direction as to route.

Emigration Department, }
Quebec. 27th July, 1853. }

A. C. Buchanan,
Chief Agent.

F

APPENDIX B

IN PRE-VICTORIAN YEARS, the Customs officials furnished the records of departures from the shores of the British Isles. As they could list only those ships to which they gave clearance, the inadequacies of their returns must be evident to any one at all familiar with the smuggling of the period or the sailings of emigrant ships from lonely shores which have been mentioned in these pages. After the development of the office that became the Colonial Land and Emigration Commission, when the government began to place emigration officers in the important British and Irish ports, an improvement in the statistical recording of emigrant departures was achieved. But in busy ports and along shores with numerous harbours, these port or emigration officers were often insufficient in number for their task. Besides they were ill-equipped with police and legal power to handle unscrupulous shippers who produced inaccurate passenger lists or took on extra cargo after receiving clearance.

After 1853 an attempt was made to record the nationality of passengers departing from the British Isles. For European-born emigrants, this change perhaps came in time, because before the fifties few such sailed *via* the British Isles. However, for distinguishing emigrants from tourists or English and Scottish from Irish emigrants, the change came late. Following the arrival of the steamboat and the drop in the cost of transportation from Ireland to Glasgow and Liverpool, the numbers of Irish emigrants sailing from those two ports alone were sufficient to vitiate the accuracy of records not only of Irish departures from Ireland but of English and Scottish departures from their respective homelands. Efforts to correct the errors arising from this and other facts have been made, notably by the contemporary emigration agent, A. C. Buchanan, and by W. F. Adams, F. Morehouse, and recent statisticians. Their conclusions have varied greatly enough to send some investigators back to the original records determined to accept what they find, though with the proverbial grain of salt.

APPENDIX B

TABLE I
EMIGRATION FROM THE BRITISH ISLES, WITH DESTINATION, 1815–1865

Year	North American colonies	United States	Australian colonies, New Zealand	All other places	Total
1815	680	1,209	—	192	2,081
1816	3,370	9,022	—	118	12,510
1817	9,979	10,280	—	557	20,634
1818	15,136	12,429	—	222	27,787
1819	23,534	10,674	—	579	34,787
1820	17,921	6,745	—	1,063	25,729
1821	12,995	4,958	—	384	18,297
1822	16,018	4,137	—	279	20,429
1823	11,355	5,032	—	163	16,550
1824	8,774	5,152	—	99	14,025
1825	8,741	5,551	485	114	14,891
1826	12,818	7,063	903	116	20,900
1827	12,648	14,526	715	114	28,003
1828	12,084	12,817	1,056	135	26,092
1829	13,307	15,678	2,016	197	31,198
1830	30,574	24,887	1,242	204	56,907
1831	58,067	23,418	1,561	114	83,160
1832	66,339	32,872	3,733	196	103,140
1833	28,808	29,109	4,093	517	62,527
1834	40,060	33,074	2,800	288	76,222
1835	15,573	26,720	1,860	325	44,478
1836	34,226	37,774	3,124	293	75,417
1837	29,884	36,770	5,054	326	72,034
1838	4,577	14,332	14,021	292	33,222
1839	12,658	33,536	15,786	227	62,207
1840	32,293	40,642	15,850	1,958	90,743
1841	38,164	45,017	32,625	2,786	118,592
1842	54,123	63,852	8,534	1,835	128,344
1843	23,518	28,335	3,478	1,881	57,212
1844	22,924	43,660	2,229	1,873	70,686
1845	31,803	58,538	830	2,330	93,501
1846	43,439	82,239	2,347	1,826	129,851
1847	109,680	142,154	4,949	1,487	258,270
1848	31,065	188,233	23,904	4,887	248,089
1849	41,367	219,450	32,191	6,490	299,498
1850	32,961	223,078	16,037	8,773	280,849
1851	42,605	267,357	21,532	4,472	335,966
1852	32,873	244,261	87,881	3,749	368,764
1853	34,522	230,885	61,401	3,129	329,937
1854	43,761	193,065	83,237	3,366	323,429
1855	17,966	103,414	52,309	3,118	176,807
1856	16,378	111,837	44,584	3,755	176,554
1857	21,001	126,905	61,248	3,721	212,875
1858	9,704	59,716	39,295	5,257	113,972
1859	6,689	70,303	31,013	12,427	120,432
1860	9,786	87,500	24,302	6,881	128,469
1861	12,707	49,764	23,738	5,561	91,770
1862	15,522	58,706	41,843	5,143	121,214
1863	18,083	146,813	53,154	5,808	223,758
1864	12,721	147,042	40,942	8,195	208,900
1865	17,211	147,258	37,283	8,049	209,801

SOURCE: *Parliamentary Paper*, 1847, XXXIII (809), 39; 1861, XXII (2842), App. 1; 1867, XIX (3855), App. 1.

TABLE II
Arrivals at the Port of Quebec from the British Isles, Europe, and the Maritime Colonies, 1829–1859

Year	England	Ireland	Scotland	Europe	Maritime Provinces	Total
1829	3,565	9,614	2,643	—	123	15,945
1830	6,799	18,300	2,450	—	451	28,000
1831	10,343	34,133	5,354	—	424	50,254
1832	17,481	28,204	5,500	15	546	51,746
1833	5,198	12,013	4,196	—	345	21,752
1834	6,799	19,206	4,591	—	339	30,935
1835	3,067	7,108	2,127	—	225	12,527
1836	12,188	12,590	2,224	485	235	27,722
1837	5,580	14,538	1,509	—	274	21,901
1838	990	1,456	547	—	273	3,266
1839	1,586	5,113	485	—	255	7,439
1840	4,567	16,291	1,144	—	232	22,234
1841	5,970	18,317	3,559	—	240	28,086
1842	12,191	25,532	6,095	—	556	44,374
1843	6,499	9,728	5,006	—	494	21,727
1844	7,698	9,993	2,234	—	217	20,142
1845	8,833	14,208	2,174	—	160	25,375
1846	9,163	21,049	1,645	896	—	32,753
1847	31,505[a]	54,310	3,747	—	—	89,562
1848	6,034[a]	16,582	3,086	1,395	842	27,939
1849	8,980	23,126	4,984	436	968	38,494
1850	9,887	17,976	2,879	849	701	32,292
1851	9,677	22,381	7,042	870	1,106	41,076
1852	9,276	15,983	5,477	7,256	1,184	39,176
1853	9,585	14,417	4,745	7,456	496	36,699
1854	18,175	16,165	6,446	11,537	857	53,183
1855	6,754	4,106	4,859	4,864	691	21,274
1856	10,353	1,688	2,794	7,343	261	22,439
1857	15,471	2,016	3,218	11,368	24	32,097
1858	6,441	1,153	1,424	3,578	214	12,810
1859	4,846	417	793	2,722	—	8,778

Source: *Parliamentary Paper*, 1836, XL (76), 8; 1837, XLII (132), 9; XXXIII (613), 74; 1843, XXXIV (109), 11; 1847, XXXIX (777), 19; 1847-8, XXVI (961), 38-9; 1849, XXII (1082), 16; 1854, XLVI (1763), 30; 1857-8, XLI (165), 20; 1860, XLIV (606), 17.

[a]From British sources. In the famine year, the Emigration Commissioners were handicapped by the lack of a report from A. C. Buchanan, emigration agent at Quebec, who was seriously ill of the emigrant fever.

TABLE III
Number of Emigrants from England, Scotland, and Ireland to the Various British North American Colonies, 1853–1860

	Canada	New Brunswick	Nova Scotia, Cape Breton	Newfoundland	Prince Edward Island	Hudson Bay
England						
1853	10,285	2,083	187	52	109	43
1854	16,821	2,973	9	27	143	—
1855	7,069	1,205	212	29	91	—
1856	10,188	416	419	203	86	100
1857	14,740	350	62	7	36	84
1858	6,109	88	18	8	16	—
1859	4,879	39	20	18	9	—
1860	5,539	52	9	8	16	—
Scotland						
1853	4,856	120	24	27	11	—
1854	6,721	65	152	3	—	—
1855	4,862	2	132	19	—	—
1856	2,812	4	38	7	—	—
1857	3,175	25	2	14	—	—
1858	1,413	18	33	11	300	—
1859	802	13	8	21	—	—
1860	972	4	21	35	—	—
Ireland						
1853	15,022	1,609	—	94	—	—
1854	16,250	532	—	65	—	—
1855	4,022	277	—	46	—	—
1856	1,768	322	—	5	—	—
1857	2,233	237	—	11	—	—
1858	1,212	203	45	119	—	—
1859	414	177	—	253	—	—
1860	2,337	238	79	422	—	—

Source: *Parliamentary Paper*, 1854, XXVIII (1833), 86–7; 1854–5, XVII (1953), 64–5; 1856, XXIV (2089), 54–5; 1857, XVI (2249, Sess. 2), 60–1; 1857–8, XXIV (2395), 70–1; 1860, XXIX (2696), 62–3; 1861, XXII (2842), 48–9.

NUMBER OF ARRIVALS AT QUEBEC[a] FROM ENGLISH, SCOTTISH AND IRISH PORTS[b], 1831-60

	1831	1832	1833	1834	1835	1836	1837	1838	1839	1842	1843	1849	1852	1853	1854	1855	1856	1857	1858	1859	1860
Aberystwith	—	—	—	—	—	—	—	—	—	—	—	—	—	—	—	—	—	—	—	—	—
Bideford	51	27	42	37	—	—	—	—	—	197	25	52	—	—	—	—	—	—	—	—	—
Bridgewater	280	60	—	—	—	16	—	8	9	142	340	191	219	190	1	46	16	—	—	—	—
Bristol	764	306	16	37	2	—	6	—	—	98	9	—	—	—	—	—	—	—	—	—	25
Carlisle	—	1836	107	64	129	283	159	4	23	535	125	139	125	173	103	34	—	358	181	—	—
Dartmouth	—	—	—	—	—	—	—	—	—	—	—	9	81	90	105	49	—	—	—	—	—
Falmouth	9	196	81	82	30	76	14	—	12	—	—	117	8	—	—	—	—	—	—	—	—
Fowey	77	107	31	59	—	11	3	17	—	195	17	140	23	—	46	—	35	—	—	—	—
Gloucester (& Frome)	—	—	—	—	—	—	—	—	—	233	63	107	95	169	320	132	—	70	—	—	—
Hull	6	—	7	10	3	22	—	—	—	94	87	—	—	—	—	—	—	—	—	—	—
Lancaster	2780	1288	655	1171	462	465	367	86	90	578	739	592	1032	289	1073	552	346	333	139	44	—
Liverpool	43	45	61	—	—	—	—	—	—	32	—	—	—	—	—	—	—	—	—	—	—
London	2261	2217	551	1060	388	3748	2247	367	—	5823	2312	4630	4167	9679	15117	5337	7805	9855	5078	4675	5464
Lynn	1135	4150	1287	1051	762	1666	987	194	83	1035	1069	927	779	167	312	339	697	1763	301	85	79
Maryport	—	86	7	—	86	810	1546	12	—	—	14	—	—	—	—	—	—	—	—	—	—
Milford	421	884	315	538	182	15	39	—	1220	—	12	11	40	52	11	—	12	12	4	5	—
Newcastle (& Berwick)	15	138	35	5	1	7	3	3	16	—	—	—	—	—	—	—	—	—	—	—	—
Newport	239	340	208	450	210	16	94	7	19	—	—	2	—	72	—	—	6	6	—	—	—
Padstow	4	—	20	1	—	—	—	—	—	—	8	—	32	50	16	—	—	—	14	7	—
Penzance	5	335	53	29	13	8	1	1	9	1173	279	520	306	30	8	14	13	16	—	—	—
Plymouth	19	28	—	12	13	—	1	—	—	7	5	13	—	—	—	—	—	5	—	6	—
Poole	474	1398	440	850	211	88	403	35	58	1207	758	1171	1534	1495	2701	2026	1673	2805	538	166	110
Portsmouth	106	150	84	1	6	74	73	52	14	13	20	—	—	7	22	19	26	—	—	—	—
Scarborough	—	932	251	163	247	778	201	123	—	—	2	—	—	—	—	—	375	—	—	—	—
(& Shields)																					
Southampton	—	12	1	49	1	14	21	—	—	39	27	—	121	13	10	—	—	—	—	—	—
Stockton	4	—	20	1	—	—	—	—	—	—	26	—	300	201	—	—	—	—	—	—	—
Sunderland	—	132	233	192	18	—	—	—	—	101	58	46	—	—	—	—	—	—	—	—	—
Swansea	86	206	40	57	16	155	36	7	41	—	—	—	18	11	—	14	13	16	—	—	—
Torquay	—	63	—	34	—	—	—	18	—	4	—	—	—	—	—	—	—	—	—	—	—
Truro	—	48	—	—	10	—	—	—	—	—	—	—	38	—	—	6	—	8	—	—	—
Tynemouth (& Wighton)	—	—	—	—	—	—	—	49	—	—	7	151	14	—	2	52	163	37	13	—	—
Whitby	471	236	46	273	—	21	—	6	—	—	—	—	—	49	24	—	4	22	49	—	—
Whitehaven	138	795	413	72	59	71	71	—	—	—	—	17	—	—	—	—	—	—	3	7	—
Workington	399	246	—	29	—	110	—	—	1	24	—	2	11	—	—	—	—	—	—	—	—
Yarmouth	514	793	171	345	203	3025	617	49	—	—	76	—	3	—	18	—	3	6	—	—	—
	10343	17481	5198	6799	3067	12188	5580	990	1586	12191	6499	9352	9276	12759	19973	8606	11421	15304	6320	500	5678

TABLE IV (*Continued*)

	1831	1832	1833	1834	1835	1836	1837	1838	1839	1842	1843	1849	1852	1853	1854	1855	1856	1857	1858	1859	1860
Aberdeen	158	478	116	647	545	696	252	147	157	495	300	182	571	693	1605	1422	845	905	246	133	2
Alloa	—	231	—	87	13	—	9	—	15	27	3	—	—	—	—	—	—	—	—	—	—
Annan	—	175	—	391	30	—	—	—	—	—	37	—	—	—	—	—	9	5	—	—	—
Ayr	40	—	24	221	—	—	11	—	—	—	—	26	—	33	—	—	—	—	—	—	2
Banff	—	—	—	—	—	—	—	—	—	—	32	—	5	80	101	—	—	—	7	—	—
Cromarty	460	638	298	276	181	545	215	—	—	—	—	—	—	—	—	—	—	—	—	—	—
Dumfries	—	—	137	—	26	—	—	—	—	—	—	—	—	—	154	21	—	—	7	—	—
Dundee	249	439	194	99	37	11	20	1	10	164	413	83	55	41	27	19	1305	1719	1022	627	988
Glasgow	176	160	168	462	80	32	45	12	63	3797	3074	2979	3554	3047	2011	2284					
Grangemouth	196	—	—	—	1	6	—	—	—	3	—	—	—	—	6	—	—	—	—	—	—
Greenock	2988	1716	1458	1140	597	519	698	145	239	546	590	412	362	480	2122	621	358	275	19	21	35
Inverness	361	—	138	—	183	—	—	—	—	—	—	344	—	337	—	—	—	—	—	—	—
Irvine	—	37	6	—	6	—	—	—	—	—	—	456	13	45	329	—	—	—	—	—	—
Islay	—	181	601	358	123	—	—	—	—	—	—	—	—	—	—	—	—	—	—	—	—
Leith	664	1145	622	661	247	45	253	41	—	150	126	38	43	15	36	—	—	—	—	—	—
Montrose	—	60	75	87	16	19	2	—	1	—	13	27	163	172	352	281	342	276	167	61	5
Peterhead	13	18	41	29	42	—	—	—	—	—	—	—	—	—	117	—	—	—	—	—	—
Port Glasgow	—	—	—	—	—	—	—	200	—	—	—	55	—	23	84	22	3	17	7	2	—
Stornaway	—	—	—	—	—	—	—	—	—	192	—	691	452	—	—	330	—	—	—	—	—
Thurso (& Kirkwall)	—	—	—	—	—	149	—	442	—	128	—	—	—	72	51	15	—	—	—	—	—
	5303	5500	4196	4591	2127	2224	1509	847	485	6095	5006	5447	5477	5038	6941	5015	2862	3216	1805	844	1032

TABLE IV (Continued)

	1831	1832	1833	1834	1835	1836	1837	1838	1839	1842	1843	1849	1852	1853	1854	1855	1856	1857	1858	1859	1860
Ballyshannon	200	86	71	164	—	122	—	—	—	34	113	—	—	—	—	—	—	—	—	—	—
Baltimore	—	184	—	—	99	166	360	—	—	198	88	—	—	—	—	—	—	—	—	—	—
Belfast	7943	6851	2637	3024	1350	1209	1999	548	1072	4636	3130	2516	851	660	914	129	—	504	227	—	—
Cork	2735	1987	925	2261	861	2588	2699	149	481	1875	417	1869	2408	2676	2897	233	116	138	51	13	1145
Donegal	—	113	—	2	—	—	113	73	70	871	302	584	94	—	—	—	—	—	—	6	—
Dublin	7157	6595	3571	5879	912	2438	2535	135	523	2081	953	2280	1287	1319	1537	—	11	—	58	—	—
Galway	452	425	190	79	—	83	—	4	18	409	78	193	14	78	265	73	167	78	441	257	591
Killala	514	—	—	—	—	288	233	—	91	392	494	327	—	—	—	—	—	—	—	—	—
Kinsale	—	—	—	2	3	118	86	—	—	—	—	—	—	—	—	—	—	—	—	—	—
Limerick	2759	1689	602	1097	641	906	1065	96	616	4021	840	7729	5555	5198	4912	1050	104	81	104	108	135
Londonderry	2888	2552	1852	1580	1041	1427	1424	204	254	2200	1126	969	451	1037	702	439	349	416	246	159	1049
Newry	1591	1374	725	945	537	144	282	17	204	1547	389	861	—	195	—	—	—	—	—	—	—
Ross	1159	926	325	278	259	208	180	12	44	653	164	1950	2840	2997	2487	1177	671	626	314	198	152
Sligo	4079	2961	657	2114	893	1687	1813	187	1378	2897	866	1402	857	487	495	201	6	—	—	—	—
Strangford	169	349	41	117	—	—	—	—	3	—	—	—	—	—	—	—	—	—	—	—	—
Tralee	114	133	67	217	42	250	286	17	100	498	131	1094	544	509	1412	714	437	445	—	8	—
Waterford	1216	877	197	1008	205	629	859	14	105	1291	320	3075	589	1133	1070	209	190	193	138	73	4
Westport	720	529	—	221	194	—	—	—	—	898	140	1225	348	308	—	120	—	—	—	—	—
Wexford	229	157	21	23	6	18	—	—	—	244	15	8	145	126	156	—	—	—	—	—	—
Youghal	210	159	53	203	65	249	246	—	—	24	47	—	—	—	—	—	—	—	—	—	—
	34135	28204	12013	19208	7108	12596	14538	1456	5113	25532	9728	26568	15983	16725	16847	4345	2095	2481	1579	844	3076

SOURCE: *Parliamentary Paper*, 1840, XXXIII (613), 73–4; 1850, XXIII (1204), 36–7; 1854, XXVIII (1833), 82–3; 1854–5, XVII (1953), 62–3; 1856, XXIV (2089), 52–3; 1857, XVI (2249, Sess. 2), 58; 1857–8, XXIV (2395), 68; 1859, XIV (2555, Sess. 2), 66; 1860, XXIX (2696), 60; 1861, XXII (2842), 46.

[a] The emigrants on ships that occasionally went up the river as far as Montreal are listed under Quebec.

[b] Ports which sent out emigrants in less than four years have been omitted, as follows: Brant, Cardiff, Chatham, Colchester, Cowes, Exeter, Grimsby, Hartlepool, Ipswich, Jersey, Llanelly, Lowestoft, Poole, Portaferry, St. Ives, Shoreham, Wighton in England; Arbroath, Campbelltown, Carmarthen, Kirkaldy, Leven, Lochinbar, Lochindoel, Skye, Stromness, Tobermorry, Troon, Wick, in Scotland; and Ballina, Bantry, Clare, Drogheda, Kilrush, Larne, Newport, and Skibbereen in Ireland. The figure given for the annual emigration, however, includes the departures from these small ports.

TABLE V
Distribution of Emigrants in Canada, by Region, 1833–5, 1842–4, 1852

	1833	1834	1835	1842	1843	1844	1852
TOTAL NUMBERS RECORDED	15,950	30,935[a]	9,800	40,505	20,924	23,000	39,176
Lower Canada	—	—	—	—	1,200	4,000	—
City and district of Quebec	1,560	1,500	825	—	—	—	1,176
City and district of Three Rivers	250	350	132	—	200	—	—
City and district of St. Francis and Eastern Townships	450	640	200	2,755	400	—	—
City and district of Montreal	1,100	1,200	790	1,175	600	—	1,100
City and district of Ottawa	—	400	350	—	—	—	2,500
Upper Canada	—	—	—	—	19,724	19,383	31,000
Ottawa, Bathurst, and Eastern districts to Kingston	1,200	1,000	2,000	4,250	4,075	2,238	—
Newcastle district and Bay of Quinté	2,750	2,650	900	—	1,539	4,181	—
Toronto and Home district	4,600	8,000	2,500	—	7,500[b]	8,009	—
Hamilton, Guelph, and Western districts and Huron Tract	2,900	2,660	1,300	—	—	1,829	—
Niagara frontier, Welland Canal, etc.	1,500	3,300	1,300	—	2,000	520	—
London district, north side of Lakes Erie and St. Clair	3,000	4,600	1,800	—	1,800	1,289	—
Canada West	—	—	—	26,900	—	—	—

SOURCE: C.O. 384/35; 42/258; Q vol. 217–3, p. 704; Public Archives of Canada, *Report*, 1900, 60; *Parliamentary Paper*, 1844, XXXV (181), 12; 1845, XXVII (617), 38; 1852–3, XL (1647), 44.

[a]Includes 800 died of cholera, 350 returned to the United Kingdom, and 3,485 gone to the United States.

[b]For 1843, 7,500 includes those gone to Toronto and Home District, Hamilton, Guelph, and Western districts, and Huron Tract.

TABLE VI

Number of Emigrants and Number of Sick at Grosse Isle Quarantine Station, with Expenditure, 1832–1851

Year	Number of emigrants	Number of sick	Gross expenditure	Source of funds for expenditure
1832	51,422	No return to be found		Expenditure paid out of a vote of £10,000 made to Board of Health, Quebec Establishment, entirely military.
1833	22,982	239	£3,233 2s. 5d.	The Quarantine Station during these seven years was under a military commandant, and the expenditure was paid by the Commissariat Department through an officer stationed at Grosse Isle.
1834	30,982	844	3,748 0 10	
1835	11,580	126	3,233 3 10	
1836	27,896	454	3,010 12 1	
1837	31,894	598	2,937 9 2	
1838	2,918	65	2,626 0 1	
1839	7,214	189	2,705 7 11	
1840	22,065	561	1,511 7 1	During this period of seven years the establishment was under a Medical Superintendent, and the expenditure was paid by the Health Commissioner and Inspecting Physician, Quebec. Steamer employed cost £550, and 50 imported iron bedsteads £133 7s. 4d.; in 1843, 50 more iron bedsteads imported £118 2s. 6d., and steamer £300; in 1844 steamer, £350; in 1845, £360, and in 1846, £520.
1841	28,060	290	1,610 18 1	
1842	44,374	488	2,284 15 4	
1843	20,714	245	1,686 8 10	
1844	24,142	388	1,790 7 0	
1845	24,640	465	1,852 12 6	
1846	32,753	892	2,380 17 0	
1847	98,106	8,691	16,000 0 0	Paid jointly by Health Commissioners and Commissariat, one of which stationed on Island.
1848	26,097	581	2,938 17 7	Expenditure again paid by Commissariat these four years; to which must be added £1,324 19s. 2d., the cost of the Steamer St. Pierre during four months of 1848, and a yearly expenditure of about £1,000 by the Board of Works.
1849	37,526	859	3,163 10 2	
1850	31,591	359	2,491 0 4	
1851	39,970	594	2,510 12 6	

Source: *Parliamentary Paper*, 1852, XXXIII (1474), 39.

TABLE VII
Passenger Vessel Quarantine at Grosse Isle in St. Lawrence River, 1845–54

Year	Number of ships placed in quarantine	Aggregate number of days all ships were quarantined	Average number of days per ship	Greatest number of days any one ship was quarantined	Aggregate number of the crews	Aggregate number of passengers
1845	17	78	4 10/19	17	340	3,504
1846	23	115	5	16	399	6,284
1847	225	1,886	8 1/2	25	4,424	74,252
1848	38	152	4 1/4	8	699	7,574
1849	50	249	5	14	1,013	10,791
1850	24	112	4 2/3	7	486	5,405
1851	20	96	4 4/5	7	346	4,574
1852	13	61	4 9/13	6	226	2,954
1853	8	32	4	6	152	2,539
1854	38	171	4 1/2	10	964	13,020
TOTAL	486	2,952			9,049	130,897

Source: P.A.C., G 14, vol. 55, Report of G. M. Douglas, M.D., Medical Superintendent.

TABLE VIII
Ships Bringing More Emigrants to Quebec than the Law Allowed, 1841

Month	Tonnage	Deck space	Passengers allowed by Act	Passengers taken	Passengers in excess[a]
May	960	2,438	247	255	8
	210	600	61	65	4
	309	—	32	175	143
June	308	1,472	150	166	16
	177	665	68	98	20
	384	1,980	202	213	11
	299	1,100	112	126	14
	275	1,450	147	155	8
	389	1,974	201	203	2
	306	1,325	135	144	9
July	873	4,473	456	509	53
	730	3,420	349	432	83
	297	1,278	129	169	40
	340	1,410	144	159	14
	309	506	52	58	7
	449	2,532	258	260	2
	203	1,036	106	125	19
	183	1,092	112	119	8
August	417	2,028	207	212	5
	275	141	144	150	7
	458	613	63	69	6
	235	855	87	120	33
	137	1,350	84	120	36
	256	1,104	113	115	3
	306	1,311	134	174	41

SOURCE: *Parliamentary Paper*, 1842, XXXI (301), 284; 5 and 6 Will. IV, c. 53.

[a] In Quebec two ships for which statistics on tonnage and deck space are lacking each paid the maximum fine, £20, for carrying passengers in excess of the law. The *Pomona* of Sligo had 250 passengers on board, 27 in excess. The *Lord Cochrane* of Tralee presented a passenger list showing 322, but had on board 399, young and old, of which 60 were adults in excess of the law. After paying the fine, the master from Tralee cleared £100 on his excess human cargo. Emigration agents, of course, contended that such a fine would not curb the lust for such profits.

TABLE IX
Income and Expenditure for the Aid of Emigrants in Canada
1842, 1843, 1852, 1855

Source of income	\multicolumn{4}{c}{Amount of income}
	1842	1843	1852	1855
	£ s. d.	£ s. d.	£ s. d.	£ s. d.
Tax collected at Quebec and Montreal	8,599 15 10	4,251 19 2	7,669 0 10	4,510 17 2
Imperial appropriation	7,908 6 8	4,293 0 0	1,825 0 0	[b]
Provincial appropriation				1,500 0 0
Payment by Commissary General	1,653 13 9	—	—	—
Balance brought down	—	115 13 8	—	—
TOTAL INCOME	18,161 16 3	8,660 12 10	9,464 0 10	6,010 17 2

Items of expenditure	\multicolumn{4}{c}{Amount of expenditure}
	1842	1843	1852	1855
	£ s. d.	£ s. d.	£ s. d.	£ s. d.
Aid to emigrants	11,607 7 4	6,717 17 10	5,477 6 0	5,308 8 7
Quarantine	615 18 0¾	—	3,701 10 2	2,527 7 10
Physician's salary, six months	—	—	—	318 6 7
Marine and Emigrant Hospital	—	—	422 15 0	500 0 0
Buildings	782 5 11	226 1 11	158 10 0	—
Agency	1,574 16 0	1,330 2 7	[a]	[a]
Balance due Military Chest	773 0 2	—	—	—
Balance unexpended	115 13 8¾	386 10 6	—	—
Expenditure over appropriation	2,692 15 1	—	343 4 4	—
TOTAL EXPENDITURE	18,161 16 3	8,660 12 10	9,760 1 2	8,654 3 0

SOURCE: Reports of Emigration Agent at Quebec, in *Parliamentary Paper*, 1844, XXXV (181), 24; 1852–53, LXVIII (1650), 10, 12; 1857, X Sess. I (14), 11.
[a] Included in main item, "Aid to emigrants."
[b] Discontinued after 1854.

APPENDIX B

TABLE X

NUMBER OF PERSONS ASSISTED TO EMIGRATE AND BY WHOM ASSISTED, 1851

Date	Vessel	Port of departure	Number receiving free passage only	Number receiving free passage and landing money	By whom assisted	Paid by Emigration Department £ s. d.	Paid by Agents £ s. d.
May 3	Laurel	London	—	43	Poor Law Unions	44 0 0	—
"	Queen Victoria	Plymouth	—	7	Parish	—	4 0 0
May 5	Dahlia	Ditto	—	8	Ditto	—	4 10 0
"	Jane Black	Limerick	—	209	Nenagh Union	144 6 0	—
"	Ditto	Ditto	—	39	Kilrush Union	28 12 6	—
"	Primrose	Ditto	—	12	Ennistymore Union	7 10 0	—
May 6	Good Intent	Fowey	—	5	Parish	—	5 0 0
May 8	Isabella	Hull	5	—	Ditto	—	—
May 10	Industry	Sligo	2	—	Ditto	—	—
May 13	Jane	Bristol	29	—	Duke of Somerset	—	—
"	Ditto	Ditto	—	1	Mr. Osborne	—	0 12 2
May 24	Belle	Padstow	26	—	Parish	—	—
May 25	Ava	Southampton	—	54	Poor Law Union	—	54 10 0
May 28	Clara Symes	Liverpool	—	30	Vere Foster	30 0 0	—
June 3	Jessy	Limerick	—	178	Nenagh Union	107 2 0	—
June 6	Dunbrody	New Ross	43	—	Landlords	—	—
"	Keirick Wood	Dublin	—	63	Ditto	—	27 1 4
June 16	Confiance	New Ross	250	—	Earl Fitzwilliam	—	—
"	Sisters	London	—	55	Poor Law Union	42 10 0	—
"	Lord Ashburton	New Ross	60	—	Earl Fitzwilliam	—	—
June 17	Governor	Limerick	—	120	Newcastle Union	57 10 0	—
"	Jane	Liverpool	74	—	Carlow Union	—	—
"	Meteor	Hull	5	—	Parish	—	—
"	Lady Campbell	Waterford	25	—	Lord Ormond	—	—
"	Collina	Gloucester	—	108	Parish	—	85 10 0
"	Rolla	Hull	11	—	Ditto	—	—
June 20	Ellison	Cork	40	30	Landlords	—	7 10 0
"	Lord Brougham	Dublin	—	89	Ditto	—	21 5 0
June 22	Ann Rankin	Glasgow	22	—	Parish	—	—
June 24	Carshalton Park	Plymouth	7	—	Ditto	—	—
June 25	California	Glasgow	90	—	Landlords	—	—
July 10	Amanda	Hamburg	30	—	Ditto	—	—
July 5	Lord Lambton	Londonderry	—	33	Derry Union	17 0 0	—
July 13	Glenlion	New Ross	10	—	Landlords	—	—
"	Empire	Ditto	10	—	Ditto	—	—
July 17	Glide	Liverpool	19	—	Hertford Union	—	—
July 26	Blanche	Stornaway	—	453	Sir J. Mathison	—	298 6 3
Aug. 2	Roderic Dhu	Cork	—	280	Newcastle Union	247 0 0	—
"	Ditto	Ditto	—	149	Killydysart Union	112 5 0	—
Aug. 5	Augusta	Sligo	5	—	Sligo Union	—	—
Aug. 15	Ann Harley	Glasgow	41	—	Landlords	—	—
Aug. 17	Perseverance	Dublin	—	35	Ditto	—	—
Aug. 18	Vittoria	Southampton	—	51	Poor Law Union	—	36 10 0
"	Leonayd Dobbin	London	—	105	Ditto	85 00 0	—
"	Chatham	Liverpool	—	21	Dunfanughy Union	7 7 0	—
Aug. 26	Jane Black	Limerick	—	225	Rathkeale Union	212 0 0	—
Aug. 30	New Zealand	Dublin	—	171	Rathdrum Union	—	114 0 0

APPENDIX B

TABLE X (Continued)

Date	Vessel	Port of departure	Number receiving free passage only	Number receiving free passage and landing money	By whom assisted	Paid by Emigration Department	Paid by Agents
Aug. 31	Industry	Sligo	—	84	Roscommon Union	84 0 0	—
"	Odessa	Dublin	93	—	Landlords	—	—
Sept. 8	Affiance	London	—	20	Parish	17 0 0	—
Sept. 10	Enterprize	Dublin	—	167	Baltinglass Union	—	150 0 0
"	Try-again	Cork	38	—	Lord Lansdowne	—	—
Sept. 17	Alert	Dublin	—	56	Strokestown Union	56 00 0	—
"	Ditto	Ditto	—	40	Other Unions	—	40 0 0
Sept. 21	Annandale	Liverpool	160	—	Carlow Union	—	—
Sept. 24	Hope	Limerick	—	202	Croon Union	172 10 0	—
Sept. 28	John Bull	London	—	8	Parish	8 6 6	—
"	Prince Arthur	Bremen	—	172	Bavarian Government	—	72 12 0
"	Jessy	Limerick	—	32	Killflyn Union	20 15 0	—
"	Ditto	Ditto	—	28	Lord Ashton	7 15 0	—
Sept. 30	Peri	Cork	67	—	Lord Lansdowne	—	—
Oct. 2	Georgiana	Limerick	—	161	Newcastle Union	126 10 0	—
TOTAL			1,162	3,544		1,634 19 0	965 15 6

RECAPITULATION

		England				Ireland				Scotland				Continent of Europe		
		£	s.	d.		£	s.	d.		£	s.	d.		£	s.	d.
Parish funds	464	386	16	6	2,179	1,704	7	6	—	—			172	72	12	0
Private	1	0	12	2	275	138	0	1	453	298	6	3	—	—		
Free passages only	83	—			896	—			153	—			30	—		
TOTAL	548	387	8	8	3,350	1,842	7	7	606	298	6	3	202	27[?]	12	0

SOURCE: *Parliamentary Paper*, 1852-3, LXVIII (1650), 17. For assistance in 1853-4, see *Parliamentary Paper*, 1854, XLVI (1763), 31.

TABLE XI
Relationship of Emigration from Ireland to Population of Ireland, 1847–63

Year	Population	Emigration	Relation of emigration to population %
1847	8,175,124	219,885	2.69
1848	7,769,440	181,316	2.33
1849	7,363,756	218,842	2.97
1850	6,958,072	213,649	3.07
1851	6,552,385	254,537	3.88
1852	6,473,601	224,997	3.47
1853	6,394,817	192,609	3.01
1854	6,316,033	150,209	2.37
1855	6,237,249	78,854	1.26
1856	6,158,465	71,724	1.16
1857	6,079,681	86,238	1.41
1858	6,000,897	43,281	.72
1859	5,922,113	52,981	.89
1860	5,843,327	60,835	1.04
1861	5,764,543	36,322	.63
1862	5,764,543	49,680	.86
1863	5,764,543	116,391	2.02

SOURCE: *Parliamentary Paper*, 1864, XVI (3341), 13. In presenting the table, the office of the Colonial Land and Emigration Commission explained that the census of 1841 was used for 1847, that the decrease shown in the census of 1851 was distributed over the four years preceding, and that the decrease of the census of 1861 was distributed over the ten years preceding.

TABLE XII
Expenditure on Emigration Officers in Ports, Colonial Land and Emigration Board, and Related Services, 1853–4

	£ s. d.	£ s. d.
Land and Emigration Board		
Chairman	1,200 0 0	
Two commissioners, at 1,000 *l.* each	2,000 00 0	
Secretary	800 0 0	
Ten clerks, from 80 *l.* to 500 *l.* per annum	2,709 11 9	
Rent and taxes	380 0 0	
Housekeeper and messengers	180 0 0	
Postage	700 0 0	
Contingencies, including copyists	500 0 0	
Arrears of postages	309 0 0	
Total Land Board		8,778 11 9
Government Emigration Officers		
Emigration officer ⎫	358 5 0	
Assistant to ditto ⎪	170 0 0	
Second assistant to ditto ⎪	150 0 0	
Third assistant to ditto ⎬ Port of London	150 0 0	
Fourth Assistant to ditto ⎪	150 0 0	
Clerk ⎪	120 0 0	
Arrears ⎭	294 14 3	
Emigration officer ⎫	400 0 0	
Assistant to ditto ⎪	250 0 0	
Second assistant to ditto ⎪	200 0 0	
Third assistant to ditto ⎪	200 0 0	
Fourth assistant to ditto ⎬ Port of Liverpool	200 0 0	
Fifth assistant to ditto ⎪	200 0 0	
Clerk ⎪	100 0 0	
Office messenger ⎪	50 0 0	
Arrears ⎭	411 0 4	
Emigration Officer at the Port of Plymouth	208 5 0	
" Port of Southampton	208 5 0	
" Ports of Glasgow and Greenock	208 5 0	
" Port of Dublin	208 5 0	
" Port of Belfast	208 5 0	
" Port of Londonderry	208 5 0	
" Port of Sligo and Outports	208 5 0	
" Port of Galway	120 0 0	
" Port of Limerick	208 5 0	
Assistant emigration officer at the Port of Tarbert	100 0 0	
Emigration officer at the Port of Cork	208 5 0	
" Ports of Waterford and New Ross	120 0 0	
Office, hire of offices, postages, travelling and miscellaneous expenses of the emigration officers' establishments	700 0 0	
Total Emigration Officers		6,318 4 7
		15,096 16 4

APPENDIX B 303

TABLE XII (*Continued*)

MISCELLANEOUS:
In aid of medical inspection, &c. towards the relief of emigrants in ships put back or wrecked on coasts of the United Kingdom	150	0	0
Cost of prosecutions under Passengers' Act	50	0	0
Religious instruction at the four depôts at Nine Elms, Southampton, Plymouth and Liverpool	400	0	0
Allowance for agency in Canada	1,500	0	0
Agency in New Brunswick	200	0	0
TOTAL Miscellaneous	2,300	0	0
GRAND TOTAL	£17,396	16	4

This Estimate is larger by 3,312 *l.* 19 *s.* 3 *d.* than last year; the following are the particulars of the additions:

	£	s.	d.
Increase to clerks' salaries from length of service	50	0	0
Increase in and arrears of postages arising from large increase of correspondence	609	0	0
Additional officers at the Ports of London and Liverpool, and increase of 50 *l.* in the salary of each of the officers at London and Liverpool, and of 40 *l.* in salary of clerk at London	1,090	0	0
Arrears of these allowances	705	14	3
Emigration officer at Southampton	208	5	0
Miscellaneous expenses of the emigration officers	200	0	0
Cost of prosecutions under Passengers' Act	50	0	0
Religious instruction at the depôts	400	0	0
Increase as compared with last year's estimate	£3,312	19	3

SOURCE: Public Archives of Canada, R. G. 7, G 1, vol. 132.

TABLE XIII
Trades and Callings of Emigrants Arrived at Ports of Quebec and Montreal, 1846–59

	1846	1853	1854	1855	1856	1857	1858	1859
Bakers	14	35	51	36	65	19	16	14
Blacksmiths, tinsmiths, braziers	61	11	16	9	18	20	61	—
Bookbinders and printers	17	21	19	13	14	22	11	12
Bricklayers and masons	60	172	228	118	115	119	52	18
Butchers	15	21	23	18	35	35	9	8
Cabinet-makers and turners	7	—	20	9	10	25	10	2
Carpenters and joiners	162	322	617	239	308	478	205	113
Cart and wheelwrights	8	15	39	36	50	44	—	—
Coachmakers	1	2	8	2	7	5	10	—
Coopers	12	9	40	27	27	21	12	3
Curriers and tanners	2	2	2	4	4	11	1	—
Dyers	1	1	4	4	19	—	3	—
Engineers	4	40	76	21	35	124	18	11
Gardeners	14	19	37	24	49	32	24	—
Hatters	1	2	3	1	12	6	—	1
Merchants and clerks	—	74	156	89	104	327	192	331
Millers and millwrights	10	48	131	88	83	127	35	13
Miners	98	119	238	35	61	156	41	10
Moulders and foundrymen	—	3	24	13	9	21	7	3
Painters and glaziers	—	15	41	19	20	24	17	9
Paper-makers	1	1	4	3	2	1	—	—
Plasterers	5	—	5	9	13	1	3	—
Professional men	—	—	—	—	—	—	—	13
Ropemakers	—	4	6	1	5	—	—	—
Saddlers and harness makers	4	15	18	11	11	15	5	2
Sail makers	—	1	5	4	2	—	3	—
Sawyers	1	5	16	6	9	21	5	5
Ship-builders	2	2	17	2	—	—	—	—
Shoemakers	87	154	358	167	227	157	52	27
Smiths	—	199	354	127	216	201	24	49
Stone-cutters	2	17	67	13	13	27	10	3
Tailors	84	176	433	153	206	207	94	61
Watch and clock makers	6	9	43	21	51	31	4	2
Weavers	—	51	85	64	65	41	23	—
Wheelwrights	—	—	—	—	—	—	9	—
Wool and flax dressers	—	3	4	9	4	10	—	4
Unenumerated	—	84	163	159	189	184	178	266
House-servants	87	146	117	26	32	134	—	—
Farmers and farm servants	4831	3974	5632	2007	2342	3518	1651	1051
Labourers	6733	6667	10448	3722	4338	6279	1593	866
TOTAL	12366	12455	19466	7309	8769	12443	4442	3081

Source: *Parliamentary Paper*, 1847, XXXIX (777), 21; 1854, XLVI (1763), 30; 1854–5, XXXIX (464), 18; 1857, X (14), 22; 1857, XXVIII (125, Sess. 2), 18; 1857–8, XLI (165), 20; 1859, XXII (218, Sess. 2), 14; 1860, XLIV (606), 16. For lack of figures from Canada for famine years, see note II (a).

BIBLIOGRAPHICAL NOTE

THE MAIN BODY of manuscript sources for this study of British emigration to British North America is to be found in government archives in London, England, and Ottawa, Canada. In 1959 some government series originally consulted at the Public Record Office in London were available in microfilm at the Public Archives of Canada in Ottawa. Of these sources among the most useful were the series, C.O. 42, original correspondence of the Secretary of State with Upper and Lower Canada, containing incoming material from the colonies, and the corresponding series, C.O. 217 and C.O. 188, for Nova Scotia and New Brunswick. Series G at the Public Archives of Canada, made up of original despatches from the Colonial Office and related correspondence, is essential as the other end of the series C.O. 42. Vital as these are for general policy, the *sine qua non* for British emigration is the series C.O. 384, original correspondence on emigration and its companion series C.O. 385, which after 1815 were separately bound and, with the appointment of agents and commissioners for emigration, became a large collection. Land Books of Upper and Lower Canada and a large series, unbound and listed as Sundries, available only at Ottawa, are also valuable.

Of various special collections of manuscript in the Public Archives of Canada, there might be mentioned the Selkirk Papers, the British American Land Company Papers, the Dalhousie Papers, the Elgin-Grey papers, the Canada Company correspondence (of which the main part is now in the Ontario Archives), and the micro-films of the Howick Papers. Though printed works are usually not to be thought of in the same breath with manuscript sources, for this study some pamphlets in the Public Archives collection deserve that honour. An account of an early government-aided emigration, not in one of the popular traveller's tales, but by a participating superintendent, rare prospectuses of little known colonization companies, hard-to-find annual reports of the great land companies are among the treasures that the Archives' nicely guarded pamphlet corner can produce.

Almost equal in importance in tracing the causes and progress of emigration are the printed reports of government commissions and select committees and special returns of correspondence or statistics called for by Parliament and offered by government departments, all roughly referred to as *Parliamentary Papers*. Beginning with the Survey and Reports on the Coasts and Central Highlands of Scotland printed in volume IV of the papers of 1802–03, this series runs to one hundred or more volumes, through the reports of select committees and commissions on the Poor Laws (*Parl. Pap.*, 1817, VI (462); 1818, V (107, 237, 358); 1819, II (529); 1834, XXVII (44)); on the distressed state of agriculture (*Parl. Pap.*, 1822, V (165, 236, 346)); on emigration from the south of Ireland (*Parl. Pap.*, 1823, XIII (401); 1825, XVIII (131)); on the possibility of emigration from the United Kingdom and parts thereof in later years (*Parl. Pap.*,

1826–7, V (237, 550); 1841, VI (182, 333); 1847, VI (737); 1847–8, XVII (415)); on the state of Ireland (*Parl. Pap.*, 1823, VI (561); 1825, VIII (129); 1825, IX (181, 521); 1835, XXXII (369); 1836, XXX (35); 1837, LI (69), XXXVIII (104)); on passenger vessels and the conveyance of emigrants (*Parl. Pap.*, 1851, XIX (632); 1854, XIII (163, 349)); through the reports of the agencies created to look into or after emigration (*Parl. Pap.*, 1831–2, XXXII (724); 1837–8, VIII (183); 1838, XL (388); 1839, IX (255); 1840, VII (30, 92); 1841, XXVII (60); including the reports of the Colonial Land and Emigration Commissioners for the years 1841 to 1865); and finally through a great number of miscellaneous papers relating to emigration to British North America, for example, *Parl. Pap.*, 1840, XXXIII (613); 1841, XV (298); 1842, XXXI (301, 373); 1843, XXXIV (291); 1844, XXXV (181); 1847, XXXIX (777, 824); 1847–8, XLVII (386, 932, 964); 1849, XXXVIII (1025); 1851, XL (348); 1852, XXXIII (1474); 1852–3, LXVIII (1650); 1854, XLVI (1763); and 1857–8, XLI (165).

The business of transporting emigrants on the high seas and the humane influence of reformers required changes in British legislation so important in this period that Acts of Parliament become an essential part of the student's references. For legislation on the passenger vessel, the minimum list would require: 43 Geo. III, c. 56; 56 Geo. III, c. 83; 58 Geo. III, c. 89; 59 Geo. III, c. 124; 4 Geo. IV, c. 84 and c. 88; 6 Geo. IV, c. 116; 7 and 8 Geo. IV, c. 19; 9 Geo. IV, c. 21; 5 and 6 Wm. IV, c. 53; 3 and 4 Vic., c. 21; 5 and 6 Vic., c. 107; 8 and 9 Vic., c. 14; 10 and 11 Vic., c. 103; 11 and 12 Vic., c. 6; 12 and 13 Vic., c. 33; 14 and 15 Vic., c. 1; 15 and 16 Vic., c. 44; 18 and 19 Vic., c. 119; 26 and 27 Vic., c. 51; on the emigration of artisans: 5 Geo. IV, c. 97; and on the Poor Law relating to emigration: 4 and 5 Wm., IV, c. 76; 1 and 2 Vic., c. 56; 7 and 8 Vic., 101; 11 and 12 Vic., c. 110.

Indispensable too are *Hansard's Parliamentary Debates*, the *Journals* of the House of Commons and of the assemblies of the colonies, the censuses of the United Kingdom and the colonies, and many collections of documents. Among the latter there should be noted, *Select Documents on British Colonial Policy, 1830–1860* (eds. K. N. Bell and W. P. Morrell, Oxford, 1930), *Select Documents in Canadian Economic History, 1783–1885* (eds. H. A. Innis and A. R. M. Lower, Toronto, 1933), *Documents Relating to the Constitutional History of Canada, 1791–1818* (eds. A. G. Doughty and D. McArthur, Ottawa, 1914), and for the years 1819–1828 (eds. A. G. Doughty and N. Story, Ottawa, 1935). Valuable also among first-hand sources for emigration are the speeches, correspondence, papers, autobiographies, and sometimes the publications of persons who influenced policy and recorded events, such men as Lieutenant-Governor John Graves Simcoe, Colonel Thomas Talbot, Lord Bathurst, Robert Lamond, John Galt, William Cobbett, Thomas Sockett, William Huskisson, R. J. Wilmot Horton, A. C. Buchanan, Dr. Thomas Rolph, Charles Buller, Colonel Robert Torrens, Lord Melbourne, Edward Gibbon Wakefield, Lord Durham, Sir Robert Peel, Herman Melville, Lord Elgin, William E. Gladstone, Lord John Russell, Henry George Grey, Viscount Howick, later Earl Grey. These and others have been mentioned and full references given in the appropriate places in the chapter notes.

Newspapers are essential in following the movements of emigrants, especially because many shipping agents and very many emigrants left no written records. For Scotland, the *Caledonian Mercury* and the *Edinburgh Evening Courant* have been helpful; for England, *The Times* and the *Morning Chronicle* (London), the *Cambridge Chronicle and Journal and Huntingdonshire Gazette*, the *Manchester Guardian*; for Canada, the *Quebec Mercury*, the *Kingston Chronicle*, the *Toronto Globe*, the Montreal *Gazette*. Painstaking work on rare newspapers by modern historians should be mentioned gratefully, for example that by W. F. Adams on Irish and F. C. Hamil on Canadian newspapers. Where such modern historians have been quoted, references for them include the newspapers they used. In somewhat the same class as the newspaper but offering more of the economic and philosophic thought of the day are the *Edinburgh Review*, the *Quarterly Review*, *Chambers's Edinburgh Journal*, the *Illustrated London News*, *Simmond's Colonial Magazine and Foreign Miscellany*, the *Spectator*, the *Scots Magazine*.

Contemporary literature useful for the study of emigration reflects the broadening business interests and the needs of the enlarged reading public of the nineteenth century, as well as the opportunities offered by the new empire. Parts of the best of these descriptions of colonial life have recently been republished in collections such as those edited by G. M. Craig (*Early Travellers in the Canadas, 1791–1867*, Toronto, 1955), by J. Hale (*Settlers: Being Extracts from the Journals and Letters of Early Colonists in Canada, Australia, South Africa and New Zealand*, London, 1950), and by E. C. Guillet (in part of *The Valley of the Trent*, Toronto, 1957).

Beyond the texts of the works with which the reader makes acquaintance in these collections, attention should be called to many significant but less popular books and pamphlets, some relating specifically to the emigration movement: J. W. Bannister's *Sketch of a Plan for Settling in Upper Canada a Portion of the Unemployed Labourers of England* (London, 1821), R. Gourlay's *General Introduction to a Statistical Account of Upper Canada, Compiled with a View to a Grand System of Emigration, in Connexion with a Reform of the Poor Laws* (London, 1822), A. C. Buchanan's *Emigration Practically Considered, with Detailed Directions to Emigrants Proceeding to British North America* (London, 1828), W. Cattermole's *Emigration: The Advantages of Emigration to Canada* (London, 1831), W. Dunlop, *Statistical Sketches of Upper Canada for the Use of Emigrants* (London, 1832), C. Barclay's compilation of *Letters from the Dorking Emigrants Who Went to Upper Canada in the Spring of 1832* (London, 1833), J. M. Brydone's *Narrative of a Voyage with a Party of Emigrants Sent out from Sussex, in 1834, by the Petworth Emigration Committee* (London, 1834), J. Buchanan's [British Consul in New York] *Project for the Formation of a Depot in Upper Canada, with a View to Receive the Whole Pauper Population of England* (New York, 1834), J. S. Buckingham's *Canada, Nova Scotia, New Brunswick, and the Other British Provinces in North America, with a Plan of National Colonization* (London, 1843), T. Rolph's *Emigration and Colonization, Embodying the Results of a Mission to Great Britain and Ireland* (London, 1844), J. R. Godley's *An Answer to the Question What is to be Done with the Unemployed Labourers of the United Kingdom*

(London, 1847), M. H. Perley's *Hand-Book . . . for Emigrants to New Brunswick* (London, 1857).

Other contemporary works, generally descriptive of the British North American colonies or the empire, would include: C. F. Grece, *Facts and Observations Respecting Canada and the United States of America; Affording a Comparative View of the Inducements to Emigration Presented in those Countries. To which is added an Appendix of Practical Instruction to Emigrant Settlers in the British Colonies* (London, 1819), J. M'Donald, *Narrative of a Voyage to Quebec and Journey Thence to New Lanark Detailing the Difficulties and Hardships Which an Emigrant Has to Encounter* (Edinburgh, 1823, 8th ed.), J. Mactaggart, *Three Years in Canada* (2 vols., London, 1829), J. Bouchette, *The British Dominions in North America, a Topographical and Statistical Description* (2 vols., London, 1831), British American Land Company, *Information Respecting the Eastern Townships of Lower Canada* (London, 1833), A. Fergusson, *Practical Notes Made during a Tour in Canada* (Edinburgh, 1834), New Brunswick and Nova Scotia Land Company, *Practical Information respecting New Brunswick . . .* (London, 1834), R. H. Bonnycastle, *The Canadas in 1841* (2 vols., London, 1841-2), [J. Abbott] *The Emigrant to North America from Memoranda of a Settler in Canada* (London, 1844, 3rd ed.), A. Gesner, *The Industrial Resources of Nova Scotia* (Halifax, 1849), J. B. Brown, *Views of Canada and the Colonists, Embracing the Experience of Eight Years' Residence* (Edinburgh, 1851), S. Strickland (ed. A. Strickland), *Twenty-seven Years in Canada West* (London, 1853), G. Patterson, *Memoir of the Rev. James Macgregor, D. D.* (Philadelphia, 1859), E. Wakefield, *An Account of Ireland, Statistical and Political* (London, 1812), J. Sinclair, *General Report of the Agricultural State and Political Circumstances of Scotland* (Edinburgh, 1814), P. Colquhoun, *A Treatise on the Wealth, Power and Resources of the British Empire* (London, 1814), G. R. Porter, *Progress of the Nation* (London, 1851, 2nd ed.), J. R. McCulloch, *A Descriptive and Statistical Account of the British Empire* (London, 1854, 4th ed.).

The appearance of books on British emigration has been mentioned in the introduction, articles in periodicals came at the same time and in greater numbers. After the First World War, an investigator felt delight to discover M. I. Adam's work on Scottish Highland emigration in the *Scottish Historical Review*, XVI (1919) and XVII (1920), or A. R. M. Lower's on Canadian immigration and settlement in the *Canadian Historical Review*, III (1922), or Frances Morehouse's on Irish emigration in the *American Historical Review*, XXXIII (1928) and on Canadian migration in the *Canadian Historical Review*, IX (1928). In the decades following, the searcher turned up almost as a matter of course discussions of Irish famine emigration to Canada by G. Tucker in the *American Historical Review*, XXXVI (1931), of Irish emigration and the emigrant traffic by O. MacDonagh in *Irish Historical Studies*, IX (1954), in the *Transactions* of the Royal Historical Society, V (1955), and in *The Great Famine* (eds. R. D. Edwards and T. D. Williams, Dublin, 1956), of emigration to Cape Breton by D. C. Harvey in the *Dalhousie Review*, XXI (1941), and to Nova Scotia by R. G. Flewwelling in the Nova Scotia Historical Society *Collections*, XXVIII (1949), of the agrarian aspects of early Victorian emigration by W. S.

Shepperson in the *Canadian Historical Review*, XXXIII (1952), of the influence of the humanitarian reforms on the conveyance of emigrants at sea by K. A. Walpole in the *Transactions* of the Royal Historical Society, XIV (1931), of Arthur Mills' colonization experiment in Canada by P. Knaplund in the *Canadian Historical Review*, XXXIV (1953).

If his interest extended to the disposal of Canadian lands, the student might use H. M. Morrison's work in the *Canadian Historical Review*, XIV (1933) and R. G. Riddell's in the same review, XVIII (1937), or the earlier findings of G. Patterson in Ontario Historical Society, *Papers and Records*, XXVIII (1932), not to mention Patterson's longer study of 1921.

On the policy of the British government regarding emigration, colonization and the empire, the articles were necessarily somewhat scattered in topic: detailed pieces on James Stephen by P. Knaplund in the *Canadian Historical Review*, V (1924), XII (1931), and in the *Journal of Modern History*, I (1929), as well as the book, *James Stephen and the British Colonial System, 1813–1847* (Madison, 1953); on the Victorians and the empire by D. G. Creighton in the *Canadian Historical Review*, XIX (1938); on mercantilism from Huskisson to Peel by A. R. M. Lower in the Royal Society of Canada, *Proceedings and Transactions*, 1937, Sec. II; on hemp and imperial defence by N. Macdonald in the *Canadian Historical Review*, XVII (1936); on Robert Peel and the party system by N. Gash in the Royal Historical Society, *Transactions*, I (1951); on the colonial policy of the Whig ministers by Helen T. Manning in the *Canadian Historical Review*, XXXIII (1952); on John Graves Simcoe's enthusiasms by G. R. Mealing in the Canadian Historical Association, *Report*, 1958; on Lord Selkirk in Upper Canada by F. C. Hamil in the Ontario Historical Society, *Papers and Records*, XXXVII (1945); on official encouragement to immigration in the province of Canada by P. W. Gates, in the *Canadian Historical Review*, XV (1934); on Edward Gibbon Wakefield in Canada by U. Macdonell in *Queen's Quarterly*, XXXII (1924–25), on a Canadian emigration commissioner in Ireland by G. R. C. Keep in the *Canadian Historical Review*, XXXIV (1953).

Since emigration springs from a variety of influences, a limited list of general references must seem arbitrarily chosen. After omitting standard national, economic, and political histories, one might retain: D. F. Macdonald, *Scotland's Shifting Population, 1770–1850* (Glasgow, 1937), A. Redford, *Labour Migration in England, 1800–1850* (Manchester, 1926), L. and C. M. Knowles, *The Economic Development of the British Overseas Empire* (London, 1924, 1930), W. H. R. Curtler, *The Enclosure and Redistribution of Our Land* (Oxford, 1920), J. L. and B. Hammond, *The Town Labourer, 1760–1832* (London, 1925), W. P. Morrell, *British Colonial Policy in the Age of Peel and Russell* (Oxford, 1930), O. A. Kinchen, *Lord John Russell's Canadian Policy* (Lubbock, 1945), *Cambridge History of the British Empire*, ed. J. H. Rose, A. P. Newton, E. A. Benians, vols. II, VI (Cambridge, 1929, 1940), E. L. Woodward, *The Age of Reform, 1815–1870* (Oxford, 1938, 1949), F. C. Bowen, *A Century of Atlantic Travel, 1830–1930* (Boston, 1930), *The Great Famine*, ed. R. D. Edwards and T. D. Williams (Dublin, 1956), J. Hannay, *History of New Brunswick*, 2 vols. (St. John, 1909), A. L. Burt, *The Old Province of Quebec* (Toronto, 1933), R. L. Jones, *History of Agriculture in Ontario, 1613–1880* (Toronto,

1946), E. Guillet, *The Great Migration* (Toronto, 1937), F. C. Hamil, *The Valley of the Lower Thames* (Toronto, 1951), B. Thomas, *Migration and Economic Growth: A Study of Great Britain and the Atlantic Economy* (Cambridge, 1954), studies by T. S. Ashton and R. M. Hartwell in the *Journal of Economic History*, IX (1949) and XIX (1959) respectively, by H. J. Habakkuk and E. J. Hobsbawn in the *Economic History Review*, 2d. ser. VI (1953) and X (1957), works of W. Cunningham, L. C. A. Knowles, J. H. Clapham.

INDEX

ACADIANS, 4–5
A'Court, Colonel E. H., 205
Addington, Henry, Viscount Sidmouth. *See* Sidmouth
Adelaide Township, Upper Canada, 184, 206
Agent-general for emigration, 95, 100, 103, 235
Agricultural Society of Quebec, 15
Agriculture: in Scotland, 19, 20, 21, 53, 175; in England, 27–9, 48–9, 173, 175; in Ireland, 35–7, 175; and Corn Laws, 174–5
Aldborough Township, Upper Canada, 116
Amboy, New Jersey, 67
American Revolution, 7, 8, 24
Annapolis Royal, 4
Annie Jane, 168
Antigonish, N.S., 21
Argyll, Duke of, 124, 126, 212
Argyll, Scotland: emigration from, 21, 27, 52, 53, 118
Arisaig, Scotland: emigration from, 20
Armagh, Ireland: emigration from, 180, 216
Arran, Isle of, Scotland: emigration from, 212
Arthur, Sir George, 101, 184
Ashley, Lord, Earl of Shaftesbury, 222
Asphodel Township, Upper Canada, 77, 78
Astle, John, 67, 91
Australia: colonization plans for, 90n, 96; emigration to, 191, 194, 195, 210; and systematic colonization, 203; and child emigration, 222
Aylmer, Lord, 136, 221, 226

BAGOT, SIR CHARLES, 126, 129, 190
Baillie, George, 140
Baillie, Henry J., 103, 124, 210
Baillie, Thomas, surveyor-general, 140
Balaquidder, Scotland: emigration from, 45
Baldoon, Upper Canada: emigration to, 119
Ballygibbin, Ireland: emigration from, 75
Ballyhooly, Ireland: emigration from, 70
Banks, Joseph, 16
Barbadoes, 126
Baring, F. T., 97, 99
Barra, Scotland: emigration from, 25, 58, 213
Bathurst, Henry Bathurst, 3rd Earl: on regulations for settlers, 40–1, 44, 122; on emigration, 58, 69, 74
Bathurst Township, Upper Canada: emigration to, 43
Bavaria: emigration from, 218, 219
Beauharnois, 105, 128, 129, 131
Beckwith, Sir Sidney, 43
Beckwith Township: emigrants to, 45
Belfast, Ireland: emigration from, 37, 38, 106, 152, 176, 213, 293; emigration agent in, 149; Atlantic fares from, 153
Benbicula, Scotland: emigration from, 213
Bentham, Jeremy, 96
Berczy, William, 114–15
Birchoff, Charles, 139
Birkbeck, Morris, 51
Bond Head, Sir Francis, 117, 184, 221

Breadalbane, Scotland: emigration from, 44–5
Bristol, England: emigration from, 149, 208, 291
British American Association for Emigration and Colonization, 125–6
British American Land Company: and co-operation with government, 102; and promotion of emigration, 124, 137, 139; organization of, 135–6; terms of charter of, 136, 138–9; under A. T. Galt, 139; and speculative era, 143
British North America: land regulations for, 42, 44, 46, 58, 113–14, 183; assisted emigrants to, 43, 60–1, 69–70, 75–6, 203–13 *passim*; attractions of, 51, 199–200; and suitability for labourers and capitalists, 58; cost of establishing emigrants in, 63, 73, 80, 189; and emigration to United States, 79, 195, 197; population needs of, 90; Goderich on assisted emigration to, 98; Durham on, 100; Stanley on, 105; against pauper emigration, 105; Grey on emigration to, 107; plans for assisted emigration to, 110; emigrant fares to, 154; growth of population in, 185, 201; and inability to absorb British emigrants, 199
Brockville, Upper Canada, 64, 185, 286
Bromley, Walter, 56
Brooks, Samuel, 137
Brougham, Lord, 178
Broun, Sir Richard, 125–6
Brutus, 154–6
Bruyère, Henry, 138
Brydone, James Marr, 127, 206
Buchanan, Alexander Carlisle, the elder; and criticism of Emigrant Society, 56; on transportation costs, 91; on British American Land Company, 137; as emigration agent at Quebec, 149–50,
182, 187; on emigrant head tax, 153; on passenger vessel law, 158
Buchanan, Alexander Carlisle, the younger: on passenger vessel law, 160, 168; on remittances, 179; on emigration and settlement, 190, 197, 199; on assisted emigrants, 207, 208, 221; on assisted foreign emigrants, 219; influence of, 224
Buchanan, James, 67
Buller, Charles: and theories of Wakefield, 96, 105, 110; with Durham mission, 100; works with Grey, 106; on North American Colonial Association of Ireland, 129; and aid for emigration, 230; on Stephen, 234
Bureau of Agriculture of Canada, 200
Burnett, Sir W., 193
Buttevant, Ireland: emigration from, 71, 75
Bytown, 223, 285

CAITHNESS, SCOTLAND, 41
Caledonian Mercury: on emigration of young men, 19; on ship agents, 20, 22; on "deluded Highlanders," 27
Callander, Scotland: emigration from, 42, 45
Cambridge, England: emigration from, 48
Cameron, Donald, 52, 122–3
Campbell, John, W. S., 42
Canada Company: in Newcastle district, 82; and co-operation with government, 102; and promotion of emigration, 124, 133, 180; organization and contract of, 132; its petitions refused, 133, 135; growth and criticism of, 135; Huron tract of, 134
Cape Breton: early policy for, 6; Loyalists to, 10; memorials from, 15; cheap Atlantic fares to, 20; destitute emigrants in, 58; as a paradise for emigrant trade, 148; Scottish emigrants to, 212

INDEX

Cape of Good Hope, 33–4, 46, 50, 73. *See also* South Africa
Cardigan, New Brunswick: emigrants to, 57
Carleton, Sir Guy, Lord Dorchester, 8–9, 10, 13
Carlisle, England, 61, 80, 173, 291
Caulfield, St. George, 214–15
Cavan, Ireland: emigration from, 38, 67
Cavan Township, Upper Canada, 57, 67, 79
Charleville, Ireland: emigration from, 70, 75
Chicago, U.S.A., 197, 286
Chelsea Pensioners. *See* Demobilized, retired, military men
Children, emigration of, 221–3
Children's Friendly Society, 221–2
Chisholm, Caroline, 168, 174
Cholera and typhus epidemics, 154–7, 163, 175, 192
Clare County, Ireland: emigration from, 37, 82, 215
Cobbett, William, 49, 51, 93, 204, 205
Cobourg, Upper Canada, 77, 133, 185, 286
Cockburn, Lieutenant Colonel, 62–3, 80, 90, 91, 92
Colborne, Sir John: on aid to settlers, 43, 63, 82, 184, 205; on Colonel Talbot, 117; and Canada Company plea, 133; in cholera epidemic, 157; and Chelsea Pensioners, 220, 221; regarding poor emigrants, 227
Colebrooke, Sir William, 142, 191
Colonial Advocate, 79
Colonial Land and Emigration Commissioners: and creation of Commission, 101; recommendation on emigration of, 102; rebuke of Cork for pauper plan by, 106; theories of, 107; and fear of depopulation of Ireland, 110; and approval of North American Colonial Association of Ireland, 129; on emigrant and passenger trade, 150, 153, 160; and consolidation and regulation of passenger law, 166; on emigration to United States, 169, 199; information work of, 182–3; on emigration balancing opportunities, 199; responsibilities of, 203, 224–5; on emigration of women, 223; budget of, 224, 302–3
Colonial Office: and plans to aid emigration, 41–2, 44, 61, 69, 74; on disposal of colonial lands, 44, 46, 96, 142, 183, 209; receipt of emigration petitions by, 50, 59, 67, 94, 105, 188, 209; and indigent emigrants, 59, 63, 214; Russell's work in, 101; Grey's work in, 107–9; and passenger vessel legislation, 147, 157; and emigrant head tax, 152; wide contacts of, 214, 221; and financial aid for emigration agencies, 225, 226; on colonial information presented, 229
Colonization Society, 96
Comrie, Scotland: emigrants from, 45
Connaught, Ireland, 35, 176
Cork, Ireland: emigration from, 45, 77, 152, 216, 293; Poor Law emigration from, 105–6; emigration agent for, 149; deaths at sea from, 164; famine in, 177, 216
Cork, New Brunswick, 142
Corn Laws, 29, 154, 163, 174, 231
Cornwall, Upper Canada, 157, 190
Crinan, Scotland: emigration from, 52
Cromarty, Scotland: emigration from, 213, 292
Cumberland, England: emigration from, 44, 188
Cunard, Samuel, 161, 170
Curwen, John Christian, 31, 33, 50, 61

DALHOUSIE, GEORGE RAMSAY, LORD, 52, 54, 63, 72
De Puisaye, Joseph Genevieve, 115

De Vere, Stephen, 164–5
Death rate on emigrant ships, 164, 166, 167, 170
Demobilized, retired, military men: colonial lands for, 4, 6, 7, 9, 41, 43; request aid in emigration of, 50; value of, 82; and Chelsea Pensioners, 219–21
Deptford, England: emigration from, 42
Devon Commission, 106, 177
Dickson, William, 123
Doneraile, Lord, and Irish emigrants, 70, 75
Doneraile, Ireland: conspiracy in, 65; emigrants from, 71, 74, 77
Dorchester, Sir Guy Carleton, Lord. *See* Carleton
Dorking, England: emigrants from, 204
Douglas, George W.: on famine emigrants, 163; reports of, 168, 296
Douglas, Sir Howard: on emigrant aid societies, 57–8; and pauper emigration, 90, 226; and agriculture, 140; and timber trade, 160
Douglas, Thomas, 5th earl of Selkirk. *See* Selkirk.
Douro Township, Upper Canada: emigrants in, 77, 78, 81, 82
Drummond, Lieutenant General Gordon, 41
Dublin, Ireland: emigration from, 38, 66, 188, 218, 293; passenger trade in, 67; emigration agent for, 149; Atlantic fares from, 153; remittances to, 179
Dumfries, Scotland: emigration from, 20, 52, 292
Dummer Township, Upper Canada: emigrants in, 82, 205
Dundas, Henry, 1st Viscount Melville, 14, 22, 37
Dunscomb, John W., 129
Dunwich Township, Upper Canada, 116
Durham, John George Lambton, 1st earl of: and colonization methods, 96, 100; on colonization companies, 127, 138; and British colonies, 231

EASTERN TOWNSHIPS, 137–9, 188, 294
Edinburgh, Scotland, 42, 133
Edinburgh Review, 22, 85, 88, 92
Egremont, Lord, 127, 205–6, 215
Eigg, Isle of, Scotland: emigration from, 20
Eighty-fourth Regiment, 9, 12
Elgin, James Bruce, 8th earl of: and emigration plans, 108–9; and needy, famine emigrants, 164, 166, 193; and colonial government, 232
Ellice, Edward, 128, 136
Elliot, Thomas Frederick: on Horton's plan, 95; in emigration committee posts, 98, 100, 102, 182, 235; on passenger vessel law, 158
Ely, Isle of, England, 48–9
Emigrant head tax: imposition of, 152, 183, 199; use of, 194, 225, 298
Emigrant ships: general, 146, 161, 167. See also *Annie Jane, Barbadoes, Brutus, James, Urania*
Emigrant (or passenger) trade: agents in, 20, 48, 150, 167; passengers in, 23, 24, 54, 148, 165, 167, 170; extent of, 67, 159–60; Atlantic fares in, 73, 91, 153–4; in cholera and famine epidemics, 154, 163–4. *See also* Passenger vessel legislation; Timber Trade
Emigration Advances Act, 104, 213
Emigration and Settlement Policy. *See* Settlement Policy
Emigration Commissioners. *See* Colonial Land and Emigration Commissioners
Emigration Committees, 89, 90–2, 147
Emily Township, Upper Canada, 77, 83
Enclosure, Acts of, 28

INDEX

England: population growth in, 27, 32; conditions leading to emigration, 28–31, 48–50, 173–4, 204–6; emigrants from, 44, 49, 182, 188, 204–6, 289–91
Enniskillen, Lord, 177
Ennismore, Lord, and emigration, 75
Ennismore Township, Upper Canada: emigrants in, 77–8
Essex, England: emigration from, 182
Eviction of tenants, 20, 21, 27, 36, 52, 76, 215

FAMILY COLONIZATION LOAN SOCIETY, 174
Famine and fever, 163, 174, 176, 192–3, 217
Fearon, Henry Bradshaw, 51
Felton, William B., 90, 136
Fermoy, Ireland, 70, 177
Finlay, Kirkman, 61
Fitzhugh, W., 91
Flint glass makers and emigration, 174
Fort William, Scotland: emigration from, 21, 25, 52
Fredericton, N.B., 6, 57
Fredericton Emigrant Society, 56
Frome, England, 204, 291

GALT, ALEXANDER T., 139, 143
Galt, John, 132, 136
Galt, Upper Canada, 185, 206
Galway, Ireland: emigration from, 177, 216, 293
Garrafraxa Road, 138, 183
Germany, emigration from, 186
Gladstone, W. E., 99, 108, 159, 231
Glasgow, Scotland: emigration from, 25, 42, 61–2, 173, 292; Irish in, 87; Atlantic fares from, 153; cholera in, 154, 163
Glasgow Emigration Society, 210
Glenelg, Charles Grant, Lord, 100, 117, 183, 222
Glengarry, Scotland: emigration from, 19, 25, 27, 213

Glengarry Fencibles, and emigration, 25
Gloucestershire, England: emigration from, 206
Goderich, F. J. Robinson, Viscount, 88, 92, 97, 98, 136
Godley, John Robert, 106, 107, 108, 178
Gore Booth, Sir Robert, 216–17
Goulburn, Henry, and emigration, 41, 47, 51, 65, 68–9, 87
Gould, Nathaniel, 136, 158
Gourlay, Robert, 96
Grand Trunk Railroad, 197
Grant, Charles, Lord Glenelg. See Glenelg
Great Western Railroad, 197, 224, 285
Greenock, Scotland: emigration from, 44, 120, 292; emigrant agent for, 149
Grey, Henry George (Viscount Howick), 3rd earl: on assisted emigration, 83, 94, 97, 99, 104, 106–7, 108, 111–12, 217; on emigrant head tax, 153; and famine emigration, 154, 164, 193–4; on empire, 232
Grosse Isle, 152, 156, 163, 192–3, 295, 296
Guelph, Upper Canada, 133–4, 185, 294

HABEAS CORPUS, 40, 60, 65
Haldimand, Sir Frederick, 9–10, 13
Halifax, Nova Scotia: emigrants in, 56, 58, 147, 192, 195; growth of, 185, 201
Hamilton, Lord Archibald, and emigrants, 31, 61
Hamilton, Upper Canada, 185, 197, 201, 286, 294
Hampshire, England: and emigration, 206–7
Harris, Scotland: emigration from, 213
Harvey, New Brunswick: emigrants to, 142

INDEX

Hay, R. W., 97, 140, 157
Hemp, 7, 16
Herbert, Sidney, 166
Heytesbury, Lord, and emigration, 205
Highland and Island Emigration Society, 213
Highland Society, 22–4, 210
Hincks, Francis, 105, 122
Hobart, Lord Robert, and emigration, 15, 25, 26, 119
Home district, emigration to, 294
Horton, Robert John Wilmot: and emigration, 69, 72, 74, 79–80, 87, 92–5; in Colonial Office, 85; and empire, 86; and Poor Law, 97, 208; on Passenger Law, 147
Howick, Viscount. *See* Henry George, 3rd Earl Grey
Hudson's Bay Company, 119–20
Hull, England: emigration from, 49, 133, 291
Hume, Joseph: on emigration, 32, 93, 103, 209; on freedom for capital and labour, 88, 148, 164
Huron Tract, and emigration, 134–5, 188, 294
Huskisson, William: and colonial connection, 86, 231; on colonial land sales, 113, 135; on passenger vessel bill, 148–9
Hutt, William, 103, 108, 128

INVERNESS, SCOTLAND: emigration from, 11, 27, 118, 213, 292
Inverness Township, 183, 212
Ireland: emigration from, 34, 38, 45, 66–7, 151–2, 188, 192, 289, 293; population of, 35, 110, 176, 237; conditions leading to emigration, 35–7, 98, 105–6, 109, 175–8; assisted emigration from, 69–71, 74–6, 213–17; parliamentary committee on, 98, 106, 177
Isle of Skye, emigration from, 18–19, 23, 26, 118, 141, 212
Isle of Wight, emigration from, 205, 208

James, 147
Jameson, Anna, 117, 180, 220
Johnson, Sir John, 9–10, 20
Johnson, Samuel, on emigration, 18, 27
Journeyman Steam Engine Makers and emigration, 174

KELP, 19, 103, 175, 210
Kempt, Sir James, 58, 147, 183, 214
Kent, England: emigration from, 182, 203, 206, 208
Killala, Ireland: emigration from, 164, 293
Killworth, Ireland: emigration from, 70, 75, 77
Kincardine, Scotland: emigration from, 45
Kingscote, Colonel, 128
Kingston, Lord, and emigration, 70, 75
Kingston (Cataraqui): emigrants in, 9, 56, 77, 79, 190; routes from, 13, 286; growth of, 185, 294
Kirkcudbright, Scotland: emigration from and its effect, 213
Knoydart, Scotland, emigration from, 20, 25, 42

LACHINE, 45–6, 57, 62, 71
Laissez-faire, 112, 113, 144, 152, 200
Lambton, John George, 1st earl of Durham. *See* Durham
Lamond, Robert, 62
Lanark, Scotland: emigration from, 31, 61–2
Lanark County, Upper Canada: emigrants in, 43, 62, 64
Lancashire, England, 28–9, 61, 173
Land system: and land grants, 42, 44, 46, 58, 198; parliamentary committee on, 99–100; and land sale, 113, 132, 136, 140, 183, 198; small allotments of, 183–4, 198
Landlord and Tenant Commission (Ireland), 106

INDEX

Lansdowne, Marquis of, and emigrants, 208, 218
Lascelles, Henry, Earl of Harwood, and emigrants, 49
Lawrence, Governor Charles, 4–5
Ledoyen, M., 193
Leeds Township: emigrants to, 183, 212
Leinster, Ireland: emigration from, 35, 176
Leith, Scotland: emigration from, 149, 292
Limerick, Ireland: emigration from, 82, 152, 188, 218, 293; emigration agent in, 149
Liverpool, Robert Banks Jenkinson, 2nd earl of, 41, 49–50
Liverpool, England: shipping interests in, 73–4, 146, 153, 160, 166, 218; emigration from, 164, 166, 169, 177, 237, 291; remittances from, 179
London, England: emigration from, 133, 208, 291
London, Canada: emigrants in, 117, 185, 189, 294
London Female Emigration Society, 224
Londonderry, Ireland: emigration from, 38, 66, 179, 180, 293
Low, Lieutenant Robert, and emigrants, 149–50, 157, 158, 166
Lower Canada, 16, 135–7, 152. *See also localities by name*

MACDONALD, CAPTAIN JOHN, 6, 11
Macdonnell, Rev. Alexander, 25
McGill, Peter, 129, 136, 137
McNab, Sir Allan, 125–6
McNab, Archibald, 53, 113, 120–2
McNutt, Alexander, 5
Magrath, F. W., on emigration, 189
Maitland, Sir Peregrine, and emigrants, 63, 71, 72, 78–9
Mallow, Ireland: emigration from, 70, 75, 176
Malthus, Thomas Robert, 31, 49, 85–6

Manchester, England, 31, 60, 173–4
Manchester Mechanics and Engineers' Friendly Society, 174
Marryat, Joseph, 146
Marshall, Captain, and emigrants, 63, 72
Matthew, Father Theobald, 176
Mayo, Ireland: emigration from, 188
Military pensioners. *See* Demobilized, retired, military men
Mills, Arthur, and emigrants, 130, 132
Moffat, George, 129, 137, 153
Moidart, Scotland: emigration from, 6
Molesworth, Sir William, 96, 101, 108, 110
Monaghan, Ireland: emigration from, 38, 67, 180
Monaghan Township, Upper Canada: emigrants in, 57, 67, 79
Monteagle, Lord. *See* Spring Rice
Montreal: routes from, 11, 57, 228, 286; emigrants in, 39, 56, 62, 71, 121, 185, 204, 225
Mull, Isle of, Scotland: emigration from, 126, 210
Munster, Ireland, 35, 73, 176
Murdock, T. W. C., 168
Murray, Governor James, 7–8

NEPEAN, EVAN, 13, 19
New Brunswick: emigration to, 53, 56, 148, 182–3, 191, 193, 223, 233, 290; immigrant policy of, 157, 166; growth of, 199–200. *See also* Timber trade
New Brunswick and Nova Scotia Land Company: and co-operation with government, 102; contract of, 140, 141–2; and emigration, 141
New York, 67, 74, 133, 204
New Zealand, 108, 194
Newcastle, England: emigration from, 188, 291
Newcastle district, Upper Canada: emigration to, 77, 82–3, 215, 294

Newfoundland, 20, 34, 66
Newmarket, Ireland: emigration from, 70, 75
Niagara, 10–11, 190, 286, 294
Nicholls, George, and emigration, 99, 209
Norfolk, England: emigration from, 182, 206–7
North American Colonial Association of Ireland: organization and plans of, 128, 129; Emigration Commissioners' approval of, 129; and Wakefield, 129–31
North American Colonial Committee, 124
Nova Scotia: emigration to, 5, 12, 18, 20–1, 27, 52, 154, 174, 195, 290; immigration policy of, 58, 152, 192, 220; growth of, 200

O'BRIEN, W. SMITH, 98, 103, 109, 159, 178
O'Connell, Daniel, 99, 106, 176
Ops Township, Upper Canada, 183
Otonabee Township, Upper Canada, 77–8, 83
Ottawa. *See* Bytown

PAISLEY, SCOTLAND, 31, 42, 173
Palmerston, Henry John Temple, 3rd Viscount, 87, 216–17
Passenger vessel legislation: Act of 1803, 24; Acts of 1823 to 1855, 146–68 *passim*; infractions and enforcement of, 151, 157, 160, 297; parliamentary committees on, 166, 168
Peel, Robert: on emigration, 38, 42, 61, 66, 68, 87, 91, 93, 99; on Ireland, 65, 176; and trade reform, 104, 111, 174
Penetanguishene, Upper Canada, 11, 221
Perley, Moses H., and emigration, 198, 200, 217, 223, 224
Perth, Upper Canada: emigrants in, 46, 63–4, 121

Perth Emigration Society (Scotland), 210
Peterborough (Scott's Mills, Plains), Upper Canada, 78, 81
Peterloo (St. Peter's Fields, Manchester), 40, 60
Petworth Emigration Committee, 205–6
Pictou, Nova Scotia: emigration to, 11, 18, 20–1, 58, 185, 212
Pinnock, J. D., 203, 206
Pitt, William, 15
Place, Francis, 32
Poor Law: and emigration in England, 28–9, 33, 89, 97, 173–4, 203, 206–7, 208, 209; and emigration in Ireland, 36, 99, 178, 215, 217
Poor Law Ragged Schools, 222
Port Stanley: emigrants to, 184, 222
Portsmouth, England: emigration from, 205, 208, 291
Prescott, Upper Canada: emigrants to, 46, 57, 62, 71, 77, 157, 184
Prince Edward Island: policy for, 6; emigration to, 6, 12, 26, 27, 118–19, 212, 290
Proclamation of February 7, 1792, 11, 113–14, 115
Prussia: emigration from, 218–19

QUEBEC: timber trade of, 16, 146, 160; emigrants in, 39, 45, 52, 66, 185–6, 190, 205, 207, 213, 215, 218, 222; routes from, 57, 108, 228, 286; cholera and fever in, 156–7, 192–3; passenger law enforcement in, 157, 166. *See also* Emigrant head tax
Quebec Emigrant Society, 56–7, 91n., 185, 188

RAILROADS, 197, 224, 228, 285
Reade, Dr. G. H., 78, 81
Remittances, 179, 199, 217
Rice Lake, Upper Canada, 44, 57, 67, 81

Richards, John, 64, 116, 146
Rideau River and Waterway, 43, 184
Rintoul, Robert S., 96
Rivière du Loup, 8, 228
Robinson, George R., 136
Robinson, Peter, and emigration, 70-2, 75, 77-8, 80, 88
Roche, E. S., and emigration, 218
Rolph, Dr. Thomas, and emigration, 105, 123-6, 178
Roscommon, Ireland: emigration from, 213, 214-15
Ross-shire, Scotland: emigration from, 11, 21, 53, 118, 213
Rubridge, Captain Charles, and emigrants, 78, 81, 184, 215
Russell, Lord John: and Ireland, 98, 99, 109, 177; and colonies, 101, 184, 231; on emigration plans, 102, 109-10, 124, 225; and Wakefield, 128

SADLER, MICHAEL, 93, 97
St. Andrews, New Brunswick: emigration to, 185, 217
St. John, New Brunswick: emigration to, 12, 39, 53, 66, 195, 201, 217; growth of, 185, 200, 201
St. Thomas, Upper Canada, 117
Scandinavia, emigrants from, 186
Scarborough, England: emigration from, 188
Scotland: emigration from, 18-21, 25-6, 42, 44, 47, 53, 61, 118-19, 137, 209-12, 289, 292; conditions leading to emigration in, 21-3, 26, 59, 89-90, 103, 175; population decrease in, 213
Scots Magazine, 59, 85
Scott's Mills, Plains. *See* Peterborough
Scrope, George Poulett, 98
Selkirk, Thomas Douglas, 5th earl of: and Scottish emigration, 22, 26, 27, 118-19; and Irish emigration, 26, 118

Senior, Nassau, 92
Settlement policy: early, 3, 6-7, 11, 13-14; of non-interference, 33, 102, 104, 106, 111, 199; of assistance, 41, 44, 46, 50, 61, 69, 74; and consideration of assistance plans, 89, 92, 102, 108, 109, 127; creation of government agencies on, 97, 100, 101, 235; and landlords' aid, 205-6, 212-16 *passim*. *See also* Land system; Poor Law
Shefford County, Lower Canada, 137
Sherbrooke County, Lower Canada, 137
Sidmouth, Henry Addington, 1st Lord, 31, 49, 60
Simcoe, Lieutenant-Governor John Graves, 11, 14-15, 113-14
Sinclair, Sir John, 22, 28
Sligo, Ireland: emigration from, 152, 164, 188, 216-17, 293
Smith Township, Upper Canada: emigrations to, 44, 77, 81, 83
Society of Brush Makers, and emigration, 174
Sockett, Rev. T. R., and emigration, 205
Somerset, England: emigration from, 50, 204
South Africa: emigration plans for, 90n., 96. *See also* Cape of Good Hope
South Australia Company, 128
Spaight, Francis, and emigration, 216
Spectator, 94-5, 108
Spring Rice, Thomas, Lord Monteagle: on Irish emigration, 103, 106-7, 177; and Grey, 108, 111, 112
Stanley, E. G., Lord Stanley: on assisted emigration, 104-5, 106, 126, 225; and land companies, 127, 136, 140; on passenger bill, 160
Stanstead County, Lower Canada, 137

Stephen, James: on Wakefield, 100; on passenger bill, 158; colonial policy of, 102, 111, 184, 234
Stewart, Thomas Alexander, 78, 79
Stornoway, Scotland: emigration from, 25, 292
Suffolk, England: emigration from, 48, 182, 206
Sunnidale Township, Upper Canada, 184
Suspension Bridge, and emigration, 197
Sussex, England: emigration from, 28, 205–6
Sutherland, Duke of, and emigration, 212
Sutherland, Scotland: emigration from, 21, 27, 41, 53, 213
Sydenham, C. E. Poulett Thomson, Baron: on assisted emigration, 125, 206, 216; and land companies, 128, 138, 143; on emigrant shipping trade, 148, 160; land policy of, 183
Systematic colonization, 95–6, 99–100, 110, 229

Talbot, Richard, 39, 45–6
Talbot, Colonel Thomas, 115–17
Telford, Thomas, 22, 23, 89
The Times, 32, 48, 67, 111, 154, 178
Thomson, C. E. Poulett. *See* Sydenham
Thurso, Scotland: emigration from, 52, 292
Timber trade, 16, 20, 74, 146, 160, 161, 162
Tipperary, Ireland: emigration from, 216
Toronto, 185, 197, 221, 226, 286, 294. *See also* York
Torrens, Colonel Robert, 96, 99, 102, 230
Treasury, 41, 56, 58, 63, 157, 164
Trent Canal and River, 82, 184
Typhus. *See* Cholera
Tyree, Isle of, Scotland: emigration from, 126, 212

Uist, Scotland: emigration from, 6, 25, 213
Ulster, Ireland: emigration from, 37, 67, 176
Uniacke, Richard, 15, 90
United Empire Loyalists, 8–10, 12, 14, 201, 228
United States: emigration to, 14, 21, 38, 41, 51, 57, 195, 197, 204; land system of, 99, 198; Emigration Commissioners on, 199
Upper Canada: bonus on hemp in, 16; growth of, 11, 185, 189, 233; assisted emigrants in, 43, 46, 62, 78, 82, 184, 206, 221; her policy on large landholders, 113–15, 117, 133; emigrants to, 189, 294. *See also localities by name*
Urania, 192

Vansittart, Nicholas, 43, 61

Wakefield, Edward, 35, 38
Wakefield, Edward Gibbon: and Horton, 95; on systematic colonization, 95–6; and parliamentary committee on colonial lands, 99–100; and Durham Report, 100; and North American Colonial Association of Ireland, 128–31; as member for Beauharnois, 105, 130
Ward, Henry George, on emigration and colonization, 99, 101, 103, 230
Waterford, Ireland: emigration from, 66, 293
Weavers, of Scotland and England, and emigration, 60, 93, 172, 209, 213
Weimar, emigration from, 218
Welland Canal, 184, 190
Wellesley, Arthur, Duke of Wellington, 63, 92
Wexford, Ireland: emigration from, 38, 188, 293

Whately, Archbishop Richard, 98
Whitbread, Samuel, 31, 33
Whitby, England: emigration from, 188, 291
Whitehaven, England: emigration from, 44, 291
Widder, Frederick, 135
Willcocks, William, and emigration, 15, 37, 114
Wilmot, Robert John. *See* Horton
Wiltshire, England: emigration from, 205, 207
Women, emigration of, 223–4

Wood, Charles, 107, 110
Wordsworth, Dorothy, and emigration, 25
Wyndham, Colonel George, and emigrants, 215–16

YARMOUTH, ENGLAND: emigration from, 208, 291
York, Upper Canada, 11, 57, 120, 205. *See also* Toronto
Yorkshire, England: emigration from, 49, 187–8, 205
Young, Arthur, 37